Global noise

MUSIC/CULTURE

A series from Wesleyan University Press

Edited by George Lipsitz, Susan McClary, and Robert Walser

Popular Music in Theory
by Keith Negus

A Thousand Honey Creeks Later:
My Life in Music from Basie to Motown — and Beyond
by Preston Love

Musicking:
The Meanings of Performing and Listening
by Christopher Small

Music of the Common Tongue:
Survival and Celebration in African American Music
by Christopher Small

Singing Archaeology:
Philip Glass's *Akhnaten*
by John Richardson

Metal, Rock, and Jazz:
Perception and the Phenomenology of Musical Experience
by Harris M. Berger

Music and Cinema
edited by James Buhler, Caryl Flinn, and David Neumeyer

"You Better Work!":
Underground Dance Music in New York City
by Kai Fikentscher

Singing Our Way to Victory:
French Cultural Politics and Music During the Great War
by Regina M. Sweeney

The Book of Music and Nature:
An Anthology of Sounds, Words, Thoughts
edited by David Rothenberg and Marta Ulvaeus

Recollecting from the Past:
Musical Practice and Spirit Possession
on the East Coast of Madagascar
by Ron Emoff

Banda:
Mexican Musical Life across Borders
by Helena Simonett

Global Noise:
Rap and Hip-Hop outside the USA
edited by Tony Mitchell

RAP AND HIP-HOP OUTSIDE THE USA

EDITED BY TONY MITCHELL

WESLEYAN UNIVERSITY PRESS   Middletown, Connecticut

Published by Wesleyan University Press,
Middletown, CT 06549
© 2001 by Wesleyan University Press
All rights reserved
ISBN 0-8195-6501-6 cloth
ISBN 0-8195-6502-4 paper

Printed in the United States of America

Designed by Richard Hendel
Set in Charter, Smack, and Meta types
by B. Williams and Associates

5 4 3 2 1

CiP data appear at the back of the book

 Contents

Acknowledgments

The idea for this book was germinated at the Eighth International Conference of IASPM (the International Association for the Study of Popular Music) at the University of Strathclyde, Glasgow, in July 1995 after a session on rap music that included contributions from myself and Ian Maxwell on rap and hip-hop in Italy and Australia. This led to discussions with Mir Wermuth, who was writing about hip-hop in Holland and the UK, and Masahiro Yasuda, who was doing research in the United Kingdom on hip-hop in France and Japan. Unfortunately none of Masa's work made it into this volume, but I am grateful for his input and correspondence. I would also like to acknowledge the global network of popular-music scholars provided by IASPM, of which I was the chairperson from 1997 to 1999, and of which all of the contributors to this book have been members. Phil Hayward, editor of *Perfect Beat,* who first published my work on hip-hop in Aotearoa–New Zealand and Maxwell's work on Australian hip-hop, was an important influence, and I am grateful to Rob Walser for his initial interest and encouragement. Ian Condry's initiative in setting up sessions on global rap music at the American Anthropological Association's Meetings in Washington, D.C., in 1997 and Philadelphia in 1998, in which Jacqueline Urla, Ted Swedenburg, André Prévos, Ian and myself participated, also provided an important fulcrum for this book. A much earlier version of my chapter on Italian rap was published in *Popular Music 14,* no. 3 (1995), while a version of Prévos's chapter on French rap previously appeared in the *European Studies Journal 15,* no. 2 (1998). Dave Hesmondhalgh and Caspar Melville presented a version of their chapter at the Tenth International Association for the Study of Popular Music (IASPM) conference at the University of Technology, Sydney (UTS) in July 1999, which I convened, and versions of Claire Levy's and Sarah Morelli's chapters were presented at the Ninth IASPM Conference in Kanazawa, Japan, in July 1997.

Tony Mitchell

Introduction

Another Root—Hip-Hop outside the USA

TONY MITCHELL

GLOBALIZING RAP

A new era . . . a more prosperous one . . . for me and my brothers. . . . I'm intoxicated because I can break into this new era where the fears that held me back don't exist any more the style has evolved from TUNIS to HONOLULU and it's coming out from the sector where it was devolved.
—Ménélik, "Another Root," on Nobukazu Takemura, *Child's View*

n his track "Another Root," the African French rapper Méné-lik marks out a new era of confident, emergent global hip-hop that has evolved from Tunis to Honolulu. He illustrates it by rapping in French on a 1994 album by the Japanese jazz musician Nobukazu Takemura, which was recorded in London, Paris, Osaka, and Tokyo. In the pages that follow, we will encounter Japanese b-boys struggling with the hyperconsumerism of Tokyo youth culture, Italian posses promoting hardcore Marxist politics and alternative youth culture circuits, and Basque rappers using a punk rock–hip-hop syncretic to espouse their nationalist cause and promote the rights of ethnic minorities globally. Rappers in war-torn Bosnia declare their allegiance with the violent lives of gangsta rappers in South Central Los Angeles, and a rap group in Greenland protests that country's domination by the Danish language. Rap and hip-hop culture's incorporation into dance music culture in Korea and Bulgaria is examined, as are its Islamic and African manifestations in France and the United Kingdom, and its indigenization in Australia and Aotearoa–New Zealand. Its adaptations in both Francophone and Anglophone Canada contrast with its growth as a commercial force in Holland's music scene.

Hip-hop and rap cannot be viewed simply as an expression of African American culture; it has become a vehicle for global youth affiliations and a tool for reworking local identity all over the world. Even as a universally recognized popular musical idiom, rap continues to provoke attention to local specificities. Rap and hip-hop outside the USA reveal the workings of popular music as a culture industry driven as much by local artists and their fans as by the demands of global capitalism and U.S. cultural domination. But the flow of consumption of rap music within the popular music industry continues to proceed hegemonically, from the USA to the rest of the world, with little or no flow in the opposite direction. This book documents and analyzes for the first time some of the other roots hip-hop has developed outside the USA, filling a vacuum in academic writing on the subject, in which the expression of local identities globally through the vernaculars of rap and hip-hop in foreign contexts has rarely been acknowledged.

The global and local manifestations of hip-hop culture in the mid-1990s coincide with what Russell A. Potter, in his book *Spectacular Vernaculars,* diagnosed as "a vulnerable time" for hip-hop in the USA, "reminiscent of rock and roll during its late-seventies lull" (1995: 147.) Despite the burgeoning commercial popularity and success of mainstream R&B-oriented and gangsta rap in the USA (in December 1998 *Billboard* noted "the genre's increasing and steady presence on the Billboard 200 charts" [Smith 1998: 27]) and the increasing number of women rappers gaining mainstream success in the USA (Oumano 1999: 25, 28, 32, 38) hip-hop's rhetorical conventions and tropes have become increasingly atrophied, clichéd, and repetitive. While the often brutalizing features of gangsta rap, with its apparent espousal of urban ugliness, greed, misogyny, capitalism, crime, homophobia, joyless sex, male physicality, and violence, appear to be declining, the bland R&B styles of Puff Daddy and others have risen to prominence. In 1996 Greg Tate, a consistent chronicler of what he refers to as the "golden age" of U.S. hip-hop from 1979 to 1991, wrote a lead article in *Vibe* magazine titled "Is Hip Hop Dead?" in which he lamented that "creatively [U.S.] hip hop [was] withering away, dying a slow, painful death," having become "spiritually and politically irrelevant." Citing the dearth of new talent "in a marketplace saturated with sucker MCs," Tate expressed the faint hope that "a revitalized underground" would emerge (1996: 35). It could be argued that this has to some extent taken place with emergent rap groups such as Slum Village in Detroit; Jurassic 5, Dilated Peoples, and the People under the Stairs in Los Angeles; and others associated with the Rawkus label in New York and the Quannum collective in the San Francisco Bay area (DJ Shadow, Latyrx, Blackalicious, Lyrics Born, et al.). More black women rappers, such as Lil' Kim, Foxy Brown, Missy Elliott, and the 1999 multi-Grammy-winning Lauryn Hill—the first rap artist to win a major album Grammy—have also entered the mainstream arena, and even mainstream white singers such as Mariah Carey have begun to incorporate hip-hop influences. Nonetheless, it is difficult to disagree with the British music writer Edwin Pouncey, reviewing 1999 releases by RZA (of the Wu-Tang Clan and Gravediggaz) and Cypress Hill, in the European avant-garde style bible *The Wire*: "With the assassination of Tupac Shakur and Biggie (Notorious BIG) Smalls, gangsta rap itself suffered a near fatal blow from which it has still to recover. Today it sounds in bad shape as it limps towards the new millennium. It'll take a rapper with superpowers to drag the genre back from the brink of its self-inflicted disaster, with their creative muscle hooked up to something more substantial than a bad mouth and a handful of 70s samples" (1999: 57).

For a sense of innovation, surprise, and musical substance in hip-hop culture and rap music, it is becoming increasingly necessary to look outside the USA to countries such as France, England, Germany, Italy, and Japan, where strong local currents of hip-hop indigenization have taken place. Models and idioms derived from the peak period of hip-hop in the USA in the mid-to late 1980s have been combined in these countries with local musical idioms and vernaculars to produce excitingly distinctive syncretic manifestations of African American influences and local indigenous elements. But these foreign developments have rarely, if ever, been acknowledged in the growing body of academic commentary on hip-hop in the USA, nor are recordings that feature them released in the parochial U.S. market, where locally produced recordings still accounted for 91 percent of the market in 1998, despite non-U.S. domestic music product reaching an all-time high of 64.6 percent in the rest of the world (Boehm 1999). This U.S. insularity is owed only in part to language barriers, as is evidenced by the increasing number of colaborations between African American and French rappers, such as Missy Elliot and MC Solaar's popular 1999 hit "All n My Grill" and Wu-Tang Clan member RZA's work with IAM and Arsenik.

Most U.S. academic commentaries on rap not only are restricted to the United States and African American contexts, but continue to insist on the socially marginal and politically oppositional aspects of U.S. hip-hop in regarding it as a coherent, cohesive, and unproblematical expression of an emancipatory African American culture of resistance. In an essay that goes sharply against this prevailing academic grain, Paul Gilroy analyzed the disappearance of any rhetoric of "freedom" from rap music in the USA since the early 1990s and its replacement by an ethos of abjection, male sexual predatoriness, and male body introspection. Using examples by artists such as R. Kelly and Snoop Doggy Dogg, Gilroy noted: " Hip-hop's marginality is as official, as routinized, as its overblown defiance; yet it is still represented as an outlaw form." He went on to identify a need to interrogate "the revolutionary conservatism that constitutes [rap's] routine political focus but which is over-simplified or more usually ignored by its academic celebrants" (1994: 51; see Mitchell 1996: 22–39 for a critique of U.S. academic analyses of hip-hop).

The origins of rap and hip-hop are usually ascribed to the Bronx in New York and to DJ Kool Herc's introduction of his "monstrous" Jamaican sound system in the mid-1970s (Toop 1991: 18–19; Rose 1994: 51–52). As Tricia Rose points out in her widely acclaimed and influential study of African American hip-hop culture, *Black Noise,* rap has important antecedents in 1960s and 1970s African American music in figures such as the Last Poets, Gil Scott-Heron, and Millie Jackson, as well as in the speeches of Malcolm X, the Black Panthers, and blaxploitation films (55). Toop paints a more complex picture in acknowledging the important influence of Jamaican sound system toasters (DJs who rapped over the instrumental dub and reggae records they played) such as Count Machouki, U Roy, and King Stitt, who were themselves influenced by the jive of 1950s African American radio DJs such as Dr. Jive and Douglas "Jocko" Henderson via the Jamaican producer Coxsone Dodd (39). This circular, diasporic influence has been invoked to justify claims that the roots of rap and hip-hop are quintessentially African American; but these roots are as culturally, eclectically, and syncretically wide ranging as they are deep. Toop lists only some of them:

> Rap's forebears stretch back through disco, street funk, radio DJs, Bo Diddley, the bebop singers, Cab Calloway, Pigmeat Marhkam, the tap dancers and comics, the Last Poets, Gil Scott-Heron, Muhammed Ali, acapella and doo-wop groups, ring games, skip-rope rhymes, prison and army songs, toasts, signifying and the dozens, all the way to the griots of Nigeria and the Gambia. No matter how far it penetrates into the twilight maze of Japanese video games and cool European electronics, its roots are still the deepest in all contemporary Afro-American music. (19)

This is not to underestimate the strong Latin American influence in breakdancing and graffiti as well as rap, and the more multicultural aspects of hip-hop culture in its manifestations in Los Angeles (see Cross 1993; Kelley 1994). The participation of Latino rappers such as Disco Wiz, DJ Charlie Chase, Ruby Dee, and Devastating Tito; graffiti artists such as Futura 2000; and breakdancers such as the Rock Steady Crew in the initial developments of hip-hop in the Bronx in the late 1970s is also an important aspect of the origins of hip-hop. The same is true of the Hispanic rap movement that developed in East Los Angeles in the 1980s led by Kid Frost and Mellow Man

Ace, although since 1993 at least five essays have appeared that give long-overdue consideration to this subject (Flores 1994, 1996; Kelly 1993; Del Barco 1996; Perkins 1996). As Cross claims, "the culture of the gang, the culture of the vato, the pachuco and westie, Eurodisco, skate culture, house, Rastafarianism and Islam all contribute to the language of hip-hop. . . . In 1993 it has become exceedingly difficult to talk about hip-hop as a unitary phenomenon" (63).

Scant attention has been given to Native American rap and hip-hop, with the exception of Neal Ullestad's 1999 survey of American Indian rap and reggae, which chronicles the "rant and roll" of the American Indian Movement activist and actor John Trudell, the "pow wow hip-hop" of Robbie Bee and the Boyz from the Rez, and the conscious rap of WithOut Rezervation (W.O.R.), who combine traditional chanting and drumming with rap, as do the Pomo–Apache Indian rapper Btaka, the Tulsa-based rapper and actor Litefoot, and Casper the Hopi reggae rapper, many of whose releases are only available on hard-to-find tapes (1999: 62–90).

In *Black Noise* Rose expresses the hope that future books on rap music and hip-hop will deal with "more globally focused projects" such as Latino rappers in Los Angeles and New York, Chinese and Japanese breakdancers in Hong Kong, and the French, German, British, and Brazilian rap scenes (1994: xiv–xv). But she seems to assume that this would involve studying the appropriation of rap and hip-hop as an essentialized, endemically African American cultural form. Potter goes so far as to suggest that the globalization of hip-hop may involve a distortion of an inherent assumed Afro-diasporic purity:

> Hip-hop . . . represents a complex weave of black Atlantic style and African American homespun. As it gains audiences around the world, there is always the danger that it will be appropriated in such a way that its histories will be obscured, and its messages replaced with others. . . . Even as it remains a global music, it is firmly rooted in the local and the temporal; it is music about "where I'm from," and as such proposes a new kind of universality. (1995: 146)

Predicating his entire argument on a misappropriation of Gilroy's concept of a "populist modernist" black Atlantic diasporic vernacular (Gilroy 1993: 45) into what he calls the "resistance postmodernism" of African American hip-hop, Potter's insistence on the authenticity of the "African American homespun" origins of hip-hop sounds like a parochial attempt to deny its appropriateness to other localities outside the USA. (It is worth recalling that Gilroy regards postmodernism as a Eurocentric notion inappropriate to black Atlantic culture, and "Afrocentrism" in the USA as more appropriately referred to as "Americocentrism" [1993: 42,197].)

Nonetheless, this book takes up Rose's challenge. I have been unable to contact any critical observers of rap and hip-hop in Hong Kong, where I was repeatedly told it did not exist, although a 1999 article by Jason Tan on the MTV Asia Web site about the eponymously titled debut EP in Cantonese of the Hong Kong rappers LMF suggests that "perhaps the first wave of hardcore hip-hop from Asia is happening earlier than expected" *(http://www.mtvasia.com)*. One thing Tan neglects to mention is that LMF stands for "Lazymuthafucka" and is a loose collective of rappers and DJs who joined forces with the Hong Kong heavy-metal band Anodize, thrash metal group Screw, and Hardcore NT to produce an expletive-ridden, declamatory hybrid sound that combines influences from Cantonese opera with hip-hop to celebrate the Street Kid Triad subculture of working-class housing estate boys *(uktsuen + sai),* and to denounce incest in a track called "Scum." Their local popularity was sufficient for them to release an album on Warner Music Hong Kong titled *Lazy Clan,* which the Hong Kong and Singapore edition of *The Voice,* HMV's monthly magazine claims "had a major impact on the local music scene, which has long been drenched in bubble-gum pop. . . . Maybe LMF is the upgraded reincarnation of forerunning Chinese rappers like [the 1960s actor] Tang Gei Chen and [Canto-pop singer] George Lam, but it has also taken its musical cues from the general hip hop movement" ("LMF, the Lazy Clan" 2000).

After selling 14,000 copies of their debut EP, LMF established themselves as virtually the sole representatives of "Canto-rap" (an alternative to the mainstream Canto-pop) in Hong Kong, attacking in their lyrics the prevalent values of Canto-pop, economic racism, and materialism espoused by the media and the younger generation. In a profile of them in the English language daily *South China Morning Post,* Kenneth Howe portrayed the group's struggle for acknowledgment of hip-hop in a climate where young people in Hong Kong are rendered conservative by a "Confucian upbringing which stifles their creativity" and do not tend to rebel like their Western counterparts. He also suggested that since the 1997 handover to China, Hong Kong youth "preferred to identify with the glamour of Canto-pop in order to distinguish themselves through material possessions from their mainland cousins." Using samples from Bruce Lee film soundtracks and 1970s Cantopop songs, the group also achieves the difficult feat of rapping in the ninetone language of Cantonese, "a linguistic Rubic's cube," although they have been criticized in some quarters for sounding forced and artificial in their attempts to combine Cantonese with hip-hop diction. Their principal rapper, MC Yan, studied French for two years in France, completed a master's degree in fine arts in Hong Kong, and draws on his knowledge of Chinese literature in his lyrics, and his rapping, influenced by the Wu-Tang Clan, is "off-rhythm, lyrics floating above and beyond the beat, in order to 'show my technique.'" In a familiar espousal of hip-hop as a vehicle for exploring and constructing youth identity, Yan claimed that "through hip-hop, we are trying to find out who we are, what we are. That's what black people in America did" (Howe 2000). But the group's 2001 EP *LMFamiglia,* with its nod to Mafia rhetoric, demonstrates a move towards the pop mainstream, with a notable absence of their trademark expletives, and tracks like "Para Salud," which they wrote for a television commercial for San Miguel beer, and "YYY," which they contributed to the soundtrack of a popular commercial film, *Gen-X Cops*. But as the first fully fledged hip-hop group in Hong Kong, they have established an important precedent.

Similarly, there is no survey of hip-hop in Brazil—where the *capoeira* fighting style originated in slave camps and developed into a dance form that was influential on breakdancing, and where violent "funk-balls" have developed where rival gangs fight it out to the sounds of hip-hop—or in other parts of Central or South America. There is no doubt that hip-hop is flourishing in this part of the world, as evidenced by the annual (since 1996) government-sponsored National Hip-Hop Conference in Cuba, which features rappers from all over Latin America. According to *The Source,* Fidel Castro regards rap music as "the existing revolutionary voice of Cuba's future" (in Ogbar and Prashad 2000: 32), and this nationalist project has been signaled by groups such as Orishas, a quartet of rappers who produced an album titled *A lo Cubano* in 1999, which was released by EMI in Spain and France and includes a track titled "537 C.U.B.A.," a rap version of "Chan-chan," the well-known opening track of the internationally celebrated *Buena Vista Social Club* album. Chile's La Pozze Latina attests to lively hip-hop activity in Latin America, as does the ironically named Colombia Rap Cartel, a collective of six hip-hop posses—formed by Carlos Andres Pacheco of the group Gotas de Rap, who released two CDs and toured Europe three times— that help emergent rappers in Bogotá, Cali, and Aguablanca. In the words of Patricia Ariza, the producer of Gotas de Rap, hip-hop in Colombia, as elsewhere in Latin America, is "a valuable cultural alternative to marginal sectors in this society" (Pratt 2000: 38).

Likewise, the Indian subcontinent and Scandinavia, both of which are reputed to have lively hip-hop scenes, will have to be left for future projects. Although such Swedish rappers as Stakka Bo, Infinite Mass, and Looptroop rap in English, sometimes even assuming U.S. accents that almost make them undistinguishable from U.S. rappers, Bjurström has made the important observation that hip-hop has functioned as a key form of resistance by youth of ethnic minorities against the white skinhead subculture and describes how the Swedish rapper Papa Dee's tongue-in-cheek claim to be an "Original Black Viking" became a rallying call for struggles against skinhead and neo-Nazi claims of Viking ancestry (Bjurström 1997: 49, 54). Other distinctive Swedish-language rappers include Mambo Kings and the female MC Feven.

There also appears to have been little critical analysis of hip-hop in Africa, apart from a 1999 master's thesis, "Tracking the Narrative: The Poetics of Identity in Rap Music and Hip Hop Culture in Cape Town," by Lee William Watkins of the University of Natal, South Africa. This ethnographic survey focuses mainly on breakdancing but analyzes the output of the Cape Town rappers Prophets of da City and Black Noise, who both espouse a global diasporic "black" identity, as well as hip-hop groups such as Grave Diggers Productions and Brasse Vannie Kaap, who identify more closely with the plight of more marginalized "colored" South Africans in post-apartheid Cape Town. The latter group raps in "a fascinating mixture of street-wise Afrikaans, English, xhosa, Arabic, ebonics and prison slang," and their use of Afrikaans "is being recognized by Afrikaans language institutions and the media as a unique rendition of the language" (Watkins 1999: 32). This official recognition of hip-hop vernacular expression as an indigenous form of cultural expression is echoed in other parts of the world, and Watkins notes intriguingly that some "colored" South African rappers identify more closely with U.S. Latino rappers than with African American hip-hop (1999: 24).

The increasing availability in some parts of the English-speaking and Francophone world of albums by the Senegalese rappers Positive Black Soul (who rap in English, French, and Wolof) and Daara J; the Moroccan posses Ahlam and Aisha Kandisha's Jarring Effects; the Algerian rappers M.B.S. (Les Micros Qui Brisent le Silence [The Microphones That Shatter the Silence]), Caravanne, S.O.S., and Le Constat (included on a 1998 Virgin France compilation, *Algerap*); and the South African rappers Prophets of da City and Zimbabwe Legit, for example, also provide evidence of a distinctive Africanization of hip-hop culture. This challenges the often shallowly rhetorical and largely imagined Afrocentricity of much U.S.-based rap music (e.g., Keyes 1996). There is also a plethora of French rappers of African origin, attested to by names such as IAM (Imperial Asiatic Man), NAP (New African Poets), Afrodiziac, and Addis Posse. As MC Solaar has commented, he and other French rappers of African origin are stigmatized as "coming from Africa or French West Indies. When a black person in the United States says,

'I'm an American,' there is evidence. But here, people think we come from Africa" (Linden 1998: 170).

As Ted Swedenburg points out in his chapter on Islamic rap in France and the United Kingdom, French Islamic rappers such as Akhenaton of IAM are also skeptical about what they see as a bogus rhetorical embrace of Islam by many U.S. rappers. Similarly, if the English journalist David Hudson's report of the hard-line militant Islamic rhetoric of the Palestinian rap group She-hadin (Martyrs) is correct, they make the rhetoric of U.S. Nation of Islam rappers seem mild by comparison. Shehadin advocate suicide and bomb attacks against Israelis and a sternly moralistic Islamic stance, expressed in a song titled "Order Your Wife to Wear a Veil for a Pure Palestine" (Hudson 1995). But as Swedenburg has argued, it is perhaps inappropriate to define the indigenous *anasheed* chanting employed by Islamic musical groups as rap music (correspondence with the author 1998).

War is frequently used as a rhetorical trope in U.S. rap. But when Chuck D of Public Enemy invokes the war in Bosnia to contrast the relatively small degree of violence rappers reflect in the ghettos of the USA (as he did in Isaac Julien's 1995 film about sexism, homophobia, and violence in reggae and rap, *The Darker Side of Black),* he might spare a thought for the Croatian hardcore rap group the Ugly Leaders. This group features DJ Pimp Tha' Ho' and Lyrical Maniac MC Condom X, whose names sound like desperate, juvenile parodies of U.S. hip-hop sobriquets. But as DJ Pimp Tha' Ho' has stated, hip-hop is the most appropriate medium of expression for war-torn Bosnia: "Rap is the form of music that had the power and directness to say what needed to be said. It fit our situation. . . . People here are also killing and dying for nothing." The Ugly Leaders are forced to write their most provocative lyrics in English; otherwise, their record label will not publish them. But their signifying (a hip-hop technique Potter defines as "repetition with a difference" [27], or versioning) on U.S. themes includes recording a Croatian-language version of Coolio's "Gangsta's Paradise" that alludes to the succession of Balkan governments and plays on the fact that "paradise" means "tomato" in Croatian (Greenwalt 1996). Similarly, the Algerian rappers M.B.S. directly invoke war-torn Algeria in their 1998 album *Ouled El Bahja,* produced in a combination of French and Arabic, and as the French reviewer Fred Guilledoux states, "They don't bother to strike any poses or hide behind the wire: the most terrible violence is right on their street corner. . . . The message is crude and chaotic, like the sound: the voices are not really mixed evenly. But a formidable vitality and a determination to fight against hatred is unleashed from these fragments, which can leave no one indifferent, either here or down there" (1998: 89; author's translation). Bouziane Daoudi has estimated that there are more than 60 hip-hop groups in Oran and about 100 in Algiers, "turning Algeria into the rap leader of Arab nations and probably the entire Muslim world despite a meagre musical output." Linguistically blending French, English, and both literary and spoken Arabic, sometimes in the same sentence, Algerian rappers display considerable verbal dexterity, and the Algiers and Oran hip-hop scenes have shifted in focus from an initial middle-class orientation toward a more underprivileged constituency (2000: 34–35).

In its recombination into local linguistic, musical, and political contexts around the world, rap music and hip-hop culture have in many cases become a vehicle for various forms of youth protest. They are also used in different local contexts to espouse the causes of ethnic minorities (e.g., in the Basque Country or Aotearoa–New Zealand) and to make political statements about local racial, sexual, employment, and class issues (e.g., in France, Italy, Germany, and elsewhere). They are also used as the basis for musical experimentations that combine local vernacular traditions and influences with break beats, scratching, MCing and signifying adapted from U.S. hip-hop. The essays in this book explore these national and regional appropriations of rap and hip-hop within their different social, cultural, and ethnic contexts. In doing so, they avoid the clichéd Eurocentric rhetoric of postmodernism too often invoked in academic attempts to explain rap inadequately in terms of pastiche, fragmentation, the loss of history, and the blurring of boundaries between "high art" and popular culture (e.g., Shusterman 1991; Potter 1995).

These essays cover local manifestations of hip-hop in most of Europe, Anglophone and Francophone Canada, Japan, Korea, and Australasia. A common feature of the hip-hop scenes in most of these countries is their multiethnic, multicultural nature as vernacular expressions of migrant diasporic cultures, which would appear to reflect the multicultural origins of rap in the South Bronx more significantly than current Afrocentric manifestations of rap in the USA. There is ample evidence here that rap and hip-hop have become just as "rooted in the local" in Naples, Marseilles, Amsterdam, the Basque region, Berlin, Sofia, Sydney, Auckland, or the Shibuya district of Tokyo as it ever was in Compton, South Central Los Angeles, or the South Bronx. The fact that in these localities it often tends to draw on a considerably wider range of musical genres, idioms, and influences than it does in the USA is surely a more appropriate argument for the locality, temporality, and "universality" of hip-hop. The few U.S. journalistic or academic commentaries that do exist on rap music outside the U.S. (Bernard et al. 1992; Cocks 1992; Jones 1994; Perkins 1996) tend to assume that it is an exotic and derivative outgrowth of an African American–owned idiom, confined to national borders but subject to continuous assessment in terms of U.S. norms and standards. Perkins, for example, in his essay "Youth's Global Village: An Epilogue," largely restricts himself to Latino rap in the USA and a footnote referring to Bernard's and others' survey of global rap that appeared in the *New York Times* in 1993 (see Mitchell 1996: 36–38), and he wrongly identifies Apache Indian as based in India rather than the United Kingdom (Perkins 1996: 269).

In its initial stages, appropriations of rap and hip-hop outside the USA often mimicked U.S. models, but in most countries where rap has taken root, hip-hop scenes have rapidly developed from an adoption to an adaptation of U.S. musical forms and idioms. This has involved an increasing syncretism and incorporation of local linguistic and musical features. Few attempts have yet been made in academic commentaries to analyze the various foreign adaptations of the genre in the context of musical and national or regional languages of individual countries, or even in terms of a global fusion of transnational influences. But it is notable that *The Source*, arguably the leading U.S. hip-hop magazine, in 1998 began to acknowledge rap music outside the USA, no doubt because it has become so prominent in major music-producing countries such as France, Japan, and Germany that it is increasingly difficult to ignore. *The Source*'s special 100th issue of January 1998 featured, along with a history of U.S. hip-hop and various top-100 lists of U.S. rap recordings, brief overviews of hip-hop scenes in London, Jamaica, Vancouver, Paris, Senegal, Italy, Japan, Holland, Spain, Hawai'i, and Cuba. Conservatively estimating that there were more than 150 rap groups in France, making it the largest market for hip-hop after the USA, Tracii McGregor argued that this global spread made hip-hop "the biggest youth-driven culture since the sixties rock movement" (1998: 109). *The Source* followed up its new global awareness in its March 1998 issue with features on Latino hip-hop and another survey of the French scene, whose title, "An American Artform in Paris" (Linden 1998), indicated a prevailingly colonialist view of hip-hop as a U.S.-owned musical subculture. Otherwise, it is left to *Billboard* to offer sporadic global market reports on rap music outside the USA, such as the cryptic coverage of hip-hop scenes in Tokyo, Munich, Paris, Milan, Amsterdam, Sydney, and the United Kingdom in its "Rap Spotlights" in November 1997, December 1998, June 1999, and December 2000.

Roland Robertson (1995) has employed the term "glocal," combining the global with the local, to emphasize that each is in many ways defined by the other and that they frequently intersect, rather than being polarized opposites. Robertson adopted this blend of local and global from its use in Japan to describe the adaptation of global farming techniques to fit local conditions and its subsequent use as a marketing buzzword to refer to the indigenization of global phenomena. In his chapter on Japanese rap music, Ian Condry notes that a Japanese rapper, ECD, uses the metaphor of "a flame flying across the ocean" to describe the hip-hop scene in Tokyo, indicating that although U.S. rap was the inspiration, the local hip-hop scene caught fire on the fuel that was already there. This "glocal" indigenizing dynamic has reproduced itself in hip-hop and rap scenes the world over, to the extent that it is arguable that rap can now surely be regarded as a universal musical language and its diffusion one that has taken root in most parts of the globe. This was confirmed by the Italian radio announcer and music critic Luca De Gennaro, who stated in the container insert of the first compilation of Italian rap music, the 1990 *Italian Rap Attack* (ironically, almost all in English): "Rap is a universal language, in whatever language it happens to be in, and whatever part of the world it is produced" (in Canevacci et al. 1993: 193). In 1996 he was echoed in the antipodes of Italy by the New Zealand record producer Alan Jannson, who was responsible for OMC's worldwide pop-rap hit "How Bizarre": "[Maori and Polynesians] can listen to a rap track from the States and straight away they can start rapping too. Rap now is not just an American thing, it's a new universal language" (Walker 1995). A 1997 release, *Kataaq*, by an Inuit rap group from Greenland called the Nuuk Posse, which Jake Barnes has described as ranging from "surreal Trip Hop to Public Enemy–style agit prop" (1997: 65), criticizes, among other things, the Danish language dominance of Greenland. This illustrates that the universality of hip-hop is spreading even to some of the world's farthest peripheries.

GLOBAL NOISE: A TOUR GUIDE

The first part of this book focuses on Europe. We begin, appropriately, in France, the world's second largest hip-hop market and the fifth largest global music market, with 7 percent of the world's music sales but an unusually high proportion of local product (Negus 1994: 159–60), although the domestic share of the French music market dropped from 48 percent to 44 percent in 1998 (Boehm 1999). Francophone rap was given a spur in the early 1990s by a decision of the French Ministry of Culture, which passed a law insisting that French-language stations play a minimum of 40 percent of French-language music. As Claude Grunitzky has pointed out, rap took root in France as early as 1983, when a national television network introduced a weekly program called *Hip hop;* "French hip hop continues to grow into a self-sufficient culture, one in which American attitudes are now deemed inappropriate and far removed from French realities" (1998). The French monthly hip-hop magazine *Groove* combines features on both U.S. and French MCs and DJs, along with CD reviews and articles on the other elements of hip-hop culture, graffiti and breakdancing, and even includes a CD featuring the artists covered in each issue. French rappers have achieved high levels of commercial success in France and often appear in the French charts. For example, MC Solaar sold more than a million copies of his second album, *Prose Combat*, worldwide in 1994, despite the language barrier (Binet 1998: 117). IAM sold an estimated 700,000 copies of their third album, *L'école du micro d'argent* (The School of the Silver Microphone) in Francophone-only markets in three months in 1997.

In chapter 1, André Prévos traces the arrival of African American rap and hip-hop in France in 1984 and the emergence of French rap during the mid-1980s. He also traces the antecedents of its linguistic wordplay (such as the reverse slang *verlan*) in earlier recordings of popular French song artists like Bobby Lapointe, Charles Trénet, Yves Montand, and Alain Bashung. He places rap in the context of traditions of appropriation of African American musical forms such as jazz and blues in France and shows how syncretism emerged in the very first French recording that made explicit use of rap techniques. This was by the group Chagrin d'Amour, who combined links with earlier French *chanson* traditions with the African American idioms of rap. He explores the "adoption" period in French rap in the 1980s, which was marked by the emergence of French recordings whose stylistic features were closely related to those of the U.S. models they tried to emulate in terms of self-aggrandizement, boasting, and attitudinizing. Prévos emphasizes the variety of ethnic origins among French rappers, from the French Caribbean to the Arab populations of North Africa in particular. Its origins in the immigrant and working-class housing projects of the *banlieues* (outer suburbs) of French cities, as displayed in Matthieu Kassovitz's 1995 film *La haine* (Hate), are also noted. A broad variety of musical inflections ranging from hardcore rap to reggae and raggamuffin distinguishes French rap from U.S. rap and gives it features more in common with British and Italian hip-hop.

The "adaptation" period of French hip-hop in the 1990s involved the growth of hardcore rap and Zuluism (based on Afrika Bambaataa's Zulu Nation). During this period U.S. models were for the most part adapted directly to French realities, but other concepts, such as Afrocentrism, could not be translated wholesale into the French context. Prévos makes the important point that French rappers such as IAM attempted to circumvent the so-called return-to-Africa ideology prevalent among some U.S. rappers in order to avoid playing into the hands of right-wing anti-Arab movements like Le Pen's National Front. Consequently, IAM constructed an elaborate "pharaohist" ideology and mythology that does not celebrate black or Arabic Africa, but rather adapts the Africa of ancient Egypt into religious symbology. They also mythologize their native Marseilles, a marginalized city with a high non-European immigrant population, as *le côté oscur* (the obscure side) of France, and they rap in Marseilles dialect. Described by Grunitzky as "by far the biggest and most consistent rap group in France" (1998), IAM have gone on to collaborate with the Wu-Tang Clan in the USA, Algerian raï singers Khaled and Cheb Mami, and the Montreal-based Francophone rappers Dubmatique, as well as releasing a plethora of solo albums by individual group members. As Steve Cannon has noted, there is in Afro-French rap "a closer physical and therefore less mythical relationship of (black) rappers in France to the *'pays d'origine'* [African homeland]" than in the USA (1997: 164.) Cannon also notes that despite the fact that only 6 percent of the population of France consists of non-European immigrants, hip-hop has become a vital form of antiracist expression for ethnic minorities:

> [S]tudies of hip hop in France in the 1980s and 1990s suggest that not only is the most numerical participation in both production and consumption of hip hop "products" among people of minority ethnic origin, but also that hip hop in France is characterized to a great extent by its role as a cultural expression of resistance by young people of minority ethnic origin to the racism, oppression, and social marginalization they experience within France's *banlieues* and in its major towns and cities. (155)

Prévos also deals with recent clashes with the law in relation to obscenity and a rhetoric of cop killing by French rappers such as Suprême NTM (also covered more sketchily in Huq 1999) and Ministère AMER. These are analyzed not as a duplication of the censorship of gangsta rap that Ice-T's "Cop Killer" encountered in the USA (see also Prévos 1998), but as a rhetorical adoption of patterns of violence that may be a more general social phenomenon in modern urban societies. That French hip-hop and rap music have become a major world force was illustrated by the participation of more than eighty rappers from France and French-speaking Switzerland, many of them African and Asian immigrants from the banlieues outside Paris, in an eight-hour freestyle marathon at the Leysin Alps Festival on 31 March 1998. Rap's rich impact on the French language was also illustrated by the publication in 1998 of a controversial dictionary of French urban slang partly derived from French rap, *Comment tu tchatches?* (How Do You Talk?) by a Sorbonne professor, Jean-Pierre Goudaillier. This charts the language of the French banlieues, known as *cefron*, "a melting pot of expressions that reflect the ethnic make-up of the communities where it is used, borrowing words from regional dialects as well as Arab, Creole, Gypsy and Berber languages" (Bell 1999). It also reveals French rappers and North African immigrant youth to be talented linguists who often speak French, *cefron*, and their native language at home, rather than the illiterate and uneducated subclass the French mass media portray. The indigenous diversity of French hip-hop was illustrated in 1999 when Manau, a white Celtic hip-hop group based in Breton, reached the top 5 in the French charts with their album *Panique celtique,* on which traditional Celtic instruments such as bagpipes and accordion are blended with scratching and rapping.

Ted Swedenburg's chapter on Islamic rap in the United Kingdom and France builds on Prévos's work on Francophone rap, extending his discussion of IAM's pharaohism and examining the work of other Muslim-influenced, rap-related musicians in France and England. Focusing primarily on the work of three prominent figures in European Islamic hip-hop—Aki Nawaz, of the U.K. group Fun-Da-Mental; Natacha Atlas, formerly of the London-based Transglobal Underground; and Akhenaton, of IAM in France—Swedenburg embeds their projects in the ethnic, political, cultural, and religious aspects of a hip-hop activist response to "Islamophobia" in Europe. Sensitive to the complexities of exoticism, political militancy, and prejudice surrounding Islamic migrant cultures in Europe, he analyzes the output of these three figures in relation to their constituencies of South Asian youth in Britain and Arab youth in France. He also discusses the critical views of the Sicilian Muslim Akhenaton on what he regards as inauthentic, "homemade" African American manifestations of Islam, despite his being influenced by U.S. Nation of Islam and Five Percent Nation rappers. Swedenburg concludes that the "transglobal Islamic underground" of Muslim-influenced rap in Europe has been almost totally ignored in the USA, despite its clear affinities with the Islamic rhetoric of much African American hip-hop culture.

Swedenburg's work on Aki Nawaz and Natacha Atlas draws on research done by David Hesmondhalgh on these artists' involvement with Nawaz's London-based recording label Nation Records (2000). In chapter 3, Hesmondhalgh and Caspar Melville expand on this work to consider manifestations of rap and hip-hop in the context of "urban breakbeat culture" in Britain. It is arguable that with a few exceptions, such as the success of the British rappers Slick Rick and Monie Love in the USA, hip-hop culture and rap music as such have never taken root in Britain, whose domestic share of the music market fell from 54 percent to 48 percent in 1998 (Boehm 1999). Surveying "Brit-hop" in *Billboard* in December 1998, Kwaku writes, "The story of British hip hop in 1998 is a mixture of sad tales of under-funded promotion by the majors, who fail to fully exploit the potential of their domestic rap acts, and ongoing struggles by small cash-strapped indie labels to keep British rap ticking over" (1998: 52). In the 1980s rappers such as Derek B. and Young MC had some degree of subcultural success among West Indian and black British communities in Britain, and groups such as Credit to the Nation, the London Posse, Eusebe, Earthling, Gunshot, and Anglo-West Indian MC Roots Manuva consolidated this subcultural following in the 1990s. But the multi-ethnic (South Asian, West Indian, African, and Anglo-Saxon) configurations of British and British-Asian hip-hop, ragga, techno, rave culture, trip-hop and drum 'n' bass have exerted a far wider influence on British listening, dancing, and subcultural behavioral practices. Rap and hip-hop are still largely perceived in the United Kingdom as U.S. imports. The Jamaican sound system culture on which U.S. hip-hop is based had already taken root in Britain before the evolution of rap and hip-hop in the USA and provided a basis on which British creolizations of hip-hop developed. This occurred through the club culture that evolved in Britain in the 1980s, often crossing boundaries of class, race, and ethnicity, and provided the social context in which they spread. Novel syncretisms evolved in combinations such as bhangramuffin (in the work of Apache Indian, Fun-Da-Mental, Kaliphz, the Asian Dub Foundation, and others), jungle, techno, ragga and scratching (DJ Krush, DJ Rap, DJ Vadim, Blade, the Herbaliser, et al.), drum 'n' bass, electronica, and trip-hop (Goldie, Roni Size, Massive Attack, Portishead, Tricky, et al.; see Johnson 1996; Eshun 1998; Reynolds 1998). While these manifestations were undoubtedly initially influenced by U.S. hip-hop, they represent a continually shifting, heterogeneous, and complex music scene in which hip-hop is displaced and often delyricized. In the process it becomes a more amorphous, abstract, and atmospherical cross-genre musical practice, engulfing a wide range of home-grown musical and lyrical influences. As Daddy G. of Massive Attack has stated: "We had the realization that trying to sound American wasn't what we were about. We had to take in all the other musical influences from where we came from — punk, new wave — so we took it all on board and were true to ourselves instead of making dodgy American-style records. Since then we've always talked about things immediately around us instead of guns and banging your 'ho'" (quoted in Holmes 1998: 5). But within the diversity and complexity of the U.K. breakbeat culture — which, Hesmondhalgh and Melville argue, cannot be simply labeled "hybrid" — diametrical ethical conflicts between black and white, "intelligent" and "stupid," ambient and hardcore, and soulless and soulful are played out as in other hip-hop scenes.

Nonetheless, recent developments in U.K. hip-hop indicate parallel developments with U.S. hip-hop. The drive-by shooting in London in July 1999 of Tim Goodman, the most influential U.K. hip-hop DJ in mainstream radio, had alarming echoes of similar occurrences in the USA. And Tricky's 1999 album *Juxtapose,* produced after a two-year sojourn in New York and featuring DJ Muggs from Cypress Hill and Grease from the Ruff Ryders, as well as the ballistic British MC Mad Dog trying to emulate U.S. rappers, displays a seemingly perverse and cryptic attempt to form a (perhaps parodic) attachment to some of the more misogynist and violent aspects of U.S. rap. Although the album's opening track, "For Real," accuses gangsta rappers of being more influenced by films than by reality, Tricky regards *Juxtapose*'s characteristically blunted beats and skewed rhythms as an attempt to make "a more commercial record" (Hitchings 1999: 23) and includes tracks titled "I Like the Girls" and "Hot Like a Sauna." These somewhat belie Tricky's claims that he is "trying to muck up the hip hop scene because it's all pretty tedious at the moment — not so much musically, more lyrically. I mean, they talk about the same things — the tough guy stuff. I don't talk about guns or girls, but there's room for a different thing" (Cyclone 1999: 14). As Peter Shapiro commented in *The Wire,* while Tricky's "willingness to confront hip hop's ugliness is laudable, his refusal to take on hip hop on its own turf is a cop out" (1999a: 58). Nonetheless, Shapiro claims, Tricky's idiosyncratic criticisms of U.S. hip-hop from an outsider's perspective, however ambiguous, are more effective than Public Enemy's onslaught against betrayers of hip-hop's values by the likes of Puff Daddy, Funkmaster Flew, and Def Jam in *There's a Poison Goin' On* (1999), which "comes over like the product of too much in-fighting" (1999b: 55). Despite its full-on attacks against the rap recording industry, *There's a Poison Goin' On,* which was made available on the Internet a month before it was released in record shops, was lauded in *Billboard* for "giving the finger to the system" and using the Internet as "an effective, direct route to potential music consumers" (Atwood 1999: 26). It would appear that however hard "renegade rappers" (Atwood 1999: 26) in the USA try to subvert or critique the regimes and institutions of rap music, they end up being effortlessly absorbed by them.

In his overview of German-language rap and hip-hop since the influx of breakdancing and graffiti there in 1983, Mark Pennay's chapter reflects upon some of the ways in which the domination of the English-speaking market has far-reaching and often subtle effects upon popular-music production in non-English-speaking countries. This occurs even in Germany, which, along with the United Kingdom, accounts for 9 percent of the global music market and is the third-largest popular-music market in the world after the USA and Japan, with a 43 percent share of domestic product in

1998 (Boehm 1999). Pennay argues that the restricted porosity of the language barrier led directly to the emergence of distinctive German performers and a fierce contestation of the domain of German rap, with lasting effects upon the genre. Drawing on discussions and debates carried out in German hip-hop fanzines and Internet sites, he analyzes the contrasting output of the most prominent German rap groups, Advanced Chemistry and Die Fantastichen Vier, who represent the hardcore and commercial poles of German hip-hop respectively. He also examines their female counterparts Cora E and Tic Tac Toe. He emphasizes the multicultural, migrant ambit of German hip-hop in the context of the increase in right-wing racist violence in the 1990s, which echoes similar manifestations in France, and its different political ramifications in East and West Germany. Since its watershed year of contestation in 1993, Pennay argues, the two poles of German hip-hop have begun to merge. A similar situation is also evident in Italy, as are certain similar continuities between hip-hop and the punk rock movements of the 1980s.

In his important 1998 article "From Krauts with Attitudes to Turks with Attitudes," Dietmar Elflein has discussed the challenges made to the "nationalisation" of the German hip-hop scene by Turkish and other "migrant hip hop" groups (1998: 255–65). As elsewhere, important primary U.S. influences on German hip-hop were Charlie Ahern's 1982 film *Wild Style* and the 1984 film *Beat Street*, produced by Harry Belafonte. U.S. role models and English lyrics predominated in Germany in the mid- to late 1980s, but in 1991 the first Turkish-language rap recording, "Bir Yabancimin Hayati" (The Life of the Stranger), was released. In the same year a compilation titled *Krauts with Attitude* was released, in which only three of the fifteen groups involved, including Die Fantastischen Vier, rapped in German; the others rapped in English. But as a result of the success of Die Fantastischen Vier's "pop rap," terms such as "100 percent German hip hop" and *deutscher Hip Hop* indicated the emergence of a rhetoric of national identity in German hip-hop. In 1995 the compilation *Cartel,* featuring predominantly the Turkish-language rap crews Karaken (who also used samples from Turkish arabesque and Pop Muzik), Da Crime Posse, and Erci C., which sold more than 300,000 copies in Turkey—though only 20,000 copies in Germany—signaled the emergence of a Turkish-German migrant rap scene, which became known as "Oriental hip-hop." Modeling itself on the U.S. Nation of Islam, this "artificially constructed ethnic minority which was supposedly 'Turkish'" (261) became something of an oppositional movement to German national hip-hop. By the mid-1990s hundreds of rap groups in the Ruhr district in southern Germany could be described as Turkish or Kurd but were unknown outside of youth community centers and escaped the attention of everyone except social workers (263). A more diverse multiculturalism manifested itself in a 1997 release, "NO! Wanna Be," by the group TCA (the Microphone Mafia), which included rappers of Spanish, Italian, Turkish, and German origin and which used musical samples from all these countries. This more diverse "immigrant hip-hop" movement, which includes the popular hardcore group Advanced Chemistry, who use West African musical samples, and Indeed, who use Korean musical samples, emphasize the multiethnicity of a national scene which Elflein describes as "by its nature, various and pluralistic" (264).

In his study of the localization of hip-hop in Frankfurt, the English academic Andy Bennett has emphasized the important role played in expressing locally relevant issues and themes by that city's North African, Southeast Asian, and Southern European immigrant ethnic minority groups (2000: 140). While the first wave of ethnic minority rappers, represented by Advanced Chemistry, made a point of rapping in German to combat racism and establish their citizenship credentials, Bennett points out that in a second wave, Turkish rappers in Germany have embraced the Turkish language and traditional Turkish music as a way of emphasizing their ethnic difference: "traditional Turkish musical styles have been fused with African American rap styles to produce a distinctive variation of the rap sound. If German language rap has come to signify the voice of the second-generation immigrant attempting to integrate into German society, then Turkish rap works to a broadly opposite effect, the whole Turkish rap movement translating into a singly defiant message aimed at the Turk's white German hosts" (145).

Pennay's brief consideration of the reception of rap music in East Germany prior to German unification leads us into Claire Levy's assessment in chapter 5 of the absorption of rap and hip-hop in the Eastern European context of Bulgaria. The influence of African American rap and hip-hop began to be felt in Bulgaria in the early 1980s, mostly through the activities of DJs in discotheques. As a result, some of the more commercially successful U.S. rappers such as Kurtis Blow, MC Hammer, Public Enemy, and Coolio became familiar to Bulgarian listeners and dancers, especially teenagers. Rap music, along with breakdancing, and other visual elements of hip-hop culture, was absorbed into the everyday lives of many young Bulgarians, especially in the larger cities. Levy analyzes the impact of rap music in Bulgaria from two perspectives: as a fashion involving the use of stereotyped images of black rappers in mainstream pop music, and as an expression of social realities in more marginal local contexts. Both manifestations exist in Bulgarian youth practices and are analyzed in relation to various pop-related activities in the Bulgarian musical mainstream. These include television entertainers who incorporate rap into their routines, television and radio commercials, and songs by composers such as Assen Dragnev, who combines a curious symbiosis of rap and regional Bulgarian folk music. The output of recent Bulgarian rap groups who have imitated black American rappers but who attempt to go beyond hip-hop fashions in symbolizing (through their lyrics, behavior, life style, etc.) the voice of a distinct social group with elements in common with the black ghetto rappers of the USA is also examined. Prominent examples are Gumeni Glavi (Rubber Heads), Nishto (Nothing), Defect, Drugite (the Others) and M'glata (Fog). As in other Central European countries, such as the Czech Republic, where groups such as Rapmasters and J.A.R. have had chart successes (see Mitchell 1996) and DJs and rap groups have proliferated in recent years, rap in Bulgaria was absorbed in the amalgamated context of pop, dance, and techno music. Its local manifestations often combine seemingly disparate and clashing musical idioms with ethnic folk music inflections in a genre-defying syncretism.

In her study of the incorporations of hip-hop in Holland, Mir Wermuth examines the ways in which young Dutch people, both white and black, have adapted hip-hop from Harlem to Haarlem and used it to create an individual and collective identity for themselves. This process has involved the creation of a relatively small space in which to produce rap music and hip-hop in the national language, known as Nederhop (see also Krims 2000). A significant proportion of Dutch rap is produced by black immigrants from the country's former colonies and is in either English (as in the case of the internationally successful Urban Dance Squad and 2 Unlimited) or Surinamese patois (*sranang tongo,* a creole language). Dutch-language rap, as produced by hardcore groups such as the Amsterdam-based Osdoorp Posse, who won the annual Dutch pop music award for 1995, had little commercial success in Holland before the mid-1990s. Wermuth deals with the role played by women in Dutch hip-hop but also argues that despite its espousal by black immigrants in Holland, Dutch rap has not tended to reflect the ethnic and political concerns of rap in other countries. Sluger (1998: 124) has noted the example of Extince, a rapper who had a string of number-1 hits in English over a ten-year career, but who in 1997 began rapping in Dutch slang in a track titled "Spraakwater." This led the way to commercial success for a number of Dutch rappers in the late 1990s. Out of this situation considerable discussion has arisen about issues such as authenticity, purity, and the adaptation and the incorporation of what is regarded by many Dutch hip-hop fans as "originally black music." Drawing on debates within British cultural studies about authenticity and its various polarities, as well as her fieldwork with Dutch hip-hop fans, Wermuth discusses Dutch-language rap in relation to

Anglophonic and African American rap and the ethical and aesthetic judgments made by Dutch fans.

Issues and pressures relating to authenticity recur in chapter 7, in which the anthropologist Jacqueline Urla provides a detailed, in-depth analysis of the work of Negu Gorriak (the Crude Winters), a punk-rock group that incorporate raps and that has represented the Basque nationalist cause in Spain. Breakdancing, graffiti writing, and rapping infiltrated Spanish cities such as Madrid and Barcelona, as elsewhere in Europe, in the mid-1980s. Spanish hip-hop posses such as BZN and the Jungle Kings were the first to release albums, to be followed later by the colorfully named Club de los Poetas Violentas, Los Verdaderos Kreyentes de la Religion del Hip Hop, and 7 Notas 7 Colores (Santos 1998: 126). But Negu Gorriak, a fiercely antistate, anticapitalist, eclectic punk-rock group based in Usurbil, drew upon the visual codes and musical forms of "nation-conscious rappers" in African American hip-hop. They combined this with punk, ska, reggae, and raï musical influences and used this syncretism to espouse the cause of Basque language and nationalism as militant political activists. Urla charts the group's development from the punk-rock group Kortatu working in the Basque tradition of "radical rock," through a lawsuit and a fine for offenses against a Spanish military officer, to their international tours. As they began to play outside Spain, they forged links of solidarity with oppressed ethnic minorities throughout Europe and South America, and they seemed to encounter few language barriers, despite their continual use of the minority Basque language. The group's bitter disillusionment with the first appearance in Spain of their idols, Public Enemy, who were ignorant of the Basque cause and preferred to play for the U.S. army rather than for what they saw as a homogenously "white" Spanish audience, is also discussed. Drawing on notions of "strategic antiessentialism" and "domestication," Urla argues persuasively for the appropriation of rap as a global idiom, with particular emphasis on its use as a political weapon to "fight the power" in specific ethnic localities.

Political activist and punkoid "combat" rappers like Negu Gorriak also exist in Italy, where extreme-left posses like Onda Rossa Posse, Assalti Frontali, and AK 47 have used similar forms of revolutionary rhetoric. But by and large the Italian hip-hop scene is less concerned than rappers in other European countries with migrant ethnic minorities, expressing instead a focus on the diversity of dialects and customs in the different regions of Italy. The earliest Italian rap recordings and performances in English gave way in the early 1990s to the use of regional dialects by individual rappers such as the Salento-born Papa Ricky and regional posses such as Almamegretta,

Africa Unite, Mau Mau, 99 Posse, Sud Sound System, and others, many of whom were associated with what has been referred to as "Mediterranean reggae." These groups were also part of a computer-linked network of underground *centri sociali*, or social clubs, which functioned as more than simply music venues. Chapter 8 offers a survey of this nationally linked but regionally diverse movement of Italian hip-hop, which combines the influence of British Jamaican ragga and African American and Latino rappers and has developed alongside a resurgence of 1970s-style mass oppositional political activity in Italy, both reflecting and providing a soundtrack for it. The importance of the centri sociali as both venues and nurturing places for the development of indigenous Italian rap styles and idioms is also discussed. In the process, contestations about the centri sociali as indicators of authenticity and street credibility against more individualistic, "funky" appropriations of hip-hop in pop contexts (for instance, Jovanotti, Frankie Hi NRG MC, DJ Flash, and Articolo 31) are examined. The musical lineage of Italian rap, which, it could be argued, extends from seventeenth-century opera *recitativo* to Mediterranean folk music and Italian punk rock, is also dealt with. Much Italian rap, although taking the form of syncretic "stylistic exercises" influenced by African American and Spanish-language rap, has also functioned as an alternative mode of social and political discourse that has spoken out about local social problems such as homelessness, unemployment, and police repression and attacked targets such as political corruption, the Mafia, and the Northern League. (It is particularly interesting to note the anti-Mafia stance of much Italian hip-hop in the context of the uncritical embrace by many U.S. gangsta rappers of Italian American Mafia role models. These have largely been adopted secondhand from the overblown stereotypes of Martin Scorsese's films; see Rodriguez 1997.) The use of regional dialects and instrumentation in Italian rap serves as a cultural repository for "tribalized" local cultural forms, and gives Italian rap a folkloric dimension which aligns it with rap music in other European countries.

From Europe we move to Asia, and in chapter 9 Ian Condry surveys the Japanese hip-hop scene, which encompasses a diversity of styles that provides yet another window on the interaction between global popular youth culture and local identity. What began as a dance fad in the early 1980s in the Hokoten "pedestrian paradise" in Yoyogi Park in Tokyo has evolved into a hip-hop scene that has both commercial and underground currents. Drawing on a year and a half (1995–97) of ethnographic research in Tokyo clubs and recording studios, Condry discusses the various styles of "J-rap" as it developed in the 1990s and argues for the importance of the club scene as the real site of Japanese rap's growth and development. Although occupying only a very small portion of the 78 percent domestic music market in 1998 (Boehm 1999) in the second-largest music market in the world (12 percent, compared with the USA's 31 percent), Japanese rap reveals significant tensions between hip-hop culture and Japanese language, ethnicity, and culture. Commercial interests are entwined in a complicated way with the music. In 1994 debate broke out among Japanese rappers about what constituted "real" Japanese rap. Was it the "party rap" or "rap lite" of groups such as East End X Yuri, which appealed to teenage girls and dealt with light-hearted love and having fun? Or was it the "underground" hip-hop of Microphone Pager and others, which appealed to teenage boys and took a more oppositional stance toward mainstream society? Party rappers have been more commercially successful, and some argue that they offer the most honest picture of Japan as a peaceful country. Underground rappers have created a more active Tokyo club scene, and their struggles to "keep it real" have involved using hip-hop culture to interpret their own experiences. For them, an oppressive system lurks behind the glossy image of Japan's success.

The depoliticization of Japanese rap relates to its history. Originally taken as a vocal style, musicians struggled with perceived deficiencies in the Japanese language, namely, a grammar that makes it difficult to produce interesting rhymes and the difficulty of giving Japanese, an unaccented language, the punctuated rhythm of rap. As the language barrier was crossed and information about the history of rap became more widely available, an increasingly holistic way of thinking about hip-hop culture came to the fore, illustrated by groups like Scha-Dar-Ra-Par, who manage to bridge the gap between hardcore rap and "rap lite." Rap and hip-hop have been appropriated in Japan within the context of a widespread dichotomy between pop-music heaven and school-and-exam hell experienced by young Japanese people. The current generation of Japanese youth grew up after the postwar economic miracle, yet face a shrinking job market after the bursting of the bubble economy of the 1980s. Japanese rap shows how they are using the idioms of hip-hop to envision a new Japan and their own identity within it.

In chapter 10 Sarah Morelli examines the reception of U.S. rap music in Korea and the social and cultural contexts of the formation of Korean rap and hip-hop. As in Bulgaria, hip-hop has developed within a predominantly pop- and disco-oriented dance-music culture. Since the onset of its popularity in Korea in 1992, rap has been overwhelmingly accepted and enthusiastically consumed by an ever-growing audience of Korean youth. Break-dancing has also provided a dream of escape from the poverty of young working-class Koreans. Hip-hop and other symbols of African American culture have also been adopted into Korean culture through the visual signs of fashion, dance, and gestures. Though phonetic considerations seemed at first to make it impossible to incorporate rap vocal styles into Korean popular music, Korean musicians have managed to do so. The result is a combination of rap with several other musical genres already popular in Korean *shinsaedae*, or youth culture. Korean rappers typically use rap in verses and combine its *sprechstimme* (speech-singing) style with melodies in the style of heavy metal, funk, rock, or even pop ballads.

This syncretism of a wide range of musical genres, often by the same group in the course of a single album, is now commonplace in Korea. One example of it is a group called Noise, whose album sleeve for *Third Revolution* describes the musical genres of each track: "Rave Dance Music," "Reggae House Music," "European Hip-Hop," "Slow Dance Music," "Techno Rave," "Disco House Music," "New Wave Rock," and "Funk Bossanova." Despite these bizarre syncreticizations ("rave" is a term used to describe a subculture or event, not a musical style, and what exactly is "reggae house" or "funk Bossanova"?), Noise's music in fact reveals itself throughout the album to be a rather homogenized blend of dance pop similar to "pretty-boy" groups such as Savage Garden. So is this Korean appropriation of hip-hop and other Western popular musical styles simply another form of global homogenization? On the one hand, rap has been appropriated as a musical idiom by Korean pop idols similar to those that exist in Japan. But also as in Japan, it has also been used to protest the educational pressures placed on young people to succeed by attending cram schools and bettering themselves by attending university.

Korean hip-hop appears to have achieved new heights of sophistication at the turn of the millennium through the small but thriving Seoul-based independent MP (Master Plan) label, which in its MP Hip-Hop Project 2000 launched "K hip-hop" recordings by Da Crew, Joosuc, Tequila Addicted, South Side AllStarz, Soul Chamber, DJ Soulscape, Side-B, and others, with raps predominantly in Korean with occasional smatterings of English. Da Crew (also know as Da Crew of Korea) in particular, a young duo consisting of producer-composer Seven X and lyricist Saatan, backed by a team of guest DJs, produced a world-class album in 2001, *City of Soul*, which blended skillful, funk-oriented beats with taut scratching, sharp, soulful samples, and seamlessly flowing raps.

In exploring the subversive and critical nature of some rap music in Korea, such as that of Seo Taiji and the Boys, Morelli argues that hip-hop has also continued to carry its implications of youth resistance, both through lyrics and music, but to a different degree from its U.S. counterpart. Like Cui Jian in China, who turned from protest rock to rap in his 1998 album *The*

Power of the Powerless (a title derived from an essay by the former dissident Czech president and rock fan Václav Havel), Taiji has suffered censorship and been ordered by the Korean authorities to cut his hair. This suggests that rap and hip-hop culture can operate as a form of musical dissidence in widely differing political contexts. The social difference it represents in Korea is due to the dynamics of indigenization, as well as to the challenge it provides to the social characteristics and the established musical order in Korean society.

But there are also socially engineered, institutionalized implications arising from the growing popularity of Korean hip-hop and pop music in Hong Kong and China. The Backstreet Boys–like pop-rap group H.O.T. (Hi-five of Teenagers), whom Morelli mentions in passing, and who became very popular in the People's Republic of China in the late 1990s, were used in 2000 as a model by the state-run mainland Chinese radio station, Radio International, to create the home-grown Chinese pop-rap groups TNT, Tinkerbell, and Annie. These ten performers were selected by Korean music industry experts from more than 5,000 applicants in Beijing and take to Seoul to be groomed and trained to sing and dance and dress fashionably. According to a report by Elisabeth Rosenthal in the *New York Times* (2001), the three mainland Chinese rap groups then performed at a concert at the Workers' Stadium auditorium, patrolled by the People's Armed Police, supervised by Party officials and fronted by a middle-aged MC in a suit and tie. Dressed in "silver tracksuits, oversized white tuxedos and Goth black tunics and pants," their repertoire set out to "develop hip-hop and R&B with Chinese characteristics," in the words of Chen Yu of TNT, and included a rap version of a traditional Chinese folksong and an expression of support of Beijing's bid to host the 2008 Olympic games. This state-sanctioned pop-rap represents the opposite end of the spectrum from the more oppositional, hardcore rap of Cui Jian, but illustrates the Chinese government's recognition of the potency of rap and hip-hop as a vernacular vehicle of expression for youth.

According to Jeroen de Kloet, Cui Jian was the first artist to adapt hip-hop to mainland China, in a track titled "Get Over the Day" that questions the wisdom of the Chinese state in relation to the 1997 Hong Kong handover (2000: 37). Elsewhere in Asia, as in Korea, rap seems initially to have been incorporated into the existing repertoires of pop singers largely as one of many Western popular musical idioms, with little specialization in rap music or hip-hop culture. In his 1998 book *Dance of Life,* which deals with popular music and politics in Indonesia, the Philippines, Thailand, Malaysia, and Singapore, Craig A. Lockard has little to say about rap and hip-hop. In Malaysia he cites the groups 4U2C and KRU, who had a following mostly among teenage girls in the 1990s, and an all-female rap group called Feminin; all three rap in Malay and, are perceived by critics as too Westernized and "un-Islamic," and their music is "value laden, attacking pollution, abandoned children, alcoholism, smoking, bad dietary habits, and other social ills, even though they carefully avoid more controversial topics that might result in increased government interference." These groups, together with MC Silva Choy and the Kopi Kat Klan in Singapore, who satirize Singapore life in English and Singlish, are, according to Lockard, "pretty tame stuff" in comparison to "American gangsta rap, or even to the hard-edged rap popular among the underclass in Rio de Janeiro or Capetown" (1998: 259), but manage nonetheless to be controversial in their countries of origin. The Malaysian hip-hop group Poetic Ammo's 2000 English-language release *The World Is Yours,* featuring Sheila Majid and D'alliance, among other local pop luminaries, received a high-profile release launch along with an interactive VCD featuring an award-winning music video, arcade games, computer downloads, and Swatch sponsorship at Tower Records, suggesting something of a mainstream coming of age for rap in Malaysia.

In Singapore the flamboyant singer and composer Dick Lee, who has also recorded and been immensely popular in Japan and elsewhere in Southeast Asia, uses passages of what C. J. W.-L. Wee has described as "a domesticated rap style befitting Lee's pro-West resistance to the West" (1996: 494) in Lee's 1991 album *Orientalism.* This expresses a positive, reverse sense of Edward Said's term describing Western exoticization of the Orient in asserting (in English) an Asian identity that aims to demonstrate that "the new Asian ready for the twenty-first century" must be assertive and combat caricatures, stereotypes, and "token yellows." Elsewhere, on his 1989 album *The Mad Chinaman,* Lee rapped in Singlish to a version of a popular Malay song, "Rasa Sayang" (To Feel Love), to express the delights of Singapore as a cosmopolitan country where "[e]verything we have has to be the best / of the fabulous East and the wonderful West . . . / we can eat, eat, eat till we nearly drop / then we all get up and we shop, shop, shop" (Wee 1996: 503). This use of rap as a rhetorical strategy to express a national and pan-Asian identity politics and to counter ethnic stereotyping is yet another example of the appropriation of rap music into political contexts of ethnic assertion.

But there has also been a reverse flow of influence from Asia to the USA in hip-hop culture, rarely acknowledged, in the form of martial arts and kung fu, which U.S. hip-hop groups such as the Wu-Tang Clan have embraced as a key activity. This cross-cultural influence is given expression in the Hong Kong filmmaker Corey Yuen's 1985 martial arts film *No Retreat No Surrender,* in which Jason Stilwell, an Anglo-American (but rather Chinese-looking) devotee of Bruce Lee, strikes up a friendship in Seattle with R.J., an African American hip-hopper and breakdancer. In a key scene in this film, R.J. takes Jason to Bruce Lee's grave, where Jason prays, in an embodiment of what Meaghan Morris has referred to as "melodrama, real melodrama, not the tortuous allegory of a Freudian case-study word which feminism found in the 'woman's film,' but festive, romping, participatory popular melodrama" (1998: 8). The influence of this "participatory popular melodrama" of Hong Kong martial arts cinema remains an underresearched aspect of hip-hop culture (see Gordon 1996: 32), although the tantalizing examples of "hip hop's eastern gaze" in Koushik Banerjea's essay "Ni-Ten-Ichi-Ryu: Enter the World of the Smart Steeper" (1998: 17) are a notable exception.

Chapter 11 moves to Oceania and Australia, where—guided by Ser Reck, a.k.a. Celsius, the narrator of Paul Fenech's 1998 film about Sydney hiphop, *Basic Equipment*—Ian Maxwell discusses the Sydney hip-hop group Def Wish Cast's attempt to forge a white, Australian-accented, Anglophonic, nationalistic hip-hop culture. Def Wish Cast are located within their performance context, in which they claim to represent their particular community, based in the socially and geographically marginalized, non-Anglo, migrant-dominated western suburbs of Sydney. Concepts of community, authenticity, Australian nationalism, and hip-hop transnationalism come into play as Maxwell examines at close quarters the processes by which cultural agents in the western suburbs of Sydney receive, abstract, translate, and apply ideas about hip-hop culture to their own situation. The fragility and underground nature of the Sydney hip-hop scene is placed in the context of an Australian self-image of peripherality, and the affective basis of the scene is analyzed in terms of inherited values of hip-hop authenticity, which are contrasted with mass-media perceptions of hip-hop as another form of U.S. cultural imperialism. Maxwell also deals with one of the few Aboriginal rap groups to have emerged in Australia, the female duo Blackjustis. (In 1998 another Aboriginal rap crew, Native Rhyme Syndicate, who are directly influenced by U.S. gangsta rap, emerged almost from nowhere after winning a Deadly Award, the Aboriginal alternative to the bland, mainstream ARIA [Australian Recording Industry Association] awards.)

Based on fieldwork carried out on the Sydney hip-hop scene, Maxwell's research concluded in 1995, before a number of more ethnically diverse rappers emerged on the Sydney scene and elsewhere in Australia. The development of a national Australian hip-hop scene was also given some degree of "official" recognition by the release by the local label Mushroom in 1995 of *Home Brews,* volume 1. This was a compilation of eleven Australian rap tracks by mostly unrecorded and almost exclusively male "bedroom" hip-hop practitioners from Sydney, Canberra, Melbourne, and Adelaide. Robert Brailsford's container insert notes expressed a prevailing sense of fragility and search for identity: "[A]part from having a hip-hop history, it is a history being built on. The main problem being Australian hip-hop suffers the same fate as English or for that matter Zambian hip-hop. The prevailing attitude is that only American hip-hop is real. . . . The main challenge for Australian hip-hop is to discover and consolidate what makes it unique. I don't really think anyone knows what that is, but Home Brews should provide some clues" (Various artists, *Home Brews* 1995). The album's diversity of styles is immediately noticeable, with trip-hop, ragga, acid jazz, and funk influences predominating. As a grouping together of exponents of a virtually invisible underground movement, it provides a valuable indicator of some of the more notable developments in an increasingly diverse national hip-hop scene. This was even more evident in the second volume of *Home Brews,* released in March 1998. As the Sydney hip-hop luminary Blaze has noted, referring to a growing number of young hip-hop crews in Sydney such as Et-nik Tribe, Beats-a-Frenik, Easybass, Fathom, MetaBass 'n' Breath, and Moonrock, a pluralist local scene is united by a single-minded dedication and commitment to hip-hop culture: "[I]t's just a bunch of kids, basically, who have the drive and initiative and they just do it in their spare time. They realise Australia's not the kind of country where you're gonna make money from it, and if you do think that way you're doomed to failure" (Blaze 1995). The Urban Xpressions Hip Hop Festivals, held over ten days in Sydney in March 1998 and three days in June 1999, which I was involved in, united many of the protagonists of the Australian hip-hop scene in a visible manifestation and celebration of its sense of a historical community, diversity, and force (see Mitchell 1999).

Hip-hop has appealed to Australian youth of non-English-speaking backgrounds as a vehicle for expressing their otherness within Australian culture. Two important recent examples of this are Brethren's 1996 eponymously titled mini-album, which includes a track in Spanish, "Pasa la cuchara" (Pass the Spoon), and *Sleekism,* the 1997 debut album by Sleek the Elite. The latter is a flamboyant and witty freestyler of Lebanese extraction who raps about Australian racism, political life, capitalism, sexual encounters, solidarity with Aborigines, and sympathies and conflicts with Lebanese culture in Australia. MetaBass 'n' Breath, an energetic Sydney crew formed in 1996 that includes two Anglo-Americans, also released a notable album of cluttered, world music–inflected hip-hop, *Seek,* in 1997, with some Spanish lyrics. Their tours of the USA in 1997 and 1998, with their highly charged, energetic, and distinctive public performances, earned them a write-up in *Billboard* in

Fijian-Australian rapper Trey. Photo by A. Gharevinia, courtesy of the artist.

1999 (Eliezer 1999: 46) in the first-ever acknowledgment of Australian hip-hop in that publication. There is also strong evidence of a Pacific Islander diaspora in the debut album by Koolism, a rap group from Canberra, which includes a track called "Juss a Brown Fellow." In it the Tongan rapper Fatty Boomstix, formerly of Easybass, maps out the diaspora of what he refers to as "Australasian rap," following a rhetorical track from Australia to New Zealand and through the Pacific Islands of Fiji, Samoa, Tonga, and New Caledonia. The Fijian rapper Trey, one of the few women MCs on the Sydney scene, expresses similar affinities with Pacific Island culture. One track on her eponymously titled tape, called "One Nation Party," is dedicated to Pauline Hanson, the Australian equivalent of Le Pen, leader of France's racist National Front; her work explores equivalences between hip-hop and Fijian musical and rhetorical formations that indicate how rap music has become indigenized in the Pacific region. As Kurt Iveson has noted, "[F]ar from representing the loss of Australian national identity in the face of global capitalism, Australian hip hop artists are engaged in the project of attempting to build a multicultural national identity in place of a racist monocultural model that is now gaining strength in Australian national politics" (1997: 47). As D'Souza and Iveson have noted, hip-hop in Australia, as in Germany and elsewhere, represents a "credible alternative" espoused by youth of non-Anglo background to the "'whiteness' of preexisting Australian youth cultures and the racism experienced by migrants." In this context, "[r]ealness . . . is defined by the ability to manipulate elements of hip-hop in an expression of place. American accents are jettisoned for Australia, talk of ghettoes is replaced with talk of the suburbs" (1999: 60).

The work of Koolism and Trey shows how the black ethnic identity markers of much U.S. rap have become "brown" ethnic identity markers in Pacific Islander rap. This is even more predominant in Aotearoa–New Zealand, my country of origin, where rap was much more easily absorbed into Maori and other Polynesian rhetorical traditions. *Patere,* in Maori, for example, means a form of abusive public discourse; one Maori dictionary even translates it directly as "rap." Maori rappers such as the Upper Hut Posse, Dam Native, Moana and the Moa Hunters, DLT, OMC, and Che Fu have thus successfully managed to combine rap with vernacular expressions of Maori militancy that sometimes incorporate the use of the Maori language. Some, such as OMC, have even managed to obtain some degree of international commercial success. Chapter 12 shows how Maori-Pakeha (white settler) biculturalism is reflected in the rap music and hip-hop culture of Aotearoa–New Zealand, where there is an increasing prominence of Maori and Pacific Islander artists adopting rap styles. This began with the appropriation of breakdancing by Maori and Pacific Islander youth and the music of the Patea Maori Club, who combined hip-hop with traditional Maori chants in the early 1980s. Most Polynesian rap music in Aotearoa–New Zealand has appropriated a variety of African American musical paradigms and blended them in distinctive and idiosyncratic ways with traditional indigenous musical forms of *waiata* (song), and idioms such as the *haka* (war dance), patere, and *karanga* (call to ancestors). Upper Hutt Posse and their leader, Te Kupu, a.k.a. D Word (Dean Hapeta) combine their powerful expressions of Maori militancy with the sentiments of the Nation of Islam leader Louis Farrakhan (see Buchanan 2000). They also incorporate *te reo Maori* (the Maori language) into their music as part of a broader cultural and political project to assert Maori sovereignty and to ensure the survival of the language. U.S. hip-hop influences have also been combined with syncretic Maori and Pacific Islander "urban Polynesian" musical idioms in the incorporation, appropriation, and indigenization of U.S. hip-hop influences by other Maori, Pacific Islander, and Pakeha groups and musicians in Aotearoa–New Zealand. King

Kapisi's "Samoan hip-hop to the world" is an important recent manifestation of this, combining with Fijian rapper Trey and the Tongan rapper of Sydney Posse Koolism to form a Pacific Island hip-hop diaspora. Elsewhere in the Pacific, the influence of hip-hop is also spreading. If, as Kirsten Zemke-White (1999) has claimed, the Hawai'ian rappers Sudden Rush's *na mele paleoleo* (Hawai'ian rap music), as expressed on their album *Ku'e* (Resist), has been influenced by Upper Hutt Posse's *E Tu* (Be Strong), there are signs of a pan-Pacific hip-hop network that has bypassed the borders and restrictions of the popular music distribution industry.

In the final chapter we return to North America, where Roger Chamberland charts the spread of hip-hop and rap throughout Canada, where there are more than 200 rap groups. Particular attention is given to Francophone rap in Quebec, where hip-hop is still expanding by way of parallel and alternative diffusion on the fringes of the commercial circulation of the Canadian music industry. Centers of production and distribution of rap music are analyzed in the larger Canadian cities such as Toronto, Vancouver, and Montreal, and on a smaller scale in Halifax and Quebec City. Chamberland argues that a sense of multicultural conviviality governs interethnic relations in Canada, a consequence of which is that other, non-ethnically bound themes are used in the discourses of Canadian hip-hop. Themes that are often of secondary importance in U.S. rap find stronger echoes in Francophone Quebec and the rest of Canada: the difficulties of finding a job, precarious living conditions, emphasis on the customs and habits of white civilization (as opposed to black or Asian communities), the collapse of the education system, and the hypocrisy of the political scene. Owing to their common struggles for acceptance by the Canadian music media and industry, a sense of national and regional underground solidarity has developed among Canadian rap groups. The success in the late 1990s of the Vancouver-based Rascalz and the Montreal-based Francophone rappers Dubmatique, building on the earlier successes of the Dream Warriors and Michee Mee, provide cause for optimism. But the Rascalz's refusal to accept their token, untelevised Canadian Academy of Recording Arts and Sciences Juno Award in 1998 for Best Rap Group indicates that Canadian rappers' struggle for acknowledgment in the shadow of U.S. rap continues (although the group was offered a conciliatory televised performance slot in the 1999 Juno Awards). Despite being in the shadow of the USA, Canadian hip-hoppers such as Dubmatique, La Gamic, Rascalz, and Swollen Members have succeeded in constructing a distinctively multicultural Canadian hip-hop nation that is increasingly being acknowledged on a global scale.

CONCLUSION: "GLOCAL" HIP-HOP AND LOCAL IDENTITY

The different hip-hop scenes surveyed here have considerable affinities as well as differences, not least in the way they all tend to seek out local roots, and they generate tensions and debates in relation to notions of authenticity, commercialism, politics, ethnicity, and language. All involve an initial negotiation with U.S. rap, followed by a return to the local, and in some cases the country of origin, emphasizing that hip-hop is about both where people are from and where they live. This return to the local also reflects the growing share that local repertoire is occupying in the global music industry (64.6 percent in 1998, up from 58.4 in 1991 [Boehm 1999]) as well as a growing sense of the superior credibility of local musical product over U.S. imports (Straw 2000). In the European, Canadian, and Australasian contexts examined here, this often becomes intertwined with the claims of displaced immigrant groups and contestations about nationality and "hyphenated" identity. Language is also an important aspect in the globalization of rap and hip-hop, with regional dialects and indigenous languages other than English coming to the fore as important markers for the vernacular expression and construction of identity.

In his essay "Music and Identity" (1996), Simon Frith has pointed out the fallacies involved in looking for direct reflections of identity or place in music; rather, musical practices need to be interpreted as processes through which identity is actively imagined, created, and constructed. Or, as Martin Stokes has put it, "Music and dance . . . do not simply 'reflect.' Rather, they provide the means by which the hierarchies of place are negotiated and transformed" (1994: 4). The reclaiming of local spaces and localities as sites for the construction of imaginary local identities through musical and subcultural practices such as rap and hip-hop is also an important aspect of what Stokes has described as an "insistence on locality and authenticity [that] contradicts a post-modernist argument in which history has disappeared in the pursuit of the instantaneous, and authenticity has been supplanted with a celebration of surfaces" (21). Hip-hop practices also become vehicles for reconstructing the "roots" of local histories, as in the use of local dialects in Italy and the Basque Country and indigenous rhetorical and linguistic practices in Aotearoa–New Zealand. In the process, "glocalization" takes place as local activities interact with the global form of rap and particular histories of different geographical scenes are constructed. The concept of the "hip-hop nation," originally used as an African American construct (although initiated in the New York *Village Voice* in 1988 and introduced into *Billboard* in 1991; see Decker 1994) has also played a role in the globalization of hip-hop. The rhetoric of the hip-hop nation has enabled hip-hoppers in more remote parts of the world to express a sense of belonging to a global subculture of breakdancing, graffiti writing, MCing, and DJing whose U.S. roots and origins are often, but not always, acknowledged. One recent example of this global connectedness of marginal hip-hop scenes is the collaboration between the Maori rapper DLT and the Canadian posse Rascalz—whose DJ and producer, Kemo, is Chilean—as well as the South African-born, German-based rapper Ono and Ryad, an Algerian-born, Paris-raised, Brooklyn-based rapper, and the innovative Paris-based Saian Supa Crew on DLT's 2000 album *Altruism* (Jewell 1999: 84–86).

After more than two decades, rap and hip-hop have moved far beyond any perceived "local" U.S. origins in the South Bronx (or South Central Los Angeles). Consisting of a syncretic confluence of musical, technological, visual, and dance forms that originated in Jamaica and Latin America, they now operate in a global conglomeration of different local contexts, where many of the same issues of roots, rootlessness, authenticity, appropriation, syncreticization, and commodification involved in notions of "world music" (see Keil and Feld 1994: 265) have again come into play. The diverse "glocal" musical and social dynamics that hip-hop scenes from Greenland to Aotearoa–New Zealand have developed in establishing their "other roots" illustrate that the globalization of rap music has involved modalities of indigenization and syncretism that go far beyond any simple appropriation of a U.S. musical and cultural idiom.

REFERENCES

Atwood, Brett. 1999. "Straight Outta.Com: Renegade Rappers Are Heard and Sold in Cyberspace." *Billboard*, 5 June, 26ff.

Banerjea, Koushik. 1998. "Ni-Ten-Ichi-Ryu: Enter the World of the Smart Steeper." In *Travel Worlds: Journeys in Contemporary Cultural Politics,* edited by Raminder Kaur and John Hutnyk (London: Zed Books), 14–28.

Barnes, Jake. 1997. Review of Nuuk Posse, *Kaataq. Wire,* April, 65.

Bell, Susan. 1999. "Talk of Town Irks Academie." *Australian,* 20 January (reprinted from the London *Times*).

Bennett, Andy. 2000. *Popular Music and Youth Culture: Music, Identity, and Place.* London: Macmillan.

Bernard, James, et al. 1992. "A Newcomer Abroad, Rap Speaks Up." *New York Times,* 23 August.

Binet, Stéphanie. 1998. "Le hip-hop ça se passe." *Source,* January, 116–17.

Bjurström, E. 1997. "The Struggle for Ethnicity: Swedish Youth Styles and the Construction of Ethnic Identities." *Young: Nordic Journal of Youth Research* 17, no. 3: 44–58.

Blaze. 1995. "Head Shot: Blaze Hip-Hop Yoda + Original Wax Junkie."
Head Shots 2, 18.

Boehm, Erich. 1999. "Global Music Business Keeps It Local." Reuters/Variety, 29 July.

Buchanan, Kerry. 2000. "A Maori Warrior Claims New Territory."
Unesco Courier, July–August, 32–33.

Canevacci, Massimo, Alessandra Castellani, Andrea Colombo, Marco Grispigni,
Massimo Ilardi, and Felice Liperi, eds. 1993. Ragazzi senza tempo: immagini,
musica, conflitti delle culture giovanili. Genova: Costa e Nolan.

Cannon, Steve. 1997. "Paname City Rapping: B-boys in the banlieues and Beyond."
In Post-Colonial Cultures in France, edited by Alec Hargreaves, and Mark
McKinney. London: Routledge.

Cross, Brian. 1993. It's Not about a Salary: Rap, Race, and Resistance in Los Angeles.
London and New York: Verso.

Cyclone. 1999. "The Unbearable Lightness of Chilling." Sydney Revolver,
16 August.

Daoudi, Bouziane. 2000. "Algerian Rappers Sing the Blues. " Unesco Courier,
July–August, 34–35.

Decker, J. L. 1994. "The State of Rap: Time and Place in Hip-Hop Nationalism."
In Microphone Fiends: Youth Music, Youth Culture, edited by Andrew Ross and
Tricia Rose. London and New York: Routledge.

De Kloet, Jeroen. 2000. "Rebel without a Pause?" Unesco Courier, July–August, 37.

Del Barco, Mandalit. 1996. "Rap's Latino Sabor." In Droppin' Science, edited by
William Eric Perkins. Philadelphia: Temple University Press.

D'Souza, Miguel, and Kurt Iveson. 1999. "Homies and Homebrewz: Hip Hop
in Sydney." In Australian Youth Subcultures: On the Margins and in the
Mainstream, edited by Rob White. Hobart: Australian Clearinghouse
for Youth Studies.

Elflein, Dietmar. 1998. "From Krauts with Attitudes to Turks with Attitudes: Some
Aspects of Hip-Hop History in Germany." Popular Music 17, no. 3: 255–65.

Eliezer, Christine, 1999. "Rap around the World: Melbourne."
Billboard, 5 June, 46.

Eshun, Kodwo. 1998. More Brilliant than the Sun: Adventures in Sonic Fiction.
London: Quartet Books.

Flores, Juan. 1994. "Puerto Rican and Proud, Boyee! Rap Roots and Amnesia."
In Microphone Fiends: Youth Music, Youth Culture, edited by Andrew Ross and
Tricia Rose. London and New York: Routledge.

———. 1996. "Puerto Rocks: New York Ricans Stake their Claim." In Droppin'
Science, edited by William Eric Perkins. Philadelphia: Temple University Press.

Frith, Simon. 1996. "Music and Identity." In Questions of Cultural Identity,
edited by Stuart Hall and Paul Du Gay. London: Sage Publications.

George, Nelson. 1989. *The Death of Rhythm and Blues*. London: Omnibus.

———. 1992. *Buppies, B-Boys, Baps, and Bohos*. London: Harper Collins.

Gilroy, Paul. 1993. "One Nation under a Groove." In *Small Acts: Thoughts on the Politics of Black Cultures*. London: Serpent's Tail.

———. 1994."After the Love Has Gone': Bio-politics and Etho-poetics in the Black Public Sphere." *Public Culture* 7, no. 1 (fall): 51.

Gonzales, Michael. 1998. "Kool Herc: The Labors of Hercules." *Source*, January, 144–53.

Gordon, Allen S. 1996. "1995 at a Glance." *Source*, January, 27–38.

Greenwalt, Alexander. 1996. "Rijekkka's Most Psycho: Ugly Rappers after the War." *Village Voice*, 3 September, 31–33.

Grunitzky, Claude. 1998. Container insert, Various Artists, *Le Flow: The Definitive French Hip Hop Compilation*. Delabel/Virgin.

Guilledoux, Fred. 1998. Review of M.B.S., *Ouled El Bahdja*. *Groove* (Paris) 21, 89.

Harvey, David. 1990. *The Condition of Postmodernity: An Enquiry into the Origins of Cultural Change*, Cambridge, Mass.: Blackwell.

Hesmondhalgh, David. 2000. "International Times: Fusions, Exoticism, and Antiracism in Electronic Dance Music." In *Western Music and Its Others: Difference, Representation, and Appropriation in Music,* edited by Georgia Born and David Hesmondhalgh. Berkeley: University of California Press.

Hitchings, Stuart. 1999. "Easy Listening." *3D World* [Sydney], 23 August.

Holmes, Peter. 1998. "The Avant-Guard." *Sydney Sun-Herald,* 29 March.

Howe, Kenneth. 2000. "New Ground Zero for Rap." *South China Morning Post,* 14 May.

Hudson, David. 1995. "Islamic Rap Tops Pop Charts with Songs of Hate. "*Sydney Morning Herald,* 6 August (reprinted from the *Guardian,* London).

Huq, Rupa. 1999. "Living in France: The Parallel Universe of Hexagonal Pop." In *Living through Pop,* edited by Andrew Blake. London and New York: Routledge.

Iveson, Kurt. 1997. "Partying, Politics, and Getting Paid: Hip-Hop and National Identity in Australia." *Overland* 147: 39–47.

Jewell, Stephen. 1999. "Under Pressure." *Pavement,* June–July, 84–86.

Johnson, Phil. 1996. *Straight outa Bristol: Massive Attack, Portishead, Tricky, and the Roots of Trip-Hop*. London: Hodder and Stoughton.

Keil, Charles, and Steven Feld. 1994. *Music Grooves*. Chicago: University of Chicago Press.

Kelley, Robin D. G. 1993. "Kickin' Reality, Kickin' Ballistics: The Cultural Politics of Gangsta Rap in Postindustrial Los Angeles." In *Droppin' Science,* edited by William Eric Perkins. Philadelphia: Temple University Press.

Kelly, Raegan. 1993. "Hip-Hop Chicano." In Brian Cross, *It's Not about a Salary: Rap, Race, and Resistance in Los Angeles*. London and New York: Verso.

Keyes, Cheryl L. 1996. "At the Crossroads: Rap Music and Its African Nexus."
Ethnomusicology 40, no. 2 (spring–summer): 223–48.

Krims, Adam. 2000. *Rap Music and the Poetics of Identity.* New York: Cambridge
University Press.

Kwaku. 1998. "Brit-Hop: London's Calling for Superstars, as Strong Talent
Struggles to Break Out." *Billboard,* 5 December, 52.

Linden, Amy. 1998. "An American Artform in Paris." *Source,* March, 167–70.

"LMF, the Lazy Clan." 2000. *Voice* [Hong Kong and Singapore], July, 12.

Lockard, Craig A. 1998. *Dance of Life: Popular Music and Politics in Southeast Asia.*
Honolulu: University of Hawai'i Press.

McClure, Steve. 1997. "Global Rap Pulse: Word from the World."
Billboard, 12 November, 40ff.

———. 1998. "Global Rap Pulse: Hip Hop around the World, from Japan to
Germany, France to the Netherlands." *Billboard,* 5 December, 48.

McGregor, Tracii. 1998. "Worldwide, Worldwide: Round the Globe at 100 bpm."
Source, January, 109.

Mitchell, Tony. 1996. *Popular Music and Local Identity: Rock, Pop, and Rap in
Europe and Oceania.* London and New York: University of Leicester Press.

———. 1999. "Another Root: Australian Hip Hop as a 'Glocal' Subculture."
UTS Review 5, no. 1 (May): 126–41.

Morris, Meaghan. 1998. "Learning from Bruce Lee: Pedagogy and Political
Correctness in Martial Arts Cinema." *Metro* 117: 6–15.

Negus, Keith. 1994. *Producing Pop: Culture and Conflict in the Popular Music
Industry.* London: Edward Arnold.

———. 1999. *Music Genres and Corporate Cultures.* London: Routledge.

Ogbar, Jeffrey O.G., and Vijay Prashad. 2000. "Black Is Back," *Unesco Courier,*
July–August, 31–32.

Oumano, Elena. 1999. "Girlz Power." *Billboard,* 5 June, 25ff.

Perkins, William Eric. 1996. "Youth's Global Village: An Epilogue." In *Droppin'
Science,* edited by William Eric Perkins. Philadelphia: Temple University Press.

Potter, Russell A. 1995. *Spectacular Vernaculars: Hip Hop and the Politics of
Postmodernism.* New York: State University of New York Press.

Pouncey, Edwin. 1999. Review of RZA, *RZA as Bobby Digital in Stereo,*
and Cypress Hill, *Cypress Hill IV. Wire,* January, 57.

Pratt, Timothy. 2000. "The Rap Cartel and Other Tales from Colombia."
Unesco Courier, July–August, 38–39.

Prévos, André J. M. 1998. "Hip Hop, Rap, and Repression in France and the
United States." *Popular Music and Society* 22, no. 2 (summer): 67–84.

Reynolds, Simon. 1998. *Energy Flash: A Journey through Rave Music and Dance
Culture.* London: Picador.

Robertson, Roland. 1995. "Glocalization: Time-Space and Homogeneity-Heterogeneity." In *Global Modernities,* edited by Mike Featherstone, Scott Lash, and Roland Robertson. London: Sage Publications, 25–44.

Rodriguez, Carlito. 1997. "The Firm: Family Business." *Source,* December, 16off.

Rose, Tricia. 1994. *Black Noise: Rap Music and Black Culture in Contemporary America.* Hanover, N.H.: Wesleyan University Press and University Press of New England.

Rosenthal, Elisabeth. 2001. "Groomed to Hip-Hop." *South China Morning Post,* 18 April (reprinted from the *New York Times*).

Santos, Aurelio. 1998. "La cosa nuestra." *Source,* January, 126.

Shapiro, Peter. 1999a. Review of Tricky, *Juxtapose. Wire,* August, 58.

———. 1999b. Review of Public Enemy, *There's a Poison Goin' On. Wire,* August, 55.

Shusterman, Richard. "The Fine Art of Rap." *New Literary History* 22, no. 3 (summer): 613–32.

Sluger, Myra. 1998. "Petje af to hip-hop." *Source,* January, 124.

Smith, Shawnee. 1998. "Rap Rips Up the Charts." *Billboard,* 5 December, 27–28.

Stokes, Martin. 1994. "Introduction: Ethnicity, Identity and Music." In *Ethnicity, Identity, and Music: The Musical Construction of Place*, edited by Martin Stokes. Oxford and Providence, R.I.: Berg.

Straw, Will. 2000. "The Political Economy of Credibility." In *Changing Sounds: New Directions and Configurations in Popular Music,* edited by Tony Mitchell and Peter Doyle. Sydney: University of Technology.

Tate, Greg. 1996. "Is Hip Hop Dead?" *Vibe,* March, 35.

Toop, David. 1991. *Rap Attack 2: African Rap to Global Hip Hop.* London: Serpent's Tail.

Ullestad, Neal. 1999. "American Indian Rap and Reggae: Dancing to the Beat of a Different Drummer." *Popular Music and Society* 23, no. 2 (summer): 62–90.

Walker, Clinton. 1995. "Pacific Pride." *Rolling Stone* (Australian ed.), June, 28.

Watkins, Lee William. 1999. "Tracking the Narrative: The Poetics of Identity in Rap Music and Hip Hop Culture in Cape Town." Master's thesis, University of Natal, South Africa.

Wee, C. J. W.-L. 1996. "Staging the New Asia: Singapore's Dick Lee, Pop Music, and a Countermodernity." *Public Culture* 8: 489–510.

Zemke-White, Kirsten. 1999. "'I Greet the Funk with My *Mauri*': Indigenous Elements in New Zealand Rap Music." Paper delivered at the Tenth International Conference of the International Association for the Study of Popular Music, University of Technology, Sydney, July.

DISCOGRAPHY

Robby Bee and the Boyz from the Rez. 1993. *Reservation of Education.* Firedrum Music.

Brethren. 1996. *Big Brother.* MXL.

Da Crew. 2001. *City of Soul*. MP Production Korea/Catalyst Action Hong Kong.

Missy Elliott featuring MC Solaar. 1999. "All n My Grill." WEA International.

IAM. 1997. *L'école du micro d'argent*. Delabel.

Cui Jian. 1998. *The Power of the Powerless*. CRC-EL.

Koolism. 1997. *Koolism*. Track Records.

Dick Lee. 1991. *Orientalism*. WEA Japan.

———. 1989. *The Mad Chinaman*. WEA.

DLT. 2000. *Altruism*. BMG.

LMF. 1999. *Lazymuthafucka*. DNA.

———. 2000. *Lazy Clan*. DNA/Warners.

———. 2001. *LMFamiglia*. DNA/Warners.

Manau. 1999. *Panique celtique*. BMG France/Polygram.

MC Solaar. 1994. *Prose Combat*. Polydor France.

Metabass 'n' Breath. 1997. *Seek*. Metabass 'n' Breath.

M.B.S. 1998. *Ouled El Bahdja*. Blue Silver/Virgin.

Noise. *Third Revolution*. Korea: Line Production.

Nuuk Posse. 1997. *Kaataq*. Sub Rosa.

Orishas. 1999. *A lo Cubano*. France: EMI.

Poetic Ammo. 2000. *The World Is Yours*. Malaysia: EMI.

Public Enemy. 1999. *There's a Poison Goin' On*. PIAS Recordings.

Saian Supa Crew. 1999. *K.L.R.* Wordplay/Source.

Sleek the Elite. 1997. *Sleekism, Featuring DJ Soup*. Sleekism Records.

Sudden Rush. 1998. *KU'E!!* Hawaii.

Takemura Nobukazu. 1994. *Child's View*. Bellissima!

Trey. 1998. *Projectile* [self-produced cassette].

———. 2000. *Daily Affirmations*. Tapastry Toons/Mother Tongues.

Tricky, with DJ Muggs and Grease. 1999. *Juxtapose*. Island Records/Universal.

Tricky. 2001. *Blowback*. Hollywood Records.

Various artists. 1991. *Krauts with Attitude: German Hip Hop*, vol. 1. Bombastic Records.

———. 1995. *Cartel*. Mercury Records.

———. 1995. *Home Brews: Extra Strength Australian Hip Hop*, vol. 1. MXL.

———. 1998. *Algerap*. Virgin France.

———. 1998. *Home Brewz*, vol. 2. MXL.

———. 1998. *Le Flow: The Definitive French Hip Hop Compilation*. Delabel/Virgin.

———. 2000. *Le Flow 2: The French Hip Hop Avant Garde*. Delabel/Virgin.

———. 2000. *MP Hip-Hop Project 2000*. MP Production Korea/Catalyst Action Hong Kong.

Chapter 1

Postcolonial Popular Music in France

Rap Music and Hip-Hop Culture in the 1980s and 1990s

ANDRÉ J. M. PRÉVOS

his essay will deal first with the steps that have marked the evolution of rap music and hip-hop culture in France in the 1980s and 1990s: their arrival in France in the early 1980s, their adoption by popular artists from varied musical and social backgrounds, and, finally, their adaptation by composers and performers to French societal and popular environments. The second goal of this essay is to locate these recent musical productions within the realms of postcolonialism. I will aim not toward a well-defined or definitive system, but at several steps that may contribute to a better positioning of these productions within realms of inquiry whose practitioners (Gilroy 1993a; Potter 1995) have already mapped out interesting inroads.

RECENT THEORETICAL CONSIDERATIONS ON RAP

The recordings produced by rap and hip-hop artists offer materials whose quality is not always remarkable but whose contents may benefit from detailed and close analysis. These analyses may also make more evident the fact that those who consume these popular productions belong not to an undifferentiated and shapeless mass, but to a multilayered and varied patchwork of subgroups, each with its own interests (Shusterman 1992: 168–70). Richard Shusterman has usefully underlined how rap artistry leads rappers to destroy the dichotomy between original creation and borrowing through the creative recombination of bits and pieces sampled from varied and diverse sources (219–20).

In the concluding chapter of *La culture hip-hop* (Bazin 1995), the author mentions three possible and complementary approaches to hip-hop culture: the empiricist approach, which underlines the new strategies, replacing the integration model with one of increased social and cultural mobility; the structural approach, which stresses the rapport between the minority groups to which the rappers belong and the prevalent societal order; and the symbolic approach, which is based upon the notions of rhythm and messianisn as leads to a new social and symbolic space (Bazin 1995: 273–74). Rap musicians and hip-hop artists who make extensive use of turntables, records, and other items of mass consumption (computers, for example) in the elaboration of their art challenge the image of the work of art by bringing these everyday objects to the fore. They also challenge the more elitist rock musical productions associated with the so-called progressive rock of the 1970s (Tucker 1982: 276). In addition, through their use of prerecorded music and by looping brief musical excerpts, rap artists have, in effect, canceled out the linearity of time and created a new "a-historical" time, a kind of "sacred time" whose characteristics resemble those of "primordial time" (Eliade 1967: 62).

The stylistic components and musical features of French rap productions are not significantly different from those of the works created by rappers from the United States or other countries. The opposition between "high" and "popular" artistic productions may have been diminished in France in the case of graffiti, since the earliest hip-hop taggers enjoyed official recognition from French artists belonging to the French "street art" school (Bazin 1995: 168). But nothing similar happened with rap productions; neither French composers nor recognized French popular artists openly supported the earliest efforts of French and Francophone rappers. They had to develop and assemble their own musical productions. During this process they used well-known techniques such as borrowing, or uncritical and almost slavish imitation; adopting, or a relocation of the borrowed items within a cultural tradition different from the one of which they once were a part; and adapting, or an innovation or modification leading to a new substyle or subtype of productions nevertheless still recognizable as rap.

RAP MUSIC AND HIP-HOP CULTURE COME TO FRANCE

There is a long tradition of U.S. cultural influence in France (Lalanne 1994: 48) as well as in other European countries (Mitchell 1995: 334). The 1920s and 1930s were marked by the discovery of jazz by French enthusiasts. Tunes from the United States — some brought by GIs during World War II — remained popular into the 1950s until the arrival of rock and roll, which overpowered French popular music, from Cora Vaucaire to Juliette Gréco or from Eddie Constantine and Henri Salvador to Georges Brassens or Léo Ferré during the second half of the decade (Rioux 1992: 91–139). The U.S.

folk revival of the 1960s and the disco wave of the 1970s also left traces in French popular musical productions (Prévos 1991). The 1980s were marked by successive changes brought on by movements from other European countries (such as punk from Great Britain) or from the USA. Such examples include disco, hard rock, "charity music," and the like (Prévos 1987) as well as original French popular styles: nouvelle chanson, "French rock" such as that of A. Bashung, and alternative music such as that of Bérurier Noir (Prévos 1991: 190–95). French and Francophone rap (the term "French rap" as used here covers these two notions) also falls into the new musical categories that emerged during the 1980s (Prévos 1992).

The years 1982–83 mark the first recording of French rap. On the B side of Fab Freddy's 12-inch 45 rpm, issued in New York City in 1982, there was a song in French: "Change de Beat" by B-Side, who later made a 12-inch under her own name (Dufresne 1994: 135). In 1982 a group of U.S. rappers toured Europe (with a few dates in France) and helped to introduce the style to new aficionados (Beckman and Adler 1991: 17). In October the French newspaper *Libération* ran a series of articles about New York rappers and their lifestyles (Thibodat 1982: 21). That same year, the French group Chagrin d'Amour recorded a long-playing album whose songs, all in French, were clearly inspired by rap techniques (Chagrin d'Amour 1982). The instant popularity of the group attracted the attention of amateurs, who even today consider Chagrin d'Amour as the first recorded example of French rap on a long-playing record.

The unexpected success of an almost unknown group was seen as both a positive factor and a disadvantage by younger rappers primarily from the northern suburbs of Paris. They were glad to see that rap, which they knew already, was gaining acceptance. But they were disconcerted because they feared that Chagrin d'Amour's innocuous rhymes would be seen as a new norm and force them to modify their own lyrics. Other French popular artists of the early 1980s used rap techniques in their recordings but did not see themselves as the originators of a new style. The group Garçons Bouchers recorded two versions of their "Rap des Garçons Bouchers" (Garçons Bouchers 1989, 1991), the style of which is close to that of the group's other recordings, but which nevertheless features "rapped" lyrics and a sampling of French-style musette music. The French comic group Les Inconnus recorded a popular sketch in which they imitated young French bourgeois attempting to imitate French rappers (Inconnus 1991); the Paris-based African jazz recording artist Manu Dibango, well known for his recording of "Soul Makossa," also turned to rap for several recordings (Mortaigne 1991: 24).

Nowadays the suburbs of Paris form a succession of residential neighborhoods, some of them made up of high-rise apartment buildings, a component of the government-subsidized popular housing administration. Some of these places, the northern suburbs in particular, have become hotbeds of violence, drugs, crime, and poverty. They have come to be seen as desolate neighborhoods where the antisocial, the criminally minded, the poor, and others on welfare live in semidesolation, a stereotype reminiscent of the U.S. ghetto.

The French branch of the Zulu Nation was established in a Parisian suburb in the early 1980s by Afrika Bambaataa, who had already created several such groups in the Bronx section of New York City (Louis and Prinaz 1990: 170). Bambaataa also used this occasion to showcase his own musical performances (Silvana 1994: 82). The Zulu movement in France helped introduce both rap music and hip-hop culture to youths in the poor suburban neighborhoods of the French capital. Since 1987 the French branch of the Zulu Nation has progressively lost most of its importance; few fictional examples (and those hardly positive) of the Zulu phenomenon have been found (Collard 1989: 197–99; Thomas 1994: 126), and nowadays only a few French rappers (Les Little 1992) claim to promote the Zulus' ideals.

It is thus clear that rap music and hip-hop culture arrived in France through borrowings and transmissions from varied sources. The first wave of French rappers included mainstream pop artists such as Chagrin d'Amour, marginal groups, and followers of Bambaataa and his teachings.

THE ADOPTION OF RAP TECHNIQUES AND IDEALS

Before considering the adoption of U.S. rap by French and Francophone popular artists, it is important to underline the fact that French popular music has had a long history of substyles focusing on puns, plays on words, and suggestive phonetic combinations. Examples from this repertoire, some dating from the late nineteenth century (the golden age of the French music-hall era), were recorded as late as the 1970s. Such is the case with "Idylle Philoménale," recorded by Yves Montand during a live show at the Paris Olympia music hall (Montand 1972). Songs whose lyrics were made up almost exclusively of alliterations, onomatopoeia, and puns were the specialty of the late Bobby Lapointe (whose complete recorded output was issued posthumously); his "Le papa du papa" provides such an example (Lapointe 1972). If these songs seldom reached the top of the French charts, they nevertheless enjoyed a respectable following. A much more popular French singer is Charles Trénet, known for his outlandish double entendre–riddled lyrics set to bouncy jazz-inspired music (Trénet 1989). Trénet, who died in 2001, is recognized today, after a singing career of more than fifty years, as a key member of the so-called classical French popular repertoire (Prévos 1991). *Prose combat,* MC Solaar's 1994 album (Le Guilledoux 1995: 18), clearly illustrates the continuity of this tradition, all the while adding an identifiable element of social and personal protest as well as an identifiable amount of "signifying" also inspired by African American hip-hop lyrics (Potter 1995: 18–53).

Produced by Labelle Noir (a subdivision of the Virgin label) in 1989, the first anthology of French rap was entitled *Rapattitudes* — a neologism and a pun combining the name of the new music and the most noticeable characteristic of its performers, their defiant attitude. Names of groups (Assassin, New Generation MC) were inspired by U.S. names such as N.W.A. ("Niggaz with Attitude," a name that clearly announces the explicit attitudinizing of its members). The groups featured on this record clearly demonstrate that they borrowed heavily from their U.S. counterparts and models. Recordings by Suprême NTM, Pouppa Claudio and Ragga, Puppa Leslie, and Gom Jabbar show that in their introductions French MCs imitated U.S. models and, like them, included a good dose of boasting and self-aggrandizement in their rhymes, as in "Rouleurs à l'heure" by the group Saï Saï (Various artists, *Rapattitudes* 1989). Claims of authenticity on the part of other performers also reminded listeners that the artists saw themselves as part of a tradition adopted in its entirety without dilution or whitewashing.

In songs and albums recorded by French rappers in the late 1980s, several artists reproduced themes encountered in U.S. and African American recordings. French rappers express opposition to the social order and to political and economic systems that have led to what they call the "oppression" of minorities (North African and French Caribbean immigrants in particular). French rappers also tell about the hardships of everyday life in the poorer suburbs, which they often characterize as "ghettos."

Antiestablishment attitudes begin with a criticism of the most evident bodies symbolizing the system (Piot 1993: 58). There are lyrics aimed at those who do not see the deepening of a generational conflict, and there are more violent and crudely worded attacks against France, the French army, and French public servants (Suprême NTM 1991). French politicians were often presented as "legal crooks" by some performers (Gom Jabbar and Puppa Leslie 1991) or as members of a political system corrupted by money (Suprême NTM 1991). Recent scandals involving high-ranking French politicians, such as the so-called blood scandal of the late 1980s involving the Socialist Laurent Fabius and members of his cabinet when he was prime minister, and illegal phone wiretaps involving members of the judicial system investigating other well-known politicians in 1994 and 1995 for the Right appear to give credence to criticisms and accusations of corruption encountered in the lyrics of French rappers.

An indirect critique of French society and of its normative forces (similar to the coded criticisms encountered in African American blues and some rap lyrics) is also found in the lyrics of songs dealing with the everyday life of French youth. The majority of French rappers emphasize that they live on the fringes of French society. They are kept outside because of forces within the societal mainstream (anti-Arab racism, poverty, police, etc.) or because of their own inability to correct the negative image they project. Calls for unity among performers and, indirectly, among their listeners are often found in the repertoires of French rappers. Such is the case with calls for a "nation" by IAM (IAM 1991) and Original MC (Original MC 1991) and for "peace and unity" by Lionel D. (Lionel D. 1990). The political agenda defended by the French movement SOS Racisme was also encountered indirectly in several recordings, including those by Saliha, one of the very few French female rappers (Saliha 1991). The least attractive activities of some members of the ghetto, drug dealers in particular, also attracted the wrath of French rappers.

By the early 1990s French rappers had truly covered most of the relevant styles found in the repertoires of their U.S. models, including more commercial styles and less vulgar lyrics, originally introduced by Chagrin d'Amour (Chagrin d'Amour 1982) and by French rap artists who, like Benny B. (1992), may be seen as having been inspired by popular U.S. styles such as those of MC Hammer.

It was also clear, even during the late 1980s, that some French rappers, in addition to their language and its stylistic or semantic inventions, were trying to inject a Gallic element into their recordings. Since most French rappers were of Arabic origin, and since their parents had fled Algeria and other North African countries because of economic hardship, they could not easily praise Africa in their songs (Phillips 1993: 45–72). In addition, Afrocentrism did not fit comfortably into their lyrics because the French extreme Right would have exhorted Arab immigrants to go back to northern Africa (Phillips 1993: 105–33) and because the rise of Arab fundamentalism in northern Africa would make it impossible for rappers to replicate their behavior in their native land. The only openly pro–black African song encountered during the late 1980s and early 1990s is "Lucy," by B-Love, in which the performer notes that the oldest skeleton found by anthropologists is that of a black African woman nicknamed Lucy who is thus "the mother of us all" (Various artists, *Rapattitudes 2* 1992).

Several artists expressed views that were developed in the first half of the

1990s. Humor, which, according to the U.S. rapper Ice-T, is often present in African American rap recordings (Ice-T 1994: 103), was more evident in French productions. Some artists included puns in their titles; such was the case with "Do the Raï Thing" (original title in English), a song by IAM (IAM 1991) in which the allusions to Spike Lee's popular film and to the Algerian musical style of Khaled and others are brought together. In 1993 IAM recorded "Le retor de Malek Sultan," in which the narrator poked fun at his own desire to become a popular performer.

The late 1980s and the early 1990s marked the end of a period of uncritical adoption of African American musical styles and repertoires by French rappers. To be sure, some continued to imitate their U.S. counterparts, while others developed either French versions of U.S. models or even invented original French popular ideologies. Three such cases are clearly identifiable today. The first two may be seen as readings or adaptations of U.S. popular ideologies; the last is truly an original invention by a French rap group.

THE CREATION OF FRENCH IDEALS

French social analysts have argued that, linguistically speaking, French rappers cannot elaborate upon a linguistic invention similar to that of their African American counterparts. Their dialect of choice (but seldom used exclusively), the so-called *verlan,* based on an inversion of the phonemes of the original French word, hampers stylistic and phonological invention owing to its heavy dependence on standard French words (Paquot 1994: 106). French and U.S. rappers both use similar musical techniques and sounds ranging from normal musical instrumental sounds to manipulations, samplings, or distortions of recorded sounds or voices. Musically, however, there is a clearer tendency among French rappers to use stylistic devices associated with reggae and raggamuffin music. In the United States there are only a handful of such artists, most of them associated with the older forms of U.S. rap, the so-called New York school (Potter 1995: 142). In France more rappers have branched out into the reggae-raggamuffin musical vein and have developed their own styles based on these Jamaican-inspired musics. One possible explanation for this particularity may be the significant percentage of French and Francophone rappers from the French-speaking Caribbean. If we are to believe U.S. musical and cultural critics, French rappers would thus have become more attuned to one of the factors in the elaboration of the rap vernacular (Potter 1995: 142). Among the most widely recognized artists in this group are Daddy Yod (Daddy Yod 1990, 1991), Saï Saï (Saï Saï 1992), and Tonton David (Tonton David 1991). Several from the southern part of France, primarily around Toulouse (Fabulous Trobadors 1995) and Marseilles (Le Guilledoux 1994: iii), have developed styles incorporating local and French regional dialects and, at times, techniques borrowed from the raggamuffin artists; such is the case with the group Massilia Sound System (Massilia Sound System 1991, 1993).

The most characteristic adaptations have nevertheless taken place on the so-called ideological level. The popularity of the gangsta style in the United States has not spread wholesale into the repertoires of French rappers simply because armed gangs and violent drug-dealing gangs in France are still very rare (Olivier 1994: 21). Even the most vocal French rap and hip-hop artists see drive-by shootings as typically U.S. occurrences (Garnier, Olivier, and Hoimian 1994: 24). Three major tendencies in the ideologies expressed by French rappers are evident: "hardcore," "zulu," and "pharaohism." As suggested earlier, two have been inspired by U.S. models, while the third is an original creation by the French group IAM.

In the ideological rap style known as "hardcore," the term, while it sometimes refers to a crude and noisy hip-hop style, is used as a characteristic more of the lyrics than of a particular political school of thought. French rappers who identify themselves as hardcore performers include Suprême NTM, Ministère AMER, and Assassin. Such groups do not pretend, nor do they try, to be simple replicas of U.S. groups linked to the gangsta rap style. Rather, they insist that what they see as their central mission is a continuation of rap as a vehicle to popularize and vent the anger and the frustrations of many disadvantaged or sometimes mistreated individuals, and to defend the cause of the poorest and least socially integrated segments of French society (Renault 1994: 32).

For members of Suprême NTM, hardcore French rap and hip-hop are one of the few possible forms of revolt given to those whose words and acts have traditionally been silenced. Hence, the hardcore performers have a clear antiestablishment slant in their lyrics and a truly oppositional attitude vis-à-vis all the representatives of the establishment or the prevalent social forces. Their lyrics sometimes include words directly borrowed from the lyrics of their U.S. examples, but once again, French hardcore rappers and hip-hop artists hardly ever mention firearms or drive-by shootings. One exception, the 1993 Suprême NTM album, features a picture of a handgun on the cover because the first song of the album deals with the suicide of a young, unemployed, and lonely individual (Renault 1994: 32). The French hardcore movement has sometimes been seen as an adaptation of the African American gangsta style because both, even though they appear to be oddities in the popular-musical repertoire, enjoy a noticeable following and an enduring success.

French hardcore performers pride themselves in their adhesion to hardcore ideology. In their song "Pour un nouveau massacre," Suprême NTM defines itself as wholeheartedly in agreement with the hardcore philosophy and the attitudes that derive from it (Suprême NTM 1993). Members of the group Assassin, in "Kique ta merde" (here one sees how English expressions are incorporated by French rappers), emphasize the fact that some critics dismissed them at first as simple imitators. They have now reached a level of popularity that allows them to be more brutal: they tell their listeners that if they do not like the song, they can always switch to another radio station (Assassin 1992). Ministère AMER, whose members also pride themselves in having clung to the values of the old style, fall squarely within the hardcore ideology. They have gone so far as to compose a song, "Brigitte (femme de flic)," about the fictional wife of a policeman who hides her amorous desires for members of the groups her husband fights (Arabs in particular) in the streets (Ministère AMER 1992, 1994).

The importance of the French branch of the Zulu Nation declined significantly after 1987, and today only a few groups adopt a clearly pro-Zulu stance. A notable exception is Les Little. Their songs suggest possible explanations for the success of the movement and for its loss of relevancy. First there were "curious" members who wanted to discover this new movement. When the group became larger there appeared "vicious" individuals and "envious" members more attracted by financial or personal gains. In addition, the Zulu movement always had to fight for its reputation because some individuals borrowed their dress code but did not adhere to their ideals. For the members of Les Little, as the title of one of their songs makes clear, "Rap Is Worth the Price of Life" (Les Little 1992).

Members of the Zulu movement also express unambiguous criticisms of the normative forces ruling the society in which they have to live. They also do not forget those among themselves whom they consider traitors or "fakes." The latter are sometimes portrayed as a "horde" of contemptible individuals attracted by monetary rewards and personal self-aggrandizement. Their contempt for these individuals, as expressed in the Lausanne-based group Sens Unik's "La horde des faux," is as powerful as that expressed toward the police or the politicians (Sens Unik 1993). As far as has been possible to ascertain, no new group claiming to promote the ideals of the French branch of the Zulu Nation has emerged in the past years, and if the history of the French branch of the Zulu Nation serves as a blueprint, it is quite likely that for the years ahead Les Little and Sens Unik will remain the two significant examples of such rappers and hip-hop artists.

The ideology promoted by the members of IAM is based upon images associated with ancient Egypt, primarily upon the mythical allusions to the pharaohs. Hence, I have decided to call it "pharaohism." This concept may be seen as a means underlining Arabic origins, all the while bypassing the popularly negative representations of North African countries gripped by Islamic fundamentalism and economic uncertainties. It may also be a means to convey positive images well known by their listeners and easily reconciled with the defense of their own Mediterranean (and especially Marseillais) attitudes vis-à-vis Paris and the rest of France. On the one hand, this attempt may be paralleled with the efforts of some Arab writers who, according to Laronde, fall within a new category he calls "neo-orientalism" (1990: 183–85). On the other, that the two productions belong to realms clearly differentiated and enjoy a rather different cultural status appears to go against a wholesale identification of these two efforts. What may be said, nevertheless, is that the efforts of the members of these two artistic groups (popular musicians and writers) are geared toward a new line of thought and an original repositioning of their efforts intended to dispel any possible linkage with ideals that could prove detrimental or harmful to their efforts.

IAM's first long-playing record was entitled . . . de la planète mars. The name Mars referred not to the planet in the solar system but to Marseilles. It helped emphasize that the group, as well as many of the people from that French city, considered themselves separated from the rest of France and, primarily, from the influence of Paris. Like the planet, which has resisted efforts of exploration and settlement, Marseilles (and other southern cities like Montpellier) has resisted integration into the Parisian sphere of influence. The financial troubles of its soccer team, combined with those of its owner, Bernard Tapie, have done nothing to soothe the Marseillais' ruffled sensibilities (Duroy 1994: 150). IAM's second long-playing record underlines these affirmations and insists upon the fact that the differences between Marseilles and the rest of France derive from the Mediterranean heritage of the region, as well as from an original interpretation of the theory of continental drift. According to the container insert text of their second album, IAM's members defend an interpretation of the theory that would have in fact separated the deltas of the Rhône and the Nile, which before that time had been joined together. This theory also helps explain the link between Marseilles and the southeastern part of France and ancient Egypt (IAM 1993).

This pharaohism is also posited as a reaction to the excesses of Western cultures. In the track "J'aurai pu croire" (I Could Have Believed), IAM claims that for the West, colonialism was sustained by the desire to improve the colonizers' powers and resulted in an artificial division of the lands invaded by colonial armies and forces (IAM 1993). Another track points up the symbolism of the number seven with beliefs associated with both ancient Egypt and the scriptures. Finally, IAM expresses the core of this new ideology. The coming of Pharaoh, presented in "Contrat de conscience," will mark the end of the decadent world we live in and an overhaul of outmoded and outdated Western ideologies and ideals (IAM 1993).

IAM's pharaohism is the clearest attempt so far at the creation of a new type of religious space, but not a church, at least in the sense that the word has come to be accepted by compilers of dictionaries. This new religious space is closer to a type of messianic space organized by the symbolic representations outlined by the artists. It contributes to the grounding of the resistance that the group has outlined in other tracks: resistance to the impact of the French capital on the lives of those living in other urban centers (as well as on those living in the entire country), resistance to the accepted interpretations of regional peculiarities (as illustrated by their revised continental drift theory), and pride in their own local idiosyncrasies.

IAM's albums are not entirely devoted to the presentation and development of this ideology. However, several tracks make it clear that, along with the positioning of their city away from Paris (hinting at reproducing the dichotomy between the Los Angeles gangsta and old New York rap schools), it is at the core of their ideals, and they intend to develop its formulation and sustain its promotion (IAM 1993). Other elements also contribute to the popularity of IAM's material. A track that refers to Spike Lee has already been mentioned. On their second album, they included two frankly humorous tracks. "La méthode Marsimil" (a pun on the Assimil technique of foreign-language learning) describes how a young American who spent two months with them ended up speaking not a word of French but, instead, their own form of local dialect, generously peppered with expletives and dubious puns (IAM 1993). "Le retor de Malek Sultan" clearly pokes fun at one of their own members, who yearns for the chance to rap in English, or so he thinks. He has gone to the USA and, like the young American in the first song, has learned more nonsensical expressions and slang than straight American English (or, at least, black English vernacular). By poking fun at themselves, the members of IAM manage to criticize those who may have fallen into this linguistic trap and warn others who may be tempted to follow such an example (IAM 1993).

FRENCH RAP AND POSTCOLONIALISM

French and Francophone rap is well into its second decade, and the past ten years have been characterized by three steps. First, French and Francophone rappers borrowed from a new African American musical form whose transfer to France was facilitated both by the development of international record distribution and by the creation of a branch of Africa Bambaataa's Zulu Nation in the suburbs of Paris. Second, these rappers and hip-hop artists adopted most of the attitudes, repertoires, and musical and performance techniques exhibited by their U.S. and African American models. Like many black U.S. rappers, they saw themselves as natural commentators and observers of a seldom seen and largely ignored world where poverty, violence, and despair are prevalent. They also saw themselves as voices of criticism of French society at large and of the establishment, as well as of its normative forces, which have led to the personal and social situations they have had to face. Third, most French popular artists involved in rap and hip-hop adapted some of the ideals, theories, and techniques of their models. They could not continue to simply transfer styles from New York City or Los Angeles, whose realities and underlying assumptions did not apply to their own situation. Their search for social relevancy and artistic activism led them either to transform preexisting ideologies (as with hardcore and Zulu performers) or to create their own in a piecemeal fashion (such as IAM's pharaohism). It also made them aware of the dual role of the media. Television and show business have seldom helped rap artists, tending instead to favor more popular forms of musical entertainment. For the group NTM, the French show business establishment lags behind its U.S. counterpart (NTM 1993). For others, the efforts of Olivier Cachin, the presenter in charge of the program *Rapline*, broadcast by the French television station M-6 (Rousseau 1990: 44), have been appreciated by artists, who have also insisted upon the limited outlets available in the French media (Les Little 1992). These steps also characterized the evolution of a French popular style whose African American and U.S. origins were undeniable. Its artistic and ideological components resulted from both a reading of preexisting popular forms by those French performers and from a process of adoption and adaptation brought upon them by peculiar socioeconomic forces not found in the societal environment (or even foreign to those in it) that had nurtured the U.S. popular productions thus deciphered and interpreted.

But developments in the summer of 1995 indicated that, after all, situations encountered in the United States with gangsta rappers appear to have emerged in France. The "Cop Killer" debate in the USA appeared after several police officers noticed the lyrics of the song, performed by Ice-T. Members of police unions and fraternal orders throughout the United States launched a well-organized campaign denouncing the performer and the lyrics of his song (Ice-T 1994). However, instead of attacking Ice-T directly, these groups and their supporters decided to pressure Time Warner, the company that owned the label that had issued the record. After several weeks of angry accusations and strongly worded rebuttals, Ice-T decided to yield to the desiderata of the police associations and issue the album without the offending song.

In France, the "Sacrifice de poulets" affair began when the French group Ministère AMER recorded the tune "Sacrifice de poulets" (literally, "Sacrifice of Chickens," though a more accurate translation would be "Sacrifice of Pigs") for an album of songs inspired by Mathieu Kassovitz's film set in the banlieues, *La haine* (Hate). The film, released in 1995, was awarded a prize at that year's Cannes Festival. It underlines the harsh living conditions encountered by the children and grandchildren of Arab immigrants living in poverty and misery in the Parisian suburbs. Kassovitz's compilation of rap tracks inspired by the film—by Assassin, Ministère AMER, Sens Unik, IAM, MC Solaar, Sté Strausz, Les Sages Poètes de la Rue, and others—does not constitute the soundtrack of the movie but instead is a group of songs specially composed (with only one exception) as a complement to the movie itself. The members of Ministère AMER made remarks expressing their contempt for the police and were quoted at length in several French popular magazines ranging from music publications (such as *Rock and Folk*) to contemporary-issues magazines (such as *Entrevue*). On 20 June 1995 the French Syndicat Indépendant de la Police Nationale (Independent Union of National Police [SIPN]) lodged a complaint of "provocation to crime" against Ministère AMER after a live broadcast of an interview with the group on French television (Bouilhet 1995: 34). On 19 July, Jean-Louis Debré, the French minister of the interior, also lodged a complaint with the French ministry of justice for "direct provocation to commit the crime of aggravated murder." A judicial investigation was launched on 14 August 1995.

This situation is not new to Ministère AMER, a group of five black rappers. Their first album, featuring "Brigitte (femme de flic)" and "Garde à vue," was also at the root of a complaint of defamation and slander by several French police unions, who asked for its removal from distribution. Nothing happened on that occasion since the complaints were made more than three months (the legally recognized period) after the original release of the record. This time the rappers were attacked not for slander but for "provocation to crime," which carries a maximum sentence of five years in prison and a fine of FF 300,000 (about U.S. $60,000). Apart from the fine, the group received a suspended prison sentence, which gave them a certain heroic status in the eyes of their fans and followers (Bouilhet 1995: 34).

This case, which pitted rappers against the so-called forces of order, provided an unmistakable illustration of the adoption and adaptation steps mentioned earlier. The complaints by the police unions illustrate the adoption stage, since both U.S. and French police forces attacked the rappers. First, French police unions do not carry enough clout, nor are they entitled, to launch a public attack against record companies; second, the U.S. counterparts to the French minister of the interior and to the French minister of justice did not become involved (Tipper Gore's work with the Parents Music Resource Center cannot be seen as equivalent). Nevertheless, the outcomes of the two cases may well be similar: Although Ice-T gained a lot of publicity and is widely remembered for the song and the controversy (Potter 1995: 112–13) in the United States, and to a lesser degree in France, he lost some popularity, and a few of his followers thought he had caved in. And although Ministère AMER might be seen as symbolizing the resilience and strength of the rap movement and its artists in France, they did not benefit from the episode in the long run and subsequently broke up, with one of their members, Passi, pursuing a solo career.

This episode underlines the lack of understanding among those in charge of law and order as well as those who analyze contemporary diasporic cultures, whether African American in the United States or Arabic or Caribbean in France (Gilroy 1993a: 120–48). Both African American and French rappers are well versed in the techniques of "signifying," using language with meanings beyond those found in dictionaries. The U.S. critics of gangsta rap often failed to see, notice, and understand the signifying encountered in lyrics that on the surface seemed simply boastful or violent but were much more meaningful to anyone who made the effort to understand what was behind them (Potter 1995: 103–4). When the members of Ministère AMER were asked about the lyrics to "Sacrifice de poulets," they answered that "young people living in the popular suburbs are not idiots, they are not going to mistake a work of art for reality" (Bouilhet 1995: 34). They also underscored the fact that their lyrics involve an element of signifying (here the "sacrificing of chickens," in addition to its coded message, also brings voodoo connotations into play), which once again hides, disguises, and amplifies their meaning. The members of the police unions (like the most vocal critics of rap) took the lyrics at face value and inferred that the rappers advocated the killing of police officers. The rappers rejected any such interpretation and argued that the wordplay of their lyrics was in tune with the prevailing attitudes of most youngsters living in the impoverished sectors of the Parisian suburbs.

This aspect of the output of French and Francophone rap artists leads us back to considerations of diasporic flows, which have been used with notable results in the analysis and criticism of popular musical forms in the United States and in the United Kingdom (Gilroy 1993b). Such considerations also help to articulate a better understanding of the productions of the French and Francophone artists involved in hip-hop productions in France as well as in other French-speaking areas of Europe.

NOTE

A slightly different version of this essay appeared in *European Studies Journal* 15, no. 2 (1998): 1–33.

REFERENCES

Bazin, Hugues. 1995. *La culture hip-hop.* Paris: Desclée de Brower.

Beckman, Jeannette, and B. Adler. 1991. *Rap: Portraits and Lyrics of a Generation of Black Rockers.* London: Omnibus Press.

Bertrand, Claude-Jean, and Francis Bordat, eds. 1989. *Les médias américains en France: Influence et pénétration.* Paris: Éditions Belin.

Bouilhet, Alexandrine. 1995. "Cette petite musique de haine qui excède les policiers." *Le Figaro,* 31 August.

Collard, Cyril. 1989. *Les nuits fauves.* Paris: Flammarion.

De Boishue, Jean. 1995. *Banlieue mon amour.* Paris: Table Ronde.

Dufresne, David. 1994. *Yo! Génération rap.* Paris: Ramsay.

Duroy, Lionel. 1994. "Loulou Nicollin, sulfureux à Paris, bienfaiteur à Montpellier." *L'évènement du jeudi,* 2–8 June, 148–50.

Eliade, Mircea. 1967. *Le sacré et le profane.* Paris: Gallimard.

Garnier, Antoine, N'Guessan Olivier, and Elia Hoiman. 1994. "Gangsta Rap." *Black News,* July, 22–24.

Gilroy, Paul. 1993a. *The Black Atlantic: Modernity and Double Consciousness.* Cambridge, Mass.: Harvard University Press.

———. 1993b. *Small Acts: Thoughts on the Politics of Black Cultures.* London: Serpent's Tail.

Ice-T, as told to Heidi Sigmund. 1994. *The Ice Opinion.* New York: St. Martin's Press.

Kuisel, Richard. 1993. *Seducing the French: The Dilemma of USization.* Berkeley: University of California Press.

Lalanne, Bernard. 1994. "Comment Le Jour J a transformé notre décor." *L'expansion,* 2–15 June, 46–50.

Laronde, Michel. 1990. *Autour du roman beur.* Paris: L'Harmattan.

Le Guilledoux, Dominique. 1994. "Marseille: Ragamuffin foot et aïoli." *Le monde,* 27 January.

———. 1995. "MC Solaar: le jongleur sans répit," *Le monde,* 22 June.

Louis, Patrick, and Laurent Prinaz. 1990. *Skinheads, Taggers, Zulus, and Co.* Paris: Table Ronde.

Mitchell, Tony. 1995. "Questions of Style: Notes on Italian Hip Hop." *Popular Music* 14: 333–48.

Mortaigne, Véronique. 1991. "L'Oncle Dibango." *Le monde,* 16 March.

Olivier, N'Guessan. 1994. "Gangsta: le langage des armes." *Black News,* 21 July.

Paquot, Thierry. 1994. *Vive la ville!* Collection Panoramiques. Condé-sur-Noireau: Arléa-Corlet.

Phillips, Peggy Anne. 1993. *Republican France: Divided Loyalties.* Contributions in Political Science 325. Westport, Conn.: Greenwood Press.

Piot, Olivier. 1993. "La rebellion du rap." *Le monde de l'education,* September, 58–61.

Potter, Russell. 1995. *Spectacular Vernaculars: Hip Hop and the Politics of Postmodernism.* Albany: State University of New York Press.

Prévos, André. 1986. "CBers and Cibistes: The Development and Impact of CB Radio in France." *Journal of Popular Culture* 19: 145–51.

———. 1987. "Singing against Hunger: French and U.S. Efforts and Their Results." *Popular Music and Society* 11: 57–74.

———. 1991. "French Popular Music." In *Handbook of French Popular Culture,* edited by Pierre L. Horn. New York: Greenwood Press.

———. 1992. "Transferts populaires entre la France et les États-Unis: Le cas de la musique rap." *Contemporary French Civilization* 16: 16–29.

———. 1993. "Une nouvelle forme d'expression populaire en France: Le cas de la musique rap dans les années 1980." *Francographies* no. special 2: 201–16.

———. 1994."La musique française aux États-Unis: Diffusion, popularité, impact." In *Les médias français aux États-Unis,* edited by C.-J. Bertrand and F. Bordat. Nancy: Presses Universitaires de Nancy.

Renault, Gilles. 1994. "Suprêmement NTM." *Libération,* 8 May, 32.

Rioux, Lucien. 1992. *Cinquante ans de chanson française: De Trénet à Bruel.* Paris: L'Archipel.

Rose, Tricia. 1994. *Black Noise: Rap Music and Black Culture in Contemporary America.* Hanover, N.H.: Wesleyan University Press and University Press of New England.

Rousseau, Frank. 1990. "Au ras du bitume." *Le Figaro,* 15 September.

Shusterman, Richard. 1992. *L'art à l'état vif: La pensée pragmatiste et l'esthétique populaire.* Collection Le Sens Commun. Paris: Éditions de Minuit.

Silvana. 1994. "International Rapper. MC Solarr [*sic*]." *Source,* April, 82.

Thibodat, Jean-Pierre. 1982. "Afrika Bambaataa, roi zoulou du Bronx." *Libération,*
    28 October.

Thomas, Bernard. 1994. *Le champ de la Butte Noire.*
    Paris: Éditions Grasset et Fasquelle.

Trénet, Charles. 1978. *Mes jeunes années racontées par ma mère et moi.*
    Paris: Éditions Robert Laffont.

———. 1989. *Boum! Chansons folles.* Paris: Éditions du Seuil.

Tucker, Bruce. 1982. "'Tell Tchaikovsky The News': Postmodernism,
    Popular Culture, and the Emergence of Rock 'n' Roll."
    Black Music Research Journal 9: 270–95.

DISCOGRAPHY

Assassin. 1992. *Le futur que nous réserve-t-il?,* vols. 1 and 2. Assassin
    Productions/Delabel.

Benny B., with DJ Daddy K and Perfect. 1992. *Perfect, Daddy K et Moi.*
    On The Beat Records.

Chagrin d'Amour. 1982. *Chagrin d'amour.* Disques Barclay.

Daddy Yod. 1990. *Raggamuffin.* Backchich Records.

———. 1991. *Redoutable.* Backchich Records.

Fabulous Trobadors. 1995. *Ma ville est le plus beau park.* Philips.

Garçons Bouchers. 1989. *Les Garçons Bouchers,* vol. 2. Musidisc.

———. 1991. *Les cinq plus grosses bêtises des Garçons Bouchers.* Island.

Gom Jabbar DC and Puppa Leslie. 1991. *Belle époque.* Musidisc.

IAM. 1991. *. . . de la planète mars.* Virgin.

———. 1993. *Ombre est lumière,* vols. 1 and 2. Delabel.

———. 1997. *L'école du micro d'argent.* Delabel.

Inconnus. 1991. *Les Inconnus.* Lederman/PEM.

Lapointe, Bobby. 1972. *Intégrale des enregistrements de Bobby Lapointe.*
    Disques Phillips.

Les Little. 1992. *Les Vrais.* Mercury.

Lionel D. 1990. *Y a pas de problème.* Squatt.

Massilia Sound System. 1991. *Parla patois.* Independance.

———. 1993. *Chourmo!* WMD.

MC Solaar. 1993. *Prose combat.* Polydor.

Ministère AMER. 1992. *Pourquoi tant de haine?* Musidisc.

———. 1994. *92500.* Musidisc.

Montand, Yves. 1972. *Yves Montand dans son dernier
    "One-Man Show" intégral.* CBS.

Original MC. 1991. *Le 21ème siècle.* Carrère.

Saï Saï. 1992. *Reggae Dance Hall.* WMD.

Saliha. 1991. *Unique*. Virgin.

———. 1994. *Résolument féminin*. Epic.

Sens Unik. 1993. *Les portes du temps*. Bondage Productions.

Suprême NTM. 1991. *Authentik*. Epic.

———. 1993. *1993 . . . j'appuie sur la gachette*. Epic.

Tonton David. 1991. *Le blues des racailles*. Delabel.

Various artists. 1989. *Rapattitudes*. Labelle Noir/Virgin.

———. 1992. *Rapattitudes 2: rap et reggae*. Delabel.

———. 1995. *La haine: musiques inspirées du film*. Delabel.

Chapter 2

Islamic Hip-Hop versus Islamophobia

Aki Nawaz, Natacha Atlas, Akhenaton

TED SWEDENBURG

he Runnymede Trust, in a 1997 report, warned of a prevailing atmosphere of "Islamophobia" in England, of growing discrimination against its 1.5 million Muslim population (80 percent of whom are of South Asian origin), and of ongoing racist violence against these so-called immigrants ("Discrimination" 1997; see also Werbner 1997: 232). Islamophobia can be equally applied to conditions in France, where the Muslim immigrant population of perhaps five million, composed primarily of North Africans, likewise faces racist hostility and structural discrimination. Among the recent dramatic instances of Islamophobia are the Rushdie affair in England and the "veil" affairs in France (see Kepel 1997).[1] Meanwhile, in both countries these "immigrants" are, increasingly, second- and third-generation citizen and legal residents who are attempting to construct cultural-political spaces for themselves as ethnicized "Muslims"[2] in Europe, and are actively involved in antiracist movements.

Among the manifold responses of European Muslims to Islamophobia has been hip-hop activism, a subject that has been largely overlooked in the relevant literature. This essay focuses on three of the most prominent figures in European "Islamic" hip-hop: from England, Aki Nawaz, of the group Fun-Da-Mental, and Natacha Atlas, from Transglobal Underground; and from France, Akhenaton, of the group IAM. By now, a considerable literature exists on "Muslims" and anti-immigrant racism in England and France, and the music press has given substantial coverage to the artists under consideration here. But studies of "Muslim" communities have generally paid little attention to popular culture, and accounts of antiracist movements (especially in England) frequently discuss popular culture but usually neglect "Islam" and "Muslim" communities.[3] The music press, finally, has not seriously examined the "Islamic" tendencies of Fun-Da-Mental, Transglobal Underground, or IAM.[4] I wish here to bring such connections into sharper focus.

AKI NAWAZ: ISLAMIC WARRIOR

Aki Nawaz (born Haq Nawaz Qureishi) was raised in Bradford by Pakistani immigrants who arrived in England in 1964 (his father worked as a bus conductor). Nawaz's first notable musical stint was in 1981–83 as the drummer for the Ur-gothic punk band, Southern Death Cult (which later transmogrified, sans Nawaz, into the Cult). Nawaz's hip-hop band Fun-Da-Mental came onto the scene in 1991, recording for Nation Records, which Nawaz had cofounded with the Afro-Caribbean Katherine Canoville. Nawaz, who adopted the performance names Aki-Stani, Righteous Preacher, and, finally, Propa-Gandhi, was the group's leader and most visible rapper. Fun-Da-Mental made an immediate impact, on the charts, in concert, and in the media, with a hip-hop sound frequently compared to Public Enemy's, an analogy that disguised the group's localized specificity.

Fun-Da-Mental's contributions should be seen, first of all, in light of the group's intervention within the Bradford "Islamic" community, and more broadly, the "Islamic" Asian community in Britain.[5] The 1980s witnessed a contest for leadership within the Bradford community involving the Council for Mosques, Muslim businessmen and professionals, and Muslim city councilors (eleven were elected in 1992). Many of the youth of Muslim background were alienated from the mosques as well as the official community leaders, especially because of the mosques' and leaders' opposition to music, dance, and videos, including bhangra, which had emerged in the 1980s as the pop music of Asian youth in Britain.[6] Fun-Da-Mental's expressions of pride in Islam appealed to Muslim youth who had been raised on British popular culture yet also felt wounded by British Islamophobia and the racist overtones of the Salman Rushdie affair. Fun-Da-Mental was also part of the new wave of early 1990s, post-bhangra Asian dance musics that, Sanjay Sharma suggests, served as "a site for the translation between diasporic Asian, Black and British identification" (Sharma et al. 1996: 40). What was unique about Fun-Da-Mental's Asian dance music was that it inserted Islam into that complicated identity configuration.

Fun-Da-Mental articulates Islamic and ethnic pride through its lyrics, musical mix, and imagery.[7] On "Meera Mazab" (My Religion, in Urdu) Propa-Gandhi raps: "I was born as a Muslim, and I'm still livin' as a Muslim / My spirituality determines reality." This song and others are peppered with lines from the Qur'an (in Arabic, but the same words are used in Urdu): "Al-lahu akbar" [God is greatest]; "Subhanallah, ilhamdulillah" [Praise God, thank God]; "Qulu allahu ahad" [Say: He is Allah, the One! (Surah CXII:1)]; and "Allahu samad" [God the eternal (Surah CXI: 2)]. The group also rejects the Western stereotype of Islam as a sexist religion: "You say Islam and its sexism / But you're blind, when it comes to global masochism." In the song "Mother India," recited by the poet Subi Shah, she names famous "strong women" from the Indian subcontinent and Arabia, including Aisha, the Muhammad's wife, and Noor Jahan, the Mogul empress. Among the ingredients Fun-Da-Mental throws into its extremely dense musical mix are the sounds of Qawwali (the Sufi devotional music of India and Pakistan)[8] and Middle Eastern beats. Publicity photos typically show Propa-Gandhi sporting an Islamic star-and-crescent medallion, a logo that also appears on the cover of the CD *Seize the Time*. Finally, Nawaz advocates a certain Islamic orthopraxy, expressing total opposition to alcohol and drug usage (Sweet 1993). It should be stressed that such "Islamic" elements are specifically South Asian (and to some extent, Middle Eastern) and are not found on the recordings of Muslim-affiliated U.S. rap groups.

Islamic community elders in Bradford were unhappy with Fun-Da-Mental's chanting of Qur'anic phrases over dance beats, which is considered *harâm* (forbidden) for orthodox Muslims (Lewis 1994: 180). Moreover, the Bradford Council for Mosques was disturbed by press reports that Aki Nawaz supported Ayatollah Khomeini's *fatwa* against Salman Rushdie, a position that undermined the council's efforts to project a moderate image of the community (Lewis 1994: 181). In fact, the press (especially music publications) had misinterpreted Nawaz, who later clarified that "he oppose[d] any attempt to kill or silence Mr. Rushdie" but understood "why Muslims are upset with the writer" (Stevenson 1994).[9] Other elements in the community were more supportive, as exemplified by this statement from the Urdu-language London daily *Jang* (7 August 1992): "Lyrics praising Islamic scriptures, Asian culture and condemning the West's oppression of them are sung in a newly released cassette single called 'Peace, Love and War.' . . . So if you are confused about your roots and your identity, it might be worthwhile giving this enthusiastic group a try" (quoted in Lewis 1994: 180).

Fun-Da-Mental's Islam is also a critical component of the group's anti-racist activity. A 1996 study of British Asian dance music, *Dis-Orienting Rhythms* (Sharma et al. 1996; see especially Kalra et al., Huq, and Hutnyk), underlines the role progressive Asian bands (such as Fun-Da-Mental, Kaliphz, Hustlers HC, Asian Dub Foundation, and, yes, Cornershop) have played in bridging the gap between locally organized self-defense and Asian political groupings and popular-front, antiracist mobilizations of the white Left, such as the reorganized Anti-Nazi League. These bands also lent significant support to the campaign against the CJA (the Criminal Justice and Public Order Act) of 1994, which allows the banning of raves and any large-scale demonstrations. Asian dance outfits, with Fun-Da-Mental in the lead, have performed and delivered speeches at antiracist benefits and carnivals, at concerts and rallies organized by the Left on anti-imperialist issues, and at leftist party conferences, and have campaigned to keep Asian issues at the forefront of antiracist struggles.

Fun-Da-Mental advocates militancy and self-defense as key elements of the antiracist struggle and mobilizes Islamic imagery to this end, as seen in "Meera Mazab":

You go for yours cuz I'm in jihad
Allahu samad . . .
So I'll be comin' around the mountain
With my Islamic warriors
Nubians wid jihad in my mind.

Here Nawaz figures the antiracist fight as a "jihad" and links local struggles to those of "Islamic" freedom fighters elsewhere. The song "Mother India," moreover, mentions in its list of strong women "Leila Khaled, freedom fighter of Palestine" (the infamous airplane hijacker from the secular Marxist Popular Front for the Liberation of Palestine). Fun-Da-Mental's "Dog Tribe" video, which was banned from daytime television in England, shows Propa-Gandhi donning a black-and-white checkered *kûfîya*, sartorial signifier of the Palestinian struggle, as he joins an antiracist self-defense group. This video imagery, predictably, raised panics in both news and music press about Islamic "fundamentalism" (Hutnyk 1996: 161–63; CARF 1994). In "Meera Mazab" Propa-Gandhi also invokes the 1990 slaughter of seventeen Palestinians at Jerusalem's Haram al-Sharif: "Massacre in the mosque, suicidal frame of mind / Take a look, can't you see, look at Palestine."

I want to emphasize that Fun-Da-Mental invokes Palestine both as a figure of global struggle and because Muslims in England experience Western support for Israel's repressive policies and the pro-Israel media slant as racism against Muslims and Middle Easterners.

Fun-Da-Mental not only inserts Asian and Islamic concerns into the antiracist front, but also works to forge unity between Asians and Afro-Caribbeans. Nation Records, as noted above, is an Asian and black-owned company, and Fun-Da-Mental is an Asian and black band whose core, since 1993, has consisted of Propa-Gandhi and the Afro-Caribbean Dave Watts, also known as Imp-D. According to Nawaz, "There should be unity between Afro-Caribbeans and Asians because the struggles are exactly the same" (CARF 1994). Although it is often claimed by antiracist campaigners in England that the category "black" includes both Asians and Afro-Caribbeans, Asian observers have noted a marked tendency to trivialize the Asian in "black."[10] This marginalization likewise extends to "Islam," which until recently had scarcely entered the scope of discussions of antiracism in England, whether on the part of activists or within the field of cultural studies. Fun-Da-Mental's novel intercession here is to posit "Islam" as a mode of Afro-Caribbean and Asian commonality by invoking both "South Asian" Islam (discussed above) and the black nationalist Islam (specifically, the Nation of Islam variety) that originated in the U.S.[11] This, I believe, makes sense of Fun-Da-Mental's frequent reference in their lyrics to such Nation of Islam (NOI) leaders as Malcolm X, Elijah Muhammad, and Louis Farrakhan (on "President Propaganda," "Dog Tribe," "Seize the Time," and "Bullet Solution").[12] For example, in "President Propaganda," we hear that "Louis Farrakhan, the Nation of Islam / That's where I got my degree from."

Moreover, Fun-Da-Mental explicitly refers to Nation of Islam (NOI) teachings, which are highly heterodox. For instance, they make reference to the conception of the white "devil" ("grafted" by the evil scientist Yaqub approximately 6,000 years ago, according to NOI teachings): "the devils that worked us out in the sunshine" ("Seize the Time"); "the devil operating through the media" ("Meera Mazab").[13] In "President Progapanda" and "Dollars of Sense," respectively, they also invoke Elijah Muhammad's claim that Islam is the "original religion" of the Asiatic black man and Christianity an inauthentic imposition:

> I'm a soldier in the name of Allah
> So put down the cross and pick up the "X" . . .
> Back in the days of the slave ships
> You had us whipped, raped and lynched
> Took away the Qur'an, you gave us the Bible
>
> Telling me Jesus is calling
> Selling me books of make believe stories
> Where people like me don't seem to have glory . . .
> They're retailing Christianity and feeding you insanity

In addition, Fun-Da-Mental ingeniously weaves samples of well-known soundbites from Farrakhan and especially Malcolm X into its multilayered, state-of-emergency dance mix.[14]

Fun-Da-Mental also attempts to educate white youth and leftists and to incorporate them into the antiracist struggle (see Yellow Peril 1995). When addressing them, Aki Nawaz attempts to "normalize" the Islamic presence in Britain as well to as explain the reasons for "fundamentalist" tendencies among Muslim youth.

> We're living on the edge and that's why there's a massive rise in fanaticism especially amongst Muslims who are joining organizations like the Kalifah. I'm not saying that's wrong, but it's a result of other things that are failing them, they're being led that way because no-one is doing anything about what should be done. Then you get the whiteman going "they're all fanatics" but he has put them in the position of having to be fanatics. (CARF 1994)

> I don't really like fanatics but I can also see that a lot of fundamentalist groups are like freedom fighters and then the people in power come along and paint them with a different and more negative brush. (Yellow Peril 1995)

Fun-Da-Mental also seems to enjoy "shaking up" young whites, as evidenced by Aki's remarks prior to performing at a Sydney concert before a crowd of mainly white indie-rock youths: "[W]e kind of look forward to going up on the stage to hordes of drunk and drugged-out indie kids and almost terrifying the shit out of them. We're like the ultimate coming down pill" (Yellow Peril 1995).

Fun-Da-Mental's uses of "Islam" are therefore central to its multipronged intervention: Islam instills religioethnic pride among Asian youth, serves as an image of antiracist mobilization, creates links between Asians and Afro-Caribbeans, and shocks and educates white leftists and alternative youth.[15]

NATACHA ATLAS: A HUMAN GAZA STRIP

Although Transglobal Underground (TGU) is not, strictly speaking, a hip-hop group, I include it here because hip-hop is one of its key constituent elements. It has been difficult, in fact, for music critics and the music industry to pin a label on TGU's music. Among the many contenders are ethno-dance, global fusion dance-trance,[16] ethnodelic, dub-hop, global groove, world dance fusion, cross-cultural funk, Arab funk, polymorphic trance, ethnic techno, radical global pop, world techno, dub-rave-dance-trance-world, cross-cultural fusion, and so on ("In Town" n.d.; Taylor 1997; Anderson 1997; Wright n.d.; Hesmondhalgh 1995). Most recently, TGU has been marketed in the United States under the category "electronica." TGU's ambiguous position at the borders of "dance" and "world" musics has given rise to criticism, in particular from John Hutnyk, who in a trenchant article titled "Adorno at WOMAD" says of TGU's performance at the 1994 World of Music and Dance (WOMAD) Festival at Reading: "How is it that white British performers can wear Nepalese masks on stage, abstracted from their social and cultural context, without critical comment?" (1997: 109). Hutnyk goes on to criticize the routinization of "global sampling" in the world-music scene as well as the depoliticized "hybridity-talk" that pervades both musical and cultural studies discourses, singling TGU out as an exemplar of such depoliticized yet critically hailed hybridity. As counterexamples of bands that are hybrid and nonessentialist yet politically progressive, Hutnyk cites Fun-Da-Mental and Asian Dub Foundation, which are both directly involved in the antiracist struggle and propagate their politics at events like WOMAD. David Hesmondhalgh (1995) raises similar issues, arguing in particular that TGU's musical sampling practices should not be hailed — as they typically are by music critics — as instances of radical postmodernism and multiculturalism but instead seen as modernist appropriations that produce primitivist, exoticist, and romanticizing significations of the other.

Without disputing that TGU has exoticist and appropriating tendencies, I want to suggest that if one focuses on "Islam," the picture looks somewhat different. I will argue, *contra* Hutnyk and Hesmondhalgh, that TGU and especially the singer Natacha Atlas do articulate a progressive politics, although not in as overtly militant a fashion as Fun-Da-Mental, and that "Islam" plays a critical role in this regard. But first, it is necessary to clarify TGU's image. It is incorrect to describe TGU as white or even predominantly white. The band member Count Dubullah, in response to such claims, notes his own Greek-Albanian background (in England, these ethnic categories are not so clearly coded as "white" as in the United States; moreover, Albanians are Muslim);[17] that Natacha Atlas has "Arabic" roots; and that, in performance, the band expands to include Africans and South Asians (Morrell 1996). Moreover, TGU is not outside the orbit of progressive Asian bands and antiracist activity, for it performs at antiracist festivals on the same bill as the "political" bands.[18] Hutnyk's model "political" band Asian Dub Foundation in fact got its start on the concert circuit by opening for TGU on several dates in late 1994 (Luke n.d.) and has since opened for Natacha Atlas's solo dates.[19] Finally, TGU recorded for Aki Nawaz's Nation Records until 1999 and has shared personnel with Fun-Da-Mental (Count Dubullah and Neil Sparkes have recorded with both groups), and several of its singles have been remixed by Aki Nawaz. For their 2001 album, *Yes Boss Food Corner,* they switched to the Mondo Rhythmica label, but they have continued their association with Nation Records.

I would argue that it would be mistaken therefore to insist on a sharp distinction between "political" Asian dance bands such as Fun-Da-Mental and Asian Dub Foundation and the depoliticized exotic-hybrid-postmodernist musical tendency (world-dance fusion) represented by TGU and Natacha Atlas. Both genres are released by Nation Records, and both Fun-Da-Mental and TGU/Atlas have made a move away from indiscriminate use of the music of the world as the source of samples and toward collaboration with "indigenous" musicians.[20] TGU could be regarded as one side of Aki Nawaz and Nation Records' multifaceted strategy for progressive cultural and political intervention within British popular culture. The trajectory of TGU's work is clearly consistent with Nawaz's broadly conceived antiracist politics, his "punk attitude," and his commitment to "reshuffling the global sound archives" while at the same time "insist[ing] on the primacy of their source material" (Toop 1993: 14).[21]

The TGU singer and solo artist Natacha Atlas is a key figure in such a strategy. She once described herself as a "human Gaza Strip," which one press account acutely glossed as referring to the "complex mélange of influences — both genetic and environmental — that have shaped her both as an individual and as a performer" ("Natacha Atlas" n.d.). Atlas's "genetic influences" are hybrid, to say the least: her father, a Middle Eastern Jew, born in Jerusalem; her grandfather, born in Egypt; a "Jewish and Palestinian mixture a few generations back" (Fruin n.d.); her mother, an English hippie, fan of Pink Floyd, devotee of Gurdjieff (Barbarian 1996; Assayas 1996). Appropriately enough, she grew up in the Moroccan and Jewish districts of Brussels, absorbing musics from both cultures and listening to her father's old Arabic records (Ali 1995:53; Assayas 1996). When her parents divorced, she relocated to England and reportedly became "Northampton's first Arabic rock singer" ("Natacha Atlas" n.d.).[22] At age twenty-four, she went back to Belgium, where she belly-danced professionally in Arab and Turkish clubs and listened carefully to the Arab classical musicians accompanying her. She describes going back to Belgium as a "return to her roots" (Barbarian 1996). By her own account, she does not suffer from an "identity problem," asserting rather that she feels equally at home in more than one culture ("In Town" n.d.).

Atlas's primary Middle Eastern "genetic" background, therefore, is Sephardi (or, to use the more politicized term, Mizrahi). Her identification with Judaism therefore is rooted in the Middle East and is affiliated (even by blood, in some complicated and unspecified way) to Islam. This is not as incongruous as it might appear from a Eurocentric or Ashkenazi perspective, for as Ammiel Alcalay so carefully shows in his *After Jews and Arabs* (1992), "Eastern" Jewry was for centuries intensely integrated into Arabo-Islamic civilization. The title of Atlas's first solo album, *Diaspora* (1997), refers, she says, not just to the "first dispersion of the Jews of Palestine but also those of all the races that have suffered injustice. . . . The uprooted are everywhere. Iraqis, Yugoslavs or Palestinians" (Barbarian 1996). It is noteworthy that all the diasporic peoples she names are Muslim (majority) peoples (assuming that that by "Yugoslavs" Atlas means Bosnian Muslims). One of *Diaspora*'s most compelling songs is titled "Laysh Nata'arak" [Why Are We Fighting?]:

Why are we fighting
When we're all together? . . .
Between me and you there is a long history. . . .
Let's return to peace
Let's make peace, we are brothers

The song addresses its call for peace to Arabs and Israelis in Arabic (the translation is mine), and therefore the primary Israeli addressees are the majority second-class Mizrahi Jews.[23] Moreover, Atlas sings, "Let's *return* to peace [emphasis added]" *[Yalla nirga' li-al-salâm]*, evoking a time, before the creation of Israel, of amicable relations among Arabic-speaking Jews, Muslims, and Christians in the Middle East.

The plaintive title cut from *Diaspora* elaborates on these themes. Atlas sings, in Arabic:

My heart is wounded, my country . . .
Without you
And my life is torture
And the pain increases

Atlas's Arabic verses alternate with Neil Sparkes's dub poetry, which addresses the English-speaking listener and emphasizes once again the rootedness of Eastern Jews in the Middle East:

The Kabbala revealed
Aramaic whispers in Jaffa and Tel Aviv
Spirits of the desert skies and plains
For what shall we mourn and grieve
Mesopotamia and Ur of the Chaldeas
Descendants of the Sephardim

Trading tolerance and unity
From Baghdad to the Promised Land
Children of Canaan
Daughter of the Maghreb

The song's achingly beautiful atmospherics evoke Atlas's feelings about her own family's "uprooting": "I don't even know how we arrived in Belgium. I feel a great sadness, a feeling of loss" (Barbarian 1996).[24] For Atlas the diaspora is contemporary, a dispersion from the Arabo-Islamic Middle East, where—until the creation of the state of Israel—Sephardi Jews were "at home." This is a Mizrahi, not an Ashkenazi, European Jewish vision of diaspora. As Alcalay (1992: 1) observes:

> The modern myth of the Jew as pariah, outsider and wanderer has, ironically enough, been translated into the postmodern myth of the Jew as "other," an other that collapses into the equation: writing = Jew = Book. By what sleight of hand? . . . Such an exclusive address . . . ultimately obscures the necessity of mapping out a space in which the Jew *was* native, not a stranger but an absolute inhabitant of time and place.

At present Atlas—as a kind of riposte to the postmodern myth?—chooses to divide her time between London and Cairo, not Tel Aviv or Jerusalem.

Atlas voices her orientation toward "Islam" on "Dub Yalil" (from *Diaspora),* where she sings the opening lines of the *idhân,* the Muslim call to prayer, "Allahu akbar, ashhadu an la allah illa Allah" (God is greatest, I witness that there is no god but God), over a dub beat. But Atlas does not *complete* the opening of the call to prayer, whose next phrase is "wa Muhammad rasûl Allah" (and Muhammad is the messenger of God). Instead, she sings, "Allah ana bahibbak" (God, I love you). The fact that she recites the idhân without mentioning the prophet Muhammad, that she *sings* this religious text rather than chants it, that her singing is set to a dub-reggae beat, and that she uses the phrase "God, I love you," all make this a highly heterodox "Islamic" production. Nonetheless, the song testifies to her Islamic affiliations. While growing up, Atlas states, her father used to tell her about Judaism and her mother about Gurdjieff, but she was not interested. Now, she asserts, "I feel myself to be very Muslim, in fact. Sometimes I go to the mosque, last year I did [fasted during] Ramadan" (Assayas 1996).

Islam is also critical to Atlas's understanding of her own and TGU's cultural intervention in Britain. I would argue that, given an overarching atmosphere of Islamo- and Arabophobia and racist violence against immigrants of Muslim origin, Atlas's and TGU's attempts to insert Arabic or

Middle Eastern music into the British public sphere attests to a progressive cultural-political agenda. Atlas has been the key figure in this subversive activity, beginning in 1990 with her work in the world-dance fusion outfit ¡Loca! (on the compilations *Fuse* and *Fuse II*), with Jah Wobble's Invaders of the Heart (for instance, on *Rising above Bedlam*), with TGU, and finally in a solo capacity (while continuing to work with TGU, although only in a production capacity since 1999). She did vocals on Apache Indian's top-20 hit "Arranged Marriage"; the music press asserts, with typical hyperbole, that she was the first woman to sing in Arabic on the television show *Top of the Pops* ("Natacha Atlas" n.d.).[25] Atlas has also worked with Daniel Ash (on *Coming Down*, 1991), and more recently with Indigo Girls on "Come on Now Social." As she has gained visibility, she has tended to use more and more Arabic in her singing, whereas her earlier recordings featured more vocals in Spanish and French (the opening track of her 1999 album *Gedida* [New] is also in French, with other tracks in Arabic and English). Her articulation of Arabic has become clearer as she has gradually gained better control over the language, and her Arabic lyrics are now also more elaborate (Small 1997). According to Atlas, "[N]ow, something more [of Arabic music] is getting through [in Britain]. It's no longer an alien sound" (Ali 1995: 50). If the Arabic sonic presence is now somewhat more normalized in Britain, this is due in no small part to Natacha Atlas's efforts.

Moreover, TGU's other core members have traveled in the Middle East and have seriously studied Arab music, in particular the Eastern modes (*mâqamât*) and melodies (Small 1997; Twomey 1997). First exposed to Arab and Iranian records by Sam Dodson (who performs under the stage name Salman Gita) of Loop Guru (until 1995 a Nation Records labelmate), later they studied with Middle Eastern musicians, including Atlas's Egyptian relative, the 'ud player and composer Essam Rashad (Small 1997). More recently, they have also collaborated with Middle Eastern musicians, including Essam Rashad (on TGU recordings and *Diaspora*) and the Tunisian artists Walid and Rafiq Rouissi (on *Diaspora*).[26] One TGU member, Alex Kasiek, claims that Arabs, especially those living in the West, are pleased with what the group is doing: "For a lot of Arabic people if you start playing Arabic music they see it as a compliment. The West is contemptuous of their culture, they see [it] being some sort of frightening 'other.' So they [Arabs] tend to find it as a mark of respect" (Small 1997).

As for audiences in the Middle East, Atlas claimed in 1997 that her solo recordings were considered too avant-garde for the mass market, but that she had won acceptance for *Diaspora* among Moroccan youth (Snowden 1997: 33). Since then both Atlas and TGU have had more impact on Middle

Eastern markets. Atlas's 1997 album *Halim* (a tribute to the canonical Egypt-ian singer 'Abd al-Halîm Hâfiz released in the United States in 1998) has been more successful, due no doubt to the fact that it sounds like a 1960s–1970s style Egyptian-Lebanese pop album, with the addition of some dub and hip-hop beats. In July 1998 Natacha traveled to Beirut to perform her single "Amulet," which has enjoyed some success in the region, on the Leb-anese television station LBC.[27] In 1997 the popular Egyptian singer Hakim, interested in expanding his sales beyond the Egyptian market, enlisted TGU's help in remixing a collection of Hakim's greatest hits. Released in Egypt in 1998, the album *(Shakl tânî/Remix)* is a remarkable fusion of Ha-kim's intense *sha'bî* vocalisms and TGU-style rhythms and deep bass. Al-though I was unable to obtain sales figures, the Hakim-TGU album seemed to be doing well in Cairo when I visited there in August 1998. *Shakl tânî* is expected to be released in Europe soon. Meanwhile, Slam!, Hakim's record company, assisted Natacha Atlas in the production of *Gedida,* which was re-leased in Europe in February 1999. (It was also released in the Arab world as *Gazouri,* minus a few tracks considered too political or sexy.)[28]

With the non-Arabic-speaking English audience, Atlas considers "Islam" the key to her success. The music press frequently called attention to the ex-otic "chiffon-draped belly dancing" she did on stage with TGU ("Transglobal Underground" 1996), and she has been criticized in some quarters for repro-ducing stereotypes of sexualized Middle Eastern women (Hesmondhalgh 1995: 9). But Atlas seems to prefer to stress her performances' spiritual ap-peal: "I love the profundity of Arabic singing and the formality of it, and the way it seems to touch on the religious. I believe the Muslim call to prayer is the sound of God, that's what ignites me and ignites Westerners who hear it and are moved by it" ("*Diaspora* Finally Available" 1997). Atlas is aware that the kids in the audience "don't know what the fuck I'm singing about, but they have a feeling." When she hits the high notes, she says, their eyes are shut, and "[t]hey look as though they're reaching for Allah. It makes them feel good, spiritual" (Ali 1995: 50).

So whereas Atlas's colleague Aki Nawaz employs "Islam" to shake up white youth, Atlas uses it to bring them into her spiritual world. The two strategies, I would argue, are complementary. The genius of TGU and Na-tacha Atlas is their sly insertion of subtle attacks on Islamophobia into a complex, multitargeted, "club-friendly" (Wright n.d.), upbeat, and dance-able mix that blends hip-hop, techno, Indian film soundtracks, African chants, and dub reggae with Middle Eastern stylings. While I think Hutnyk and Hes-mondhalgh raise important criticisms regarding the exoticizing effects of

TGU-Atlas performances and mixes and their appropriations of uncredited samplings, I do not agree that TGU and Atlas simply produce images of unmarked otherness and depoliticized notions of hybridity. Instead, their hybridized music is heavily "Islamicized" and, therefore, politically charged.

AKHENATON: 100 PERCENT MÉTÈQUE

Akhenaton, the rapper and chief spokesperson for the Marseilles rap group IAM, was born Philippe Fragione, the son of immigrants from the region of Calabria in southern Italy who settled in Marseilles. When IAM burst onto the French rap scene[29] with its 1991 release . . . *de la planète Mars* (. . . From the Planet Mars), one of its most notable features was what André Prévos dubs its "pharaohism." Four of the group's six members go by ancient Egyptian names (Imhotep, DJ Kheops, Divin Kephren, and of course Akhenaton), and IAM's lyrics are full of references to ancient Egyptian civilization. Prévos argues astutely that pharaohism permits IAM to assert connections to the contemporary Arab world in an indirect, coded way: "The concept [of pharaohism] underlines Arabic origins while bypassing negative representations of North African countries gripped by Islamic fundamentalism and economic uncertainties" (1996: 721).[30] The jacket of IAM's second CD, *Ombre est lumière* (Shadow Is Light) even asserts that in ancient times, Egypt was connected to Marseilles, but the continents subsequently drifted apart. I would take issue, however, with Prévos's claim that IAM's pharaohism is an original development that demonstrates French rap's growing independence from U.S. hip-hop hegemony (Prévos 1996: 719, 721–722). According to Akhenaton, the name IAM (standing for Imperial Asiatic Men)[31] was chosen after he read the Senegalese writer Cheikh Anta Diop, one of Afrocentrism's leading theorists, who spurred Akhenaton's preexisting interest in the Asiatic Middle East as the origin of the monotheistic religions and in Egypt as the (black) cradle of civilization. "Egyptianism," in fact, is a long-standing theme of Afrocentric thought, dating back to the nineteenth century (see Gilroy 1993: 60, 208–9). I would argue that the real ingenuity of IAM's pharaohism is that it gives Egyptianist Afrocentricity a Mediterranean inflection, asserting a kind of "black Mediterranean."

And more precisely, a black *Islamic* Mediterranean. From IAM's inception, Akhenaton's fascination for ancient Egypt and the Middle East was largely religiously motivated; he consciously took his stage name from the first *monotheistic* pharaoh. Although Akhenaton only formally converted to Islam in 1993, IAM was already making positive references to Islam on . . . *de la planète Mars* in 1991:

Allahu akbar, protect us from absolute darkness
Like King Raz said to whom I say salaam [peace, an Islamic greeting]
Ulemas [Islamic learned men] we are, souls of Islam.
  ("Red, Black and Green")

According to Akhenaton, the process by which he arrived at Islam was a lengthy one. His mother used to read the Bible to him as a child, stressing its "Oriental" dimensions (Jorif 1995: 25). Almost all his friends in polyglot Marseilles are Muslims; their celebrations of Ramadan made him want to learn more about the religion. He found in Islam an attitude that was very rational and scientific, but most importantly, mystical (Péguillan 1995). It is Islam's mystical dimension that Akhenaton finds most appealing, that he stresses in interviews (Cachin 1995: 22; Robert 1995: 26; Dufresne 1991: 151), and that emerges most clearly from the lyrics of IAM and Akhenaton's solo work.[32] While clearly Akhenaton's mystical tendency is, in part, a product of personal predilection, it is significant that, given an atmosphere of intense hostility on the part of the French toward immigrants who, even more than in Britain, are figured chiefly as "Muslim," he chooses to espouse a spiritual as opposed to a political Islam. In interviews, he underlines that his Islam makes a separation between religion and politics—in unstated opposition, for instance, to the FIS, the Islamist political opposition in Algeria. In the track "J'aurai pu croire" ("I Could Have Believed," on *Ombre est lumière*), IAM takes both Saddam Hussein and Iran's ayatollahs to task for their hypocritical politicization of religion:

Saddam you don't make me believe in you
When you pray in front of cameras
Do you at least know that to display [your portrait] everywhere
Is forbidden by our holy book the Qur'an?
And you blaspheme and blaspheme and blaspheme

Akhenaton emphasizes that the Islam he espouses is tolerant and characterized by a mystical beauty, and that he is neither a "fundamentalist" (*intégriste*) nor a *provocateur* (Péguillan 1995). At a time when right-wing extremists such as Jean-Marie Le Pen and his followers are railing about the threat of an "Islamic invasion" and winning local elections, when FIS "terror" cells have been operating inside France, and when the mainstream press frequently depicts rap music itself as incendiary (exemplified in the harsh actions taken against hip-hop groups such as NTM; Prévos 1997), it is little wonder that Akhenaton publicly advocates a transcendental and nonconfrontational brand of Islam.

But while he stresses its spirituality, Akhenaton's Islam is in fact neither quietist nor apolitical. Promoting "Islam" in fact is part of IAM's general effort to widen the space of tolerance for Arabo-Islamic culture in France, through its lyrical subject matter, its deployment of Arabic words and expressions, and its musical mixes, splattered with Middle Eastern rhythms and samples of Arabic songs.[33] For Akhenaton/Philippe Fragione, moreover, Islam represents a reconnection to his Italian roots, a return that he invests with an antiracist inflection. Here again Akhenaton demonstrates his creativity in putting forward a vision of a pan-Mediterranean black Islamic culture, a position that resonates with the reality of polyethnic Marseilles.[34]

In interviews that appeared around the release of his solo album, *Mètèque et mat,* released in 1995, Akhenaton discussed his conversion to Islam and its relation to his Italian heritage. Although it is little known, he says, Sicily was an Islamic state in the tenth century, and southern Italians have Arab blood, although they have forgotten this fact (Cachin 1995: 21; Jorif 1995: 25).[35] The barbarian Lombards invaded from the north, carried out an inquisition and massacres against the Muslims, and forcibly converted them to Christianity (Jorif 1995: 25). (Akhenaton here both refigures Gramsci's "Southern Question" as an "Arab-Islamic Question" and reverses hegemonic Italian notions regarding northern Italian "superiority," expressed most recently by the Northern League.)[36] He goes on to assert that one still sees churches in the south that were originally mosques. He also claims that some Muslim sects in Italy practiced *taqiya* (dissimulation), and that therefore some (secret) Muslim groups still exist in Sicily today (Jorif 1995: 25).[37] Commenting on how his solo album investigates his Italian roots, Akhenaton asserts: "I realized that on the one hand, like all humanity, our cradle was African, on the other hand that the Arab race was present and influential in our blood and our customs. . . . *Mètèque et mat* is that: the idea that my roots as an Italian from the south are in symbiosis with two others" (Robert 1995: 24). The cover of *Mètèque et mat* offers a brilliant visualization of Akhenaton's efforts to yoke together these various cultural strands (African, Italian, and Arabo-Islamic). A sepia-toned photograph shows a middle-aged Italian seated behind a chessboard whose king piece is an Egyptian pharaoh. The design that surrounds the name, Akhenaton, is Islamic, and the courtyard of the house that spreads out behind the chess player appears both Italian and Arab. The title of the CD, moreover, is a brilliant, multilayered pun. *Mètèque et mat* rhymes with *echec et mat,* the expression for "checkmate." *Mètèque* means "wog," and so the literal translation of the title is "Wog-mate." Furthermore, the word *mat* comes from the Arabic *mât,* meaning "to die," and, contrary to normal French rules but following the word's Arabic origins, the "t" is pronounced (the English "checkmate" carries the same Arabic etymology).[38]

Akhenaton clearly regards Islam as a kind of potential but occulted cultural bridge linking Italian communities, the products of earlier waves of immigration to France, to Maghrebi-Islamic communities, the more recent arrivals. When he converted to Islam, Akhenaton says, his own family was very tolerant, and he realized then that Catholicism and Islam are closely related religions. Besides common cultural roots, Italians and Arabs share similar experiences as immigrants, as Akhenaton emphasizes in interviews and on his solo CD. Both are métèques or "wogs," in the view of dominant French culture. Both groups have suffered from racism, and many métèques responded by attempting to integrate so quickly into French life that they forgot their own culture (Péguillan 1995). In "L'Americano," Akhenaton notes the assimilationist tendency among Italian immigrants and pokes fun at the "types aux origine truquées" (guys with "doctored" origins), immigrants who changed their last names from Malano to the Frenchified Malan (Cachin 1995: 21), just as some assimilated Arabs changed their names from Boubaker to Bob. As a result of such cultural losses—hence the nostalgia-drenched sepia of the CD cover and container insert—Italians have forgotten their traditions. Arabs meanwhile have become so Frenchified that those living in state-funded high-rise apartment blocks (the dreaded HLMs) do not know their own neighbors (Cachin 1995: 22). "Car mat est le métèque / Fascinés par le mirage des idéaux de modernité" (For checkmated [dead] is the métèque / Fascinated by the mirage of modernity's ideals), raps Akhenaton on "Métèques et mat." People of the "south" (African, Arab, or Italian), Akhenaton asserts, are losing their characteristic hospitality and assuming a posture of aggressiveness. When the south loses its culture, Akhenaton warns, it becomes vulnerable to Americanization (FLX 1995: 57). The métèques, therefore, need to reinvent community life and to develop a sense of personal responsibility (Cachin 1995: 22). But such a common effort can succeed only if Italians remember why they immigrated to France: to escape fascism and repression. "I'm one of those whom Hitler called the niggers of Europe" (Je suis un de ceux qu'Hitler nommait nègres de l'Europe), he chants on "Métèque et mat." Akhenaton is "pissed off" that Italians have been involved in racist murders and that many Italians are voting for Le Pen, forgetting their own past sufferings (Cachin 1995: 21; Péguillan 1995).

Akhenaton asserts that IAM is antipolitical, in the sense of wanting nothing to do with the state: "On ne me traitera pas de soumis à ce putain d'état" (They won't call me submissive to this whore of a state; from "Non soumis à l'état," on . . . de la planète Mars). But he goes on to say that the group is political only insofar as it actively opposes Le Pen and his National Front's racist politics. IAM, whose members are variously of Madagascaran, Senegalese, Algerian, Spanish, and Italian background, plus one white French "native," advocates a multiethnic antiracism, one that reflects the diverse nature of Marseilles and the *banlieues,* the suburban zones of the immigrants and lower class in France.[39] Although the French banlieues are multiethnic, they are heavily racialized in official discourse. And the symbol of all that is "other" in France is, most centrally, the young, "immigrant" Arab Muslim, the *zonard* of the banlieue (see Bazin 1995: 116).[40] Unlike in the United States, where racial and ethnic difference is structured around a black-white polarity, in France the principal opposition is between white native and immigrant Arab other. Since the main thrust of racism in France is anti-Arab and anti-Islamic, IAM's successful insertion of Islam and Middle Eastern music into the space of popular culture (as with Fun-Da-Mental and Transglobal Underground) is ultimately political. IAM is also critical of "global" racism. The track "Tam tam de l'Afrique" (. . . *de la planète Mars),* for instance, decries the West's enslavement of Africans. In interviews, IAM has also disparaged the West's war against Iraq, stressing that the conflict originated from disputed boundaries drawn by the colonial powers, and in the track "J'aurai pu croire," they blast U.S. conduct in the 1991 Gulf War: "They intervened in Kuwait for oil and money / The rights of man have nothing to claim for the country of the Klan." "Le soldat" (from *Ombre est lumière)* exposes the horrors of war from the point of view of a soldier, no doubt referring to the Gulf War, to which France contributed troops. In "J'aurai pu croire," IAM takes Israel to task for its repression of Palestinians, mentioning, among other examples, the 1982 massacres at the Sabra and Shatila refugee camps in Lebanon, and states: "But bullets against pebbles, cannons against stones / Border raids, I can't shut up / The child David has become Goliath." As in Britain, Muslims in France experience such instances of Western imperialism in the Middle East as racism. It should be noted as well that the anti-Arab hysteria that erupted in France during the 1991 Gulf War, in which anti-Saddam fever intersected with deep-seated antagonism toward domestic Arabs, was a particularly horrible experience for Maghrebis in France (see Gross et al. 1996: 146–47; Ben Jelloun 1991).

IAM's 1997 album *L'école du micro d'argent* (The School of the Silver Microphone) represents a more political move on the part of the group. Full of vignettes on daily life in urban France, *L'école* presents a much darker view than 1994's *Ombre est lumière,* which contained its share of danceable and humorous numbers. The shift was prompted by the increasing influence in the south of Le Pen's fascistic Front National (FN), as exemplified by the

1995 murder of Ibrahim Ali, a Comoran teenager who belonged to BVice, a hip-hop group close to IAM, by an FN activist, and by the election of FN mayors in several urban centers in the south (Davet 1997). It was IAM's "sound architect," Imhotep (né Pascal Perez), who was most instrumental in pushing the group in a more overtly political direction. Imhotep/Pascal was born in Algiers in 1960 to a *pied-noir* family of Spanish origin who were close to the Arabs and despised by the rightist Colón terrorist organization, the OAS, and who supported the Left when they moved to France in the wake of Algerian independence. According to Imhotep, *L'école du micro d'argent* represented an effort to rekindle the spirit of revolt in France, against the FN and against racist immigration laws, as well as to educate the youth. In particular, IAM is working to encourage young people to vote so as to turn back the FN electoral tide. IAM also participated in a counterdemonstration organized on the occasion of Le Pen's visit to Marseilles (de Monicault 1997) and contributed to the rap single "11'30" contre les lois racistes (Eleven Minutes Thirty seconds against Racist Laws), produced at the initiative of Madj (of rap group Assasin) and in collaboration with the grassroots antiracist organization MIB (Mouvement de l'Immigration et des Banlieues). The single, aimed at raising the consciousness of youth regarding racist immigration laws, had netted 500,000 francs for MIB by October 1997 ("Rap: Les producteurs . . ." 1997; Fara C. 1997).

Finally, I want to mention IAM's connections to U.S. hip-hop, and especially U.S. "Islamic" rappers. Although Akhenaton's Islamic orientation is mystical and not political, he is well versed in the teachings of black Muslims. He was influenced in this regard partly by his mother, whom Ahkenaton describes as having a rather "revolutionary" tendency and as someone who read Angela Davis. As a teenager, Akhenaton spent summers visiting relatives in the United States, where he read the works of leading African Americans such as Marcus Garvey, Malcolm X, Huey Newton, and Elijah Muhammad. Having been exposed to Nation of Islam teachings, he is critical of what he calls the "home-made" religions of the United States (Dufresne 1991: 151), which he distinguishes from the more "authentic" Islam practiced in France. Other IAM members of the group equally understand the gap between the Islam of black North Americans and the Islam of French Maghrebis and Africans. According to Imhotep, a Muslim in Marseilles would find black Muslim discourse "bonkers." IAM's dancer and sometime rapper Algerian Malek Sultan discusses the Five Percent Nation of Islam, whose members style themselves Gods,[41] noting that the celebrated U.S. rapper Rakim is a member. Malek Sultan regards their beliefs as a "sacrilege" (*profanation*) (Dufresne 1991: 151). Yet while IAM marks the distinction between the local, more "orthodox" Islam and the black nationalist Islam of the United States, it is nonetheless heavily influenced by U.S. "Islamic" rap styles. Of the three groups under consideration here, IAM is the most prototypically hip-hop, and its musical style is the closest to U.S. rap—although, as Akhenaton is careful to note, IAM's sound is slower, uses Oriental music and rhythms, and so on (Dufresne 1991: 15). Asked in 1995 by the music magazine *L'affiche* to list his ten favorite albums (Cachin 1995: 22), Akhenaton's choices were all U.S. rap releases. Five of his favorites were by artists who belong to the Five Percent Nation (Raekwon, Eric B and Rakim, Wu-Tang Clan, Nas, and Mobb Deep); a sixth was by A Tribe Called Quest, two of whose members are orthodox (Sunni) Muslims. Akhenaton has elsewhere expressed his admiration for Raekwon of the Wu-Tang Clan (FLX 1995: 54). Moreover, the U.S. rap group Sunz of Man, who belong to the Wu-Tang "family" and are also Five Percenters, guest on "La Saga," a cut from *L'école du micro d'argent,* throwing in some recognizably "Islamic" raps:

'Bout to take it to another chamber
From Medina to Marseille . . .
Never ate ham, never gave a damn
Television tells lies to your vision
So, beware of the trick-nology set off to fool the mind

Medina, in Five Percent argot, stands for Brooklyn. Not eating ham is a reference to Five Percent and Nation of Islam injunctions against the consumption of pork, a ban shared by orthodox Muslims. Describing television as something that "tells lies to your vision" is typical Five Percent wordplay; "trick-nology" is a Nation of Islam term for deceitful "white" teachings. The IAM album on which "La Saga" appears, moreover, can be seen as a kind of artistic tribute, or analogue at least, to the influential vision of the Wu-Tang Clan, Five Percent rappers whose work is heavily invested with samples from karate films and references to the ideology of Oriental martial arts and who call their native Staten Island "Shaolin." The cover of *L'école du micro d'argent* features armored Chinese warriors, and raps on the album feature numerous references to martial arts, Taoist philosophy (IAM's other lead rapper, Shurik'N Chang-ti, is a Taoist), and even to Shaolin.

Although IAM's second release, *Ombre est lumière,* was, in Tony Mitchell's judgment, "in many ways the unacknowledged masterpiece of Francophone rap" (1996: 41), it seems to have had no impact on the U.S. market, and therefore the group's subsequent release, *L'école du micro d'argent,* is almost impossible to obtain in the USA. IAM's collaboration with Sunz of Man and the group's links to other Five Percent rappers, especially the Wu-Tang Clan, have therefore gone virtually unnoticed in the USA. Nonetheless, they bear testimony to a kind of "transglobal Islamic underground" of cultural flows and affinities that exist despite deep-seated differences over the nature of "Islam."

CONCLUSION

I want to conclude by arguing for the importance of paying close attention to popular cultural manifestations of "Islam" in Europe, given the ethnic, political, and cultural importance of "Islam" to youth of Islamic background in Britain and France. While we should by no means ignore Islam's religious appeal to this youth, we also must situate that appeal in relation to ethnic, political, and cultural factors, which in many instances may carry more weight than the religious. Through such a focus, we will also expand our understanding of the extremely heterogeneous nature of "Islam" in Europe and shift attention away from a single-minded focus on issues (such as the veil, female genital mutilation, *hallal* diets [of meat from ritual Islamic slaughter], etc.) that often have contributed to stereotyping rather than to an understanding of Muslims. Cultural and political interventions such as those of Aki Nawaz, Natacha Atlas, and Akhenaton are likely to continue to be of critical importance for young Muslims as part of larger efforts to create new spaces for multifaceted Islamic identities and as weapons in the battles against racist violence and Islamophobic discrimination. There are similar manifestations elsewhere in Europe: for instance, a 1995 Turkish-German compilation called *Cartel,* which included Karakan, Erci C, and another high-profile German rap group called Da Crime Posse, composed of two Turkish immigrants, plus a German and a Cuban, who have injected Turkish music styles into rap and have addressed anti-Turkish racism (Robins and Morley 1996; Soysal 1997: 521, 527; Elflein 1998).[42] And 1996 saw the release of the French rapper Yazid's album *Je suis l'arabe* (I Am the Arab), a militant assertion of Arab issues and Arab identity. On "Je suis l'arabe," Yazid raps:

I'm the Arab, stopping oppression is my mission. . . .
The country of secularism doesn't tolerate Islam
Unemployment ravages, they talk of immigration
And when the banlieue burns, they talk of integration

On another cut, "Islam," Yazid defends and explains his religion. He asserts both his ethnic and his religious identity much more forcefully than has been seen before in French rap.

We have not witnessed the emergence of such popular cultural phenomena in the USA, where "Islamic" hip-hop has chiefly been a black nationalist articulation and where Muslims have not been "ethnicized." But perhaps a portent of the future is a new figure in New York City's "illbient" (dark ambient, instrumental hip-hop) DJ scene, a young Egyptian women named Mutamassik ("tenacious" in Arabic).[43] Mutamassik has recorded remixes that drop in samples from Egyptian pop for the 1996 Arto Lindsay releases *Mundo Civilizado* and *Hyper Civilizado* and has performed on the same bill as South Asian DJs. Illbient Islam, anyone?

NOTES

Thanks to David McMurray for supplying hard-to-locate French articles on French rap and specifically Akhenaton/IAM; to Joan Gross for French translation advice; to Mike Woost for first turning me on to Fun-Da-Mental; to Tony Mitchell for alerting me to *Dis-Orienting Rhythms* and for furnishing the Hesmondhalgh article and hard-to-find music; to Saba Mahmood and Kamran Asdar Ali for help with Urdu; to John Peel, whose BBC World Service radio program alerted me to the existence of Natacha Atlas and Transglobal Underground when I lived in Cairo; to Nirvana Tannoukhi for assistance with Natacha Atlas's Arabic; and to Beatrice Nibigi for help in transcribing IAM's lyrics. All translations of lyrics, quotations, etc., are by the author.

1. A spectacular example of Islamophobia, well remembered by Arab residents of France but hardly recalled outside those circles, was recently brought to public view by the Papon affair. It is by now well known that Maurice Papon was accused of responsibility for the deportation of 1,560 Jews to Germany's death camps between 1942 and 1944, when he was in charge of Jewish affairs in Bordeaux. During Papon's trial it also emerged that he had served as the Paris police chief at the time of police murders of 200 (and possibly more) Algerians in Paris during protests on 17 October 1961. Scandalously, Papon's involvement in the 1961 massacre has received little coverage in the United States (but see Singer 1997; *Guardian Weekly*, 2 November 1997, 5; Einaudi 1997). Interestingly, Didier Daeninckx's crime novel *Murder in Memoriam* (1991) called attention to these connections (deportation of Jews, massacre of Arabs) in the Papon affair when first published in France in 1984. Good sources on the 1961 massacre are Aïchoune 1991; Ben Jelloun 1984; Cockburn 1991; Einaudi 1991; and Hargreaves 1989.

2. I employ quotes around "Muslim" and "Islam" to call attention to the fact that these are not natural, homogenous categories, but rather social constructions of heterogeneous and processual phenomena.

3. The major exception is John Hutnyk.

4. One finds a similar avoidance of "Islam" in the coverage of U.S. rap; see Swedenburg 1996.

5. On Muslims in Bradford, see Lewis 1994.

6. On bhangra, see Banerji and Baumann 1990; Huq 1997.

7. I refer here chiefly to the group's first album release in the United States, *Seize the Time* (1995).

8. An amazing tribute to the most famous Qawwali singer, Nusrat Fateh Ali Khan, appeared in 1997. *Star Rise* is a collection of remixes of the work of Nusrat Fateh Ali Khan by key figures in the Asian dance scene, including Aki Nawaz, Fun-Da-Mental, Asian Dub Foundation, and Talvin Singh.

9. Lewis (1994: 181) repeats uncritically the press accounts of what Aki Nawaz is purported to have said regarding Rushdie.

10. An example of this marginalization within cultural theory is *Black British Cultural Studies: A Reader* (Baker et al. 1996). The selection of authors (Stuart Hall, Paul Gilroy, Kobena Mercer, Rachel Carby, and others) and subject matter produces a distinctly Afro-Caribbean version of British blackness. Only Dick Hebdige (1996: 139) touches on Asian popular culture (Indi pop and bhangra); the only Asian author is Homi Bhabha, but his essay, "The Other Question," scarcely touches on "Asian" issues. For a critique of Paul Gilroy in this regard, see Hutnyk 1997: 127.

11. Although the Nation of Islam is reportedly active in the Afro-Caribbean community in Britain, it appears to have made few converts. I have been unable to track down any information on this subject.

12. I believe that an analytical focus on "Islam" begins to make sense of what Sharma et al. (1996: 53–54) describe as the confusing eclecticism of Fun-Da-Mental's politics.

13. It should also be noted that Fun-Da-Mental gives the rap expression "G" a South Asian inflection. Although "G" is often thought to mean "Gangsta" in hip-hop dialect, it originated as a form of greeting used between members of the Five Percent Nation of Islam, standing for "God." Fun-Da-Mental uses the expression "Ji" (which sounds exactly like "G") as an Urdu (or Hindi) term of address to denote respect between friends or lovers. (For instance, "Ah . . . people say I've gone and lost my mind 'cause I'm not afraid to die 'gee'"; from "Dog Tribe.")

14. While I do not consider Fun-Da-Mental's invocation of NOI ideology unproblematic, it should be understood as motivated in part by the group's punk provocateurism, in part by an effort to forge a kind of unity between Afro-Caribbeans and South Asians in England.

15. More recently, Fun-Da-Mental's scope of activity has extended to Pakistan; see "Interview with Aki" 1997.

16. Natacha Atlas offers this label in Twomey n.d.

17. The Count's ingenious stage name, combining "dub" and "allah," no doubt refers to his Albanian roots. Hesmondhalgh notes that the name "draws upon Caribbean [musicians'] parodies of British aristocratic titles, such as Prince Buster

and Prince Far-I" (1995: 10), to which I would add that inasmuch as "Count Dubullah" sounds like "Count Dracula," the name also evokes exotic Eastern Europe.

18. TGU performed at the antiracism festival at Finsbury Park in July 1996, along with the "political" bands Fun-Da-Mental, Chumbawamba, Kaliphz, Credit to the Nation, and Asian Dub Foundation. Posting to <http://www.uk.music.rave> by Andrew Cowper (acowper@dvcorp.co.uk), "Re: Finsbury Park" 19 July 1996.

19. For instance, in Paris, January 1996. Newsgroup posting (found through Deja News) by Serge.Boue@p1.f310.n320.z2.fidonet.org, "Concert de janvier," 25 January 1996.

20. Hesmondhalgh shows how the issue of sampling vs. collaboration with live musicians was a point of tension and struggle inside the Nation group and a factor in the departure of Loop Guru from the label (1995: 13).

21. In the course of an interview in which the issue of Aki Nawaz's media visibility came up, Atlas remarked, "He's a good speaker, actually" (Fruin n.d.). Given that Nawaz's media interventions are always political, her statement should be understand as an expression of support for his positions.

22. Since Atlas began to stress her "Arab" roots only later in her career, I doubt that she stressed her Arab side in her punk rock phase.

23. On the position of "Eastern" Jews in Israel, see Swirski 1989.

24. It should also be noted that TGU has played at WOMAD in Israel, and also in Taba and Eilat. *The Rough Guide to Rock,* probably referring to the Israel gigs, states, "As Transglobal Underground's turbulent gigs in the Middle East confirmed, cross-cultural musical references invite political debate" (Wright n.d.). I have been unable to uncover more details on TGU's experiences in Israel.

25. Atlas's singing style on "Arranged Marriage" (on Apache Indian's CD *No Reservations)* sounds more "South Asian" than "Middle Eastern," and I cannot detect the use of any words that sound Arabic. In fact, her vocalizations serve the purpose of providing this reggae song with its South Asian ambience (see Taylor [1997: 159–65], who curiously never mentions Atlas in his detailed analysis of the song).

26. Hesmondhalgh notes that employing live musicians is much more expensive than using samples, and that this has compelled the "independent" Nation label to make marketing agreements with larger recording companies (1995: 13).

27. During a visit to Amman, Jordan, in summer 1997, I came across a locally produced cassette collection that included Atlas's single "Amulet" (the song is called "Maarifnash" on *Halim).* I was told that the collection was an example of "Eastern-Western" *(sharbî-gharbî)* music.

28. For an online video of Natacha Atlas dancing in concert, see <*http://www.paleo.ch/audio.video.html#23*>.

29. See Cannon 1997 and Prévos 1993, 1995, and 1996 for overviews of the French rap scene.

30. I noted the general and somewhat surprising absence of "Arab" themes in French rap in a study originally done in 1992; see Gross et al. 1996: 143–44. Prévos's argument helps make sense of this nonappearance and of the fact that "Arab" is a kind of "absent presence" in the work of IAM.

31. IAM also stands for (1) "I am" [in English]; (2) Invasion Arrivant de Mars; and (3) Indépendantistes Autonomes Marseillais (see Dufresne 1991: 149 and Bazin 1995: 256–57 for an exegesis).

32. An example of IAM's mystical side, which makes no overt reference to Islam, is "Cosmos," on *Ombre est lumière*.

33. On the massive Arab presence in French popular culture, see McMurray 1997.

34. It should be pointed out, although the point cannot be developed here, that a sizable proportion of blacks in France are Muslims from West Africa, and so such appeals to Islam can be a way of asserting links between Arabs and blacks.

35. The Muslim conquest of Sicily lasted from 827 to 902 A.D.; Muslim rule in Sicily lasted until the Norman conquests (1061–1091); and the last Muslims were expelled from the island in 1246; see Ahmad 1975.

36. In fact, it was the German emperor Frederick II who eliminated the Muslims from Sicily (Ahmad 1975: 82–87). Akhenaton is correct, however, to see the Islamic influence in Italy as "civilizing."

37. Akhenaton's attempts to uncover and expose the Arab roots of southern Italy recall similar efforts by the Spanish novelist Juan Goytisolo and the music group El Lebrijano, who seek to bring to light Spain's Arab (Andalusian) origins.

38. Thanks to Joan Gross for help with teasing out these meanings.

39. A good sense of Marseilles's polyethnic atmosphere can be gained from the *policiers* (detective novels) of Jean-Claude Izzo; see, e.g., Izzo 1995.

40. On the banlieues, see Aïchoune 1991; Jazouli 1992; and Hargreaves 1995. See also Mathieu Kassovitz's powerful 1995 film *La haine* (Hate), now readily available in the United States on video.

41. On the Five Percent Nation in U.S. rap, see Swedenburg 1996.

42. Thanks to Resat Kesaba for telling me about *Cartel* and to Martin Stokes for alerting me to the Robins and Morley article.

43. The music press insists on translating *mutamassik* as "fanatic," which is unfortunate, but perhaps this is DJ Mutamassik's own translation, her effort to refigure "Islamic fanaticism."

REFERENCES

Ahmad, Aziz. 1975. *A History of Islamic Sicily*. Edinburgh: Edinburgh University Press.

Aïchoune, Farid. 1991. *Nés en banlieue*. Paris: Editions Ramsay.

Alcalay, Ammiel. 1992. *After Jews and Arabs: Remaking Levantine Culture*. Minneapolis: University of Minnesota Press.

Ali, Lorraine. 1995. "Fruits of the Desert." *Option* 65 (November–December): 48ff.

———. 1997. "Mutamassik: Vinyl Threat." *Option* 75 (July–August): 63.

Anderson, Jason. 1997. "Color Your World: Natacha Atlas and Transglobal Underground's Crosscultural Funk." *Eye* (3 July), <*http://www.eye.net/eye/issue/issue_07.03.97/music/anderson.html*>.

Assayas, Michka. 1996. "Djinn Tonic." *Les inrockuptibles*, 21–27 February, 20–22 (cited in McMurray 1996).

Baker, Houston A., Jr., Manthia Diawara, and Ruth H. Lindeborg. 1996. *Black British Cultural Studies: A Reader*. Chicago: University of Chicago Press.

Banerji, Sabita, and Gerd Baumann. 1990. "Bhangra 1984–8: Fusion and Professionalization in a Genre of South Asian Dance Music." In *Black Music in Britain*, edited by Paul Oliver. Milton Keynes: Open University Press.

Barbarian. 1996. "Natacha Atlas ou l'autre monde." *Libération*, 22 February.

Bazin, Hugues. 1995. *La culture hip-hop*. Paris: Desclée de Brouwer.

Ben Jelloun, Tahar. 1991. "I Am an Arab, I Am Suspect." *Nation*, 15 April, 482–84.

Brah, Avtar. 1996. *Cartographies of Diaspora: Contesting Identities*. London: Routledge.

CARF. 1994. "Fun-da-mentally Sound: An Interview with Fun-da-mental." *CARF* [Campaign against Racism and Fascism] 22, September–October. Posted on various electronic newsgroups by Arm the Spirit (ats@etext.org), 22 July 1995.

Cachin, Olivier. 1995. "Akhenaton: IAM à la première personne." *L'Affiche*, November, 20–23.

———. 1996. "IAM: La puissance vient du soleil." *L'Affiche hors-série* 2: 85–86.

Cannon, Steve. 1997. "Paname City Rapping: B-boys in the Banlieues and Beyond." In *Post-Colonial Cultures in France*, edited by Alec Hargreaves and Mark McKinney. London: Routledge.

Cockburn, Alexander. 1991. "Beat the Devil." *Nation*, 23 December, 802–3.

Daeninckx, Didier. 1991. *Murder in Memoriam*. Translated by Liz Heron. London: Serpent's Tail.

Darling, Cary. 1997. "Natacha Atlas Fans Get an Earful." *Orange County Register*, 26 February. <*http://www.newstimes.com/archive/feb26*>.

Davet, Stephane. 1997. "Rappers Capture Marseille's Mix." *Manchester Guardian Weekly*, 23 March, 18.

De Monicault, Frédéric. 1997. Interview with Imhotep. *Le Figaro grandes écoles et universités*, 22 May. <*http://www.iam.tm.fr/archimed/itw-eco/figrandun.html*>.

"*Diaspora* Finally Available in Canada." 1997. Napadogan Music press release, 26 March. <*http://www.napadogan.com/atlas_pr.htm*>.

"Discrimination against Britain's Moslems Becoming More Extreme." 1997. AFP report, 22 October. Posting on newsgroups from C-afp@clari.net.

Dufresne, David. 1991. *Yo! Revolution Rap*. Paris: Ramsay.

Einaudi, Jean-Luc. 1991. *La bataille de Paris, 17 Octobre 1961*. Paris: Editions du Seuil.

———. 1997. "Papon's Career Built on 'A Pack of Lies.'" *Guardian Weekly*, 9 November, 14 (translated from *Le monde*, 25 October 1997).

Elflein, Dietmar. 1998. "From Krauts with Attitudes to Turks with Attitudes: Some Aspects of Hip-hop History in Germany." *Popular Music* 17, no. 3: 255–65.

FLX. 1995. "Akhenaton: Via con me." *L'indic*, December, 54–57.

Fara C. 1997. "Les balles verbales de IAM." *Humanité dimanche*, 15 May. <*http://www.iam.tm.fr/archimed/itw-eco/humdum.html*>.

Fruin, Pete. N.d. "Transglobal World Atlas." <*http://www.london-calling.co.uk/ matlas*>.

Gilroy, Paul. 1993. *The Black Atlantic. Modernity and Double Consciousness*. Cambridge, Mass.: Harvard University Press.

Gross, Joan, David McMurray, and Ted Swedenburg. 1996. "Arab Noise and Ramadan Nights: *Rai*, Rap and Franco-Maghrebi Identity." In *Displacement, Diaspora, and Geographies of Identity,* edited by Smadar Lavie and Ted Swedenburg. 119–55. Durham, N.C: Duke University Press.

Hargreaves, Alec. 1995. *Immigration, "Race," and Ethnicity in Contemporary France*. London: Routledge.

Hargreaves, Alec, and Mark McKinney, eds. 1997. *Post-Colonial Cultures in France*. London: Routledge.

Hebdige, Dick. 1996. "Digging for Britain: An Excavation in Seven Parts." In Houston A. Baker, Jr., Manthia Diawara, and Ruth H. Lindeborg, *Black British Cultural Studies: A Reader*. Chicago: University of Chicago Press.

Hesmondhalgh, David.1995. "Nation and Primitivism: Multiculturalism in Recent British Dance Music." Paper delivered at the International Association for the Study of Popular Music Conference, July, Glasgow.

Hunt, Ken. N.d. "Fun-Da-Mental." *The Rough Guide to Rock*. <*http://www. roughguides.com/rock/entries/FUN-DA-MENTAL.html*>.

Huq, Rupa. 1997. "Asian Kool? Bhangra and Beyond." In *Dis-Orienting Rhythms: The Politics of the New Asian Dance Music,* edited by Sanjay Sharma, John Hutnyk, and Ashwani Sharma. London: Zed Books.

Hutnyk, John. 1996. "Repetitive Beatings or Criminal Justice?" In *Dis-Orienting Rhythms: The Politics of the New Asian Dance Music,* edited by Sanjay Sharma, John Hutnyk, and Ashwani Sharma. London: Zed Books.

————. 1997. "Adorno at WOMAD: South Asian Crossovers and the Limits of Hybridity-Talk." In *Debating Cultural Hybridity: Multi-Cultural Identities and the Politics of Anti-Racism,* edited by Pnina Werbner and Tariq Modood. London: Zed Books.

"In Town: Bellydancing Natacha Atlas Sings Arab Funk." N.d. <*http://www.riv.nl/yuliana/postcard/week41/atlas.htm*>.

Izzo, Jean-Claude. 1995. *Total Khéops.* Paris: Gallimard.

Jazouli, Adil. 1992. *Les années banlieues.* Paris: Editions du Seuil.

Jorif, Sylvia. 1995. "Akhenaton: La mère méditerranée." *B Mag*, December, 24–27.

Kalra, Virinder S., John Hutnyk, and Sanjay Sharma. 1996. "Re-Sounding (Anti)Racism, or Concordant Politics? Revolutionary Antecedents." In *Dis-Orienting Rhythms: The Politics of the New Asian Dance Music,* edited by Sanjay Sharma, John Hutnyk, and Ashwani Sharma. London: Zed Books.

Kepel, Gilles. 1997. *Allah in the West: Islamic Movements in America and Europe.* Translated by Susan Milner. Stanford: Stanford University Press.

Lewis, Philip. 1994. *Islamic Britain: Religion, Politics and Identity among British Muslims—Bradford in the 1990s.* London: I. B. Tauris.

Luke, George. N.d. "Asian Dub Foundation." *The Rough Guide to Rock.* <*http://www.roughguides.com/rock/entries.Asian_Dub_Foundation.html*>.

McMurray, David. 1996. "La France arabe." Paper delivered at the annual meeting of the Western Society for French History, 1 November, Charlotte, N.C.

———— 1997. "La France arabe." In *Post-Colonial Cultures in France,* edited by Alec Hargreaves and Mark McKinney, 1997. London: Routledge.

Mitchell, Tony. 1996. *Popular Music and Local Identity: Rock, Pop, and Rap in Europe and Oceania.* London: University of Leicester Press.

Morrell, Anna. 1996. "Transglobal Underground." *Retroactive Baggage,* June. <*http://www.warwick.ac.uk/~maurj/issue13/tgu.html*>.

"Natacha Atlas." N.d. <*www.beggars.com/atlas/atlasbio.html*>.

Nickson, Chris. 1997. "Transglobal Underground/Natacha Atlas: If You're Dancing, You're Dancing." *CMJ New Music* 43 (March): 18–19.

Owen, Frank. 1997. "Women Step Up to the Decks." *Village Voice,* 2 December, 30–33.

Péguillan, Frédéric. 1995. "Le pharaon de Marseille." *Télérama,* 23 December, 91.

Prévos, André J. M. 1993. "Une nouvelle forme d'expression populaire en France: le cas de la musique rap dans les années 1980." *Francographies. Actes II,* 201–16. New York: La société des professeurs français et francophones.

————. 1995. "Création, transformation, américanisation: Le rap français des années 90." *Francographies* 2: 170–209. New York: La société des professeurs français et francophones.

————. 1996. "The Evolution of French Rap Music and Hip Hop Culture in the 1980s and 1990s." *French Review* 69, no. 5: 713–25.

————. 1997. "Hip-Hop, Rap, and Repression in France and in the U.S." Paper delivered at the annual meeting of the American Anthropological Association, November 22, Washington, D.C.

"Rap: Les producteurs du single 11'30 contres les lois racistes." 1997. *Le monde,* 18 October, Culture section.

Rigoulet, Laurent. 1997. "Saga rap." *Libération,* 19 April. <*http://www.iam.tm.fr/archimed/itw-eco/lbrtn19497.html*>.

Robert, Richard. 1995. "L'armée des ombres." *Les inrockuptibles,* 15–21 November, 22–26.

Robins, Kevin, and David Morley. 1996. "Almanci, Yabanci." *Cultural Studies* 10, no. 2: 248–54.

Schmidt, Cecile. 1998. Interview with Natacha Atlas, 23 July (in French). <*http://www.sonicnet.ch/special/metafiles/natacha56.cam*>.

Sharma, Sanjay, John Hutnyk, and Ashwani Sharma, eds. 1996. *Dis-Orienting Rhythms: The Politics of the New Asian Dance Music.* London: Zed Books.

Singer, Daniel. 1997. "France on Trial." *Nation,* 10 November, 5.

Small, Craig. 1997. "Transglobal Underground: An Interview with Natacha Atlas." *HiFi*, March. <*http://www.spwa.com/hifi/articles/html/trans.html*>.

Snowden, Don. 1997. "Dancefloor Osmosis." *Rhythm Music* 6, no. 5: 30–34.

Soysal, Yasemin Nohoglu. 1997. "Changing Parameters of Citizenship and Claims-Making: Organized Islam in European Public Spheres." *Theory and Society* 26: 509–27.

Stevenson, Richard W. 1994. "Rapping, and No Apologies for a Generation's Rage." *New York Times* (international ed.), 12 August.

Swedenburg, Ted. 1996. "Islam in the Mix: Rap Lessons of the Five Percent." Paper delivered at the annual meeting of the American Anthropological Association, November, San Francisco.

Sweet, Stephen. 1993. "Fear and Loathing in Pakistan." *Melody Maker,* 13 November, 8–9.

Swirski, Shlomo. 1989. *Israel: The Oriental Majority.* Translated by Barbara Swirski. London: Zed Books.

Taylor, Kim. 1997. "England's Transglobal Underground Stirs U.S.: Ethno-Dance Collective Rides Electronica Wave." *Allstar,* 26 February. <*http://www.allstarmag.com*>.

Taylor, Timothy D. 1997. *Global Pop: World Music, World Markets.* New York: Routledge.

Toop, David. 1993. "He Wants to Change the World: Nation of Desire." *Wire,* December, 12–14.

"Transglobal Underground." 1996. <*http://www.geocities.com/SunsetStrip/ Alley/5444/ Transglobal_Underground.html*>.

Twomey, Chris. 1997. "Natacha Atlas and Transglobal Underground." *Exclaim!* J uly. <*http://exclaim.shmooze.net/features/9707/f/1txt.htm*>.

Werbner, Pnina. 1997. "Essentialising Essentialism, Essentialising Silence: Ambivalence and Multiplicity in the Constructions of Racism and Ethnicity." In *Debating Cultural Hybridity: Multi-Cultural Identities and the Politics of Anti-Racism,* edited by Pnina Werbner and Tariq Modood. London: Zed Books.

Werbner, Pnina, and Tariq Modood. 1997. *Debating Cultural Hybridity: Multi-Cultural Identities and the Politics of Anti-Racism.* London: Zed Books.

Wright, Chris. N.d. "Transglobal Underground." *The Rough Guide to Rock.* <*http:// www.roughguides.com/rock/entries/TRANSGLOBAL_UNDERGROUND.html*>.

Yellow Peril. 1995. "Fun-Da-Mental: A Revolution of the Consciousness." *3Dworld.* <*http://www.cia.com.au/peril/texts/features/Fundamental.htm*>.

DISCOGRAPHY

Akhenaton. 1995. *Métèque et mat.* Delabel.

Apache Indian. 1992. *No Reservations.* Mango.

Ash, Daniel. 1991. *Coming Down.* Beggars Banquet.

Atlas, Natacha.1997. *Diaspora.* MCA.

———. 1998. *Halim.* Beggars Banquet.

———. 1999. *Gedida.* Mantra/Beggars Banquet.

———. 2001. *Ayeshteni.* Mantra.

Fun-Da-Mental. 1995. *Seize the Time.* Beggars Banquet/Mammoth Records.

———. 1998. *Erotic Terrorism.* Beggars Banquet.

———. 2001. *There Shall Be Love.* Nation Records.

Hakim. 1998. *Mukhtarât shakl tânî/Remix.* Slam!

IAM. 1991. . . . *de la planète Mars.* Labelle Noire/Virgin.

———. 1993. *Ombre est lumière,* vols. 1 and 2. Delabel.

———. 1997. *L'école du micro d'argent.* Virgin.

Jah Wobble's Invaders of the Heart. 1991. *Rising above Bedlam.* Atlantic.

Nusrat Fateh Ali Khan and Michael Brooks: Remixes. 1997. *Star Rise.* Real World.

Transglobal Underground. 1994. *International Times.* Epic.

———. 1996. *Psychic Karaoke.* MCA.

———. 1998. *Rejoice Rejoice.* Nation Records.

———. 2001. *Yes Boss Food Corner.* Mondo Rhythmics/Arkzi Records/Universal.

Various artists. 1989. *Fuse: World Dance Music.* Nation Records.

———. 1991. *Fuse II: World Dance Music.* 4th and Bway.

Yazid. 1996. *Je suis l'arabe.* Play It Again Sam Records.

Chapter 3

Urban Breakbeat Culture

Repercussions of Hip-Hop in the United Kingdom

DAVID HESMONDHALGH & CASPAR MELVILLE

frican American cultural commentators have rightly taken pride in the influence hip-hop has exerted on popular culture across the globe. But the direct impact of hip-hop on non-U.S. musical cultures is often exaggerated. In this chapter, we want to argue that the most significant passages of hip-hop from the United States to the United Kingdom should not be understood as localization, whereby a U.S. musical mode is adapted, with minor modifications, to British themes and accents. The most important developments in recent British popular music indeed have many of their origins in hip-hop, but we aim to show that they represent such a transformation of these origins that the term localization, with its connotations of local adjustment to a still-intact form, hardly seems valid.

There have been, it is true, attempts to develop U.K. versions of rap and hip-hop that are strongly influenced by U.S. versions, but that make reference, verbally and musically, to distinctive situations faced by black and white Britons. We trace some of these rich creolizations in the first part of this chapter, including appropriations of hip-hop by British South Asian musicians. In cases such as these, the term "localization" seems apt. But a more significant legacy of hip-hop, in our view, is to be found in the experiments of various musicians, from the late 1980s onward, with key elements of hip-hop music, most notably breakbeats and sampling. These practices have been adapted for use in very different performative and institutional circumstances from those to be found in the USA and have led to a profusion of new genres (often uncomfortably bracketed under the category "dance music"). They mark a further stage in the creative appropriation of consumer and semiprofessional playback technology initiated by disco and hip-hop.

Analyzing the complex legacies of hip-hop in the United Kingdom raises important issues about the journeys and lineages of sounds in the global era, and about disruption and continuity in black musical traditions. At what points do sounds, technologies, and performances become detached from their origins in particular places (as "U.S." or "Jamaican" or "Indian")? How do they become reconfigured as different kinds of cultural interventions, based on, in the U.K. case, new relationships between diasporic ethnicities, city and suburbs, center and periphery?

Our investigation of these issues begins with an outline of the economic, political, and cultural conditions specific to Britain that are most relevant, in our view, for understanding the way in which hip-hop elements became adapted and, eventually, transformed in the U.K. context. We then discuss the impact of U.S. hip-hop culture in the United Kingdom in the 1980s. As it has elsewhere, U.S.-produced rap has been popular in Britain, and hip-hop culture has resonated with black and white British youth. In terms of musical production, however, the impact of U.S. hip-hop on British music making has been complex and diffuse. In spite of the undoubted talent of many British hip-hop musicians, British rap has been marginalized and to some extent impoverished by an overreverential attitude toward U.S. rap, by the attempt to reproduce styles and languages developed in very different contexts. Rather than seeing U.S. hip-hop as a point of origin — an approach likely to make British versions appear implicitly parasitical — we argue for a view that sees black cultures in Britain, the Caribbean, and the United States as linked in a complex network of cultural flows. The productive syncretism of diasporic cultures is further demonstrated by the creative use British Asian musicians have made of hip-hop as the basis of musical-cultural statements about how they are negotiating new ethnic identities. Here again, hip-hop is only one node in a complex web of postcolonial cultural elements.

Finally, we (artificially) divide our discussion of the new musical genres produced in this post-hip-hop and dance culture into two overall categories: jungle/drum 'n' bass; and trip-hop. These terms are journalistic tags that do little justice to the complexity of the cultures concerned. But the categories provide a means of organizing an account of how hip-hop became one of a number of key elements in a highly distinctive set of musical practices that we want to call, following the Metalheadz label, "urban breakbeat culture."

BLACK BRITISHNESS, SOUND SYSTEMS, AND CLUB CULTURE

Urban breakbeat culture draws inspiration from U.S. hip-hop culture but is ultimately the product of national conditions specific to the United Kingdom. This diasporic music emerges from the particular confluence of a number of diasporic cultural flows in 1980s and 1990s Britain. It is, ultimately, black music; but as black British cultural studies have shown (e.g., Gilroy 1993b; Mercer 1994), there are particular ways in which blackness is inflected in Britain, and these have a crucial bearing on understanding the new musical cultures. Black people have been present in Britain for many centuries (Fryer 1984), but most of the nonwhite population of the United Kingdom is the result of postwar migration from Britain's former colonies. One in every twenty Britons defines himself or herself as nonwhite. Nearly 1.5 million people have their family origins in India, Pakistan, and Bangladesh. Half a million are African Caribbean. There are also very large groups of migrants from Africa (including African Asian people) and China.

Postwar migration to Britain was the result of labor shortages. Black immigrants were welcomed and given full citizenship rights as subjects of the British Commonwealth. Gradually, though, immigration policies became increasingly restrictive and racist. Immigration figures declined significantly after the early 1970s. The vast majority of young black British people were born in Britain.[1] As a result, a whole generation of migrants' children are dealing with the experience of being British and black. They have roots in former colonies such as Jamaica and India, but have been exposed to a myriad of other media and cultural influences. In Britain, hip-hop provides only one set of ways in which identity is constituted and negotiated musically. Its practices, technologies, and aesthetics have been merged and recombined with those of two other crucially important musical-cultural phenomena: sound system culture and club culture.

SOUND SYSTEM CULTURE

Les Back (1996) has argued that the rejection of black migrant workers by white working-class leisure institutions during the postwar period fostered the creation of autonomous black cultural spaces. Amongst the Caribbean community, the gambling house and the sound system were particularly significant. The latter, originating in Jamaica, is a massive hi-fi, operated as a small business and taken from venue to venue by its operators to play music for dancing at youth clubs, "blues parties," and all manner of Caribbean community events from weddings and christenings to "sound clashes" (where two or more systems would compete in front of a crowd on the grounds of volume and originality of record selection). The emphasis in sound system aesthetics has been strongly on the production of booming, powerful, syncopated bass runs, which is significant in understanding later developments, in particular jungle.

CLUB CULTURE

Sound systems represent a distinctive British Caribbean black practice. The importance of club culture to British musical life cuts across classes and races, but it is still vital for understanding the urban breakbeat cultures we describe. This importance in turn derives from particular social, economic, spatial, and political conditions. In her study of British club culture, Sarah Thornton has suggested that "the widespread significance of dance clubs to growing up may be unique to Britain" (1995: 16) and that the importance of "going out dancing crosses boundaries of class, race, ethnicity, and sexuality" (1995: 15). The centrality of club culture to British life derives, as Thornton points out, from the drive to escape from the "tyranny of the home" (1995: 18, citing Mary Douglas). Many British homes are very small, and domestic culture is heavily television oriented. Pubs, clubs, and "the street" have been important alternative venues. Dance clubs are often based in town centers, which remain relatively well served by public transport. But even as young people have gained increasing access to cars, the importance of the dance club has not declined. Trips to other boroughs, towns, and cities and to out-of-town venues have become more important, which has only added to the importance of the dance club in British life.

For many years, many young British people viewed dance clubs with suspicion, as "cattle markets" (i.e., places devoted mainly to sexual pairing off), sites of an artificial glamour, or white dominated (Asian youth often attended "daytimers" rather than nighttime events). The 1980s saw the popularity and importance of clubs spread into new constituencies, including those in higher education and just out of it, and to sections of the working class previously disinclined. By the late 1980s, the club had for a number of reasons become the locus of a new popular cultural politics. This was to have complex repercussions for ethnic relations in cultural spaces, and it had the most profound effects on British music making. We explore these changes in more detail below.

The importance of sound systems and club culture does not, however, negate the great importance for British youth of U.S.-produced hip-hop. We begin, then, by tracing the particular ways in which that culture was received in Britain before going on to discuss how it was transformed.

THE EARLY IMPACT OF U.S. HIP-HOP IN THE UNITED KINGDOM

Almost as soon as it moved from the street corner to the recording studio, hip-hop, along with rap, found a sympathetic audience in the United Kingdom. And right from the start, hip-hop in Britain was a cross-racial scene. It is important to remember that the various ethnic groups in Britain tend not to live in segregated areas. Even in the areas with the highest proportions of ethnic minorities, such as the northwest London borough of Brent, white people still form a majority. There are a number of places in Britain where white, Caribbean, and Asian youth share much cultural interchange: Bristol, Birmingham, and southeast London, to name but three. These are spaces where, in spite of institutional racism and the persistence of poverty amongst ethnic minority populations, a "rigorously syncretic youth culture" (Back 1996: 123) is being created.

Hip-hop in the United Kingdom was largely pioneered by DJs on the racially mixed "rare groove" scene, a loose network of DJs and clubs with origins in the soul and R&B scenes of the mid-1970s whose musical milieu combined rare U.S. soul and jazz dance with slicker soul, disco, and funk. And hip-hop practices, such as breaking, graffiti, and the various DJing techniques, were adopted by not only Caribbean youth, but also by whites and Asians.

It is significant that hip-hop was only one of a number of styles being played in British dance clubs in the 1980s. Clubs devoted exclusively to hip-hop were rare. Black British culture already had a musical, stylistic, and social structure—the reggae sound system culture described earlier—that to a certain extent obviated the need for wholesale conversion to hip-hop. By the early 1980s, according to Back (1996: 187), sound systems operated in all the major regions of London where black young people lived, and he provides a list of twenty-two sound systems functioning in southeast London alone in 1981 (1996: 286). So the United Kingdom already had its own version of an emancipatory black practice, a Caribbean-derived cultural formation with music at its epicenter that fostered black expressivity and organized and channeled critiques of institutional racism and neocolonialism. In other words, sound system culture did for black British urban populations what hip-hop did for African Americans. Many black British clubbers and consumers picked up U.S. hip-hop but incorporated it into their preexisting diet of reggae.

This process is best understood via Paul Gilroy's now-familiar but still enormously productive concept of the black Atlantic (1993a) as the site of complex cultural flows among the African diaspora in Europe, the Caribbean, and North America. U.S. hip-hop is itself the product of the physical and cultural traffic between Jamaica and New York (Toop 1991), an influence embodied in the figure of Clive "Kool DJ Herc" Campbell from Kingston, one of hip-hop's founding fathers. The very sound system culture that was exported from the Caribbean to Britain in the 1950s was the basis of much of U.S. hip-hop. Rapping, while clearly based to some degree in African American oral tradition, borrows heavily from the development of the Caribbean's myriad creolized languages.[2]

Reggae, meanwhile, was heavily informed by U.S. R&B (Hebdige 1987). Twenty years later hip-hop had a profound effect on Jamaican music, influencing the development of a harder style of reggae rapping known as ragga (or dancehall), which became popular amongst Caribbean audiences in the United Kingdom. According to one prominent U.K.-Jamaican toaster, Leslie Lyrix, Jamaican and British dancehall tapes circulated widely amongst U.S. hip-hop producers, and the fact that many prominent U.S. rappers were explicit about their Caribbean parentage (e.g., Grand Puba) or consciously fused hip-hop with reggae and Jamaican vernacular forms (e.g., Shinehead, and Boogie Down Production's *Criminal Minded*) should serve to guard against a model that insists on the national integrity of genre or on one-way patterns of musical influence.

This does not negate the possibility that musical forms can be innovative, nor that they might be associated with particular groups. Hip-hop is clearly music of mainly black origin(ality). But the black Atlantic histories outlined above make it impossible to speak of the effect of hip-hop on U.K. music in terms of a direct, one-on-one influence. That influence is mediated, distorted, amplified, and fractured because of the complexity of the international flows of musical culture.

It is for this reason, perhaps, that British hip-hop can be considered to have failed where it has overenthusiastically imported African American attitudes to hip-hop, along with the music and style. There have been numerous attempts to forge a British version of rap drawing directly upon U.S. models. A number of acts emerged from pockets of U.K. hip-hop activity, concentrated primarily in multiracial areas of south London such as Brixton and Peckham: the London Posse, Sindecut, Dodge City, Big Ted, the She-Rockers, the Cookie Crew and Monie Love, and Ty and Shortee Blitz. In commercial terms the most significant outlet for the music was the independent label Music for Life, run by hip-hop fan Simon Harris. From the beginning there was a lively debate within U.K. hip-hop regarding the extent to which U.S. rap should serve as a model. The issue was twofold: a question of accent (style) and one of content. Should a British rapper adopt the U.S. drawl of the Brooklyn badboys (an enterprise doomed to failure) or stick to an English accent that might sound strange? Should a U.K. rapper adopt the Uzi-packing, carjacking, bitch-smacking lexicon of U.S. rap or develop a "vocab" more in step with the British context, where guns are rare, few youths can afford cars, misogyny is perhaps slightly less acceptable, and the prevailing British diffidence renders public boasting (or "bigging yourself up") relatively uncommon and frowned upon?

While many rappers could not help but begin by imitating the styles and accents of their U.S. heroes, there were many who realized that to merely transpose U.S. forms would rob U.K. hip-hop of the ability to speak for a disenfranchised British constituency in the way that U.S. hip-hop so successfully spoke to, and for, its audience. As the frankly derivative early efforts of many of these rappers failed to ignite the imaginations of the record-buying public and were met with derision by a U.K. rap market that tended to value authenticity above all else, many U.K. rappers began to subscribe to the sentiments expressed by the rapper Dizzi Heights: "I'm sick of English rap kids saying fresh and def and hard. Those words come from America. We've got— 'it's well 'ard' and 'it's cool' lots of slang words. . . . You can make much better raps using words you know and that's where we could really come in" (quoted in Back 1996: 208). Attempts were made by U.K. rappers to develop styles more obviously rooted in British linguistic practices—Rodney P of the London Posse deliberately chose a London accent—although many succeeded only in adopting a slurred hybrid that located the rap somewhere in the middle of the Atlantic Ocean.

British rap throughout the 1980s tended to eschew the cartoon braggadocio and gunplay of U.S. rap in favor of more recognizable U.K. themes. One obvious way this was achieved was to (re)import into the U.S. rap framework styles and terms from Caribbean culture. Many U.K. rappers such as Blak Twang and Rodney P drop frequent references to, and echoes of, British Caribbean style into their rapping styles and have arguably, therefore, cast a more authentic version of U.K. rap by acknowledging that allegiance to an Afro-American form need not supersede or replace black British links to the Caribbean. Classic British hip-hop tracks like the London Posse's "How's Life in London?" (London 12-inch, 1990) explicitly incorporate "cockney lyrics" and references to familiar London situations, such as riding the number 37 bus and collecting unemployment benefits. Blak Twang's "Red Letter" (Jammin' 12-inch, 1997) features a chorus sung in a reggae-toasting style, all about receiving final-demand (red) bills through the post. Both are attempts to refit hip-hop to a specific black British situation.

British hip-hop has, in our view, been less successful where it has taken a

Rodney P. Photo by Ken Passley.

purist attitude toward U.S. models. In their determination to remain "true to the game," "keep it real," and ally themselves with the kind of Afrocentric politics represented by, for example, the Native Tongues wing of U.S. hip-hop, British hip-hop has flown in the face of the complex transnational processes that birthed it, and this has disallowed its participation in the creative flux of the U.K. music scene in general. While many participants in U.K. hip-hop culture have taken their skills into other genres (examples include the scratch DJ Pogo, who DJs with the jazz saxophonist Courtney Pine's band, and the producer DJ Krust, who emerged as a significant figure on the jungle scene), purists tended to be left on the sidelines complaining about a lack of respect. By adhering too closely to a set of precepts, a sense of correctness, that emerged in very different circumstances, under different racial and social conditions, British hip-hoppers have, it seems, largely succeeded in marginalizing themselves. Hip-hop continued to thrive in Britain in the late 1980s with the emergence of the "second wave" of New York rap (Eric B and Rakim, Public Enemy, Gang Starr, etc.). But in terms of British production, rap was one of a number of styles that could be fused eclectically to make new genres, rather than constituting a goal in itself.[3]

Hip-hop, however, exerted a huge influence on U.K. music making primarily in relation to DJing (scratching and mixing) and production techniques. The sale of samplers rose exponentially during the late 1980s. In particular, that period saw the rise of the breakbeat phenomenon: the development of a subculture based around searching for rare breaks on soul and funk records and sampling and reconstructing beats using Atari computers with sequencing programs and Roland 808 drum machines. This began to lay roots that would come to fruition in the early 1990s.

BRITISH ASIAN HIP-HOP

The major exception to the developments noted above, whereby the attempt to develop distinctive U.K. versions of hip-hop had largely been abandoned by the early 1990s (and British artists proved unable to adapt rapping as a form), was the continued adoption by British Asian musicians of hip-hop forms. Again, this has important implications for the issues of ethnicity and cultural legitimation we raised at the beginning of this chapter. British African Caribbean musicians struggled to gain the respect accorded to their African American counterparts. This applied to British Asian musicians working in the field of hip-hop too. But the very novelty of young Asians, traditionally portrayed in racist lore as relatively passive and subservient, adapting the urban musical languages of hip-hop served to provide a (limited) space in which such musicians could gain a certain (limited) access to the musical public sphere.

Many young British Asians were involved in breakdancing and graffiti from the early 1980s on, but very few were rapping and scratching. It was only in the early 1990s that a number of hip-hop-influenced acts emerged from within the various constituencies of the Asian diaspora in Britain to a greater national prominence, in the form of television coverage and deals with major and large independent record companies. Kaliphz, for example, formed in the early 1980s in Rochdale, were signed to London Records in 1992 and achieved some success (including an appearance on the BBC show *Top of the Pops* with the boxer Prince Naseem Hamed). The label Nation Records, based in West London, has served as a hub for a number of British Asian acts, influenced by hip-hop in a variety of ways. Perhaps the best known of these is Fun-Da-Mental, consisting of Nation's co-owner and manager, Aki Nawaz, and his partner, Dave Watts (who is Caribbean in origin). Fun-Da-Mental demonstrated an explicit allegiance to African American Islamic radicalism and to the black separatist politics of groups such as the Black Panthers, which led to their being labeled "the Asian Public Enemy"— a label Nation adopted for its own publicity. Their third single, "Wrath of the Black Man" (Nation 1993), for example, is built around a sample of a speech by Malcolm X. While African American radicalism provided political inspiration, the themes of the raps and spoken samples were concerned with Asian and British Asian issues. The band's name reflects this—a controversial invocation of Islamic fundamentalism, even while the hyphens in the name indicate another purpose, that of combining pleasure ("fun") with thought ("mental"). The band's symbol is a crescent, to evoke not only Islam, but also the Pakistani flag (Aki Nawaz's mother was a leading British activist for Benazir Bhutto's Pakistan People's Party).

Hustlers HC and Asian Dub Foundation, both of whom released records on Nation, demonstrate other affiliations. Whereas Fun-Da-Mental's Aki Nawaz discovered rap late and found "its politics more sorted than its music,"[4] Hustlers HC had a long-standing allegiance to hip-hop culture that preceded its pedagogical turn in the mid- to late 1980s. Like many other hip-hop fans, they were drawn to aesthetic and cultural features of the form as much as to the direct expressions of political anger contained within certain versions of it. Given the greater allegiance of Fun-Da-Mental to black nationalism, it is ironic that while Fun-Da-Mental found greater recognition amongst white audiences and institutions, Hustlers HC have gained much more positive reactions from British Caribbean hip-hop crowds. Such crowds

Hustlers HC. Courtesy of Nation Records.

tend to have a strong sense of hierarchy about who can best perform and play rap: African Americans tend to be most favored, followed by British African Caribbeans. So for a Sikh band to gain the respect of an African Caribbean hip-hop crowd is no mean feat.

Just like U.S. rap acts that were more obviously engaged politically, such as the Disposable Heroes of Hiphoprisy or Consolidated, Fun-Da-Mental's appeal was more to white student populations than to the less-educated urban poor addressed by hardcore rap. Perhaps for this reason the political messages of Fun-Da-Mental have been granted considerably more coverage in the student-oriented British music press (such as *New Musical Express*) than any other British rap act. Other South Asian acts influenced by hip-hop have struggled to receive airplay and media attention. Hustlers HC adopted a different approach to music and black identity from Fun-Da-Mental. Their raps were rarely political, in the direct sense. Their aim was to show that Sikhs are as influenced by hip-hop culture as by the temple, and that they are as capable of producing high-quality rap as are British Caribbean bands. For many, this is a sufficiently strong political aim in itself, because it resists stereotypes of Asian life as composed only of traditional elements.

Indeed, it could be said that what unites British Asian acts influenced by rap is precisely such a desire to assert a more complex sense of identity than that assumed by many media representations of the South Asian diaspora in Britain. (See Sharma et al. 1996) But there are important differences in how various acts go about asserting this complexity. Fun-Da-Mental borrowed extensive samples from Indian film music, particularly from the string sections. Through their juxtaposition with hip-hop rhythm tracks and angry raps, such samples are reconfigured, and a new hybrid Asian identity is emphasized. Hustlers HC, however, made extensive use of Indian instrumentation on only one track: "Let the Hustlers Play," which was the B side of their "Big Trouble in Little Asia" single. Hustlers HC (Nation 12-inch, 1993) did use samples from Asian records, but they tended to listen mainly for sounds that can be perceived as distinctly un-Asian. As one of their associates at Nation, Simon Underwood, put it, Hustlers HC were "not a fusion band."

Like Fun-Da-Mental, Anirhudda Das, of the former Nation act Asian Dub Foundation, similarly sees his band's use of "Indian sounds" as symbolic of certain experiences for second-generation British Asians: "When we use Indian sounds or stuff out of Hindi films, it's reflecting our upbringing, that we heard these sounds, always, in the background, on the telly, on the video." But the band merges such sounds with appropriations of the electronic dance music that exploded in the United Kingdom from the late 1980s onward, partly under the influence of hip-hop, but also because of separate developments (which we treat in the next section). There is a further level of defiance too: they incorporate the kind of rock instrumentation that, at least until the "big beat" phenomenon in dance music in the mid-1990s, was shunned by many dance musicians: "We're expected to be sitting there playing tablas or sitting there playing sitar and all of that, and we're saying, 'nah, nah, that's for hippies.' I'm playing bass guitar, Steve's playing distortion guitar, and we're more Asian than you are in what we're playing."

The range of uses of hip-hop by British Asian musicians, then, suggests once again that the most fruitful way of telling the story of hip-hop is not as a musical form that has spread across the world from U.S. origins, but rather as one of a number of elements that can be recombined to make important statements about cultural identity. This is not to disrespect the astonishing creativity of U.S. rap musicians and those who have attempted to stay close to their example. Rather, it is to pay proper attention to the creativity of those who have transformed that resource in new and adventurous ways.

ACID HOUSE AND AFTER: THE BREAKBEAT ERA

We now turn to what we consider to be the most fruitful and exciting adaptations by British musicians of hip-hop musical components. These new genres, we believe, can be understood only by reference to changes in British club culture in the 1980s and early 1990s.

It is difficult to convey to outsiders the profound effects on British popular music of the rise of dance music culture in the late 1980s and early 1990s. As we have seen, the dance club already had an unusual importance in British youth culture. For many people increasingly drawn to electronic dance music in the wake of hip-hop, rave culture confirmed the subversive populism of dance.[5] Its dangerous reputation was sealed by a kind of moral panic in the national press about the drugs associated with the scene, especially ecstasy. Accompanying this panic, though, was an especially strong utopian discourse of collectivism and equality within club culture, that stressed the breaking down of ethnic, class, and gender differences. Dance events had long been viewed as rituals of togetherness and inclusion, but the new dance culture went further, and the rhetoric, at least, was genuinely democratizing: "No performers, no VIPs, we are all special" was one typical slogan from a club flyer.

The music comprised, at first, rhythmic offshoots of disco, imported mainly from Chicago, Detroit, and New York City. House, techno, and garage were the principal forms. Pop producers, increasingly dance oriented since the early 1980s, picked up on these black U.S. subcultural styles, and dance music's centrality to the most popular songs intensified. Ironically, the "acid house" moment meant that hip-hop production techniques hit the pop charts in the form of a postmodern, cut-and-paste technique of sampling and mixing — for example, in the huge 1987 hit by MARRS, "Pump Up the Volume" (4AD 12-inch, 1987; see Manuel 1995 for an analysis). The emphasis was much less on the sampling of breaks than on melodic samples, but the hip-hop influence was reinforced by the fact that many key phrases were being sampled from U.S. hip-hop tracks. (MARRS's "Pump Up the Volume," for example, drew on Eric B and Rakim's "I Know You Got Soul.")

But in spite of the basis of the music in hip-hop and in black U.S. offshoots of disco, and even though there was a widespread rhetoric of racial unity on the scene as a whole, many black Britons perceived rave as a white thing, especially as the music of black Chicago and Detroit became supplanted or supplemented by Euro-house from Italy and the "colder" strains of German and Belgian techno. While a few club nights retained their traditional soul and R&B formats, some "blacker" house and rave clubs (such as Confusion in central London) retained an emphasis on traditional "black" practices by injecting breakbeats into the mix and featuring toasting (the practice, originating in Jamaica, of rapping, often at remarkable speed, over a track played on a sound system). A post-rave subgenre of techno called hardcore (or 'ardkore) simmered underground. This musical synthesis of techno and hip-hop, with the addition of reggae and ragga influences, transmuted into jungle.[6] It is here that breakbeat experiments continued in musical production.

JUNGLE AND DRUM 'N' BASS

There are important influences, connections and continuities between U.S. hip-hop and jungle. Jungle is a musical genre dominated by DJs and producers (rather than live performers), whose formal techniques—the use of samplers and sequencers and the high value placed on drum patterns and volume—borrow heavily from models established by U.S. hip-hop practitioners. Also, jungle, rather than using the repetitive kick drum that characterizes house music, borrows hip-hop's reliance on *breakbeats*, the jerky, interrupted rhythmic pattern that underpins hip-hop. Jungle also shares a number of themes and attitudes with hip-hop, particularly with gangsta rap and the crazed and blunted productions of Cypress Hill and the Gravediggaz. Jungle introduced dark, scary chords frequently derived from horror movie soundtracks, gangsta references (gunshots, police sirens, and vocal samples like "who's the badbwoy"), and the kind of nihilistic attitudes to violence that are associated with U.S. gangsta rap acts such as N.W.A.

The explosion in popularity for this new musical form (around 1993–94), particularly among British Caribbean youth in London, was also the occasion for the emergence in the press of the kind of moral panics and racialized narratives that gangsta rap provoked in the United States. Familiar positions were that jungle glorified violence and drugs, that it was too "dark" and downbeat, that it was not musical, and that it had spoiled the utopian possibilities of rave. Clearly, these anxieties about the "darkness" of jungle were racist responses to a music that was defiantly "black," whose core market was very obviously black, and whose structure reintroduced elements of black musical forms and practice—the figure of the MC-rapper is a ubiquitous presence at jungle clubs—that had been noticeable by their absence from the previous five years of rave music.[7]

The influence of hip-hop is discernible at every level of jungle: lexicological, technological, and textual. In addition to jungle's elevation of the producer-DJ and MC-rapper, junglists (as they became known) clearly drew on U.S. models for their nomenclature—for instance, DJ Hype, DJ Die, Spinback, Shy FX, and Reprazent. This was often inflected with British and West Indian slang (reflected in names such as Ed Rush, A Guy Called Gerald, and Ganga Kru). Jungle also shared with hip-hop a thematic emphasis on "inner-city pressure" (the title of a Goldie track from 1995) and a fascination with technology, weaponry, and science fiction and horror movies.

On the textual level, in terms of the music itself, the links are even more obvious. Take, for example, the track "Danger" by Special K, released as a 12-inch single in 1996 on the small south London independent Trouble on Vinyl. The cut begins as out-and-out hip-hop, with a thick ("phat") slow breakbeat and chugging bass line and with subtle echoes of reggae in the sung chorus and a stabbing keyboard riff. There is no lead rap, just some repeated vocal hooks. This basic form loops for over two minutes until, suddenly, the tune stops and a vocal warns, "You've heard the tune now hear the remix." The track suddenly shifts up in speed: a huge subbass line wobbles on to the soundscape riding an uptempo reggae-inspired repeated figure, and the breakbeat quickens to almost double the original speed. The texture of the bass line particularly is rough and distorted, pushing the reproduction technology (and your speakers) to the limit, a practice Tricia Rose (1994: 74) has defined within hip-hop as "working within the red." Hip-hop thus is transformed, by a change of tempo and the (re)introduction of reggae, into jungle.

Trouble on Vinyl tend to specialize in jungle and drum 'n' bass in the "jump up" and "tech step" subgenres (drawing heavily on reggae in the first instance and techno and hardcore in the second). This is quite different from the more jazz- and funk-tinged jungle and drum 'n' bass of acts such as Roni Size and 4 Hero. Yet here too hip-hop provides an important reference point. Roni Size's "Brown Paper Bag" (Talking Loud 12-inch, 1997), for example, employs a live double bass in place of the electronic "Hoover" subbass of Special K's "Danger." This is an explicit reference to jazz as well as to the jazzy hip-hop of A Tribe Called Quest and the Roots. But both tunes employ meticulously crafted breakbeats that, when slowed down, reveal themselves as hip-hop beats.[8]

One of the biggest jungle club tunes at the time of writing is Shy FX's "Bambaata" (Ebony 12-inch, 1998), a tribute to the hip-hop DJ Afrika Bambaata employing a pitched-up Latin percussion–influenced beat that once again ups the ante amongst jungle producers and introduces another source from which to draw rhythmic inspiration. Changes of tempo, pitch, and style, as well as importations from hip-hop and reggae and house, coexist in jungle in an unstable and continually evolving mix. So, although jungle has an enormous range of subgenres, from those drawing on reggae and ragga (General Levy and DJ Red) to more techno- and rave-inspired hardcore (Grooverider and Ed Rush) to styles influenced by jazz and funk (Roni Size and Squarepusher), all jungle shares common ground with hip-hop. Even where the overt influence is minimal, the basic materials and production practices (breakbeats and bass lines, samplers, drum machines, microphones, and sequencing program) are the same. Tricia Rose's detailing of the fundamental elements of hip-hop production applies equally well to jungle: "Rhythmic complexity, repetition with subtle variations, the significance of the drum, melodic interest in bass frequencies and breaks in pitch and time"

(1994: 67). But if jungle is the "first truly *British* black music" (Collin 1997: 260; original emphasis), and if it shares so much with U.S. hip-hop, then is it not useful to label it, as Benjamin Noys (1995) and others have done, British hip-hop? The problem is that this move reproduces the parochial categories of U.S. histories and ultimately undermines the view that jungle is truly both an integration and something new. To be fair to Noys, his characterization of jungle as British hip-hop can be read as a strategic rhetorical move: in aligning jungle with hip-hop, Noys is implicitly making the case that what might be considered peripheral or ephemeral should instead be treated as an important object of study. Certainly his conclusions—that jungle has "drawn together the subcultures of hip hop, techno and rave," which leaves the future open and "complicates questions of racism and sexism in its integration of a series of unstable cultural and musical hybrids" (Noys 1995: 331)— mitigate against any easy incorporation of jungle into a simplistic model of hip-hop.

In crucial ways, jungle is not hip-hop at all. Musically, it would be wrong to think of breakbeats as a unique product of hip-hop. While hip-hop places much emphasis on breaks and achieves levels of volume, distortion, and juxtaposition that were not available before some of the recent innovations in studio technology, the actual form of breakbeats has been around in black Atlantic music for a very long time. Hip-hop breakbeats are sampled reconstructions of the same kind of interrupted rhythms found most obviously in James Brown's music, in jazz recordings from previous generations, and in Brazilian and Afro-Caribbean rhythms. Breakbeats, then, cannot be taken as the defining characteristic of hip-hop, as *belonging* to hip-hop in some way, nor as evidence that jungle is U.K. hip-hop.

Most significantly of all, perhaps, jungle has purposefully avoided an ethnocentric account of its own origins. In place of declarations of black particularity (be it "The Blues Matrix" [Houston Baker] or "The Signifyin' Monkey" [Henry Louis Gates]) or the kind of black nationalism espoused by Ice Cube or Poor Righteous Teachers, junglists have tended to emphasize the racial openness of their scene. Again, the distinctive social conditions of the United Kingdom need to be forefronted here. In Britain, interracial alliances within musical subcultures, such as those that prevailed on the "rare groove" scene, offer perhaps more hope for cross-racial collaboration than the fiercely polarized racial dynamics and segregated patterns of leisure of the United States. Black junglists including Goldie, Roni Size, and Jumping Jack Frost have claimed that jungle transcends race. As MC Conrad says frequently while MCing, "It's not a black thing, it's not a white thing, it's a multi-culture, interracial dance thing" (Wiser 1993). So, both in terms of its musical raw materials (hip-hop, techno, and ragga) and its political narratives, jungle must be read not as U.S. hip-hop adapted, but as hip-hop transformed, a musical expression of new black (and other) British identities, or perhaps a frame within which these identities are produced.

Recently there has been much cross-pollination between hip-hop and jungle. The U.S. producer and remixer Timbaland, for example, one of the hottest properties in hip-hop at the time of this writing (1998), has developed a style that, although with a slower character of its own, draws heavily on jungle's redistribution of labor between the drum and the bass. This kind of cross-pollination and syncretism should alert us to the material reality of Paul Gilroy's model of the black Atlantic. Jungle is an Afro-diasporic soundtrack that narrates the continual flow among the United States, the Caribbean, and the United Kingdom. Syncretism, rather than the expression of some form of racial essence, is at the center of black musical practice. The restless musical development that is one signal feature of British club culture and musical production, which folds black musical genres, wherever they are from, into new and imaginative fusions, shows no signs of abating. New genres have sprung up incorporating elements of hip-hop aesthetics and culture, but fused with musics that are not defined by "blackness," in particular with indie and alternative rock and pop. One such genre is ambient jungle, or its near kin, intelligent drum 'n' bass, which represents a fusion of jungle breakbeats with the mood and tenor of ambient music. For many this is an adventurous step forward; for others it constitutes a gentrification of an earthy street sound.[9]

The form that has made the most impact in the British musical public sphere, though, is a style that has been labeled "trip-hop." There is space only for a brief survey here, but trip-hop helps to demonstrate further the distinctive ways in which hip-hop was adapted in the United Kingdom. If jungle shows the results of the unexpected collision of post–house club culture with hip-hop, trip-hop demonstrates other odd fusions. Here, the key influence is sound system culture.

TRIP-HOP

Trip-hop is a flimsy journalistic tag punning, badly, on the fusion of hip-hop with "trippy" psychedelic styles. As with most journalistic tags, "trip-hop" was strenuously resisted as a descriptive term by those engaged in producing the music itself. However, the term does serve to illustrate the fact that this subgenre modeled itself as a version of hip-hop. Conventional journalistic surveys of trip-hop center on the music, which emerged from Bristol, a port city in the southwest of England.[10] While any implication that Bristol was the only place where such innovation was occurring would be false, and with due wariness of the projection of location as an apparently stable and unified guarantor of authenticity that Will Straw (1991) has warned persuasively against, it is useful to revisit the Bristol music scene in the early 1990s to draw out some of the key themes of trip-hop. This will also serve to illustrate how studies of popular music must remain aware of the processes — aesthetic and social — that bring particular musical forms and techniques together in surprising ways and unlikely places.

In common with cities such as Liverpool with long-standing black communities such as London and Birmingham, where waves of migration created new British Caribbean communities, Bristol has a deeply rooted sound system culture. An important center of the eighteenth-century slave trade, Bristol has a black population that has been defining what it means to be black British for several centuries, as well as a large mixed-race population, and, alongside greater racial tensions, a well-integrated youth culture based around St. Paul's and schools where black and white children shared classes and befriended each other. Reggae culture and rastafarianism provided anti-imperialist narratives and a vocabulary with which to resist institutional racism. The cafés and youth clubs of St. Paul's and West Knowle were a gathering point for Bristol's black and progressive communities, and they provided cheap entertainment for unemployed youth. Bristol never had a highly developed club scene comparable to London's, so the musical culture was dominated by the sound systems and the blues parties, where reggae and soul provided the soundtrack throughout the 1980s.

Under the influence of the first wave of U.S. hip-hop in the early 1980s, many of Bristol's youth, black and white alike, became converts to hip-hop culture, adopting its style and outlook as well as names such as the Fresh Four and the Wild Bunch. Hip-hop was immediately fused with elements of black music that already had roots in the United Kingdom: dub, dancehall, and soul. The peculiar socioracial characteristics of Bristol, however, also meant that "white" forms, particularly punk, had a strong influence too (early 1980s Bristol bands such as Pop Group and Rip Rig and Panic found fruitful correspondences between punk, funk, and jazz). In the early 1990s, a succession of Bristol bands — some brand new, others merely reconfigurations of crews who had been around for years — began to release material that clearly relied heavily on the influence of hip-hop production techniques, while seemingly uninhibited by the potential for comparison with U.S. acts.

Among the bands to emerge from the Bristol scene — and virtually all interviews with supposed representatives of this scene have denied its existence — are Massive Attack, Tricky, Portishead, Smith and Mighty, Cool

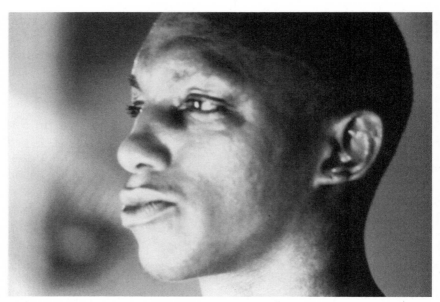

Tricky

Breeze, Earthling, and Roni Size/Reprazent. The music, though disparate, in general is laid back, downbeat, even "miserabilist." In the mid-1990s it provided a very different soundtrack to the brash optimism of Britpop guitar bands. But even as its sounds encoded a cool detachment, trip-hop unmistakably displayed a new confidence in its black Britishness. Tricky's debut album *Maxinquaye* (Island, 1994) is perhaps the most remarkable (and therefore, admittedly, atypical) example of this. Tricky was inspired by hip-hop, but he whispers and squeaks where U.S. rappers aim at a loud-and-clear, articulate flow. Against the assertion of an overcoherent biopolitics of individualized sexuality (analyzed so powerfully in Gilroy 1994) in recent U.S. R&B, Tricky offers a polysexual angst, dressing as a woman on the sleeve of his record, confessing that he comes too quickly. It is his female singing partner, Martina Topley Bird, who sings a version of Public Enemy's "Black Steel in the Hour of Chaos," rather than Tricky. Male rebellion is deflected, made uncertain, and yet is more defiant through this very deflection. The beats are equally confident in their portrayal of confusion and fucked-upness: they slide in tantalizingly, disappear unexpectedly. Grooves are found, only to be abandoned.

But the sexual dimensions of the album should not distract the listener from the racial dynamics of the music. There is an interest in memory and continuity (for example, in the track "Aftermath") that many commentators have noted in Afrodiasporic music. Tricky shows his debt to hip-hop aesthetics by recontextualizing samples and slices of both the most respected black music (Public Enemy) and the tackiest pop (quoting David Cassidy's "How Can I Be Sure?"). Tricky is exceptional in that he has become a recognized "artist" whose albums are now awaited as statements of a continuing music development (and whether this ultimately detracts from the power of his music is a moot point).

Trip-hop as a whole, however, can be divided into two basic types. The first might just as well be called instrumental hip-hop: dense constructions of breakbeats, samples, drum patterns, and incidental squiggling that draw heavily on the production styles of Premier, Muggs, and Pete Rock. In its earliest "dark" manifestation, this first type favored a cinematic mode that imported the sweeping strings and horror chords of movie soundtracks along with snatches of dialogue from "gangsta" movies such as *Scarface*, *Goodfellas*, and *The Warriors*. The mood was "blunted," heavy with the smoky ambience of dub as well as the more horrific hip-hop of Cypress Hill, Onyx, Geto Boys, and Lords of the Underground. Much attention was given by the producers to the cutting and splicing of found sounds, the phatness of the beats (which usually quavered at fewer than 100 beats per minute, much slower than most hip-hop). It is this form of instrumental hip-hop that inspired a whole generation of U.K. producers and labels, such as Mo' Wax, Wall of Sound, Hard Hands, Sabres of Paradise, and Pressure Drop.

The second strain of trip-hop can be understood as a synthesis of hip-hop sensibilities with the format of conventional (including "alternative") rock. *Dummy*, Portishead's debut album (Go! Beat, 1994), is perhaps still the prime exemplar of this form. Over the heavy drumbeats meticulously assembled by the producer, Geoff Barrow, and the subtle scratching of the DJ, Andy Smith—both hip-hop fanatics and archivists—is laid the querulous, chain-smoking, exquisitely fragile vocals of Beth Gibbons. Portishead thus bridges the gulf between the cultural milieus of (implicitly black, U.S.) hip-hop and (implicitly white, English) "student" rock. In the wake of the huge commercial and critical success of *Dummy*, a rash of trip-hop "bands" were signed, each to some degree indebted to the Portishead format: Moloko, Lamb, Sneaker Pimps, Morcheeba, and Olive. As with other white appropriations of musics of black origin, this can be seen as exploitation rather than tribute. It is important to remember that Barrow worked as an engineer with the multiracial Massive Attack and that the music emerges from a scene where white and black musics and musicians were in a constant process of exchange and cross-fertilization. This is not to deny the continued existence of power dynamics in the British music industry. But trip-hop represents something a little more complicated than the mere transposition of hip-hop techniques to student and young middle-class audiences. And, like jungle, it represents an important and distinctive strand of British music making that cannot be understood simply as the descendant of hip-hop.

REPERCUSSIONS

However much it has been taken up by whites, hip-hop can be seen as primarily a form of black cultural expression. But as the work of Paul Gilroy and others has shown, to be black and British is very different from the model of black experience often assumed by African American commentators. Nearly all discussions of U.S. hip-hop begin by locating its origins in the South Bronx. An overemphasis on such origins can lead to difficulties in accounting for other variants of hip-hop culture, not only on the U.S. West Coast, but in Houston, in Jamaica, in Britain, and elsewhere. The very different economic, political, and cultural dynamics that obtain in Britain produce different sounds, encoding different worldviews. Urban breakbeat culture does not constitute the adoption of an imported language. It builds on the technologies and attitudes of hip-hop but transforms them according to particular national diasporic conditions. As should be obvious now, discussing the racial dynamics of these diasporic conditions of British musical production is fraught with difficulty. Jungle and drum 'n' bass are both multicultural, in terms of the ethnicity of producers and consumers, and black, in the sense that black styles and traditions clearly play a more important role within jungle than they did in rave.

Trip-hop, too, represents the outcome of interactions between the syncretic youth cultures that Back (1996) so effectively draws attention to. One of the most interesting aspects of urban breakbeat culture is the way that it challenges assumptions about origins and confuses notions of cultural boundaries between one style and another, between one group of people and the next. Ironically, while some U.S. commentators, unaware of or uninterested in these developments, have overplayed the direct influence of rap music in Britain, British commentators have downplayed the importance of hip-hop and other distinctive forms of Afrodiasporic musical expression in the development of the new genres discussed here. The U.K. music press tends instead to overemphasize the influence of rave culture on genres such as jungle (and on more recent emergent genres such as speed garage) to the point where the influence of black cultural practices on dance-music culture is hardly considered at all (except as a mere precursor, in the form of black gay clubs in U.S. cities). To celebrate the global spread of hip-hop is an understandable assertion of pride in the continued vitality of African American cultural expression. And to point out the vitality of post-1980s dance-music culture is to resist a mainstream conception of youth culture as trivial, insignificant, and uncreative. Both of these positions represent partial viewpoints and particular interests and are inadequate to understanding the complex weave of influences and origins that make up these new cultural forms.

None of the above should be read as a claim that the transformations and recombinations we have been examining are superior to those of U.S. hip-hop itself, or that Britain has a monopoly on distinctive forms of intertextuality. Our aim has been to provide a case study of the particular way in which flows of culture have merged in new, unexpected, and often exciting ways in the 1990s. Within cultural studies, this kind of approach is hardly innovative: an emphasis on the complexity of flows as a resistance to ethnic and national particularism has become something of an orthodoxy. However, studies of such flows are often asociological and ahistorical, finding evidence of them in analysis of the ambivalence of cultural texts. We have tried instead to show how a particular nexus of cultural institutions—club culture and sound-system culture—serve to create situations where new ways of making meaning through music and dance are tried out and experimented with, and from which new sounds are eventually produced. We would want to distance ourselves too from a position lurking beneath some recent cultural studies that might implicitly see cultural hybridity as an easy answer to or adequate compensation for long histories of racial and class division.[11] It is these conflicts that ultimately lie behind the particular ways in which a new generation of musicians have sought to create pleasure and meaning. This does not mean celebrating all forms of music equally. But we have tried to suggest that the creativity of black British musicians, comparatively marginalized in the global public sphere (see Gilroy 1993b: 61), merits the kind of respect and consideration previously granted only to black U.S. music.

NOTES

1. The 1991 census reported that 75 percent of the working-age ethnic-minority population in the United Kingdom was born abroad, but that the figure for the under-sixteen group was only 14 percent (Central Office of Information 1997).

2. This is not even to mention the unique contributions made by Hispanic Caribbeans to hip-hop culture, especially in breakdancing and graffiti.

3. An important attempt to craft a version of U.K. rap emerged from the "acid jazz" scene when some of the more self-consciously radical, intellectual British rappers hooked up with jazz musicians to create a jazz-rap fusion. Of this wave, which included MC Mello and Urban Species, U.S.3 was the most successful, hitting the charts in both the United Kingdom and the USA with "Cantaloop" (Blue

Note 12-inch, 1993). With the demise of jazz-rap, the hopes of developing a truly British hip-hop virtually withered away.

4. All quotations in this section, where not attributed in the main text, are taken from interviews conducted by David Hesmondhalgh as part of his fieldwork at Nation Records in 1994 and 1995. See also Hesmondhalgh (2000).

5. "Rave" was a term used for big, often unlicensed dance events, usually held out of town. In the early 1980s, parties in abandoned warehouses had been the subject of extensive and glamorous coverage in the U.K. "style press" (i.e., magazines such as *Face* and *i-D*). Raves extended this movement away from the restrictions of licensed city-center premises, out into the unregulated outer-city and rural areas of Britain.

6. There was a brief controversy over the notion that "jungle" — also thought to originate from "junglist," a reference to the inhabitants of Kingston, Jamaica — was thought to have primitivist racial connotations (cf. Thompson 1998: 99), and for a while the term "drum 'n' bass" was used as an alternative by some. In general, though, the two terms tend to be used interchangeably.

7. Many of the major figures within jungle are black British: the MCs Det, Navigator, GQ, and 5-o; and the DJs LTJ Bukem, Brockie, Fabio, Roni Size, Goldie, Grooverider, Bryan Gee, and Krust; as well as many of the label owners and staff at prominent labels such as Reinforced, V Recordings, Trouble on Vinyl and Good Looking/Looking Good.

8. It is common practice for U.K. hip-hop and breakbeat DJs to play jungle 12-inch singles at 33 rpm, (re)presenting them as instrumental hip-hop.

9. See, e.g., the debates in the pages of the avant-garde music magazine *The Wire*, following Simon Reynolds's critique in the June 1995 issue of the search for "depth" and "maturity" amongst some drum 'n' bass musicians.

10. The best journalistic survey is a book-length treatment by Johnston (1997); it provides good background on Bristol and intelligent analysis of key figures. See also Reynolds 1998: 313–34.

11. Hybridity has been a key concept in recent cultural theory, and no doubt many readers will be tempted to label the cultural formations we have described as hybrids. We want to resist using the term here, because its overuse has come to flatten out the differences between very diverse forms of recombination and intertextuality.

BIBLIOGRAPHY

Back, Les. 1996. *New Ethnicities and Urban Cultures:*
    Racism and Multicultures in Young Lives. London: UCL Press.
Central Office of Information. 1997. *Ethnic Minorities.*
    2d ed. London: Stationery Office.

Collin, Matthew. 1997. *Altered State: The Story of Ecstasy Culture and Acid House*. London: Serpent's Tail.

Fryer, Peter. 1984. *Staying Power: A History of Black People in Britain*. London: Pluto.

Gilroy, Paul. 1993a. *The Black Atlantic: Modernity and Double Consciousness*. London: Verso.

———. 1993b. *Small Acts: Thoughts on the Politics of Black Cultures*. London: Serpent's Tail.

———. 1994. "'After the Love Has Gone': Bio-Politics and Etho-Poetics in the Black Public Sphere." *Public Culture* 7, no. 1: 49–76.

Hebdige, Dick. 1987. *Cut 'n Mix: Culture, Identity, and Caribbean Music*. London: Routledge.

Hesmondhalgh, David. 2000. "International Times: Fusions, Exoticism, and Antiracism in Electronic Dance Music." In *Western Music and Its Others: Difference, Representation, and Appropriation in Music,* edited by Georgina Born and David Hesmondhalgh. Berkeley: University of California Press.

James, Martin. 1997. *State of Bass: Jungle, the Story So Far*. London: Boxtree.

Johnston, Phil. 1997. *Straight out of Bristol*. London: Hodder and Stoughton.

Manuel, Peter. 1995. "Music as Symbol, Music as Simulacrum: Postmodern, Pre-modern, and Modern Aesthetics in Subcultural Popular Musics." *Popular Music* 14, no. 2: 227–39.

Mercer, Kobena. 1994. *Welcome to the Jungle: New Positions in Black Cultural Studies*. London: Routledge.

Noys, Benjamin. 1995. "Into the 'Jungle.'" *Popular Music* 14, no. 3: 321–32.

Reynolds, Simon. 1998. *Energy Flash: A Journey through Rave Music and Dance Culture*. London: Picador.

Rose, Tricia. 1994. *Black Noise: Rap Music and Black Culture in Contemporary America*. Hanover, N.H.: Wesleyan University Press and University Press of New England.

Sharma, Sanjay, John Hutnyk, and Ashwani Sharma, eds. 1996. *Dis-Orienting Rhythms: The Politics of the New Asian Dance Music*. London: Zed Books.

Straw, Will. 1991. "Systems of Articulation, Logics of Change: Communities and Scenes in Popular Music." *Cultural Studies* 5, no. 3: 368–88.

Thompson, Ben. 1998. *Seven Years of Plenty*. London: Victor Gollancz.

Thornton, Sarah. 1995. *Club Cultures: Music, Media, and Subcultural Capital*. Cambridge: Polity.

Toop, David. 1991. *The Rap Attack 2*. London: Serpent's Tail.

Wiser, Jo, producer. 1993. *A London Somet'ing Dis*. Transmitted by Channel 4 (U.K.).

DISCOGRAPHY

Records and tracks are cited by label and year in the main text. What follows is a very brief supplementary discography for those who wish to listen more widely. For a much fuller discography of jungle, see the recommended listening in James 1997, and in Reynolds 1998, a much fuller analysis and history of post-rave dance music and culture.

U.K. Hip-Hop

Blak Twang. 1998. *19 Longtime* [LP]. Jammin'.
Courtney Pine, featuring DJ Pogo. 1996. *Modern Day Jazz Stories* [LP]. Talking Loud.
History and Science, vol 1 [compilation EP]. 1998. Response Records.
London Posse. 1990. *Gangster Chronicles* [LP]. Island.
————. 1990. *How's Life in London?* [12-inch]. London.
U.S.3. 1993. *Hand on the Torch* [LP]. Blue Note.

British Asian Hip-Hop

Fun-Da-Mental. 1994. *Seize the Time* [LP]. Nation.
Hustlers HC. 1993. "On a Ride/Vigilante" [12-inch]. Nation.
Kaliphz. 1993. "Vibe da Joint" [EP]. London.

Jungle or Drum 'n' Bass

4 Hero. 1994. *Parallel Universe* [LP]. Reinforced.
Goldie. 1992. "Terminator" [12-inch]. Metalheadz.
————. 1995. *Timeless* [LP]. ffrr.
M-Beat featuring General Levy. 1994. "Incredible" [12-inch]. Renk.
Photek. 1996. *Natural Born Killa* [EP]. Metalheadz.
Roni Size. 1997. *New Forms* [LP]. Talking Loud.
Routes from the Jungle [compilation LP]. 1995. Circa.

Instrumental Trip-Hop

Cuts: Flexistentialism [compilation LP]. 1996. Ninja Tunes.
Headz [compilation LP]. 1995. Mo' Wax.
Hustlers of Culture. 1996. *Many Styles* [LP]. Wall of Sound.
Lesson One [compilation LP]. 1997. Scenario Records.

Vocal Trip-Hop

Earthling. 1995. *Radar* [LP]. Cooltempo.
Lamb. 1997. "Gorecki" [12-inch]. Fontana.
Massive Attack. 1994. *Protection* [LP]. Circa.
————. 1998. *Mezzanine* [LP]. Circa.
Moloko. 1996. *Do You Like My Tight Sweater?* [LP]. Epic.
Portishead. 1997. *Portishead* [LP]. Go! Beat.

Chapter 4
Rap in Germany
The Birth of a Genre

MARK PENNAY

ne point that should be made abundantly clear by this collection of essays is that genres of popular music can transcend linguistic and cultural barriers. This is not to say, however, that such barriers are fully transparent; indeed, it is contended here that musical transmission is better modeled as a selective osmosis. Through a consideration of the emergence and development of German-language rap, I attempt in this essay to illustrate the importance of both language and cultural differences for the fortunes of a musical genre outside of the monolithic English-speaking market for recorded music.

Beginning with a brief résumé of the significance of heterogeneity within a musical style, I sketch the history of rap and hip-hop culture in Germany since 1983, seeking an explanation for the watershed in the popularity of the former that occurred a full decade later in the specific cultural context of post-reunification Germany. Subsequent developments are then considered in the light of the proposed explanatory factors.

Although there is now a healthy mainstream strand to German-language rap, with most major labels having two or three German rap groups under contract by the late 1990s (K.M.S. 1997), a significant proportion of the music remains closely tied to a hip-hop subculture that is less accessible to an outsider. In this study I have attempted to compensate for a necessary bias toward the readily accessible by consulting hip-hop fanzines such as *MZEE* (in 1993) and Internet sites dedicated to the subculture (in 1997), and through the use of citations from interviews with practitioners from within the "underground" hip-hop scene.

GENRE AND MARKET

One of the first issues that confronts us when we move outside of the English-speaking market for recorded music is to establish whether or not the discrete musical genres we know from that market are fully congruent with similar divisions in other pop worlds. This is important in two ways. First, although no single country comes close to matching the amounts spent on recorded music in the United States, these markets are nonetheless economically significant. Germany, for instance, is the largest single market in Western Europe, with estimated annual sales of U.S. $3.74 billion in 1996. This represents around 30 percent of reported U.S. sales and makes Germany the third biggest music market in the world.[1] Developments in the local market since reunification are also on an internationally significant scale. Techno, for instance, a relatively new genre with a high proportion of locally produced recordings, accounted for 8.8 percent of total recorded music sales in Germany in 1996 (Henkel and Wolff 1996: 91). At a national level, the marked increase in the locally produced segment since reunification (the share of the domestic market more than doubled in the first six years, increasing 40 percent in 1994 alone [Smith 1995]) compelled the then conservative federal government to begin to acknowledge the role of record companies in the country's economy. The meeting between the president of the German Federal Republic, Roman Herzog, and leading record-industry figures in late November 1997 was the first of its kind (Gray 1997). When such a market begins to display trends that diverge from the U.S. pattern, the question of the congruence of genres clearly assumes a degree of at least economic significance.

Second, it is important to remember that genres are defined in flux and are subject to constant revision and refinement in the face of the continuing stream of fresh recordings. Such revisions apply in both temporal directions, with the proliferation of new subgenres (e.g., gangsta rap) and the simultaneous reclassification of existing oeuvres ("old-school," for instance). This should remind us that genres are not defined simply on the basis of a list of characteristic features distilled from a plethora of particular concrete artifacts; rather, each release is, as it were, an utterance in a continuing conversation that positions itself in relation to what has gone before and is subject to repositioning in the light of what follows.[2]

To put it another way, rapping is an expression of culture. In order to assess rap music in Germany, we thus need to perform something of a genre analysis, that is, to treat the genre as a kind of social activity realized at least partly in language and existing within social, cultural, musical, and linguistic parameters. It is necessary, then, to consider the wider cultural context in which German rap has emerged and the conversation that was taking place at the time rap was overheard from another (Anglophone) conversation and then restated in a local idiom.

At the outset, it is obvious that major differences separate the circumstances of the underprivileged urban Americans who created hip-hop and those of the relatively wealthy, monocultural youth who form the main body of German popular-music consumers.[3] Some of these discontinuities are explicitly recognized by rappers in Germany. For instance, in the view of one new-school group renowned for their political texts, Main Concept,

> the Americans . . . are not united by hip-hop, but rather by the fact that they are black, and through this alone they manage to establish a community. In the first instance, for them it is not about hip-hop but about blackness. That is the identification point for them. Here, with us, the identification point is hip-hop, and therefore people have such set opinions in comparison to the States. Apart from that, the freaks here are extremely envious [of one another]. . . . The Americans are simply more tolerant in this regard and thus they do not have such a narrow view of the whole thing. (Hülsmann 1997)

Second, who these rappers are is also an important factor:

> [i]n contrast to New York, where the ghetto kids try via hip-hop to achieve a breakthrough into the culture scene of white America, youth from all social groups belong to the hip-hop movement in Berlin. (Henkel and Wolff 1996: 53)

A third major difference is one of language. Whereas for English speakers, even those unfamiliar with the genre, the idioms employed by U.S. rappers are relatively comprehensible, for German youth, in particular those living in the former East Germany, where English was not part of the school curriculum, this argot often remained impenetrable.[4]

As will emerge in the next sections, these differences have had consequences that are clearly discernible in the pattern of popularity that characterized hip-hop's early years in Germany and that have continued to affect the ways in which the genre has developed.

A HISTORY OF RAP IN GERMANY

The niche currently occupied by rap music in Germany, and existing tensions within the genre, have much to do with the reception of hip-hop during the 1980s. This section first sketches the origins of rap in both East and West Germany before considering its wider historical background and the development of a vibrant German-language rap scene in 1993.

The First Waves

The fortunes of rap in divided Germany follow what is at first sight an unusual pattern, with two clear impulses from the United States in and around 1983 and 1989 leading to a brief and widespread flurry of interest that on both occasions then dwindled to an underground following. A closer examination of the context should, however, help explain this path of development.

It should not be surprising that television and cinema appear to have been the crucial vectors for the initial communication of the hip-hop subculture into Germany. The international appeal of early breakbeat music appears to have been closely tied to a fascination with the associated cluster of activities such as breakdance and graffiti, which could only effectively be communicated via visual media. What is surprising is how differently this trend from urban USA was received in (as they still were) East and West Germany.

One of the very few documentations of the history of hip-hop in West Germany (Jacob 1992) emphasizes the enthusiasm for but paucity of information about a genre with roots in a culture very different from that of the German middle class as a restraining factor on the development of the subculture. Jacob describes a brief flare of novelty-value interest in the early 1980s around such figures as Grandmaster Flash and essentially centered on breakdance. Cora E, "the token German female rapper" (Henkel and Wolff 1996: 96) from Kiel, confirms this assessment in an interview in the fanzine *Zap,* where she states: "One should keep in mind that hip-hop in Germany only became known at all through breaking . . . actually B-Boying. . . . When this wave from the USA reached Europe ten years ago, rap music was simply breakdance music" (Gonzo and SPoKK Mind Squad 1993b: 11). Similarly, Henkel cites the Rock Steady Crew, New York City Breakers, and Mr. Robert as seminal influences in 1983–84 (Henkel and Wolff 1996: 70). She does, however, mention mid-1980s dance-offs in Berlin and interestingly notes that these took place between crews divided along the lines of citizenship, that is, into Germans and foreigners. This latter phenomenon could be seen as an attempt to create some kind of parallel for the competitive, racially polarized context of the source culture in the local context.

Credence is lent to the view that the initial interest in hip-hop among West Germans was simply a manifestation of a more general Americanophilia and that the movement (as in the USA) was interpreted locally as little more than a craze: "There was a period where it was the uncoolest thing possible if you said you listened to hip-hop or possibly even breakdanced. . . . By at the latest 1985 [it was] deemed ridiculous" (Absolute Beginner, in Gonzo and SPoKK Mind Squad 1993b: 12). There do not appear to have been any local record releases during or following this first *Beat Street*–inspired phase. Echoing the visual fascination with breakdance as the initial carrier of the music into a German context, Henkel identifies the shelving of the VIVA *Free Style* television program presented by Nils Robitzky, himself an avid breakdancer, as a significant contribution to the decline of hip-hop's popularity (Henkel and Wolff 1996: 71).[5] Once the breakdance craze passed, it became increasingly obvious that there was very little common ground between the underprivileged urban U.S. home culture of early rap music and the experiences of West German youth; the fact that raps were in a foreign language appears to have rendered the emerging political elements of the genre opaque.

The reception of hip-hop in East Germany, however, was very different. Once again, the visual catalyst was the film *Beat Street,* which proved sufficiently potent to prompt state intervention: following the showing of the film in East German cinemas, automobile spray-paint cans had to be withdrawn from sale (Henkel and Wolff 1996: 56).

East German authorities, however, were particularly sensitive to the political potential of music, and their responses to such influences were carefully considered, with no small element of *realpolitik* (see Wicke and Shepherd 1993 for an excellent account of the German Democratic Republic [GDR] state's responses to and attempts to control rock music). Thus, the film first became part of the annual Christmas television programming, as a "warning example of 'capitalist competition'" (Henkel and Wolff 1996: 72–73), which all but assured its achievement of cult status and its emulation throughout the entire GDR. Then, after further consideration, officials in the sports-oriented East revised their ideological assessment of the trend and acknowledged breakdance "not as an expression of western decadence but rather as a 'combatant sport art of the culture of the repressed masses in America'" (Henkel and Wolff 1996: 73). There were apparently some objections to the association of hip-hop with sport, and East German substitutes were found. Henkel goes on to report a series of international and well-attended breakdance contests in the Eastern bloc in the mid-1980s (Henkel and Wolff 1996: 73) and videos and television coverage featuring East German dance crews. However, any such cultural activity was obliterated in one fell swoop by the fall of the Berlin wall, which left the aspiring stars with a string of now useless connections and no hope of further funding in the midst of a total administrative collapse (Henkel and Wolff 1996: 74).

Support for the contention that hip-hop met with a qualitatively different reception in the East from that of the West is offered by the remembrances of Cookie of Fresh Force (from Leipzig), who claims, "Hip hop was for us true identification, because—we were at the bottom. . . . Hip hop was never merely a fashion for us, but rather truly a chance to break out" (*MZEE* 3/93: 18). This source describes those East German youth who did manage to discover a little of the original context and elements of hip-hop as forming a tight community that distributed rare records smuggled from the West, handed on dance moves learned—without the benefits of video replay—from illegally watched West German television, and even reproduced spray-paint art styles on T-shirts using toothbrushes in the absence of aerosol cans. He also mentions, however, the absence of rappers, citing the lack of English as a deciding factor in this regard (*MZEE* 3/93: 18).

What was common to both Germanies during this first phase was the dearth of information that came across about hip-hop culture, a scarcity exacerbated by the language barrier. The perceptions most Germans had of hip-hop were restricted to the glimpses conveyed by occasional chart appearances (and their accompanying videos). The transmission, in terms of both content and the radically disparate contexts of the movement's source and sites of its reception, was imperfect enough to preclude any attempt to transplant the subculture wholesale. In the West, the "music to breakdance to" slipped into obscurity with the demise of that particular fad, while isolated teenagers in the East sought to take advantage of qualified state approbation for the "culture of resistance" to covertly indulge in the forbidden.

An interregnum followed in which young people in both Germanies appear to have remained ignorant of almost all further developments in rap music. Jacob (1992: 167) names Run-DMC as the only rap act to achieve wider recognition in the five years between 1984 and 1989. Then, however, came the second, "by all means necessary," wave of interest, which was picked up by DJs and by city and lifestyle magazines in the West as potentially "the next big thing" (Jacob 1992: 167).

Henkel implicitly identifies another film as launching the second surge of widespread interest in hip-hop: Dennis Hopper's 1988 *Colors* (Henkel and Wolff 1996: 57). Jacob (1992: 170), on the other hand, arguing that the musical style itself was not popular and had to be actively packaged and marketed, sees the roots of the revival in the cross-genre experiments of Public Enemy and Anthrax. Once again, and probably for the reasons Jacob suggests, the widespread enthusiasm was short lived.

West German engagement with the overtly political pronouncements of the U.S. rap stars of the time is seen by this latter commentator as a kind of consumerist posturing. He claims the radical statements of U.S. rappers were felt to be sufficiently divorced from the German situation to be safely parroted; German youth were content to wish the American blacks well in "*their* struggle" (Jacob 1992: 172; original emphasis). Against this background of a general ignorance of and lack of serious engagement with rap as a medium of political expression, Jacob does mention a few earnest figures, many of them immigrants in the West, who turned to rap as an alternative to the dominant musical direction of a "Laibach—Nick Cave—[Einstürzende] Neubauten—REM mainstream" (Jacob 1992: 167) and actively sought out details of the associated hip-hop culture. The handful of recordings made between 1988 and the time at which Jacob was writing mostly feature English texts, in keeping with a tendency in Germany for local groups to develop an English repertoire in the hope of capturing the ear of the predominantly Anglophone international audience.[6]

There is a dearth of evidence of how, or even if, the phase of active interest in U.S. rap in 1989 was experienced in East Germany, embroiled as it was at the time in deep economic, social, and political crisis. It does appear, however, that the fledgling hip-hop culture Jacob documents seems to have thrived better in the East, even if it remained unrecognized in the immediate wake of German reunification. One small indication of this is Henkel's claim that it was East German sprayers who made the eastern side of a preserved section of the Berlin wall one of the most fiercely contested aerosol-art surfaces in Germany (Henkel and Wolff 1996: 56). Another indicator is the fact that the East German rappers Down Town Lyricz (their original moniker, East Side Voice, was prohibited by the state authorities) were in a position to conduct a tour of West Germany and Switzerland shortly before splitting up in 1990 (*Out~side* 1997).

Thus, in Germany up until late 1992, imported U.S. rap had been the subject of two brief film-launched crazes that had not led to any widespread local engagement with the hip-hop subculture. This outcome might have been predicted on the basis of the disparity between the life circumstances of the rappers and the German record-buying public, but it also demonstrated that on the other side of a language barrier the inherently political dimensions of the genre could be better held at a distance or ignored. It is also important to note, however, that contact with hip-hop had set off a spark among a tightly-knit club of disaffected Eastern youth and some small clusters of immigrants around major industrial centers in the West (Jacob 1992: 167).[7] Notable also was the distinct lack of locally recorded material.

The Background to 1993

In order to explain at least one strand of the next phase, it becomes necessary to widen the focus and to consider some of the broad sweeps of historical change affecting Germany at this time. By 1993 reunification was in full swing. The West German Treuhand authority was supervising the privatization of East German industries, and a massive infrastructure rollout, funded by special tax surcharges, was visibly under way, repaving streets and autobahns and installing new telephones, digital exchanges, and fiberoptic cables. A timetable had been established for the achievement of wage parity in East and West, a special office had been created to allow citizens access to the records of the former East German secret police, and an unparalleled building boom was being planned in the new capital, Berlin. There was also an alarming, and well-documented, upsurge in the amount of violence perpetrated by the right wing.[8] In 1993 asylum seekers and Turkish families died in arson attacks, homeless people and left-wing sympathizers were beaten to death, and neo-Nazi groups managed to stage unrestricted public demonstrations.

The underlying causes of this right-wing and racist violence were of course extremely complex, but the continuing internal rapprochement between the first and second worlds of West and East Germany was implicated. The political confusion following their incorporation into a larger, capitalist economy was cited at the time as grounds for the prevalence of right-wing opinions among East Germans. But the wave of racist violence was not confined to the "new states" of the former East Germany, and right-wing parties such as the Republicaner party also polled better in by-elections in the West. (The necessarily high taxation and budget restrictions imposed upon the West at a time of economic downturn in order to finance infrastructural reform in the East must be considered as a possible contributing factor to these reactionary developments.)

There were also some attempts to portray the perpetrators of right-wing violence as impressionable and misguided youth. The adequacy of this portrayal is questionable in the light of, for example, the clearly documented inaction, and in extreme cases approbation, of bystanders or police during such attacks, but it served some utility in deflecting the stigma onto a vulnerable subgroup within the German population.[9] It also dictated the form of much of the response to the right-wing upsurge in Germany.

Because of the history of the right wing in Germany, there exists a core of public opinion firmly committed to a repudiation of any perceived initiatives from this side of the political spectrum. The motivations of such opinion are diverse, but the participants in the social movements of the late 1960s play a significant role as articulators. For youth audiences, however, this generation is of an age identified as belonging to the cadre from which parents, teachers, and large sectors of the status quo are drawn.

With underprivileged youth constructed as the deluded victims of right-wing ideology, popular music naturally became one of the cultural arenas employed by those who wished to do something to inhibit this movement as well as by those who wished to appear to be doing something. The year 1993 was characterized by a prodigious output of ostensibly antiracist recordings and press statements from a broad spectrum of musicians and music groups.

Unfortunately, or perhaps predictably, much of this musical response proved rather lame, tending toward the formulaic and the didactic (Beck 1993). This can be attributed in part to the deficiencies of mainstream pop as an expressive medium, particularly in the light of the complexity of the underlying causes of the problem. Successful groups with established reputations (such as Die Toten Hosen, from Düsseldorf, or the reconfigured Ärzte) were able to deliver sharp political messages in German, but only at the cost of criticism for misusing their popular appeal in order to preach to their audiences (see, for instance, Becker 1993: 46–47).

At this point, when the crisis of 1992–93 had accentuated the need to be able to articulate complicated political ideas and arguments in an accessible form, a new pop genre emerged that seemed to offer precisely such an opportunity (Pennay 1993). In late 1992 a seminal album and a 12-inch single appeared that represented two poles of what was to become "almost overnight" the German rap scene. The maxi was an old-school single by the group later acknowledged as the scene's most senior representatives (see, e.g., Jessewitsch 1997), Advanced Chemistry. The album was the second solo release by four young men from Stuttgart who make up what is still easily the best-known rap group in Germany, Die Fantastischen Vier (the Fantastic Four). One can argue that these two catalytic records represent two distinct constellations around which German-language rap has since burgeoned.[10] They are examined separately below.

1993: THE BIRTH OF GERMAN RAP

In 1993, in the absence of a significant push from the USA but at a time of great domestic change, German-language rap entered the mainstream with a vengeance. It has been hailed as the year of German hip-hop, and countless reports about this "new" scene among German youth appeared. A good example is the report in *Wiener* (Strasser 1993), an established magazine, which included a section titled "What Is Hip-Hop? Let's Start from Scratch," clearly demonstrating the background lack of awareness of hip-hop culture in Germany. One indicator of this efflorescence can be found in the number of local rap recordings released at the time in Germany. Prior to 1993, a total of twenty releases are reported by Cracc, whereas in 1993 alone at least forty-one recordings hit the market.[11]

But Günther Jacob, in a criticism of the pale and imitative efforts of fledgling rap groups in Germany in 1992, noted that "the endless stream of excellent imports reduces all [local] efforts to nil, as long as one only imitates. . . . [F]or something independent one needs a good political idea, comparable perhaps to punk" (Jacob 1992: 196). His words, in the light of the political context outlined above, proved prophetic. Against the background of a need to articulate convincingly an alternative viewpoint to the right-wing groundswell, one 12-inch single shone out among the pedagogic and trite attempts of the German (pop) musical status quo. It was a rap with clear debts to the U.S. old school by a trio of Heidelberg youths of Italian (Toni L.), Ghanaian (Linguist), and Haitian (Torch) backgrounds, who described in clear German what it was like to possess German citizenship but be treated like a foreigner on the basis of appearance. Advanced Chemistry's "Fremd im eigenen Land" ("Foreign in My Own Country") brought into sharp focus a level of widespread and implicit racism that was in clear danger of being ignored if not actively denied in the face of overt racist attacks.

The video of the single, which achieved wide airplay on MTV Europe, was successful because rather than preaching to right-wingers in an attempt to convert them, it spoke directly to the broad middle mass and confronted them with an uncomfortable view of life from the perspective of a minority. This was rap with a real political message, not a pale imitation of the sort criticized by Jacob. In the words of Toni L., "I find it . . . important that [my work] reflect my 'own' reality, and not an imaginary world modeled on America that doesn't exist here. Through the fact that I talk about my own world and reality, an independent style is also created" (K.M.S. 1997). At the same time, Advanced Chemistry quite explicitly linked themselves to the unfashionable hip-hop enthusiasts of the 1980s and were in turn lionized by the hip-hop community. Toni L.'s 1998 solo release acknowledges his nickname of "der Pate" (the Godfather) (Alternation/Intercord), while Torch has been described as "the merciless chief ideologue of the German hip-hop scene" and leader of the German chapter of the Zulu Nation, and the group as a whole are for the same writer "unequivocally the spearhead of the movement" (Strasser 1993: 34–35). What Strasser refers to as "the movement" is a body of hip-hop enthusiasts united in their aims of "communicating hip-hop culture alongside socially critical texts" (Eissfeldt, in Gonzo and SPoKK Mind Squad 1993a: 11). Many trace their involvement in hip-hop culture (as opposed to rap music alone) back to the two waves of interest in particular rap acts outlined above.[12] Despite a modicum of chart success in and after 1993, many of these acts remain on independent labels. It took three years for Advanced Chemistry to be able to release an album, for instance, owing to problems with their label (K.M.S. 1997). These hard-core hip-hop groups have in common a credo that does not permit the separation of a rapped delivery style from the trappings of what is believed to be the true hip-hop culture, incorporating breakdance, graffiti, freestyling, and a code of honor. They are thus strongly opposed to the trend begun by Die Fantastischen Vier.

The second hinge upon which the market opened to embrace German-language rap could also have been inspired by Jacob's dismissive criticism, barring the elision of one key term, "political." Die Fantastischen Vier, based in Stuttgart in Germany's conservative south, were also among the first German rap groups to experiment with German lyrics in combination with "breakbeats and grooves. . . . real . . . funky hip-hop" (Jacob 1992: 195). In their own account, Smudo and Thomas D from Die Fantastischen Vier were inspired to begin rapping in German following a six-month visit to the United States, where it became apparent to them that they had nothing in common with the rappers of Los Angeles and that U.S. rappers were speaking of a real environment containing elements totally foreign to the essentially middle-class world of the Vier. The group subsequently decided to concentrate on issues they saw around them, using their own language, rather than aping American styles (Nink 1993; Strasser 1993: 34).

The resulting debut, *Jetzt geht's ab* (Here Goes!), was the first album to feature exclusively German-language rap. Released by Sony in 1991, the listing of the title track as a "radio edit" made clear the commercial intentions behind the album. The rap texts were notably trite, however, and *Jetzt geht's ab* and an earlier, Marlboro-sponsored compilation on which Die Fantastischen Vier were also featured *(Krauts with Attitude)* were in fact the specific releases lambasted by Jacob in the critique cited above. In particular, he noted, "[w]hoever takes hip hop/rap seriously must also be interested in German-language raps, because rap is 'word' and 'message' (and not just the groove) and because both deserve to be understood. The problem is, however, that the Fantastischen Vier have grasped this idea, but . . . have nothing to say (Jacob 1992: 195; ellipsis in original).[13] Nonetheless, the group launched their second album with a single deliberately written to achieve radio airplay (Nink 1993) and with the full backing of a major label. It was a runaway success. By February 1993, half a million copies of *Vier Gewinnt* (literally, "Four Wins"; see note 19) had been sold, and a second single had joined the first in the top 40. In comparison to Advanced Chemistry, the texts rapped by Die Fantastischen Vier were anything but political, but they had, perhaps unknowingly, had "a good . . . idea."[14]

What Die Fantastischen Vier did, I would argue, was to successfully transfer rap's potential to communicate strong emotions and shared experiences into the German sphere by shifting its subject matter. Despite being young and articulate at a time of massive change and huge social problems, the Vier began to rap about the world of personal relationships, about intimacy, one of the few arenas in the materially comfortable (at least in the former West) lives of young Germans in which powerful feelings could be indulged without sanction. By grasping at a universal theme, it could perhaps be argued that they attempted to circumvent the divisions and stresses of the collision of the two political worlds, seeking escape in the "exchange of bodily fluids" rather than ideologies.[15]

Through their enormous success Die Fantastischen Vier acted as the vanguard for a home-grown German rap industry that actively divorced itself from traditionalists such as Advanced Chemistry and Cora E and their insistence that rap was inseparable from hip-hop. They made commercially accessible music centered on the traditional pop themes of feelings and relationships, coupled with the distinctive "new" feature of spoken German lyrics and some highly polished breakbeat stylings. By 1999 their wave of popularity had shown no sign of abating: their album *4:99* went to the top of the German charts, and their single "MFG" *(Mit freundlichen Grussen,* "With Friendly Greetings" i.e., "Yours Sincerely") also ranked highly.

It needs to be emphasized that the events of 1993 thus challenge the picture drawn by some commentators from the English-speaking world, who position "European rap" as a response to "the social problems and political uncertainties facing Europe in the nineties [which] make great source material for hip-hop" (Harpin and Wenner 1993: 58). Rap was not, as has been claimed, experienced in the early 1980s as an exciting and relevant means of self-expression, and Europeans did not "rapidly" learn its power derived from speaking about one's own experiences in order to draw upon their own language and national influences.[16] At least in Germany, it took a decade for the (in the English-speaking world inescapable) political dimension of rap to gain any foothold, and even then it was accompanied — indeed, in sales terms, completely overshadowed — by an appropriation of these musical styles for traditional pop themes. Further, the initiators of this appropriation themselves recognized the need to draw upon their own environment in order to make the genre relevant and appealing.

THE CURRENT SITUATION

Since 1993 German rap has securely established itself as a significant element in the spectrum of local German musical output, albeit as a piebald creature in which the seminal legacies of the two records discussed coexist.

On the one hand, there are the old-school hardcore heirs and peers of Advanced Chemistry, who are able to trace their roots back to those marginalized enthusiasts who took the "fashion" waves of the 1980s to heart. On the other can be found the more commercial and accessible perpetrators of the "lovers' rap" trend begun by Die Fantastischen Vier, who rap about personal relationships, with little or no recognition of a wider hip-hop culture. Absolute Beginner, a new-school group from Hamburg whose album *Bambule* (Ruckus) reached number 17 on the German charts in 1998 (see Weinert 1999: 40), summarized the connection between the two traditions as follows: "Through the Fantas [Die Fantastischen Vier] the interest has been raised, the media are picking up German-language hip-hop, some are letting themselves be pulled along, but the old-school is raising its forefinger and saying 'Beware, do not let this happen to you' because they have the experience of former times [where the trend was just as quickly abandoned]" (Gonzo and SPoKK Mind Squad 1993a: 12). Naturally, selecting two single recordings as representative forerunners of a divided tradition can only offer an oversimplified picture, with numerous inherent distortions.[17] For instance, fans of "serious hip-hop" (as opposed to rapping pop stars) continue to include Die Fantastischen Vier in their genealogies and discographies, whereas the more blatantly commercial offspring of their shift to the interpersonal are excised.

At the same time, parallels can be found with other musicians. Among female rap stars, a similar distinction could be drawn between Cora E on the one hand and Tic Tac Toe on the other. Cora E was one of the very few old-school acts to have been taken on by a major record label following two singles on Bruback. Her first single with EMI, "Schlüsselkind" (Latchkey Kid), released in December 1996, achieved wide airplay and features a relatively unpolished production style and traditional delivery, with lyrics that attempt social criticism via personal experience, linking a description of her own childhood to the problems of children of working parents. The parallels to Advanced Chemistry should be fairly clear. Further, Cora E was the only female rap star who penned her own texts (Henkel and Wolff 1996: 77), and she is adamant that she was not a rapper, but rather a hip-hopper (Gonzo and SPoKK Mind Squad 1993b: 11).

Tic Tac Toe, on the other hand, do not "do hip-hop" (Gonzo and SPoKK Mind Squad 1993b).[18] The three young women from the industrial Ruhr valley area, Jazzy, Lee, and Ricky, are in their early twenties and made their chart breakthrough in 1996 with two platinum singles (including a number 1 with "Verpiss' dich") and an eponymous first album that also went platinum. They also won a VIVA Comet award for Newcomer of the Year, while a third single, "Warum?" (Why?) went to number 1 within two weeks of release in February 1997. The trio are famous for their direct, vernacular speech ("Verpiss' dich" translates roughly as "Fuck off"), and also for the fact that "a message is contained in every song in a nice, guaranteed effective way" (according to their record company, BMG [BMG 1997]). Topics that they have tackled include safe sex ("Leck mich am A, B, Zeh" [Kiss my A, B, C]), drug abuse ("Warum?"), and even child sexual abuse ("Bitte küss' mich nicht" [Please Don't Kiss Me]), but their repertoire also encompasses such sentiments as "Ich wär' so gern so blöd wie du" (I wish I Were as Stupid as You Are), and "I sit on your lap and my dreams grow large."

Tic Tac Toe are clearly heirs to the Fantastichen Vier tradition. Even their name is a play on the title of the latter's first successful album.[19] In discussing how "Verpiss' dich" is more than a settling of accounts with an ex and also reflects "true feelings," Lee tellingly states, "Unhappiness in love [Liebeskummer] is a topic with which everybody can empathize, which is why the song is so effective" (BMG 1997). Similarly, "'Warum' is about dependency, sorrow, pain, and doubt" (BMG 1997). This explicit recognition of the need for emotional honesty, rather than political instruction, seems to have become part of an unofficial credo for German-speaking rappers outside the hardcore tradition. One of the most poignant new acts to emerge after 1993 were the Rödelheim Hartreim Projekt (Hartreim = "hard-rhyme"). Moses Pelham and Thomas Haas, who come from Rödelheim, a satellite town near Frankfurt, identify "the idea and the wish to give expression to our feelings and thoughts in our language, with our music" as a central element of their undertaking (RHP 1996). Their sound is a mixture of rap braggadocio with laid-back grooves and slick production and makes use of their regional accents (a marker of class as well as geography).[20] Their first album, Direkt aus Rödelheim (Straight out of Rödelheim), has been described as the "phattest" and "heaviest" German hip-hop recording to date, with debts to R&B, N.W.A., and even some string arrangements. On the tail of their 1994 hit "Keine ist" (No One Is), similar in subject matter to "Nothing Compares 2U" but with a softly spoken rap over a mellow understated backing track, they introduced their second album, Zurück nach Rödelheim (Back to Rödelheim), with statements that

> [h]ip-hop is not Soul, but it must have soul. What use is a rap that just tells me that the rapper has done his homework (or not even that)? A rapper has to be able to describe how he ticks, and how the people around him tick. He must find a language for this. He must be able to turn himself inside out like a glove. Expose his heart. He must rap his autobiography

without blushing. He must be able to chronicle his milieu, his people, but without constantly sounding like a social worker. He must not fear the independent life of his own words. He must have soul. . . . Only when someone comprehends his own situation and finds words for it can others find their own situation in them. (RHP 1996)

There is a melancholy to the hit "Keine ist" that found its echo in one of the "discoveries" of 1997, Freundeskreis (Circle of Friends). This group of four from the Stuttgart region combined and synthesized a number of elements from the various strands of the German rap tradition, in keeping with their definition of hip-hop:

For me it depends upon (a) the sound and (b) what the people are trying to achieve with their music. Hip-hop is also a healthy competition, and anybody who releases a record looks to see that it is better than what has gone before. It is a spur to study the other MCs and then to make something which goes a step beyond that. And that's something I can't see with many of these commercial pop rappers; instead they clearly serve a listenership who have no idea of hip-hop and no point of comparison. (Schröder 1997)

The group incorporates overtly political texts but justifies them on the basis of their own personal politicized upbringings (the two rappers were raised in a Black Panther household and a Marxist collective, according to the sleeve notes of the group's album *Quadratur des Kreises* [The Circle Squared]. They switch between languages but retain genuinely poetic lyrics: their first single was entitled "Leg' dein Ohr auf die Schiene der Geschichte" (Lay Your Ear on the Rail of History). In it they call for a greater hermeneutic awareness, asking the listener to contemplate and bear in mind the broad political and historical context in which they find themselves. Their second single, about a relationship, featured the full melancholy and phat production of the Rödelheim sound (its subtitle translates as "Every Time It Rains") but was promoted with a violent video, depicting interrogation and torture in a setting reminiscent of Vietnam, that achieved high rotation on MTV Europe. Their debut album, on the label founded by Die Fantastichen Vier, was, not surprisingly, hailed as one of the definitive German hip-hop recordings to date (Schröder 1997).

Another figure who must be mentioned in a brief résumé of key acts that have emerged since 1993 is Sabrine Setlur, who is of Indian extraction. Originally recording as Schwester S (Sister S., with a minialbum titled *Hier Kommt die Schwester* [Here Comes the Sister] and closely allied to the Rödelheim Hartreim Projekt, Setlur has hardcore credentials and an emotional focus tinged with the *tristesse* of her producers' sound, but in her more aggressive numbers she begins to resemble Tic Tac Toe. Admittedly, rather than shouting "Verpiss' dich!" Setlur more quietly states, "Du liebst mich nicht, Du liebst mich einfach nicht" (You don't love me, you just don't love me), but a more recent single features electric guitar solos and a video showing Setlur raging in a glass cage and turning into a panther. (In January 2001 she was reported in the international media to be having an affair with tennis star Boris Becker.) Her output is further evidence that the two clearly distinguished styles of German rap that existed at the outset are hybridizing, as the hardcore school begins to embrace the emotional tropes of the pop idiom and demonstrates the potential perils and gains of this move quite clearly. Her new record company is definite about which side of the fence Setlur belongs on: "One could . . . begin to create incredibly highflown constructions, perhaps attempt to enlist all manner of half-fermented intellectual piffle in order to avoid that which it is actually about: to come close to them, to capture them—FEELINGS" (Sony 1997).

A strain of pure pop rap has persisted, however, as Maximilian, of Freundeskreis, laments in the quote above. Some of its purveyors are intelligent and articulate, with real cult followings, such as Fettes Brot ("Stoned Bread"; literally, "Fat Bread"), whose long-term residency on the youth radio station of the former Eastern zone, Fritz, successfully transferred to television. It is indicative of their love of wordplay that the radio program was known as "Trout Tea," and the television follow-on as "Trout TV." Their first big hit at the end of 1995 was a "party rap" (in the words of their label, *MZEE* 1997) titled "Nordisch by Nature" (i.e., Nordic) and included a collage of playful steals from across the board, such as a poor falsetto rendering of the Bee Gees' "Night Fever" as "Nacht Fieber," a translation that retains chiefly the medical connotation. A more recent release rather surrealy tells of "silverfish in my bed." If Fettes Brot have a political message at all, it is little more than advice to loosen up and not take an essentially corrupt world too seriously.

This very clearly puts them at the other end of a spectrum from such groups as Blumfeld or Anarchist Academy, who in the summer of 1997 participated in a podium discussion with leading pop-music journalists (including Günther Jacob) about the music business as part of a major southern German festival in honor of Franz Degenhardt.[21] Anarchist Academy's first concert in their hometown of Lüdenscheid, in 1992, led to a local ban on performing in public on the basis of their "child-endangering texts," and Die Fantastischen Vier have also refused to share a bill with these uncompromising offshoots from the autonomous/punk scene. They are also linked to an illegal anonymous pressing in 1993, *Partisanen gegen Deutschland* (Partisans against Germany). In 1993 it looked as though Anarchist Academy's branch of rap had a promising future, particularly given the political upheavals of the time and the explicit recognition by some of the groups involved that rap offered them a perfect medium for the dissemination of their oppositional views (Pennay 1993). However, as Wegener (1996) succinctly observes in a review of *Anarchophobia* (1994): "They cannot become the German Public Enemy, as there is no need for discussion at their [i.e., Public Enemy's] level here anymore."

Whether one agrees with this political assessment or not, the conversation that is German rap has clearly moved on. Even the old-school appear to be recognizing the need to change and to broaden the pool from which they draw their influences, although Advanced Chemistry carefully justify this on the basis of only now being able to reveal the full breadth of their inspiration with their new label and the freedom to release albums (K.M.S. 1997). Perhaps German rap came of age in 1997 after four years in the mainstream, as the strident defense of Freundeskreis's frontman Maximilian appears to indicate: "One can no longer say 'you are just imitating' because since I was sixteen I have been listening to hip-hop and that is just as much a part of my cultural understanding as it is for an American who has been doing this for longer" (Schröder 1997).

Despite Main Concept's caveat that "we live after all in Germany, where nobody accepts somebody else trying to tell him something" (Hülsmann 1997), it does seem that the stars of the German rap scene are beginning to listen closely to each other, and that the influence of recordings even from other poles within the genre, and from other schools, are starting to carry greater weight than those from overseas. Perhaps the champions of the original waves of inspiration are beginning to recognize that the transmission of hip-hop culture was necessarily incomplete, and that although they, by virtue of their social situation, had grasped an essential element that had evaded the main body of record buyers, what they saw was still only a snapshot—the real message, irrespective of style or genre, was one of self-expression. It could even be that the enormous upsurge in locally produced recordings and the emergence of German rap are linked by this metamessage.

CONCLUSIONS

In this essay I have shown that generalizations made about the characteristics of a genre on the basis of its development within the English-speaking market cannot be transferred wholesale to other national contexts, and that although this market does act as a reference point for the entire world, the trends it exhibits are always subject to local reinterpretation. In the particular instance of rap music in Germany, a clearly imperfect transmission of the cluster of ideas surrounding this genre has led, as shown, to the evolution of a related but unique genre, marked by its own internal dynamics and reference points. Regrettably, the flow of new ideas and stylistic innovations in popular music is nearly always from the English-speaking market, and not to it. But this must be balanced against a growing independence and confidence among young Germans that they can create music in German for Germans —the most positive development within post-reunification Germany of a renaissance within the local music scene, and one within which the transmuted and initially contested genre of rap has played a key role.

NOTES

Acknowledgments are due to L'Age d'Or Records of Hamburg for their helpful provision of material related to this topic, to Phil Hayward for initial guidance and support, and to Tony Mitchell for encouraging me to undertake an update. All quotations are my translations from German originals.

1. Reported sales were U.S. $3.2 billion, estimated by the German reporting body to represent 85 percent of all sales. This equates to over 300 million soundcarrier units. Based on statistics from the HMV Music Business Research Site at Westminster University (HMV 1997).

2. Sometimes this positioning is explicitly aided by the self-identification of the artists. At other times, how a new recording is classified in a large music store can provide intriguing insights into the implicit categories at work. For instance, Yothu Yindi, an Australian Aboriginal group who created a novel combination of traditional songs and instruments with contemporary rock, dance, and reggae elements and production values, was filed under "reggae" in a large record store in Berlin.

3. At least in the West. Despite the fact that the surface "assimilation" of East Germans has been most marked and most rapid among the youth, significant differences did persist in the years immediately succeeding reunification; these I return to later.

4. See, for instance, the July–August 1993 issue of *MZEE,* which carried an interview with an East German group where the history of hip-hop before reunification was discussed; the group (Fresh Force) confirmed that "no one could speak English" and that this stymied the development of a local rap scene (*MZEE* 3/93: 18). Henkel reports that even after reunification, East German rappers outside Berlin showed a clear preference for German (Henkel and Wolff 1996: 17).

5. VIVA is a German music television station similar to MTV. Through its support

for local acts and content in general it is seen as playing a significant role in the boom in music produced for the German domestic market. Another, short-lived, hip-hop program was *Wild Style,* on German state television (ZDF).

6. Cracc (see note 11) lists twenty releases between 1988 and 1992, sixteen of them in the last eighteen months of that period.

7. The three larger hip-hop fanzines of the early 1990s were all published in Cologne and Hamburg (Jacob 1992: 211), and none in largely nonindustrial Berlin. These cities, together with Frankfurt, Stuttgart, and Düsseldorf, have remained centers of the hip-hop scene.

8. See, e.g., the cover story of *Der Spiegel* 50 (1992): 22–54.

9. *Stern* 21 (1994), 34 ff., for instance, continued this trend when it carried dramatic photos from the infamous "Ascension Day Hunt" in Magdeburg showing foreigners being pursued through the center of the city by right-wing youths assisted by the police.

10. A third strand, which relates directly to the punk tradition and which also flourished in 1993, has proved less vibrant, although exponents such as Anarchist Academy are still active. It is discussed in Pennay 1993.

11. These figures are based on the extensive discography of German rap recordings assembled at one of the best World Wide Web sites devoted to German hip-hop, *Out~side*/Cracchouse. The trend continued in 1994 with forty-seven releases and has remained high ever since.

12. In fact there is something of a rift between those who have kept the flame alive since the early 1980s and those whose enthusiasm dates from the second wave, the so-called old and new schools.

13. The first and best known single from *Jetzt geht's ab,* "Hausmeister Thomas D" (MC Thomas D), opens with the lyrics

We are the Fantastischen Vier
and we're here
with plenty of beer
and lots of women
they haven't shot through
they're here
to watch our show.
    (Roth 1995–97)

14. In fact it was disparagingly described as "hip-hop for Manta drivers" (Strasser 1993: 34), Manta being a dated General Motors production line "sports" car and a symbol of lower-income conventionality.

15. A translation of a line from one of their early hits, "Saft" (Juice).

16. This seems a common trope among writers about rap. Henkel argues along

very similar lines from within the German scene that the success of rap in Turkish by the groups involved in the *Cartel* project is dependent upon an "essential moment of identification for the kids . . . the recognition of their own problems or everyday reality in the texts. . . . [I]t will not take long until other national minorities in Germany begin to rap in their mother tongue" (Henkel and Wolff 1996: 76).

17. Toni L., describing how the group's status has changed, himself notes that "everything that belonged together with hip-hop was all at once apparently us. Everything commercial was the Fantastischen Vier" (K.M.S. 1997).

18. As quoted on the official Tic Tac Toe fan homepage (TTT 1997). It should be noted that the group split in 1998, with Jazzy and Lee continuing under the name of Tic Tac Two, but they reformed in 2000, after Sara had pursued a brief solo career.

19. "Vier Gewinnt" is the name under which the quasi-3D variant of noughts and crosses (tic tac toe) known as "Connect Four" is marketed in Germany.

20. Moses Pelham is known as the bad boy of German hip-hop (Woldach 1997) because of his uncompromising language and his working-class manner. The epithet was originally earned when he assaulted a VIVA presenter.

21. Franz Joseph Degenhardt is a respected singer-songwriter from the socially critical, nonconformist tradition of the late 1960s. A 1998 Anarchist Academy single was a cover version of one of his songs.

REFERENCES

Beck, Christian. 1993. "Die Tra-la-la-Offensive." *Zitty* 3, 8–11.

Becker, Andreas. 1993. "Wir nützen den Persilschein." *Zitty* 20, 46–47.

BMG. 1997. <*http://www.bmg.de/tictactoe/tttbi001.htm* and *tttbi002.htm*>. [Biography of Tic Tac Toe on the official BMG World Wide Web site.]

Dufresne, David. 1992. *Yo! Rap Revolution*. Translated by Jutta Schornstein. Neustadt: Buchverlag Michael Schwinn.

Gonzo and SPoKK Mind Squad. 1993a. "Die absolute Wahrheit über Hiphop und Gottings." *Zap*, 1 August, 10–12.

——— (with thanks to Steffen W.). 1993b. "Hard Cora." *Zap*, 1 September, 10–12.

Gray, Andrew. 1997. "German President Meets Popsters as German Rock Booms." Reuters, 26 November.

Harpin, Lee, and Martina Wenner. 1993. "European Rap." *i-D* 116, 58–60.

Henkel, Oliva, and Karsten Wolff. 1996. *Berlin Underground: Techno und HipHop zwischen Mythos und Ausverkauf*. Berlin: FAB Verlag.

HMV. 1997. The HMV Music Business Research Site at Westminster University. <*http://www.wmin.ac.uk/media/music*>.

Hülsmann, Stefan. 1997. "Niemand hat angefangen Hiphop zu hören, weil er die

Texte geil fand." MK ZWO. *<http://www.media-online.de/hhnet/main.htm>*. ["Hiphop net" Web site.]

Jacob, Günther. 1992. "Up-date zur deutsche Ausgabe." In David Dufresne, *Yo! Rap Revolution.* Neustadt: Buchverlag Michael Schurinn.

Jessewitsch, Dirk. 1997. Online review of Der Pate. *Discover* [online magazine] at KWS online. *<http://www.kws.de>*.

K.M.S. ([Kold Man See]). 1997. Toni L: Der Pate des deutschen Rap. *Out~Side* [online hip-hop fanzine]. *<http://www.htwm.de/~mvogel1/outside.htm>*.

MZEE. 1997. *<http://www.planetsound.com/label/mzee>*. [Homepage of MZEE records.]

Nink, Stefan. 1993. Interview, Die Fantastischen Vier. *ME/Sounds*, May.

Out~side. 1997. *<http://www.htwm.de/~mvogel1/outside.htm>*. [Major World Wide Web site devoted to German hip-hop; includes authoritative discography.]

Pennay, Mark. 1993. "Rap and racism in Germany." Unpublished manuscript.

RHP. 1996. Rödelheim Hartreim Project Official page. *<http://www.pelhampowerproductions.de/rhp/>*. In particular, *<http://www.pelhampowerproductions.de/rhp/supporter/bandinfo/bio/bio.html>*.

Roth, Markus, with Smudo. 1995–97. Fantastischen Vier Homepage. *<http://www.bawue.de/~markus/fanta4.html>*.

Schröder, Matthias. 1997. "Die Facetten des Lebens." *Subway* (October). *<http://subway-net.de/magazin/1997/10freund.htm>*.

Smith, Gary. 1995. "The German Market Report." *Music Business International*, August 1995. Online version, *<http://www.dotmusic.co.uk>*.

Sony. 1997. *<http://www.sonymusic.de/music/progressive/SabrineSetlur/welcome.htm>*. [World Wide Web page devoted to Sabrine Setlur on the Sony German site.]

Strasser, Eva. 1993. "Deutscher Hip Hop." *Wiener* 2, 32–36.

TTT. 1997. Die offizielle Tic Tac Toe-Fan-Homepage. *<http://www.tictactoe.de>*.

Wegener, Thomas. 1996. Review of *Anarchophobia. Discover,* 26 January. *<http://www.discover.de/discalt/a/anarchist.htm>*.

Wicke, Peter, and John Shepherd. 1993. "'The Cabaret Is Dead': Rock Culture as State Enterprise: The Political Organization of Rock in East Germany." In *Rock and Popular Music: Politics, Policies, Institutions,* edited by Tony Bennett, Simon Frith, Lawrence Grossberg, John Shepherd, and Graeme Turner. London: Routledge.

Weinert, Ellie. 1999. "Rap Around the World: Munich." *Billboard* 5, June, 40.

Woldach, Stefan. 1997. "Ein unhipper Rapper auf dem Weg in den HipHop-Erfolg." *Berliner Morgenpost,* 28 April.

DISCOGRAPHY

Absolute Beginner. 1998. *Bambule*. Universal.

Advanced Chemistry. 1992. *Fremd im eigenen Land*. MZEE.

———. 1996. *Das Album!* 360°. Marketing/distribution by Intercord.

Anarchist Academy. 1994. *Anarchophobia*.Tribehaus/IRS.

———. 1994. *Solingen . . . Willkommen im Jahr IV nach der Wiedervereinigung*. Tribehaus/Community.

———. 1997. *Spiel nicht mit den Schmuddelkindern*. Tribehaus/Community.

Anonymous. 1993. *Partisanen gegen Deutschland*. Unregistered pressing; no publisher indicated.

Ärzte. 1993. *Schrei nach Liebe*. PMS/Metronome.

Cora E. 1996. *Schlüsselkind*. EMI.

Cora E (and Marius No. 1). 1993. *Könnte ihr mich hör'n*. Buback.

———. 1994. *Nur ein Teil der Kultur*. Buback.

Fantastischen Vier. 1991. *Hausmeister Thomas "D."* Sony.

———. 1991. *Jetzt geht's ab*. Sony.

———. 1992. *Die Da!* Sony.

———. 1992. *Hausmeister Thomas "D" '92*. Sony.

———. 1992. *Saft*. Sony.

———. 1992. *Vier Gewinnt*. Sony.

———. 1999. *4:99*. Columbia.

Fettes Brot. 1995. *Auf einem Auge Blöd*. Yo Mama/Intercord.

———. 1995. *Nordisch by Nature*. MZEE.

———. 1997. *Silberfishe*. Yo Mama.

Freundeskreis. 1996. *(A.N.N.A.) Immer wenn es Regnet*. Four Music.

———. 1997. *Leg' dein Ohr auf die Schiene der Geschichte*. Four Music.

———. 1997. *Quadratur des Kreises*. Four Music.

———. 1999. *Esperanto*. Four Music.

Mastino. 1993. *Brüder und Schwestern*. Age d'Or.

Rödelheim Hartreim Projekt.1994. *Direkt aus Rödelheim*. MCA.

———. 1994. *KEinE iSt*. MCA.

———. 1996. *Zurück nach Rödelheim*. Pelham Power Productions/MCA.

Setlur, Sabrine. 1997. *Die neue S-Klasse*. MCA.

———. 1997. *Du liebst mich nicht*. MCA.

Thomas D. 1997. *Solo*. Four Music.

Tic Tac Toe. 1996. *Ich wäre gern so blöd wie du*. BMG.

———. 1996. *Leck mich am A, B, Zeh*. BMG.

———. 1996. *Tic Tac Toe*. BMG.

———. 1996. *Verpiss' dich*. BMG.

———. 1997. *Bitte küss' mich nicht*. BMG.

———. 1997. *Klappe die 2te*. BMG.

———. 1997. *Warum?* BMG.

Toni L. 1997. *Der Pate*. Alternation/Intercord.

Toten Hosen. 1992. *Sascha (ein aufrechter Deutscher)*. Virgin.

Various artists. 1991. *Krauts with Attitude*. Boombastic.

———. 1993. *Hip Hop Hurra!* Prinz.

———. 1993. *That's Real Underground: 100% German Hip Hop*. Rap Nation.

———. 1995. *Cartel*. Mercury Records.

Chapter 5

Rap in Bulgaria

Between Fashion and Reality

CLAIRE LEVY

ap music is usually seen as one of the four elements of the broader field of hip-hop culture, along with graffiiti, break-dancing, and DJing (Garofalo 1990, 1996; Rose 1994). Having emerged in the mid-1970s among young black and Latino urban youth living in the South Bronx (a neighborhood in one of New York's five boroughs) initially as a local street movement, hip-hop and rap music can no longer be defined as an isolated local practice. Today they constitute a global urban subculture that has entered peoples' lives and become a universal practice among youth the world over. Listening to contemporary urban soundscapes, whether in shops, in discos, or from the open windows of passing cars, the throb of low-frequency beats under rapping voices is ubiquitous. Looking at some of the predominant visual signs of urban youth in the streets of Sofia, New York, or Tokyo, it is easy to recognize the casual fashion styles of oversized, baggy pants, sloppy T-shirts, baseball caps, and other accessories associated with hip-hop. These sounds and signs bear witness that, contrary to the brief existence many predicted, rap music has not only taken root firmly in the vocabulary of contemporary popular music, but defined itself as a specific artistic idiom in both visual and musical terms. From a local fad among black youth in the Bronx, it has gone on to become a global, postindustrial signifying practice, giving new parameters of meaning to otherwise locally or nationally diverse identities. In attempting to trace the global role of hip-hop as a complex music-dance-behavior style in the 1990s, the impact of rap could be compared with the global impact of jazz since the 1920s and rock music since the 1950s and 1960s. Along with jazz and rock, rap and hip-hop have represented a major contemporary youth

Graffiti in Sofia. Photo by Momtchil Titzin.

lifestyle since the 1980s and have to a considerable extent shaped the identity and development of contemporary popular music and culture.

In this chapter I will discuss the influence of rap on popular music in Bulgaria and how it has interacted with local social and cultural realities. As a Balkan country that has traditionally experienced multicultural interactions with the "oriental" East and the "civilized" West, Bulgaria, especially over the last century, since national liberation, has provided a highly symptomatic example of how these two cultural formations battle for dominance. In other words, the influence of rap needs to be seen as one of the various local manifestations motivated by the joining-the-civilized-world syndrome that has inevitably intensified dialogue with, or rather the cultural movement of Bulgarians toward, Western values.

Drawing on the dialogic approach to popular music history advocated by Keith Negus (1996), I will take a pluralistic approach to the dynamic nature of what is a discontinuous process, connecting the past and the future, melting fragments from outside and inside, combining global and local influences, to focus on events taking place in a given particular space and during a given specific time. I wish to emphasize the global-local dialogue — or, rather, that what has been happening in Bulgaria is not a matter of passive local responses to the global impact of rap, but a question of interaction in which the artists who participate in the process of appropriation take an inevitably dynamic position. Before analyzing this process of interaction, I would first like to interpret briefly the idea of rap as a globalized style.

RAP MEANINGS AND THE GLOBAL CONTEXT

It is hardly possible to talk about rap as a global practice in the sense of any clear stylistic characteristics. Yet rapping is a vocal (verbal) activity, and this general characteristic suggests the conveyance of meaning expressed through words. It is no coincidence that the meanings of rap often give rise to more questions than answers. Since the time of its emergence many different forms of expression have been added, and many different social and cultural filters have contributed to multiply the meanings of rap. Puzzled by the morass of rap-related meanings, one could ask, What is rapping actually about? Is it about sexism and violence, as some observers claim, or it is a folklike protest music of socially charged comment? Is it about the messages produced by marginal voices or a highly commercialized form of mainstream musical production? Is it about swaggering masculinity or racial inferiority? Is it about competitive verbal skills or silly rhymes? Is it about a sense of humor or bad boys' badass behavior? Is it about dull, repetitive rhythms or a joyful, highly danceable beat? Is it about stereotyped racial, social, political and gendered images or provocative creativity? Is it music or noise? One could go on and on like this, but none of these questions can be answered satisfactorily without bearing in mind the particular contexts in which different forms of rap are created.

In analyzing the nature of African American rap, Tricia Rose (1994) looks at the complexity of the phenomenon in the context of the postindustrial age, based on rearticulated African American cultural priorities and their interaction with modern technology. Rose explores the innovative, alternative forces of hip-hop culture, identifying some general stylistic characteristics (flow, layering, and rupture). Similarly, Portia Maultsby defines rap as "rhymed poetry recited in rhythm over prerecorded instrumental music." Rapping is rooted, she claims, in the black oral tradition of storytelling, toasting, boasting, signifying, and the "dozens (the ritualized word game based on exchanging insults)." The performance style of rappers employs rhyming couplets, rhythmic speech patterns, and the rhetorical styles of the DJs, who talk, or "rap," over music (1995: 104). However, as Rose has pointed out,

> the oral aspects of rap are not to be understood as primary to the logic of rap nor separate from its technological aspects. Rap is fundamentally literate and deeply technological. To interpret rap as a direct outgrowth of oral African American forms is to romanticize and decontextualize rap as a cultural form . . . The lyrical and musical texts in rap are a dynamic hybrid of oral tradition, postliterate orality, and advanced technology. (1994: 95)

In other words, as a vernacular form associated primarily with African American culture, rap must be seen from a pluralistic, nonessentialist perspective (Gilroy 1993). Such a perspective would enable this cultural form to be conceived of not as something frozen, in the vague sense of "that black thing" or "ethnic absolutism," but in the context of a continuum of permanent cultural exchanges in which rap has innovated, revised, and refreshed, for instance, the bluesy flavor of what other African American styles such as funk, doo-wop, or bebop formulated in earlier years. In addition, I would point out that rap music has emerged as a component of urban ghetto life. It articulated its initial marginal meanings in close collaboration between creators and consumers, bringing "the community's knowledge and memory of itself" (Rose 1994: 95). What happens, however, when the same material is mediated by MTV or other global, mainstream-oriented outlets? Rap's meanings cannot remain the same, if only because of the different cultural backgrounds of its new consumers and their different perceptions. As a result the "innocent" folklike messages implicit in boasting, signifying or the "dozens," which are rooted deeply in black oral traditions, cannot be easily understood and tend to be exaggerated, simplified, stereotyped, or perceived merely as crude sexism, for instance. Rap's verbal complexity could be regarded as foolish rhyming, its sense of humor as nonsensical, and its music as noise. Because of their strong links with the "real life" of distinct communities, rap meanings, especially social meanings, which are often expressed in a specific kind of slang, remain enigmatic to a large part of the rest of the world, even for those whose native language is English. The context of black ghetto existence remains for many behind a curtain and even becomes a source of stereotyped imitations.

In other words, the globalization process that characterizes and in many ways unifies the world today, hardly works in favor of any deeper understanding of what musical meanings, whether they come from the Bronx or

Sofia, are really about. Often this process delivers at best a series of vague, superficial notions about "others." For many young Bulgarians, for instance, rap embodies a dreamlike, Western way of life. And their fascination with black Americans' participation in rap music is hardly motivated by any sympathy for or understanding of the realities of black urban ghetto life. This fascination is much more aligned with "pinky," stereotyped ideas of the USA that can be traced back to the years when another young generation in Bulgaria had their eyes opened by rock music. America is still seen as the Promised Land, where life is easy, you can party all the time, and even crime is a matter of having fun. What today's Bulgarian teenagers see in Coolio's "Gangsta's Paradise" or in Notorious BIG's messages is little more than the power of the music and its specific rhythmic and sonic patterns. Words, lyrics, and other vocal components are heard almost exclusively as part of a purely sonic discourse.

Often these fragmented ideas feed cultural dialogues and perhaps determine the postmodern logic and cultural mosaic of our times. As I have already noted, these superficial, fragmented ideas of others' culture in rap music are inevitably fueled by the commodified production of MTV. This is an argument for interpreting the multilayered, flexible, and sometimes controversial scale of rap meanings as one that gravitates between the poles of mainstream and commodified rap production, on the one hand, and the messages emanating from local cultures, on the other. This does not necessarily mean a gravitation between positive and negative polarities. Dick Hebdige (1979) has argued that there is no absolute distinction between commercial production and creativity, but it is worth bearing in mind that mainstream culture often facilitates the stereotyping of visual and sonic messages. It is well known that black music entered MTV on a regular basis in 1983, and by the late 1980s rap had become integral to MTV's programming (Garofalo 1990; Maultsby 1995). Today MTV, which began broadcasting in Bulgaria only in 1996, is perhaps the most influential global mediator of rap imagery and sounds worldwide, but hardly the most truthful one. The point here is that in talking about local rap-influenced manifestations, we must be aware of the role that MTV has played as a dominant influence. We must be aware, in other words, of the specific nature of the cultural dialogues at play in these local manifestations.

LOCAL DISCOS: WHERE IT ALL BEGAN

Bulgarian audiences were first exposed to rap music by DJs in discos. At the time, in the early 1980s, there was no MTV in Bulgaria, nor any substantial form of access to Western pop music. The national media (there was no public or private radio or television) followed a strategy of devoting no more than 30 percent of air time to Western pop or rock music. Nonetheless top international hits (usually the most commercially successful) were finding their way to young Bulgarians. The black market in Western recordings was flourishing, and DJs were able to get "into the flow" and play "hot" material. Despite restrictive state controls on disco music repertoires, enacted in the interest of ensuring that a stable portion of national music products were played, DJs regularly broke the rules. Music selection processes were very much in their hands, and they played a leading role in the dialogue with disco audiences. But it remained a dialogue only insofar as the DJs had to be competitive in accommodating dancers' preferences. Having discovered that soul- and funk-oriented music was more appealing, more attractive, and more danceable, DJs had begun playing the hits of Michael Jackson, Terence Trent Darby, James Brown, Tina Turner, and others. It was no coincidence that one of Bulgaria's most successful DJs of the early 1980s called himself Petko the Funky.

It was this funk-oriented repertoire that developed a taste for broken or ruptured dance rhythms and for a specific, elusive, bluesy flavor. As a result, when rap entered the discos in 1984, sounds such as those of Kurtis Blow, for instance, were not perceived as unusual. The public was ready for them, while teen audiences were much more preoccupied with learning the fashionable breakdancing steps made popular by videos circulating in private clubs and by movies like *Flashdance*.

I recall a particularly symptomatic episode that sums up this shift in dance tastes. It was in the mid-1980s, at a DJ contest in a disco in a small Bulgarian town called Haskovo. The town was famous for its relatively wide ethnic diversity, which included Turkish and Gypsy communities, and the contest featured DJs competing from all over the country in front of a live audience of enthusiastic dancers. The event was striking for the dance styles it revealed: there were multiple reproductions of Michael Jackson's dance routines, and brilliant imitations of his moves were mixed with elements of breakdancing. The majority of those on the dance floor assumed the role of supporting background, while the soloists in this spontaneous happening performed acrobatic moves such as backspinning and headspinning. The supporting crew simply jumped and moved their legs, but they adopted the new breakdancing style. Watching this event I realized that something had profoundly changed on the dance floor. The style was different, the dance steps were different, and, of course, the rhythm was different—different from, say, the established flat disco rhythm of the 1970s (represented largely in Bulgaria, for instance, by groups like Boney M), and characterized by

Garofalo as "rhythm without blues" (1996). Watching the crowd dancing, I also noticed that ethnicity was not quite irrelevant to what was going on the dance floor. The ethnic backgrounds of the dancing teenagers were hardly recognizable, and the government policy at the time of national integration appeared to be working effectively, but still I noticed, without being unnecessarily ethnocentric, that the Gypsies were much more skillful dancers. Their solos were more creative, and they appeared to contribute more effectively to the local appropriation of this new dance style. They were clearly bringing into play a natural sensitivity that openly celebrated their pleasure at participating in both music and dance. Of course, this sensitivity was not unfamiliar. It was another expression of what African American music, since the days of the minstrel shows in the nineteenth century, has continued to give dancers all over Europe (Mutsaers 1998), blended in this case with a local "oriental" dance tradition that has survived among the Gypsy population in Bulgaria. This sensitivity, usually interpreted by Europeans in terms of "emancipating the hips and the body," is closely related to local belly-dancing *(kjuchek),* which—although in a different stylistic way—also stimulates enjoyment in moving the body.

This episode served as a reminder of the beginning of the appropriation process of one particular dance-music-behavior activity among Bulgarian youth and also indicated some of the similarities between the inventors of hip-hop and their counterparts and followers in this distant region of Bulgaria. As in the South Bronx, breakdancing was the first hip-hop element to be adopted by Bulgarian youth. The craze was so widespread that for a while special breakdance schools were opened. And again as in the South Bronx, DJs led this hip-hop movement. Because of the increasingly important role of discos as a special terrain for social contacts in Bulgaria from the mid-1970s on, DJs had become important artistic figures. Some of them were real entertainers, gaining pop-star status, which motivated them to be more competitive and inventive. Soon the practice of mixing different recordings and "rapping" live over them became fashionable. In this way DJs began to intervene in the process of music making, adding distinctive scratching, breaking, and rupture effects. Although modern DJ technology was still a luxury, over time a kind of formalistic techno approach became common practice amongst Bulgarian DJs. Discos created the climate necessary for local rap-influenced music production to emerge. They changed public music tastes, updated styles of dancing, and introduced a different, techno-based approach to music making.

It is interesting to note that at the same time, DJs used a diversity of material. Because of the mixed disco audiences, they were playing mostly dance music, but not necessarily the "hottest" tracks all the time. The repertoire needed to be predominantly familiar and was usually a mosaic of British, American, French, Italian, Russian, and Bulgarian music. In the course of an evening you could hear, say, Duran Duran, Elvis Presley, Little Richard, or the Italian popular artists Adriano Celentano and Mattia Bazar, along with Bulgarian pop, rock, and even traditional folk, pieces. Within this mosaic, soul, funk, and rap music represented just some of the most energetic inflections. But this is the context in which rap music influenced Bulgarian practices. Today soul, funk, and rap are not as immediately evident in the music made in Bulgaria, at least not in any direct stylistic sense. But they have been definitely incorporated into the vocabulary Bulgarian artists and performers use in their music. They give an updated sense of color to the mosaic of Bulgarian music, in which blended voices coming from different cultural dialogues can be heard.

CULTURAL DIALOGUES

In my attempt to outline the directions in which the influence of rap has developed in Bulgaria, I find it useful to apply Negus's classification of three different types of musical dialogue that may go on at any time, in any place (1996: 145). Negus suggests that "popular musicians can be identified as genericists, pastichists and synthesists." According to this classification, "genericists" are "those performers who accommodate their musical practice and performance to a specific genre style at a particular time and stay within this," which means that "they compose and perform within the codified convention of a generic style." "Pastichists" are "those artists and performers who recognize that a new style has appeared or has become popular and so include this in their set as yet another style to be performed as part of a varied repertoire—a practice that involves the combining of stylistic heterogeneity with little coherence or logic other than the fact that some songs are popular with some people some of the time." This also relates to the way "music genres are adopted in a broad context and played among cabaret and club circuits around the world." The third category, the "synthesists," who are seen as more creative, are those "who draw on the elements of an emerging generic style but blend them in such a way so as to create a new distinct musical identity. These are not unique individual geniuses but synthesists working at the fuzzy boundaries where generic codes and stylistic conventions meet and create new musical patterns." It is often through the hard work and skilled routines of synthesists that "generic boundaries are broken and remade" (1996: 147). These different forms of dialogue suggest that different musical meanings determine the dynamic, relative, and flexible nature of cultural exchanges, and of the interactive process of music making. The categories can be identified among rap-influenced artists in Bulgaria, the most visible sector of which is the pastichists. Rap idioms and influences in Bulgaria have mostly penetrated the broad field of various pop-related musical styles. They can be heard in the music of pop singers, on some television and radio entertainment shows (sometimes involving social and political comment), quite frequently in commercials, and even in some songs included in music textbooks. The genericists, or artists operating as straight rappers only, are relatively few and belong to a distinct social niche.

THE GENERICISTS: VOICES FROM THE MARGINS

Rap "made in Bulgaria" first appeared in the early 1990s. Although not very visible on the surface of contemporary popular culture in Bulgaria, these rappers adopted a position that claimed to express the teenaged "voice" of a distinct subculture. Through their rather crude lyrics and unruly behavior and lifestyle, they largely imitate MTV-derived stereotyped images. Because of the language barrier, they are scarcely able to reproduce the humor involved in black male boasting and expressed through black slang. Instead, they openly glorify ugliness, violence, and masculinity, with little awareness of the real social contexts that create some of the socially charged African American rap messages. Addressed to teenaged audiences, this kind of Bulgarian rap from the margins reveals little more than a sense of inferiority, which is understandable in terms of the psychology of teenagers. Such attitudes among teenagers are motivated not so much by hip-hop influences as by the harsh local social environment in which increasing rates of crime, violence, unemployment, and poverty make some young people, especially in the urban areas, feel vulnerable and helpless.

A more prominent representative of the genericist trend is the Varna-based male rap group Goumeni Glavi (Rubber Heads), who released four albums between 1994 and 1997. Musically, their most recent album, the title of which translates as *For More Money* (1997), is their most successful in terms of getting the "right" rap sound. Their stick-to-the-rules techno approach and use of pop and dance samples, including ABBA's "Money, Money" and the 1950s track "Tequila," show them to be seeking a wider local audience, and the album also includes some material reminiscent of the recent local ethnopop fad, also known as *chalga*. But in ideological terms the album represents another apology for vulgar, crude sexism and pornography. The position it takes could be read as a reflection of confused values in a time of transition. Since the "big change" in Bulgaria that has taken place since

Goumeni Glavi (Rubber Heads). Courtesy of Payner Record Company.

1989, moral values have been seriously questioned and often dismissed as old fashioned or as a residue of the defeated socialist ideology of the former regime. The new value system espouses a vulgar pragmatism that is seen as leading Bulgarians into the "civilized" world. Similar ideologies can be observed in ethnopop, which nonetheless interprets the expansion of pragmatism with a sense of humor and from a clearly expressed ironic perspective (Kurkela 1997).

But in the case of Goumeni Glavi, the values of the new pragmatism are brutally manifested and expressed in a vocabulary that has the capacity to scandalize even people who consider themselves open-minded and non-puritanical. It is obvious that Goumeni Glavi use this vocabulary as a self-promotional challenge; the cover of one of the band's albums bears the warning "Parents, watch out! Dirty words!" The question, of course, is not merely one of dirty words. It is well known that many forms of folkloric music (so why not modern pop?), including Afro-American and Bulgarian folk, in both its rural and urban forms, contain similar vocabulary. It is interesting to note that in the 1930s, for instance, urban folk forms, blended with the then-modern popular music of the West, gave birth to some new hybrid forms of popular music in Bulgaria. But compared to the way today's Bulgarian rappers use dirty words, suggesting a form of verbal onanism, the old "dirty folk" music seems rather innocent. Whereas the verbal forms in Bulgarian "wet" folk involve witty verbal tricks and a strong sense of humor, Goumeni Glavi do not rely on any sense of irony or creative imagination, and their messages are delivered in a straightforward, serious fashion. And unlike the traditional dirty rural or urban folk repertoire, which was most often performed in private, their dirty messages are presented in public.

Goumeni Glavi's rapid rise in popularity, despite their rather poor production values, was followed by a similarly rapid decline of interest in them. This is reminiscent of the post-1989 epoch, when, in an immediate reaction against former taboos in the mass media and Bulgarian culture as a whole the magazine market was flooded for a while with both hard- and softcore pornography displayed openly in public. But as the saying goes, "Any miracle only lasts three days." Thirsty for ideological freedom and sensation, Bulgarian readers of pornography soon lost interest in this pseudo-independent, if modern, form of mass consumption. In observing the spread of rap in Bulgaria, parallels with the era of punk ideology in the early 1980s can be easily drawn. It seems as if, sooner or later, almost any destructive form of youth subculture that flaunts and challenges adult cultural conventions will inevitably be embraced by Bulgarian youth.

THE PASTICHISTS: RAP AS A FADDISH ACCESSORY

Other Bulgarian rap-influenced examples of musical production, which I would relegate to the category of pastichists, are associated not with any essential appropriation of rap as a distinctive cultural formation, but rather with fragmented borrowings of elements of rap music and its creative technologies. These borrowings can be found mostly in Bulgarian pop music, especially dance music, but also in rock subgenres or in ethnopop, which combines different local folk and ethnographic material. The common traits of these rap usages display two main tendencies: partial rapping over prerecorded instrumental music, performed in a more polished, "clean" way than most other rap music, and a combination with other generic and stylistic characteristics, where rap patterns are incorporated to provide a modern taste, as a faddish accessory to update the musical perspective. Two prominent pop-music composers have made a substantial contribution to this first type of appropriation of rap: Vladimir Naumov, a songwriter working mostly with his wife, the pop singer Elvira, and Assen Dragnev, one of the pioneers of the new technologies introduced into Bulgarian pop-music production, who works closely with Bogdan Tomov, a pop singer and host of television entertainment programs. These two composers explore territory in which the late female songwriter Zornitza Popova left significant creative traces. It is interesting to note, however, that they are influenced in a secondhand way, rather than directly, by U.S. rappers. They follow motifs used by pop groups such as New Kids on the Block or East 17 or by pop stars such as George Michael. Naumov and Dragnev have been active for a number of years and demonstrated a creative approach that aims to update their music by blending in elements of the hottest tendencies in Western pop. Since the beginning of the 1990s, and especially over the last few years, they have appropriated rap to give their songs a special flavor.

"Rapping actors" describes another trend of pastichists, one associated with the music presented on television shows produced in the style of political cabaret. The music of one such show, called *Kanaleto*, includes songs that could be described as political satire, which are sometimes based on rap elements and display an intelligent sense of humor. Usually the musical material incorporates a local, recently revived ethnographic flavor, and the result conveys a clearly identified sense of place and time. One of the recent hits on *Kanaleto* was a cover version of "I'll Be Missing You" by Puff Daddy sung in Bulgarian, substituting comical lyrics about the 1998 World Soccer Championship in France. In it, the rapping actors parodied images of some of the most popular Bulgarian soccer players. Rapping actors also fronted another popular television show in a political cabaret format, *NLO* (UFO), which also succeeded in keeping alive some of the best Bulgarian carnival and comedy traditions, including street improvisation.

Rap music patterns and techno effects have also penetrated the practice of a number of other Bulgarian actors and pop singers, as well as ethnopop —a field revealing unpredictable intercultural interpretations and freely combining diverse ethnic material, including "oriental" material. Yet, for the present at least, I would hesitate to suggest that there are sufficiently strong Bulgarian examples for it to be classified as an organic expression of a rap-influenced synthesis, at least not in the way some observers see such examples in France or Italy (e.g., Mitchell 1998). However, at the time of writing a video clip premiere has appeared on television presenting a new rap piece performed by two charming children (in English) and written by a DJ calling himself "Dance Machine." The piece is impressive not so much because of its use of a Bulgarian folk tune, but rather because of its other audiovisual aspects, which correspond to a sense of local identity in a quite organic way. Called "Katerina," perhaps in search of an echo of "Macarena," it gives cause for hope that real Bulgarian rap synthesists will appear soon, most probably from the ranks of the most skilled and creatively attuned pastichists. At the end of 2001, there are signs that this is occurring. The frontman of Goumeni Glavi, Misho Shamara (Misho the Slap) has embarked on a solo career, and rap in Bulgaria appears to be a much more creatively developed practice. New local groups have mushroomed, including Upsurt (a humorous slang metamorphosis of the word "absurd"), Momcheshki Sviat (Boy's World), Romanetza I Enchev (the Romanian and Enchev), and Igrachite (The Players), a group with a strong female presence, among many others.

REFERENCES

Frith, Simon. 1981. *Sound Effects: Youth, Leisure, and the Politics of Rock 'n' Roll.*
    New York: Pantheon Books.
———. 1988. *Music for Pleasure.* Cambridge: Polity Press.
Gaitandjiev, Gencho. 1990. *Populjarnata muzika: pro? contra?*
    Sofia: Narodna Prosveta.
Garofalo, Reebee. 1990. "Crossing Over: 1939–1989." In *Split Image:
    African-Americans in the Mass Media,* edited by Jannette L. Dates,
    and Williams Barlow. Washington, D.C.: Howard University Press.
———. 1996. *Rocking Out: Popular Music in the USA.* Boston: Allyn and Bacon.
George, Nelson. 1988. *The Death of Rhythm and Blues.* New York:
    Plume/Penguin Books USA.

Gilroy, Paul. 1993. *The Black Atlantic: Modernity and Double Consciousness.* London: Verso.

Hebdige, Dick. 1979. *Subculture: The Meaning of Style.* London: Routledge.

Jones, LeRoi. 1963. *Blues People: Negro Music in White America.* New York: Quill.

Kurkela, Vesa. 1993. "Deregulation of Popular Music in the European Post-Communist Countries: Business, Identity, and Cultural Collage." *World of Music* [journal of the International Institute for Traditional Music] 35, no. 3: 104.

————. 1997. "Music Media in the Eastern Balkans: Privatized, Deregulated, and Neo-Traditional." *Cultural Policy* 3, no. 2: 177–205.

Levine, Lawrence W. 1977. *Black Culture and Black Consciousness.* New York: Oxford University Press.

Levy, Claire. 1996. " African-American Music: A Generator of Dominant Music Idioms." *Bulgarsko Muzikoznanie* 3–19.

————. 1998. "Popular Music and National Identity: Bulgarian Radio in Transition." In *Music on Show: Issues of Performance,* edited by Tarja Hautamäki, and Helmi Järviluoma. Tampere University, Department of Folk Tradition.

Maultsby, Portia. 1995. "Music in African-American Culture." In *Mediated Messages and African American Culture: Contemporary Issues,* edited by Venise Berry, and Garmen Manning-Miller. Thousand Oaks, Calif.: Sage Publications.

————. 1996. "Music." In *Encyclopaedia of African-American Culture and History,* vol. 4, *1888–1907,* edited by Jack Salzman.

Middleton, Richard. 1990. *Studying Popular Music.* Buckingham: Open University Press.

Mitchell, Tony. 1998. "Questions of Style: Notes on Italian Hip Hop." In *Music on Show: Issues of Performance,* edited by Tarja Hautamäki, and Helmi Järviluoma.

Mutsaers, Lutgard. 1998. "Audience and Performer Roles During Dance Crazes." In *Music on Show: Issues of Performance,* edited by Tarja Hautamäki, and Helmi Järviluoma.

Negus, Keith. 1996. *Popular Music in Theory.* Hanover, N.H.: Wesleyan University Press.

Robinson, Deanna Campbell, Elizabeth Buck, and Marlene Cuthbert, eds. 1991. *Music at the Margins: Popular Music and Global Cultural Diversity.* Newbury Park, Calif.: Sage Publications.

Rose, Tricia. 1994. *Black Noise: Rap Music and Black Culture in Contemporary America.* Hanover, N.H.: Wesleyan University Press.

Small, Christopher. 1987. *Music of the Common Tongue: Survival And Celebration in Afro-American Music*. New York: Riverrun Press.

DISCOGRAPHY

Elvira. 1993. *Nai-hubavite pesni* [The Best Songs]. Musa/Mega Sofia.
Goumeni Glavi. 1994. *Kvartal # 41* [District No. 41]. Melomania.
———. 1995. *Goumi vtora upotreba* [Second-Hand Tires]. Melomania.
———. 1997. *Za poveche pari* [For More Money]. Payner.
Gypsy Aver. 1994. *Imam li dobur kusmet?* [Do I Have Good Luck?]. Video Total.
Kanaleto. 1997. *Francia zdravei!* [Hello, France!]. Bulgarian Music Company.
Tomov, Bogdan. 1993. *Za malki I golemi* [For Kids and Adults]. Unison Records.
Popova, Zornitca. 1993. *Chestni sini ochi* [Pretty Blue Eyes; songs performed by Bulgarian pop singers]. Balkanton.

Chapter 6

Rap in the Low Countries
Global Dichotomies on a National Scale

MIR WERMUTH

ince the early 1980s, rap music has become a worldwide phenomenon from Senegal to Tokyo, Paris, and Amsterdam. With its own unique hip-hop lifestyle (including specific codes of dress, hairstyles, footwear, and dance, as well as ways of walking and talking), rap has invaded global popular culture and has had an enormous impact on both pop and rock music.[1] In this chapter I want to explore and explain the popularity of hip-hop within a particular national setting. I am interested in how young Dutch people experience rap music, why they are involved in hip-hop culture as fans or artists, and how their fandom is constructed. Rap music and its accompanying hip-hop lifestyle has been mostly discussed by academics as a U.S. subculture or mass product within the boundaries of the U.S. context (see, e.g., Rose 1994; Toop 1984; George 1993; Kelley 1994; Shusterman 1991). Only a few attempts have been made to place European or Asian rap on the global map (e.g., Jacob 1993; Baker 1990; de Kloet 1993; Gilroy 1995; Sharma et al. 1996; Heijmans and De Vries 1998). The lack of attention given to the international reception of rap attested to by this relatively small amount of writing compared to articles and books on the production and reception of other forms of popular culture, such as television soap operas in different countries (Katz and Liebes 1985; Ang 1985; Herzog Massing 1987) is surprising and disappointing. In terms of rap's popularity, historical tradition, and cultural significance, it is time its cultural conditions outside of the USA received more attention. One reason for the academic neglect of European rap lies in discussions about authenticity. In general most popular culture is judged in terms of "authentic" versus "unauthentic." As Iain Chambers has put it:

Buried deep inside the criticisms and condemnation of "mass culture" is an underlying belief in the idea of "authenticity." Use of the word authenticity implies that there exists the possibility of a direct relationship between our actions and our ideas, that the former express something that is essentially immediate and natural. It is against this particular measure of the "truth" that modern culture [particularly popular or mass culture] is found to . . . be fundamentally "false, and therefore unnatural." (Chambers 1990: 313)

The result of this view on popular culture (see Theodor Adorno's 1941 article on pseudo-individualization in popular music [Adorno 1941]) is that popular culture has often been associated with negative values.

The outcome of discussions about authenticity is more specific if we look at the importation of American goods into Europe after World War II, owing to Europeans' perceived desire to imitate U.S. styles (van Elteren 1994). Imitation is always considered unreal, unauthentic, and unnatural. But discussions about authenticity are not only carried out in academic projects. Pop fans also judge their idols as "sincere," spontaneous, "real," and "direct" (Lewis 1992; Vermorel and Vermorel 1990). According to Negus (1992: 70), it is "the irony of consumption that, as audiences, we acknowledge that our favorite artists, whether Bob Dylan, Public Enemy or Madonna, are studied, calculated and hyped in various ways, but at the same time we accept them as 'real'."

Within the rap community this ambiguous relationship with authenticity is also an issue, one that takes on specific forms in the context of a small European country such as the Netherlands. In this chapter I want to describe how discussions about authenticity appear in particular dichotomies relevant to the Dutch rap community: the local versus the global, artistic integrity versus sellout, masculine versus feminine, and black versus white, whereby each first-mentioned term is associated with the good and positive qualities of the music. In analyzing these dichotomies, I hope to show how a U.S. cultural product acquires meaning within a different national context. I will also discuss how the dichotomies interact with commercial success, racial awareness, and acceptance of the genre on a national level.

If we consider authentic cultural expressions real, natural, and original, Dutch hip-hop cannot, by definition, be authentic. The answer to the question of where rap is really from, where its roots lie, is that it is perceived as a U.S. phenomenon, or often, more specifically, as an African American phenomenon. How do Dutch hip-hoppers deal with this knowledge? What does it mean to be involved in a subculture that cannot be "original"? These questions have been central to my research into the role of the media in the construction of subcultural identities, and in particular the hip-hop subcultures of the United Kingdom and the Netherlands. This research has consisted of interviews with rap producers and audiences and participant observation in record shops; at rap, swing beat, ragga, and jungle music concerts; and at other meeting places such as cafés and shopping malls. I have also done qualitative content analyses of rap videos and the representation of rap in daily newspapers, music magazines, and fanzines. A third aspect of my research has involved quantitative content analysis of the share of U.S., Dutch, and (other) European rap hits in the national Dutch charts between 1980 and 1998. Discussions about authenticity have played an important role, in all three parts, but they are most striking in the interviews I have done with Dutch rappers, DJs, and fans. Most of the examples and illustrations in this chapter are taken from these interviews.

THE COMMODIFICATION OF RESISTANCE

Despite its small size, Holland, together with Great Britain and Germany, is one of the biggest European markets for U.S. pop music. Dutch audiences spend a relatively large amount of money on records (with a turnover of 1.113 billion guilders—about U.S. $500 million—in 1996, the Netherlands are among the top ten countries in the world market). In addition, Holland plays a leading role in U.S. artists' breaking into the rest of Europe. Only 29 percent of the artists in the Dutch pop music charts are Dutch: "Dutch consumers spend much more money on foreign-originated recordings than on recordings by 'homegrown' musicians" (Rutten 1991: 114; Rutten and Oud 1991: 123). There is also a considerable market for black dance music; 16 percent of the Dutch chart music between 1960 and 1985 can be called African American, and 64 percent originates from the United States (Rutten 1991: 103). Black dance music (soul and reggae in the 1970s, and more recently rap, swing beat, and ragga) is very popular among Afro-Caribbean people from the former Dutch colonies Surinam and the Dutch Antilles.[2]

A long period of time ensued between the beginnings of U.S. rap and its adaptation by black Dutch youth in the early 1980s. But after rap was finally adopted by black communities, Afro-Caribbean youth in Holland began to follow closely the latest developments in rap, ragga, jungle, and rapso.[3] The subcultural capital Dutch hip-hop connoisseurs acquire by reading international hip-hop magazines as well as local underground fanzines (such as *Art. 12*) makes them different from other Dutch subcultures as well as from nonsubcultural youth, and also—and this creates some ambiguous feelings—different from their U.S. hip-hop counterparts (see Thornton 1995 on subcultural capital in the house music scene). The Dutch hip-hop subculture is nowadays "in the know," but it was some time before hip-hop really took off in the Netherlands, especially when we consider the general eagerness of Dutch music fans to adopt new Anglo-American popular-music trends.

One reason for Holland's slow adaptation of U.S. rap lies in the development of U.S. rap itself. U.S. hip-hop in its early days (1975–79) emerged within a relatively small community of African American youth living in urban ghettos. Rappers, b-boys, writers, DJs, and their audiences formed a subculture based on a set of values and attitudes toward life and toward poverty, unemployment, drugs, inadequate housing, and so on. But it took a couple of years for rap to become established and adopted—or incorporated —by a wider audience. This incorporation of rap also implied a commodification. By the time the Sugar Hill Gang became popular in the USA and Western Europe, hip-hop had begun to reach a more international audience. In Holland, the Sugar Hill Gang's single "Rapper's Delight" (1980) was number 1 in the national charts. Other raps that became very popular in Holland in the early 1980s were Blondie's "Rapture" (1981) and "Wordy Rappinghood" (1981) by the Tom Tom Club (two members of the Talking Heads). These two latter hits are examples of works by white rock artists who appropriated rap in a more commercial rock idiom.

The commodification of rap has been a prerequisite for the export of rap to other countries. Rap in Holland has only become known, experienced, and produced on a national scale because of the export of U.S. records and artists as well as commercial Hollywood movies such as *Colors*, *Breakdance*, and *Electric Boogaloo*.

HAARLEM, HOLLAND, VERSUS HARLEM, NEW YORK

Being a rapper or hardcore rap fan has not been easy in Holland. Outsiders are constantly pointing out that rap is American, and so if you are not you must be an imitator. This discussion is as old as Dutch rock history (see van Elteren 1994). The USA has played a dominant role in the global production and distribution of consumer articles and is still important in dispensing "America" around the world. But after forty years of homemade pop music in the rest of the world, it is nonsensical to dismiss appropriations outside the USA as mere imitation. The whole Western world (and, increasingly, other parts of the globe too) has become fascinated by popular culture. Since the USA has the longest traditions and the largest and most numerous popular-culture industries, Americans have been able to export more of it to the rest of the world. This is simply a reflection of the economic and political power of the United States.

U.S. popular culture has become global popular culture. But globalization does not mean uniformity. All global popular culture genres have national and local variants (see Wallis and Malm 1984). And the more globalized the world gets, the more popularly oriented local culture becomes. The unification of Europe, which will reach its peak with the introduction of the Euro in 2002, has culminated in widespread discussions about the survival of the national identities of the countries involved and led to a resurrection of local folklores. Dutch soap operas are far more popular in Holland than the U.S. soap *The Bold and the Beautiful*. And not only soap operas, but also other forms of popular culture, including sports, are gaining in popularity. So one cannot speak of a mere opposition between the local and the global, since they augment each other. Except perhaps in the case of homemade rap. Until the late 1990s, the Dutch record-buying audience did not take much to rap from the Low Countries. Perhaps this was because it was too hardcore or too "black." There have only been a few black Dutch artists, such as the pop singer Ruth Jacott, who have achieved any degree of popularity and fame.[4] Rap is a genre with a strong black awareness, and this may be too threatening for Dutch music consumers. But at least we buy black American records: the Wu-Tang Clan, Tupac Shakur, and the Fugees have all found a ready market in Holland.

In almost every other European country there are devoted rappers who rap in their own language, although it may not be their first language. This is the case in France (MC Solaar, NTM), Germany (Die Fantastischen Vier, *Krauts with Attitude*), and Spain (Tzaboo). Even British rap has its own local and national input using regional accents, such as the cockney-inflected London Posse. Dutch rap, however, is almost completely based on American slang (e.g., 24K, Def Real, Postmen, Da Grizzlies). There have been some extremely negative reactions in Holland to non-U.S. rap. Dutch rapper Boosta: "You have to stick to the rules of hip-hop. Hip-hop has its origins in America, so you have to rap in American slang. That's the rule." Another reason for this apparent hostility toward the national language may be that compared with other European countries, Dutch people lack strong feelings of national identity in general. Owing to foreign influences in both the past and the present, the Dutch language is larded with French, German, and English words.

Only since the mid-1990s have things begun to change in the Dutch rap community. A growing number of black and white rappers have begun to write their rhymes in Dutch as, for example, on the compilation CD *Nederhop groeit* (Netherhop Grows). This is the result of the growing popularity, mainly outside the Randstad, of the white Dutch crew Osdorp Posse (OP), named after a district of Amsterdam. The Osdorp Posse not only rap in Dutch, but also refer to typically Dutch social and cultural events and people, such as the Dutch royal family in their track "Willem, de hardcore koning" (William, the Hardcore King). Various media commentators have referred to OP's lead rapper Def P as a serious contemporary urban poet, which is remarkable, since his streetwise Amsterdam slang is not understandable to all. But the popularity of homemade rap could only expand if it became more Dutch in content and form. By content I mean lyrics written in Dutch or lyrics about Holland; by form I mean the iconography (Goodwin 1993: 32–36) of artists' performances, such as music videos shot in a Dutch landscape, or rappers wearing a Dutch soccer cap instead of an American baseball cap.

This is exactly what has happened since 1994. Although the Osdorp Posse still play an important role in the Nederhop subculture, they have remained relatively unknown to a mass audience. They prefer to stay underground and remain signed to an independent label, and in 1998 they set up their own independent label, Ramp Records. Owing to their distrust of the national public pop-radio station, Radio 3, and other similar commercial outlets, they have never released a hit single, and as a result have never appeared in Dutch record charts. But a number of other rap acts have: Extince, Odie3, E-Life, and the Postmen are examples of both male and female, black and white, and Dutch- and U.S.-influenced hip-hop acts that have reached the charts. Apart from Odie3, a female rap act produced by two dance-oriented musicians (known from their earlier worldwide hit "Rock Me Amadeus"), all these acts have had a long history in the hip-hop underground but have managed to cross over to a wider audience. There are two main reasons for their success. One is that since the mid-1990s, hip-hop has generally become more popular among a mass Dutch audience, which has smoothed the way for Dutch rap and hip-hop. The other reason lies in the attractiveness of typical Dutch elements interwoven into the iconography and performance of these hip-hop artists. Extince's extremely humorous rhymes flow in a very soft southern accent (southern Dutch is more fluent and softer and has more regional dialects than the Dutch of other regions of Holland). His first hit single, "Spraakwater," weaves a single extended metaphor around the theme of delivering his rhymes. The title is a play upon the word "mouthwash." The 1998 hip-hop surprise in Holland was the Postmen, whose song "Cocktail" was enormously successful. Their style is a mixture of reggae and rap, and their video was shot in the sunny Dutch Caribbean, generating the right ingredients for a summer hit. And although their musical style attracts a wider public than does the Dutch hip-hop underground, they still hope to appeal to that niche audience with their combination of Rastafarianism and message rap lyrics. As their frontman, the Anonymous Mis, states:

> In our rap lyrics we address particular people [reggae and rap fans]. Our rhymes are meant to be positive, as opposed to most American lyrics. By rapping about guns and shit like that, I try to warn people about violence. It's not as dangerous here as in the Bronx, but there's a lot of criminality in Amsterdam and my hometown Rotterdam. Drugs and guns are everywhere, and we rap about watching your back, about Rotterdam street knowledge. I understand that people want to adjust to Babylon, to the system, just to survive, but in our music we try to show that there are alternatives, positive things to get out of your life. Postmen are not three angry ghetto homeboys, but we are very serious guys.[5]

The solo rapper E-Life also celebrated his first chart success in 1998. His single "More Days to Come" is also a mixture, but this time of R&B and hip-hop. But his success is not so surprising if we consider the global popularity of Puff Daddy and his offspring. This brings me to the question of whether chart success merely dilutes underground musical styles.

SELLOUT VERSUS ARTISTIC INTEGRITY

A group of Dutch rap diehards has generated an ongoing debate about whether rap has sold out and which rap crews remain true to the original intentions of hip-hop culture. Will E-Life and the Postmen be accepted by their hip-hop peers? Extince was savagely dissed after the release of "Spraakwater" by his former friends the Osdorp Posse: the OP released a parody of "Spraakwater" called "Braakwater" (*braak* = vomit). The discussion has its roots in the founding years of Dutch hip-hop. After a period of imitating U.S. breakdancing and rapping over popular and well-known beats (1980–82), Dutch rappers started writing their own lyrics. Later a number of DJs began producing their own beats and samples. They considered themselves to be innovators and original artists on the Dutch rap scene. By 1982 the Dutch hip-hop subculture had arrived, and local rappers had progressed past the imitation phase. Until the mid-1980s, rappers and breakdancers were able to earn considerable sums of money by performing in clubs. But the club audiences gradually drifted away when the appeal of hip-hop began to fade. The period that followed was a tough one. On the one hand, U.S. rap had developed into hardcore rap, with deafening beats and a tendency toward black political awareness instead of bragging and party raps. This new form of rap was no longer popular in clubs because it was hard to dance to, and the message

rhymes were too difficult to sing along with. On the other hand, performing conditions and record deals were entering a difficult period in the
Netherlands.

Between 1982 and 1988, as a result of the growing unpopularity of hardcore rap, the Dutch rap community consisted of a couple of hundred homeboys and fly girls scattered around the country. They remained based mainly
in the urban areas of the Randstad (economically the most developed part of
the Netherlands and also the region where most of the people from the former Dutch colonies and other migrants live) but chose to retreat into a kind
of isolation. Dutch rappers began to organize their own parties and contests
and created their own meeting places. As a result this group of individuals
organized themselves into a permanent subculture with specific rules. In its
subcultural reaction to poor production conditions and its response to developments in the genre in the USA, Dutch rap became synonymous with
"bass—how low can you go?" and "as hardcore as you can get."[6] Dutch rappers tried to get as close as possible to what they perceived as the origins of
rap. They were also strict in following hip-hop's subcultural rules of behavior, dress, and music preferences.

Any rapper who shook off this yoke and tried to come up with something
different was accused of selling out. These accusations intensified when,
from 1988 on, hip-house became popular in Holland.[7] Suddenly talent scouts
began showing up at rap concerts looking for new MCs who could rap one-
liners over hip-house records. A number of rappers signed deals with commercial producers, hoping that after one hit they would be able to record
their own more hardcore material. Usually this turned out to be an illusion.
Up to the mid-1990s there was only a handful of hardcore rappers who enjoyed any (relative) success with their records (e.g., King Bee, Osdorp Posse,
DAMN, and 24K). The most successful Dutch rap records were crossovers between rap and other more popular genres, such as house (e.g., Tony Scott's
hip-house), pop (MC Miker G's "Holiday Rap," based on Madonna's hit
"Holiday"), or rock-metal-funk (Urban Dance Squad's fusion of all these
genres). Hardcore rap was modified or mixed with other genres by talent
scouts, artist and repertoire managers, and record producers working within
the popular-music industry to make it more attractive in commercial terms.

The appropriation of subcultural signs by the mass media and the popular culture industries has always been ambiguous. Hebdige (1979: 94) identifies two forms of recuperation: the conversion of subcultural signs into
mass-produced objects (the commodity form) and the ideological labeling
and redefinition of deviant behavior by dominant groups such as the police
and the mass media (the ideological form). One form of this commodifica-

tion of Dutch subcultures was recordings by artists who modified hardcore rap. According to many Dutch rap fans, these modifications—such as using the Dutch language—made these rap artists and their music less authentic. As Pitch Master Skeen, the DJ and producer of the Dutch rap crew Da Grizzlies, put it: "My idea of hip hop is that you are wack if you rap in the Dutch language. It may sell more copies, but it ain't the real shit. The people who listen to the Osdorp Posse are not b-boys. These roughnecks listen to all kinds of music."

The same dynamic can be seen in the spectacular dress style of hip-hoppers. By the time subcultural Lugz boots began to appear in ordinary sports and shoe shops, hardcore rap fans no longer wanted to wear them. This longing for uniqueness matches the homogenous, spectacular character of subcultures. A collective identity is built up around exclusiveness and membership. But there is another form of commodification, one neglected by both subcultural theorists such as Hebdige and "real" fans: hardcore rap is released by major record companies without demands for softening the music or other mechanisms to appeal to a wider audience (which is often the function of crossover music). It fits perfectly into the rock discourse of authenticity, autonomy, and originality. On the one hand there is commodified, unauthentic rap (rap in a pop format), on the other there is hardcore rap (rap in a rock format), and both sell well in the United States. The fact that it is possible for a lot of U.S. rap acts to remain faithful to subcultural values and at the same time sell millions of records to hip-hop and other audiences is difficult for Dutch hardcore fans to accept. Rapper Boosta: "It is the Dutch media who are to blame most. They are always derogatory about hip-hop. The media have never acknowledged hip-hop as real music. That's why rap in Holland can never be as big as it is in the U.S." Subcultural diehards blame the recording industry for making rap a sellout and accuse the mass media of negative coverage, but they have no answer to the commercial success in Holland of hardcore artists such as Public Enemy, Nas, or Paris. Among Dutch hip-hoppers there is a tendency to stick to the dichotomy of commercial versus anticommercial.

Most of the Dutch hip-hoppers who perceive themselves as part of an underground subculture constantly struggle with the clichés of what hardcore is. According to them, hardcore hip-hop is something you can immediately distinguish. It is constructed in the sound, the lyrics, and the performance of "pure" hip-hop. And a commercial sound can likewise be deconstructed: "you know it when you hear it," as many Nederhoppers point out. Only when so-called pure hardcore Dutch hip-hop reaches the charts and its exponents are signed to a major record label does the dichotomy between hardcore and commercial turn out to be a paradox, since commercial music can also be rebellious, original, and authentic. Underground hip-hop has also been discovered by the high arts. Educational programs make use of rap, there are cultural debates between the Osdorp Posse and the Dutch minister of culture, and volumes of "street poetry" are the order of the day (Beryl 1997: 1998). Hardcore may still be the opponent of commercialism, but hardcore popular culture itself may turn out to be the next high culture (see also Hebdige's [1979] comparison of punk and Art).

GHETTO FEEL VERSUS FAKES

Not only has Dutch rap been restrictive in terms of its musical development, as I have shown above, but within the hip-hop subculture there is pressure to remain authentic and a longing for political correctness, which presuppose a ghetto background. In an interview the three members of West Klan all stress the importance of a streetwise bad-boy image: "We rap about things we experience in our daily lives, things from the street. Hip-hop is about real life, what is going on out there." This is one of popular music's most important myths: the notion that its musicians come from "the street." Goodwin (1993: 116) has also found that the urban fantasies of street knowledge are often to be found in rap videos.

A number of old school Dutch rappers (those who became involved in the early years) do have this kind of ghetto background. Most of them are black (e.g., Surinamers and Antilleans) and live in poor urban neighborhoods such as Bijlmer in Amsterdam or Schilderswijk in The Hague. They fit many other rap stereotypes, too: dropping out of school, being poor, coming from single-parent families, and so on. These similarities between the backgrounds of the American "originals" and their Dutch followers are not as odd as they may seem. A significant number of black Dutch youths found the role models they were looking for in U.S. hip-hop. The reggae subculture of their older brothers and sisters was not "flash" enough for the 1980s; white Dutch rock was not an acceptable option, and traditional ethnic music such as the Surinamese *kawina* and *kaseko* was out of the question because of the generational conflict between black Dutch adolescents and their parents' culture. So it was this group of Dutch hip-hop originals with their specific ghetto backgrounds who played a decisive role in laying down the rules. Several times I heard from hip-hop fans that "if you didn't have that ghetto feel, you were a fake. If you're down with hip-hop you may be white, but at least you must be part of a posse or gang from 'da hood.'" The only white youths included in this metropolitan rap image are those from the same socioeconomic background, so-called white trash. All other groups or individuals are excluded. Style, attitude, and sociodemographic characteristics determine the core of the Dutch hip-hop scene.

Most fans acknowledge that the image the subculture projects to the outside world has to be coherent and distinctive from other subcultures and non-subcultures. Raw G, a rapper from the north of the Netherlands (far away from the center of the Dutch subculture in the Randstad) sometimes feels the contempt of other, more committed rappers: "Rappers from the Randstad are more into laid-back gangster rap, that's the dominant form nowadays. Here in the north, we're more into uptempo rap. So those rappers think we are not really down with hip-hop. We are not accepted by the subculture, we are in their opinion just peasants."

The importance of such distinctions between an inner group (the right style and ghetto feel) and an outer group is essential because without these distinctions there would be no subculture at all. Rappers and fans who do not play the game according to the exact rules are the ones who are blamed most by the inner group. They project the wrong image of the subculture to the world, and so they have to be punished; they are not the real thing. For the "originals" the subculture can only exist with a clear reference to a true, original image, the image of authenticity. As Rapper Malice of Da Grizzlies stated: "You have a lot of niggers who wear baseball caps and Chipie jeans. Well, if you wear Chipie, you are not a real homeboy! And then you have all the skaters: they listen to hardcore stuff, but the skate culture is not the same as hip-hop culture. Skate culture is just fashion, it has no content."

The image of authenticity is only recognizable if a fan wears the right brands of clothes, buys records by the Wu-Tang Clan and Jeru the Damaja, watches MTV's *Yo!* and listens to the hip-hop show on VPRO national radio. All these products and media are available and accessible to anyone in Holland, but this fact does not seem to be a contradiction for the "real fan." The distinction between a real fan and a phony is difficult to define. Even for an outsider it is easy to dress and behave in the correct style, because of the availability of the products. The mechanisms of inclusion and exclusion are almost invisible, but Dutch rap diehards constantly draw distinctions between their subculture and others. The rate of circulation of subcultural goods is very rapid. The strategy of defining and redefining the subculture has resulted in a very small number of real fans. Even for the devoted fan, it is difficult to keep up with the latest trend. This has led to a very small inner group and a large group of mere "listeners." The listeners have the same knowledge (cultural capital) about rap music but do not belong to the subcultural lifestyle. Listeners in this group are the biggest spenders and thus very important in the process of commodification of rap as mainstream music.

In Holland debates about political correctness have hardly gained a hold. You can see this in the way rappers always present themselves as "Negroes" and not as African Caribbeans. Discussions about blackness (and who is included in and excluded from the concept "black"), multiculturalism, and ethnic nationalism tend to be purely academic (see, e.g., Fennema and Tillie 1994; Gilroy 1995). Recently there has been some debate in the rap world about the "wigger" phenomenon (a contraction of the words "white" and "nigger"). Dutch audiences at performances of Ice Cube, Cypress Hill, and other black U.S. rappers, are predominantly white. White middle- and upper-class kids are down with hip-hop, skating, and graffiti without being involved in the subculture. They dress in the right style and talk about the latest Jurassic 5 album, but they are not "homies" (homeboys). Rap would never have grown as much as it has in the past few years without being received by this musical avant-garde, with its open attitude toward all kinds of new music. A lot of black rap fans see the difference between the so-called white coats (white avant-garde) and black lower-class youth in terms of class difference: "Because of their rich parents, they can afford an exclusive rap style." Black fans explain the differences only in terms of class, not in terms of ethnicity. This is very different from the situation in the United Kingdom, where both class and ethnicity are problematized by rappers.

In many Dutch discussions on ethnicity and racism two groups look at each other and simply say "live and let live." This kind of approach is often found in multiculturalism (see, e.g., Donald and Rattansi 1992 on multiculturalism and antiracism), which assumes that different ethnic groups can live peacefully together. I find this view of multiculturalism too optimistic and individualistic. Although issues concerning migration are at the top of most Dutch citizens' lists of national problems, and black youth are confronted with more and more racism every day, there is hardly any stimulus for discussion in the rap subculture. In the days of "message rap" in the mid- and late 1980s, there were some Dutch rappers who rhymed about ethnic-minority issues, but once the popularity of politically conscious raps had waned, they drifted into the background.

Kees de Koning, the founder of Top Notch, the record label to which Extince is signed, states:

> There used to be a lot of solidarity in the scene. Through hip-hop I became friends with Surinam, Antillean, and Turkish people. But eventually cultures become separated, that is how our society works. In America the separation between blacks and whites is bigger of course, but it's

growing in the Netherlands. In Amsterdam you can see a kind of ghetto-ization. There is no such thing as a multicultural society. For a very long time I had this multicultural dream, because I lived in quite an ethnically mixed scene. What is striking is that now two of the three most famous Dutch rappers (Extince, Def P, and Rudeboy) are white. Most of the record-industry people are white, and so are the hip-hop journalists. There is a "whitening" tendency in hip-hop culture.

I have a lot of discussion with black hip-hoppers. Sometimes they ac-cuse me: "wat weet jij nou van hiphop, kankerblanke?" [what do you know about hip hop, white asshole?]. Or: "being down with hip-hop is a luxury for you and other white people. If it ain't working out good for you, society will always have some space left for you. For us blacks, hip-hop is the only opportunity to win a place in the sun." I don't believe in a multicultural solution; the core problem is that qualified black people just don't get the opportunity to prove themselves. (Interview by the au-thor 1996)

De Koning's observations about the changes in the Dutch hip-hop commu-nity are accurate. Since the popularity of the Dutch-language "metal rap" of Osdorp Posse and their friends, there has been a growing separation in the Dutch hip-hop subculture. Generally speaking, the audience for metal and noise rap consists mostly of white fans, while soul-, reggae-, and R&B-oriented hip-hop attracts mostly black audiences.

"SLACK" LYRICS VERSUS FEMINIST AWARENESS

Opposition between masculinity and femininity fits neatly into discus-sions about authenticity. In almost every genre of popular music, males pre-dominate as the originators. Male artists in any given genre are usually the first to become successful. The output of women artists is often seen as an imitation of male versions. Male artists are regarded as true, original, and authentic. Masculinity is usually associated with rock, femininity with pop.

In the case of rap the situation is not much different. After twenty years of American rap there are far more male than female rappers, and new sub-genres are mostly developed by men. Like U.S. rap, most Dutch rap has been gangsta rap and rap boasting about male sexual prowess. In the early days there were large numbers of all-female crews, but as time went by a lot of these fly girls moved out of the subculture. They now have children or boy-friends or have become involved in more female-friendly music styles such as swing beat and R&B (Wermuth 1994b). Swing beat could be seen as a pop variant of black dance music. So the division between male and female appears little different from that in other countries where hip-hop exists, including the USA. In a video documentary I made in 1991, female rappers stated that rap had made them more independent, stronger, and more equal to men. In spite of the negative images of women in rap, hip-hop gave these girls a feeling of empowerment (see also Lewis 1992; Guevara 1987; Roberts 1990). Empowerment can be understood as the construction of identity and authority (Hermes 1989: 289). The latter refers to institutional power and to an individual, subjective "form of knowledge" (control of specific areas of knowledge, i.e., the hip-hop subculture). The investment female fans make in rap music gives them a certain feeling of control over their personal lives, in terms of both ethnicity and sexuality. Rap fan Boogie remarks:

> There are a few girls into hip-hop, but there's not that many. I think it has to do with girls reaching a certain age when they don't want to jump around any more, they want to be more feminine. When girls get older, they prefer to go to soul and swing beat clubs. I don't like dressing up, that's the reason why I don't go to swing beat clubs. Usually you have to dress up and you get the women coming in there, jewels, miniskirts. I could be like that if I wanted to, but I don't feel comfortable with that. I feel comfortable in hip-hop crowds.

What has often been said about women in the pop-music industry—namely, that all they need is a pretty face and a well-shaped body—does not apply (if it is true at all) to Dutch female rappers. Women rappers caught the public eye when hip-house was popular, and with 2 Unlimited, the combination of a male and female rapper was very successful; but by the mid-1990s a Dutch Salt 'n' Pepa or Queen Latifah had still not emerged. A couple of female rappers (Nasty and Odie3) did hit the charts in the late 1990s with raps in the Dutch language. Although they are still in the minority, some space has been developed for women who want to enter the hip-hop business. But this space is very limited. Both Nasty and Odie3, as well as the more hardcore hip-hop act Bitchez and Cream, have had to fulfill certain stereotypes of either the virgin (the cute little girls of Odie3) or the femme fatale (the sexy outfits and rough look of Nasty and Bitchez and Cream). The range of female imagery within the hip-hop genre is not very wide, but—surprisingly enough—the lyrics of both virgins and femmes fatales are very explicit about the other gender and sex. Male rappers may prefer to brag and boast about bumping and grinding, or about a gun—which is, as a phallic symbol, also sexually oriented—but female rappers have emancipated themselves to the same level of sexually explicit lyrics:

We know damn well what they do with little chicks like us
They have sexy sexy bodies and that makes me happy
More and more is what boys want
Short skirts and tight tights over my ass
That hungry look can't be stopped any more
One step closer and I'm gonna scream real loud
  (Odie3, "Jongens" [Boys])

As these lyrics show, female rhymes can be quite explicit, especially when we consider the age of the rappers (between twelve and sixteen), but in the end the virgin stereotype is maintained: if the boy comes any closer the girl will start screaming.

But this explicitness is not something peculiar to female rap in the Netherlands. Once or twice a year a female pop artist with tacky lyrics will hit the Dutch charts, mostly around Carnival or summer. So neither the "slack" lyrics nor the relatively small number of female artists are specifically bound to hip-hop, and the strong feminist awareness present in some U.S. hip-hop has still not found a Dutch counterpart. The way female crews such as Nasty or Bitchez and Cream perform can be considered empowering and self-conscious, but if this is the only positive result of more than fifteen years of Dutch hip-hop, it is not very substantial. There are far more and better examples of empowering female singers, DJs, and producers within Dutch R&B and techno music.

SOME CONCLUDING THOUGHTS

I have shown how rap music, as a major product of popular culture, reflects certain dichotomies in debates about popular music: commercial versus independent, authentic versus artificial or imitation, local versus global, male versus female, and, last but not least, white versus black. Most of these dichotomies can be summarized in the opposition between rock and pop (Tetzlaff 1994: 101). According to Tetzlaff "each term [i.e., pop and rock] not only denotes a category of musical style, but also a certain context of production and distribution . . . , particular fan formations, reception contexts and interpretative attitudes" (96–97). He distinguishes several dichotomies between pop and rock:

Pop	Rock
Artifice	Authenticity
Commercialized	Anticommercial
Stars and idols	Autonomous artists and community representatives

Hi-tech	Antitechnology
Banality	Poetics
Private pleasure	Cultural and political significance

The distinctions Tetzlaff uses can also be found in discussions about differences between art and mass culture. Popular music has had to defend itself for years against the low-high dichotomy, which has entered popular-music criticism itself. The double articulation of authenticity, both in relation to art and in itself, has made discussions within popular music about authenticity very complex.

Most of the dichotomies mentioned in this article are not characteristically Dutch, or even typical of the position occupied by rap in popular culture. But issues of commercialism and authenticity are interconnected with debates about the differences between pop and rock. How these dichotomies work depends on sociocultural conditions such as space (geographical locations), gender, class, and ethnicity.

In this chapter I have tried to show that the national context of the Netherlands has resulted in a very particular form of fandom among Dutch hip-hoppers. In terms of authenticity, Dutch rap fans appear to be more Catholic than the Pope. Dutch rap may resemble U.S. rap in many ways, but this has more to do with the current state of global popular culture and the absence of adequate black role models in Dutch society than with the idea of simply imitating U.S. rap. In some ways African Caribbeans living in the diaspora (e.g., Surinamers and Antilleans living in Holland) have more in common with African Americans than they do with indigenous Dutch people. The absence of black role models in Dutch music has made Dutch hip-hoppers more persistent in following the subcultural codes of hip-hop.

The Dutch national context limits similarities between U.S. and Dutch rap. Dutch rap has tended not to be as commercially successful as U.S. rap, for two reasons. Firstly, only a few Dutch pop groups have ever managed to break through to an internationally successful career. Secondly, the Dutch rap market is not as big as the British or U.S. market. It is easier to appeal to a wider audience if you already have support from your own ethnic community. Compared with support for *kaseko* music, there is little or no support for rap from the Surinamese community in Holland.

Dutch rap has also been weak politically. "Conscious" U.S. rappers have dealt with issues of race (Native Americans, Hispanics, African Americans, et al.), the educational system, welfare, class, poverty, and so on. Ice Cube's views on the Los Angeles riots in the wake of the Rodney King verdict were widely discussed in the U.S. media. But Dutch rappers have tended to neglect this aspect of rap music and have concentrated more on individual upward mobility. If they wished to belong to a subculture that was proud to be black and attempted to solve dichotomies between black and white on a national level, they would have been better off joining forces and starting a rational debate about race relations in Holland. But in their everyday lives, most black (and white) Dutch rappers have been too busy surviving and making a living. As E-Life has put it:

> I want the cash, cause I'm on that mo' money trip
> I want the 850 Beemer [BMW] and all that other shit
> Word either way, I'm gonna get my own crib
> Doin' crime or bustin' rhymes illegal or legit
>   ("Stacked with Honors")

Between 1994 and 1998, Dutch hip-hop improved considerably and became more complex musically, largely as a result of following the latest hip-hop trends, such as fusion with R&B, drum 'n' bass, and British "big beat" (e.g., Junkie XL and the veteran rapper Rudeboy). There has also been funky rap performed in Dutch, and metal rap played with live instruments. Rap from the Low Countries has grown up and matured, like any other musical genre that has been around for a while. U.S. rap is still very influential, but that is not exceptional either in the Netherlands or in global rap. But apart from the global input, a completely independent national and local hip-hop culture industry has emerged. Nederhoppers are no longer dependent on MTV or *The Source*, but have developed their own hip-hop magazines (*Art. 12* and *Magic Sounds*), radio and television programs (City FM and *The Pitch*[8]), indie labels (Ramp Records, Fat Shit Productions, Cruise Control, and Top Notch), and rap contests. The platforms rappers are able to use are more widespread and highly visible to a larger audience. This national visibility, combined with a stretching of musical boundaries and, more importantly, a gradual awareness that reaching the charts is not per se bad for their subcultural attitude, is very promising, both nationally and internationally. The dichotomies between pop and rock seem to be slowly but steadily disappearing, and dance music (not only hip-hop, but also house) has also played a very important role in bridging this gap. And perhaps black Dutch rappers have already become too Dutch, too well integrated: as the famous Dutch saying goes, "They act normal, because that is crazy enough."

NOTES

1. In subcultural theories developed by British cultural studies writers such as Stuart Hall, Phil Cohen, Paul Willis, Dick Hebdige, Iain Chambers, and others, the

four core elements of a youth subculture are dress, slang, rituals, and music (and dance). See Hall and Jefferson 1976; Hebdige 1979; Chambers 1985.

2. In 1992 there were 280,000 people of Surinamese ancestry in Holland and 92,000 of Antillean or Aruban ancestry. The total population of Holland in 1992 was around 15 million.

3. Jungle (drum 'n' bass) is a combination of "tribal" beats (related to house), ragga, techno, and hip-hop. Rapso is a mixture of Trinidadian calypso and rap.

4. There are some black stars in other popular areas, such as the soccer players Frank Rijkaard and Ruud Gullit.

5. Interview in *Live XS*, Nov. 1998.

6. "Bass how low can you go" refers to the lowest tones you can play on the bass guitar. The lower the tone, the heavier the sound. A heavy sound is considered original, true, and noncommercial. The same applies to the phrase "as hardcore as you can get."

7. Hip-house is a combination of house music and rap. In the early 1990s there were a lot of hip-house artists who had hit singles in Europe. The music of such Dutch groups as 2 Unlimited, Snap, Culture Beat, and the like is the offspring of early hip-house.

8. *The Pitch* is a weekly hip-hop program on TMF, a twenty-four-hour Dutch music video channel.

REFERENCES

Adorno, Theodor. 1990 [1941]. "On Popular Music." In *On Record: Rock, Pop, and the Written Word,* edited by Simon Frith and A. Goodwin. New York: Pantheon.

Ang, Ien. 1985. *Watching Dallas: Soap Operas and the Melodramatic Imagination.* London: Methuen.

Baker, Houston. 1990. "Handling Crisis: Great Books, Rap Music, and the End of Western Homogeneity." *Calaloo* 13, no. 2 (spring): 173–94.

Berger, Arthur A., ed. *Television in Society.* New Brunswick, N.J.: Transaction Books.

Beryl, Emerald, ed. 1996. *Double Talk,* vol. 1. Amsterdam: Arbeiderspers.

———. 1997. *Double Talk,* vol. 2. Amsterdam: Arbeiderspers.

Chambers, Iain. 1985. *Urban Rhythms: Pop Music and Popular Culture.* London: Macmillan Education.

———. 1990. "Popular Music and Mass Culture." In *Questioning the Media: A Critical Introduction,* edited by John Downing, Ali Mohammadi, and Annabelle Sreberny-Mohammadi. Newbury Park: Sage.

Donald, James, and Rattansi Ali. 1992. *"Race," Culture, and Difference.* London: Sage.

Elteren, Mel van. 1994. *Imagining America: Dutch Youth and Its Sense of Place*. Tilburg: Tilburg University Press.

Fennema, Meindert, and Jean Tillie. 1994. "The Extreme Right as Perverse Cargo Cult: Ethnic Nationalism, Social Efficacy, and the Extreme Right in the Netherlands." Paper read at the workshop "Political Communication," Politicologenetmaal, Soesterberg, 27 May.

George, Nelson. 1993. *Buppies, B-Boys, Baps, and Bohos*. New York: Harper Collins.

Gilroy, Paul. 1995. *The Black Atlantic: Modernity and Double Consciousness*. London and New York: Verso.

Goodwin, Andrew. 1993. *Dancing in the Distraction Factory: Music Television and Popular Culture*. London and New York: Routledge.

Guevara, Nancy. 1987. "Women, Writin' Rappin' Breakin'." In *The Year Left 2: Towards a Rainbow Socialism: Essays on Race, Ethnicity, Class, and Gender*, edited by Mike Davis, Manning Marable, Fred Pfeil, and Michel Sprinker. New York: Verso.

Hall, Stuart, and T. Jefferson. 1976. *Resistance through Rituals: Youth Subcultures in Post-War Britain*. London: Hutchinson.

Hebdige, Dick. 1979. *Subculture: The Meaning of Style*. London: Methuen.

Heijmans, T., and F. de Vries. 1998. *Respect! Rappen in Fort Europa*. Amsterdam: De Balie/de Volkskrant.

Hermes, Joke. 1989. "Sommige dingen doe ik alleen op uit vrouwenbladen en niet uit de praktijk. Over het gebruik van vrouwenbladen en empowerment" [Some Things I Only Learn from Women's Magazines, and Not from Practice: About the Use of Women's Magazines and Empowerment]. *Massacommunicatie* 17, no. 4: 283–304.

Herzog Massing, H. 1987. "Decoding Dallas: Comparing American and German Viewers." In *Television in Society*, edited by A. A. Berger. New Brunswick, N.J.: Transaction Books.

Jacob, Günter. 1993. *Agit-pop: Schwarze Musik und weisse Hörer*. Berlin: ID-Archiv.

Katz, Elihu, and Tamar Liebes. 1985. "Mutual Aid in the Decoding of Dallas: Preliminary Notes from a Cross-Cultural Study." In *Television in Transition: Papers from the First International Television Studies Conference*, edited by Phillip Drummond and Richard Paterson. London: BFI.

Kelley, Raegan. 1994. "Kickin' Reality, Kickin' Ballistics: The Cultural Politics of Gangsta Rap in Postindustrial Los Angeles." In *Droppin' Science: Critical Essays on Rap Music and Hip Hop Culture*, edited by William Eric Perkins. Philadelphia: Temple University Press.

Kloet, Jeroen de. 1993. "The One and Only Reason Is Fun Fun Fun??? Youth Cultures in China." Master's thesis, University of Amsterdam.

Lewis, Lisa A. 1992. "Being Discovered: The Emergence of Female Address on MTV." In *Sound and Vision: The Music Video Reader,* edited by Simon Frith, Andrew Goodwin, and Lawrence Grossberg. New York and London: Routledge.

Negus, Keith. 1992. *Producing Pop: Culture and Conflict in the Popular Music Industry.* London and New York: Edward Arnold.

Osdorp Posse. 1998. *Tien jaar O.P. en het ontstaan van de Nederhop* [Ten Years of the Osdorp Posse and the Origins of Nederhop]. Eindhoven: DJAX.

Pels, D. 1997. "Wat Nou!? Een studie naar de ontwikkeling van Nederhop" [What Now!? A Study of the Development of Nederhop]. Master's thesis, University of Amsterdam.

Roberts, Robin. 1990. "Music Videos, Performance and Resistance: Feminist Rappers." *Journal of Popular Culture* 252: 141–52.

Rose, Tricia. 1994. *Black Noise: Rap Music and Black Culture in Contemporary America.* Hanover, N.H.: Wesleyan University Press.

Rutten, Paul. 1991. *Hitmuziek in Nederland, 1960–1985.* Amsterdam: Otto Cramwinckel.

Rutten, Paul, and Gerd-Jan Oud. 1991. *Nederlandse popmuziek op de binnenlandse en buitenlandse markt* [Dutch Pop Music on the National and International Market]. Rijswijk: Directoraat-generaal Culturele Zaken van het Ministerie van WVC.

Sharma, Sanjay, John Hutnyk, and Ashwani Sharma. 1996. *Dis-Orienting Rhythms: The Politics of the New Asian Dance Music.* London: Zed Books

Shusterman, Richard. 1991. "The Fine Art of Rap." *New Literary History* 22, no. 3 (1991): 613–32.

Tetzlaff, David. 1994. "Music for Meaning: Reading the Discourse of Authenticity in Rock." *Journal of Communication Inquiry* 18, no. 1: 95–117.

Thornton, Sarah. 1995. *Club Cultures: Music, Media, and Subcultural Capital.* Cambridge: Polity Press.

Toop, David. 1984. *The Rap Attack: African Jive to New York Hip Hop.* London: South End Press.

Vermorel, Fred, and Judy Vermorel. 1990. "Starlust." In *On Record: Rock, Pop, and the Written Word,* edited by Simon Frith, and A. Goodwin. New York: Pantheon.

Wallis, Roger, and Kristen Malm. 1984. *Big Sounds from Small People.* New York: Pendragon Press.

Wermuth, Mir. 1990. "Clockin' Knowin' What Time It Is: A Study of the Hip Hop Culture in Holland." Master's thesis, University of Amsterdam.

———. 1991. "Meanwhile, at the Other Side of the Ocean, Hip Hop Culture in

Holland." *Nothing Bloody Stands Still: Annual Magazine of the European Network for Cultural and Media Studies* 1, no. 1: 62–65.

———. 1993a. "Weri man!. Een studie naar de hiphop-cultuur in Nederland" [Weird man!. A Study of the Hip Hop Culture in the Netherlands]. In *Kunst en beleid in Nederland,* no. 6: 63–112. Amsterdam: Boekmanstichting/Van Gennep.

———. 1993b. "Van pogo tot pose: Socialisatie, participatie en popmuziek" [From Pogo to Pose: Socialisation, participation and pop music]. *Boekmancahier* 5, no. 15: 38–44.

———. 1993c. "Let's Talk about Sex, Baby: Fly Girls in de Nederhop." *Lover* 20, no. 4: 224–27.

———. 1994a. "Rap from the Low Lands, 1982–1994: Global Dichotomies on a National Scale." In *Popular Music studies in a New Dutch Perspective,* edited by Lutgard Mutsaers. Amsterdam: IASPM-Benelux en Dutch Rock Foundation.

———. 1994b. "Bubbelen voor pinko's en vanilla's. Etniciteit en seksualiteit in zwarte dansmuziek" [Bubbling for Pinkos and Vanillas: Ethnicity and Sexuality in Black Dance Music]. *Tijdschrift voor Vrouwenstudies* 57: 63–78.

———. 1998. "Zwaai je handen. Over de bedrijvigheid van immigranten in de wereld van de (populaire) muziek" [Throw Your Hands Up: Immigrant Activities in the World of (Popular) Music]. In *Rijp en Groen: Het Zelfstandig Ondernemerschap van Immigranten in Nederland,* edited by Jan Rath and Robert Kloosterman. Amsterdam: Het Spinhuis.

DISCOGRAPHY

Da Definite No Remorse. 1995. *Cocktail Party*. DJAX Records.

De Posse. 1994. *Nederhop groeit* [compilation album]. DJAX Records.

———. 1996 and 1997. *Deel twee en drie* [compilation albums]. DJAX Records.

Deams. 1995. *Set It Off.* Xray Records.

Def Real. 1993. *Versatile.* Future Music Dance Department/PIAS.

———. 1995. *Potdamn, Here It Is!* Via Records.

Divorze. 1990. *Remove the Chains.* Runnetherlands CDs.

Dutch Masters. 1995. [Compilation album]. Radiola Records.

E-Life. 1998. *More Days to Come.* Dead or E-Life Records.

———. 1998. *Stacked with Honours.* Dead or E-life Records.

Empress. 1995. *This Is What You Want.* CMC Records/Soul Relation.

Extince. 1998. *Binnenlandse Funk.* Top Notch/Virgin Benelux.

Glaze. 1998. *Leviticus, the 9-Day apocalypse.* Leviticus/EMI.

Family Jewels. 1995. *Family Style.* Endorphin Records.

King Bee. 1990. *Back by Dope Demand.* Torso Dance Records.

Marvin D. 1997. *Ruvadantuv*. BMG Ariola.

Neuk. 1997. *Dopeheid troef*. DJAX Records.

No Sweat. 1997. *Dutch R&B Flava* [compilation album].
Amsterdam: Dutch Rock Music Foundation.

Northside Stylaz. 1990. *Escape from the Fridge*. Demo Produkties.

.nuClarity. 1996. *Regardless*. Off da dome Wreckords.

Onderhonden. 1998. *Subwoefers*. Ramp Records.

Osdorp Posse. 1992. *Osdorp stijl*. DJAX Records.

———. 1992. *Roffer dan ooit*. DJAX Records.

———. 1993. *Vlijmscherp*. DJAX Records.

———. 1994. *Hardcore Leeft*. DJAX Records.

———. 1994. *Ongeplugd*. DJAX Records.

———. 1995. *Afslag Osdorp*. DJAX Records.

———. 1995. *Commercieelste Hits*. DJAX Records.

———. 1996. *Briljant, hard en geslepen*. DJAX Records.

———. 1997. *Geendagsvlieg*. DJAX Records.

———. 1998. *Oud and Nieuw* [best-of album]. DJAX Records.

Ouderkerk Kaffers. 1994. *Wie zijn wij?* DJAX Records.

Phat Pockets. 1998. *The Hustle Goes On*. DJAX Records.

Postmen. 1998. *Documents*. Top Notch/V2 Records.

RollaRocka (a.k.a. Shy Rock). N.d. *No Stress*. Blue Funk/Dureco.

Spookrijders. 1997. *De echte shit*. DJAX Records.

Sprooksprekers. 1997. *Eindhalte fantoomstad*. DJAX Records.

Surkus. 1990. *Mind*. Torso Dance Records/Columbia.

TOF. 1995. *Funk It Up*. Xray Records.

24K. 1989. *No Enemies*. DJAX Records.

Umfufu. 1995. *Who's a Friend, Who's a Foe*. Mercury Records.

Various artists. 1996. *Rap van Tong* [compilation album]. Arcade.

———. 1988. *Rhythm and Rhyme*, vol. 1 [compilation album].
Amsterdam: Dutch Rock Music Foundation.

———. 1992. *Rhythm and Rhyme*, vol. 2 [compilation album].
Amsterdam: Dutch Rock Foundation.

West Klan. 1995. *Taal van de straat*. DJAX Records.

White Wolf. 1995. *Hondsdolheid*. DJAX Records.

Yukkie B. 1997. *Wat Nou!* Top Notch Records/Virgin Benelux.

Zombi Squad. 1995. *Rough and poetically*. Vinyl Vendetta.

Zuid Oost. 1995–96. *Deveterror*. DJAX Records.

Chapter 7

"We Are All Malcolm X!"

Negu Gorriak, Hip-Hop, and the Basque Political Imaginary

JACQUELINE URLA

If you want to draw lines and mark yourself off, you have to be willing to reconnect; if you want to celebrate borders, you have to learn how to build bridges and know about the alternatives.
—Juan Flores (1994)

or Basques, as for many other diasporic indigenous and minority groups, music has been an important terrain of cultural politics. In many different contexts across the globe, music is "a weapon in battles to create a cultural basis for new nations, to transform alliances and identities within already existing states, and to unmask the power imbalances that give regions, languages, and ethnic groups very different relations to the state they supposedly all share" (Lipsitz 1994: 151). In the Basque Country, musicians representing various genres, from folk to heavy metal, have played dual roles as activists in the ongoing struggle for autonomy and basic cultural rights. While a full exploration of this rich history remains to be written, here I will be focusing on the musical vision, lyrics, and style of one particular group, Negu Gorriak. One of the most popular groups of the early 1990s, Negu Gorriak has always been clear about its strong affinity with Basque nationalism and Basque language revival, which it supported by singing exclusively in Basque. Until they disbanded in 1996, one of the distinctive features of this fiercely antistate, anticapitalist group was the way they drew upon the visual codes and musical forms of nation-conscious rappers in African American hip-hop, as well as punk, ska, reggae, and raï music. In seeking to cultivate political awareness and cultural pride, Negu Gorriak used these resources to fashion a new image of a militant Basque nation that was simultaneously transcultural, hybrid, and media driven.

171

Negu Gorriak. Courtesy of Esan Ozenki Records.

What Negu Gorriak accomplished takes on added importance because the group is not unique. Many politicized white groups like Negu are tapping into the global attraction the sounds and signs of hybridized African American and diasporic music hold for youth. Some are more hardcore and politically confrontational like Negu Gorriak, while other ethnorap groups such as Les Fabulous Trobadors from Toulouse are more playful.[1] We are clearly faced with a practice that is quite extensive. How do we understand these kinds of formations? More specifically, what politics are at stake in these hybrid forms of minority cultural expression? To date, the most common framework of analysis has been that of cultural imperialism. Such theories often represent linguistic or cultural minorities as victims of a relentless and inescapable process of cultural homogenization promoted by the international marketing of mass-produced popular music.[2] It is important not to underestimate the power of the global music industry; minority-language musicians talk about it and about the pressure to reproduce Anglophone musical formulas all the time. While there is no doubt that a small number of multinationals exercise a great deal of control over the cultural pleasures and tastes available to us in mainstream culture, this chapter sides with a growing body of work in cultural studies that argues for a more paradoxical and complicated state of affairs.[3] At the same time that mass-mediated images and aesthetic or musical forms may be contributing to uniformization, they are also affording an array of semiotic resources to be appropriated and reworked into new synthetic or creolized cultural forms. Rather than assume cultural difference or identity to be a preexisting entity that is eroded or defended in response to foreign-dominated media, I want to suggest that we might more fruitfully look to the alternative music scene as an arena where political imaginaries are tentatively forged—sites where differences and affinities are produced, and power relations illumined, in and through various mechanisms of what Néstor García Canclini (1995) calls cultural reconversion. I will argue that far from being an example of Basques "losing" their tradition, Negu Gorriak is an example of how young people are engaged in a dynamic conversation about tradition, exploring and defining for themselves what it means to be Basque in the present. And I want to look specifically at how intercultural borrowing affords the radicalized youth of postindustrial Basque cities a means of rearticulating the project of Basque national liberation in synchrony with other progressive social movements and international struggles for social change.

Global flows of people, media, and music have made processes of cross-cultural borrowing a salient issue for theorists who want to understand their complex and often contradictory cultural and political significance. If cultural theorists' love affair with hybridity and transnationalism has taught us anything, it is that meanings do not reside solely in operations of the signs themselves. Rather, they are generated in the interactions that local actors, located in specific historical, social, and political circumstances, have with translocal and mass-marketed commodities, images, and processes. Hip-hop is a good example. Rap travels not only among youth of the African diaspora, but beyond them as well. And as it travels, it is picked up by youth of many different social strata, including ethnic-minority Basques, war-torn Croatians, North African immigrants in France—people who may share no historical relationship with blacks but who find in hip-hop a language, a set of resources, and knowledge with which to articulate similar but not identical struggles and concerns. And as hip-hop travels the global circuit and is incorporated into distinct musical forms and contexts, it too is transformed. Hip-hop sounds different and means different things in the Basque Country, in Paris, in the white suburbs of the United States, and in Puerto Rico. Understanding how the mass-mediated sounds, images, and signs of hip-hop acquire the social and political messages that they do for Basque youth requires contextualization. It requires looking at the social struggles, the ethnic tensions, the texture of social life, and class and gender interests that musicians and their audiences bring to the music. Secondly, we want to understand how these local circumstances place constraints on fusion. Postcolonial and minority theorists have argued with clarity that culture is not a grab-bag for everyone. As the case of Negu Gorriak will show, appropriations and border crossings are always inflected by histories of power that shape when cultural, ethnic, or linguistic boundaries are asserted, when they are transgressed, and when they are misunderstood.[4]

ROK RADIKAL EUSKALDUN

When Negu Gorriak emerged in the late 1980s, they were building upon two and a half decades of an active popular-music movement that began with the singer-songwriter movement of the 1960s and 1970s and was followed by the musical phenomenon that came to be known as Basque Radical Rock (Rok Radikal). The group takes inspiration from both of these movements. Negu Gorriak's name (the Crude Winters) is taken from a track by Mikel Laboa, one of the most innovative figures of the New Song movement, and the group shares Laboa's penchant for experimenting with musical style as well as his commitment to the Basque language.[5] Musically, the band is clearly related to the combative punk rock groups that preceded it—in particular Hertzainak, Baldin Bada, and Kortatu. Two members, the Muguruza brothers, had played in Kortatu, while the guitarist, Kaki Arkarazo, had played in the eclectic but short-lived group M-AK, prior to forming Negu Gorriak. With the exception of the bass guitar player, Mikel Cazalis, a.k.a. Anestesia, who wears the long hair of a thrasher, the rest of the group members sport the close-shaved hair, bomber jackets, jeans, and army-style boots associated with the punk movement. And like the radical rockers before them, they would address in their music many of the social problems facing their generation—problems of unemployment, drugs, and alienation. But they differ from a large segment of the punk rock scene in that their politics are neither nihilistic nor antisocial (Lahusen 1993). Rather than opting out of participation in civil society, they call for activism, militancy, and Basque cultural pride. Indeed, to call them "punk," as some authors do, is problematic at best. For while Negu would continue to reflect the musical influence of punk, thrash, and hard rock music in their work, in their political rhetoric and iconography they shifted the frame of reference, aligning themselves more with nation-conscious rappers such as Public Enemy, Ice-T, and the Disposable Heroes of Hiphoprisy.[6]

This was emphatically announced in their debut album, *Negu Gorriak*, released in 1989. The influence of Public Enemy, at the height of its popularity in 1987–90, was everywhere on the album, as was Spike Lee's film about racial conflict in New York City, *Do the Right Thing*. As Fermin explained, "[W]e had been listening to a whole lot of music, especially linked to the rap explosion. We were shocked by Public Enemy, by the force that the rap movement had, its power to criticize in the same way we had been by the punk movement in 77" (quoted in Ross 1993). In militant rap and its denouncement of North American race relations, these young Basque radicals found a new and potent language of protest. In a society deeply divided over the question of armed struggle, young militants found meaning and lessons in the African American community's debate over Martin Luther King and Malcolm X. If any of their tracks could be called the anthem of the group, it would be "Esan Ozenki," their adaptation of James Brown's funky declaration of cultural pride: "Say it loud: I'm Basque and I'm proud" (Esan ozenki: euskalduna naiz eta harro nago).

Negu Gorriak was not only saying it loud, they were saying it in Basque. Negu Gorriak is one of a handful of groups in the Rok Radikal Basko movement to extend its nation-conscious radicalism to language. Although most of the radical groups gave themselves Basque names—Zarama, Eskorbuto, Kortatu, Kontuz—and included some identifiably Basque words in their album packaging, and possibly even include an occasional track in Basque, few actually sang much in Basque (for an exception, see Espinosa and López 1993 on Hertzainak, one of the earliest *euskaldun* [Basque] punk groups). Token use of Basque is very common throughout alternative youth culture. Sprinkling in a few Basque words, talking about the *txakurrak* (dogs, police), going to the *gaztetxe* (youth house), or using Basque spelling conventions in Castilian words (e.g., *k* for *c*, or *tx* for *ch*) in *barrikada*, or *la martxa*, functions as a badge of oppositionality, allowing speakers to speak Castilian while distancing themselves from its associations with the language of the state (Urla 1997). When Negu Gorriak appeared singing only in Basque, it made a huge impact. In part, this was because two of the group members, Fermin and Inigo Muguruza, had up until then been singing primarily in Spanish in the group Kortatu. The Muguruza brothers' language background was not unlike that of many Basques living in the predominantly Castilian-speaking cities of the industrial north. Basque (Euskera) was spoken by their grandparents, but they grew up *erdaldunak* (Spanish speaking) and had to learn Basque by attending a community *euskaltegi* (adult Basque language school).

The group's decision to dissolve Kortatu at the height of its popularity, and to reemerge as *euskaldun berriak*, the term for new Basque speakers, was a deliberate political choice aimed at bringing together language militancy and nationalist pride with the oppositional culture of radical rock and rap. This was visually literalized in the way they printed the lyrics to their tracks of their first album. The words to "Radio Rahim" (a reference to a character in *Do the Right Thing*) and "Esan Ozenki" (Say It Loud) were superimposed on a facsimile of a newspaper carrying a review of Public Enemy's

It Takes a Nation of Millions to Hold Us Back by Xabier Montoia, a well-known Basque musician and poet from the group M-AK. Also in the background were a review of Spike Lee's *Do the Right Thing*, two articles on black-white relations in the United States, and two articles reporting on Basque-Spanish language politics. The parallels were intentional, and the effect on the youth music scene was explosive. Fermin, the charismatic spokesman for the group, explained their decision to the press as a question of principle: how could they continue to hold themselves up as *abertzales*, Basque patriots, and not use the language of the nation?

In the first chapter of *Black Skins, White Masks*, titled "The Negro and Language," Frantz Fanon writes that every colonized subject must face the problem of language: "Every colonized people — in other words, every people in whose soul an inferiority complex has been created by the death and burial of its local cultural originality — finds itself face to face with the language of the civilizing nation" (Fanon 1967: 18). Indeed, it was precisely Fanon's goal in this pathbreaking book on colonialism to describe how this sense of inferiority becomes attached to and expressed in everyday uses and attitudes toward language. To the degree that the colonized subject comes to perceive the language of the colonizer as more civilized, beautiful, sophisticated, or elegant than her own, she is on the path toward the profound alienation and sense of lack that, for Fanon, were defining features of a colonized psyche.

Negu Gorriak's analysis of Basque language politics follows in a very similar vein. By singing exclusively in Basque, they were throwing down the gauntlet, challenging self-identified radicals to take language domination seriously and to view it as an integral part of the struggle for Basque cultural pride and independence. They are asked about this choice in virtually every interview. What will singing in Basque mean for their distribution possibilities? How will it affect their ability to tour or reach broader audiences? In their interviews and in their praxis, group members challenge the assumption that Basque is an obstacle to communication. "For me," says Anestesia, "Euskera is a symbol of identity. I like that we can carry Euskera from place to place via our music. When we toured Italy, Switzerland, France, and Norway, we flipped out at finding that people knew the words to our tracks." As other group members point out, people are used to hearing music in languages they do not understand. Why should Basque be any different?

Nevertheless, from its formation, Negu Gorriak understood that its music would probably not be marketable through any of the normal commercial recording houses. Nor did they want it to be. From the beginning, the group has had a keen sense of the importance of financial autonomy for maintaining their political vision. They have opted for the D.I.Y. (Do It Yourself) movement growing among other alternative groups. As Fermin Muguruza explained to a British journalist:

> In the end, we record our records ourselves, release them ourselves and decide how to promote them, and we decide when we go on tour. We are the masters of our own labour. And instead of buying shares in the arms industry or in petrochemicals, as most multinational corporations do, we invest the small profit we make in our record company, Esan Ozenki, to support other groups singing in the Basque language. In order to see how different we are from the dinosaurs of rock, you have to see us play live. Nothing we've done has ever appeared on MTV. I can't imagine why. (Bousfield 1994)

In organizing their own tours through Europe, Latin America, the United States, Quebec, Japan, and Cuba, Negu Gorriak cultivated an audience in self-governing alternative communities, free radio, and squatters' buildings, and at political rallies. In San Francisco they played at the Basque Community House, while in Washington, D.C., they played at a benefit concert with Fugazi and the British group Chumbawamba and stayed with Positive Force, a nonprofit collective helping inner-city youth. They gave interviews to alternative magazines, music 'zines (e.g., *Maximum Rock and Roll*), and local radio stations. They tended to tour and play with groups that shared their political vision: Banda Bassotti from Italy, Mano Negra (now Radio Bemba) from Paris, Urban Dance Squad from Amsterdam, and Wemean, a women's rock group from Switzerland. They also played with the Occitan group Massilia Sound System and with Anhreín, the Welsh-language political rock group. Esan Ozenki also helped to create a new label, Gora Herriak, to distribute the work of alternative international groups like Wemean within the Basque Country.

In keeping with their understanding of music as a tool of consciousness raising and counterinformation, Negu came up with an interesting strategy for turning music consumption into political organizing. They did this by encouraging fans to form themselves into "brigades" rather than fan clubs. Brigades formed in Irun, Madrid, Valladolid, Galicia, Paris, and Rome. The largest of them, the Catalan Nationalists in Barcelona, raised money selling T-shirts and buttons with Negu logos, and they produced a 'zine that carried interviews with the group members, newspaper reports from various parts of the world about their tours, articles about language politics, and comics. Defying the notion of fans as passive consumers of a prepackaged image, brigade members took part in analyzing, extending, and carrying forth the task of radical social critique, to not be passive consumers, but, to use one of their slogans, "get out of the ghetto, organize your hate!" Negu Gorriak's praxis, then, was more like free radio than a music group. As conceptualized by anarchotheorists such as Felix Guattari, the idea of free radio was that of creating a communal space of discourse that would turn consumers into producers of counterinformation capable of creating sodalities that cut across boundaries of state, race, and nation (Urla 1997).

IDEIA ZABALDU (SPREAD THE WORD)

Negu Gorriak is decidedly nationalist and strongly supports the Basque language revival. But the kind of nationalism espoused by the group is one based on anti-imperialism, class consciousness, and solidarity with other national liberation struggles. Through the lyrics, music, and visual imagery deployed by these young musicians, the Basque struggle for self-determination and language revival is placed into a broader dialogue with other social movements within and beyond the Basque territory. Their tracks address a wide-ranging set of issues, from police repression and the torture of political prisoners to the alienation of life under the rule of time clocks, mortgages, and consumerism. Their track "Stop Hipokrisy," for example, speaks to the persecution of communists and homosexuals. Franco, the church, and the Spanish state are clearly some of their targets. But the group makes clear that it is Spain the state, not the Spanish people, that is their enemy. And their tours reveal that they have sympathizers despite the deluge of anti-Basque press (see Bousfield 1994).

Their critiques brought them trouble as well as fame. Taking on corruption in the Spanish Civil Guard, as they did in one of their earliest tracks, "Ustelkeria" (Rottenness), landed the group a lawsuit and a large fine of 15 million pesetas (approx. U.S. $125,000) for defamation of character of the lieutenant colonel (now a general) named in the track. Prohibited from singing the track in public, the group fought back with a new CD of the same title and a megaconcert in October 1995 titled "Hitz Egin!" (Speak!) to raise money for the fine and for the legal costs they expected to incur as they took their appeal to higher courts. Their efforts have met with a large popular outpouring of support from both Basque and non-Basque writers, intellectuals, journalists, and musicians against this infringement of freedom of speech.[7]

Like African American rappers, Negu urges its audience not to believe the hype. Like many Basque radicals, they have a deep suspicion of what passes as official knowledge. Radicals sympathetic to the goals of Euskadi Ta Askatasuna (ETA) have found themselves maligned in the press and victims

4.Zk.   **Maiatza 91+1**   100pzta.

Poterea Borrokatu

Fight the Power: Negu Gorriak fanzine. Courtesy of Esan Ozenki Records.

of a state-sponsored dirty war that for years was officially denied. Songs such as "What History Has Taught Us," from their first album, speak to this history of distortion and call upon Basques to remember that history is always written by the victors. As the track tells us, in order to "fight the power," history must be unlearned and the enemies identified. These multiple enemies are described in all of their albums, but with special clarity in

"We Are All Malcolm X!" : 179

their 1993 release "The Executioner Has a Thousand Faces." Negu Gorriak's tracks celebrate not corrupt official knowledge but popular knowledge and alliances gained through common experiences with oppression. "JFK," written by Fermin, is a track about rejecting Kennedy, to whom many Basques had looked as "our American friend." In "JFK," the "America" that Kennedy represented is cast aside as a media fiction, and new American friends emerge: Angela Davis, Che Guevara, and Simón Bolívar, among others.

This strategy of aligning themselves with others is not new. Radical Basque nationalists have a long history of linking themselves to other liberation struggles. ETA political papers from the 1950s and 1960s frequently drew examples and lessons from the Cuban and Algerian revolutions. Negu Gorriak continues in this tradition, establishing through their lyrics and visual imagery solidarity between the Basque struggle and the contemporary liberation struggles they perceive around them: that of blacks in the United States and South Africa, Native Americans, Zapatistas, and liberation movements in Central America. The track "Napartheid," from their first album, for example, establishes a line of solidarity between South African blacks and Basque speakers who find themselves fragmented into language "zones" and separate juridical entities. The track was written at a time of mass mobilization against apartheid and seizes upon worldwide attention to racial inequality and apartheid as a way of drawing attention to other forms of inequality, in this case linguistic. Through a complex layering of metaphors, the Basque towns of Navarre are renamed Soweto and Pretoria, while the white man has become the representative of Spanish nationalism and language domination. Expressions of solidarity and identification with blacks appear repeatedly in their subsequent albums, such as *The Executioner Has a Thousand Faces*, in tracks such as "Living Color" [Kolor Bizia], a diatribe against racism, xenophobia, and fascism in which they call out, "Let's not forget that we are Afro-Basques and that we will defend our sisters and brothers: Ali, Mohamed, Kepa, Ismael, and all the tribes of Zimbabwe. We will attack the misery."

Lahusen (1993) has argued that the achievement of punk-inspired Basque radical rock was to create semiotically a syllogism between the oppositions punk:society and Basque:Spain. Negu Gorriak as euskaldun radicals has added to this equation not only Euskera:Erdera (Basque:Non-Basque) but also, to some extent, a fourth pairing, nonwhite:white. Blackness, which most often stands in as the signifier of the nonwhite, works here as a key symbol of the militant. In other instances, we find the Native American in battle, as an equivalent signifier of militancy. In both cases, blackness and Aboriginality function as signs of oppositionality, more than race.

In appropriating rap, in calling themselves "Afro-Basques" and becoming, for a moment, outlaw rappers, Negu Gorriak's members are not pretending they are black. Nor are they saying, Our struggles are identical. Theirs is not a claim to a blood tie or even a common identity. In fact, in some of their tracks, such as, "We Are All Malcolm X" (a collaboration with the Galician group Os Resentidos), they even laugh at the whole idea of "blood"—the infamous Rh-negative factor that presumably differentiates Basques and has made them of such interest to human genome researchers. Like the black youth in Spike Lee's film who cry out, "We are all Malcolm X," Negu Gorriak is engaging in what Lipsitz (1994) has called "strategic anti-essentialism." They are asserting a claim of identity based on what Ralph Ellison called a shared identity of passions, not biology (quoted in Gilroy 1987: 159). Negu Gorriak's performances of a hybrid Basque hip-hop may be better understood not as Americanization or imitation but as a strategic deployment of signifiers that affords youth a window into their own situation and what it shares with that of racialized minorities.

In borrowing the image or sounds of rap, the group is also spreading the word to youth for whom issues of racism, like those of homophobia, may not seem relevant to their concerns with independence. When two members of the Malcolm X Foundation in the United States visited the Basque Country, Jarrai, the radical nationalist youth group that sponsored their visit, asked Negu Gorriak's singer, Fermin, to interview them (with the assistance of a translator) at a local free radio station. In several of their interviews, the group mentioned that the touring they do helps them not only to spread the message of the Basque struggle abroad, but also to better understand struggles going on in other parts of the world. Through touring, the group built a web of contacts with small independent producers, concert promoters, and groups who "share a common wavelength, even if we have different musical styles."[8] Are these the signs, asks the rock critic Jakue Pascual, of a Frente Popular Rockero? Perhaps, says Fermin. The groups communicate and help each other with organizing concerts and with distribution. Negu also makes direct contact with political groups. In 1994, the group went to El Salvador at the invitation of the Fronte Farabundo Martí de Liberación Nacional (FLMN), where they played under armed protection to appreciative crowds. Keenly aware of how their activities are ignored by mainstream media, the group and its brigades have been engaged in meticulous self-documentation and in so doing, have been creating a record of their politics and their tours. They regularly produced a 'zine with press clippings and interviews with foreign journalists that conveyed a sense of the larger international dialogue they are engaged in and the intercultural alliances they form. They also boast about the positive reception they have outside of Euskadi, even in the Spanish state, despite the fact that their music gets virtually no airplay.

Through what they learn, and through the status that Fermin and his group have cultivated among politicized youth, Negu Gorriak brings to Basque youth an understanding of these other struggles and modes of domination taking place beyond their borders or even in their own backyard. In an interview about the group's most recent album, *Ideia zabaldu*, Fermin explains:

> On our tour Stop Hipokrisi, we spent two months in Argentina, Chile, and Uruguay, even El Salvador. I started writing in Tijuana, Mexico. It was a few days before the Zapatista uprising began. We've traveled over most of Europe and a good part of America too. We've developed close relations with the Arab community in Europe. The lyrics talk about the Arabs we have in Euskal Herria and the ones we came to know in other parts of Europe. I had a ton of material in my head so I just started writing. (Agirre 1995: 25)

This influence is reflected in their track "Salam, Agur," dedicated to the Arabic-speaking workers who cross by the thousands through the Basque Country en route to jobs throughout Europe, or who are now increasingly settling in Basque towns like Tolosa. Although tension with Gypsies is long standing, racial conflict has not been as salient an issue in the Basque Country as it has been in Barcelona, Paris, Marseilles, or London. Negu Gorriak is probably one of the very few groups to bring questions of racism to the attention of Basque youth. The track begins with Sadia Aitelkho, a young woman from Casablanca the group members met via SOS Racism, a European antiracist organization. Though Sadia is neither a singer nor a musician, the group was nevertheless very keen on including her on the album. "These last years we have developed close relations with the Algerian community of Tolosa and Paris and we wanted to include the problems of the Arabic-speaking community on the album" (Agirre 1995: 24). Echoing the style of "JFK," "Salam, Agur" ends by calling out the names of Arab peoples—Morrocans, Libyans, and Algerians—saluting them with a bilingual Arabic-Basque greeting (*salam* and *agur*) and bringing them effectively into the transnational community of friends and comrades Negu draws around itself.

These intercultural alliances are claimed, as we have seen, through the content of the lyrics and through the incorporation of other voices on the album. They are also evoked through a hybrid set of visual and musical codes. Visually, the group borrows, as we have noted, from the iconography of black militancy. This is visible throughout their 'zines and especially in their identifying symbol the X. If we look closely, the X is formed by two axes. The ax, *aizkora,* was originally a farm tool and is used today in Basque log-chopping competitions. It is also widely associated with ETA, whose symbol is an ax encircled by a snake (see Zulaika 1988). Negu Gorriak's X visually unites the symbol of militant Basque nationalism with the X of Malcolm X, about whom they sing and whose ideas of violence as self-defense they find instructive. The cover of their album *Ideia zabaldu* is an equally dense reconfiguration of symbols. We see the figure of a woman holding a *laia,* or two-pronged spade. Like the aizkora, the laia is a traditional tool of Basque farming, here reconfigured into an emblem of resistance. The outline of a woman's body is covered with designs like the *lauburu* (a symbol of Basque identity that many people wear as a pendant around their neck), the black eagle, and the ax—all recognizable symbols of Basque nationalism. But these are painted in a design that might recall African printed cloth. The colors are those of the Basque flag (red, white, and green) with black and yellow, colors from the black nationalist flag added in. Inside the CD is a design modeled on the work of the artist and AIDS activist Keith Haring. On the back cover of the album is one of Negu's favorite images: a Yanomami man, woman, and young boy, each sporting a Negu Gorriak T-shirt.

Negu's visual borrowings transgress boundaries of the urban and the rural, first world and third world, and tradition and modernity to create a new hybridized context in which to articulate the group's concerns and alliances. Rhythmically, the group knows no bounds. They borrow liberally from rap, soul, ska, reggae, and raggamuffin without relinquishing their more classic hard rock origins. Overall, they have expanded the musical boundaries of radical rock and seem willing in their later work to let go of the more aggressive, rough sound to make room for more ballads and melodic tunes. Negu, like many other groups today, refuses categories, preferring to mix rhythms and genres on their albums. *Borreroak* (1993) was described in one interview as having a "core [that] is still rap, but there is soul, ska, salsa! heavy metal." In their latest album, hip-hop still figures as an important component, but there are more funk, fandango, and salsa. There are even some Curtis Mayfield–style falsettos from Javier Pez, a house music–acid jazz performer from the group Parafunk. The group is also known for the way in which they have inserted traditional Basque music and instruments, like the button accordion *(trikitixa),* into their tracks, and created new mixes by combining Basque improvisational poetry *(bertsolaritza)* with rap into their well-known track "Bertso Hop." They have toured with Tapia and Leturia, one of the most innovative accordion-tambourine duos, and they have promoted the group Lin Ton Taun, a group that is also creating a new fusion of pop rock and trikitixa.

Rebelling against the constraints of tradition that have relegated Basque musicians to the realm of folklore, Negu Gorriak exemplifies what Flores and Yudice (1990) have called "the art of brazen neologism," mixing rhythms and styles at will. The list of acknowledgments on their second album gives thanks to musicians as diverse as Juan Mari Beltran (a Basque ethnomusicologist), De La Soul, and Aretha Franklin, clearly indicating the transnational nature of their musical heritage.

While the group sings in Euskera, the album as a whole is a heteroglossic speech community of social movements that speak a common language of social liberation in multiple tongues. We hear this most clearly in the opening to *Ideia zabaldu*. Assisted by Manu Chao, a friend and frequent collaborator of the group, Negu begins the first cut, "Hitz Egin!" (Speak!), with a thirty-second *errefrito* (stir-fry) called "Hitzaurrea" (Preface), consisting of a collage of voices—African, Basque, English—and sounds layered on top of one another. Also on this album we get a short sampling of Spanish-language music from Silvio Rodriguez, a key figure of the Cuban New Song movement. English is everywhere—in the titles of tracks and injected as spoken and written slogans like "Power to the People" or "Do the Right Thing" in their lyrics, in 'zines, and in the videos of their tours. The voices of African Americans are also audibly present through sampling of tracks such as En Vogue's "Free Your Mind," and other prerecorded bits of rap, blues, R&B and soul music. The number and type of collaborators and hence voices on the group's albums have also expanded. Most notable is the inclusion of female vocalists, until recently markedly absent from the world of Negu Gorriak (as they have been from Basque Radical Rock as a whole). On *Spread the Word,* we find Irantzu Silva, Sorkun "Kashbad," and the Algerian singer Sadia Aitelkho, who sings in Arabic on the cut "Salam, Agur." We also have a fiercely angry critique of sexist men, "Potroengatik," written by the twenty-year-old female *bertsolari,* Estitxu Arozena.

CONCLUSION

How do we assess the new meanings hip-hop acquires as it travels to places like the Basque Country and is incorporated by musicians in various settings? How do we describe the recombinant cultural signs that are generated in the hybrid forms of rap we encounter? Are youth drawing upon, resorting to, appropriating from, assimilating, parodying, distorting, or subverting hip-hop? Are these Eurorappers, as one *New York Times* writer suggested, simply poor imitations of a fashion trend?

Perhaps some are. But it seems that the more fruitful questions can be asked only if we stop trying to separate what is authentic from what is not;

these are categories that make little sense in the current cultural context, and probably never did in the past either. Cultures in and of themselves are neither authentic nor contaminated; they are meaningful systems that are constantly evolving and contested. "Who is to say," the guitarist Kaki Arkarazo told me, "what is and is not our musical patrimony? John Mayall or Eric Clapton is as much a part of my musical culture as the trikitixa accordion." Rather than try to sort out the autochthonous from the borrowed, we need to consider the uses musicians make of hip-hop, how they understand its relationship to their own condition, and what new meanings are generated by its use.

It is important to be clear. Negu Gorriak has never tried to be a Basque rap group: their musical influences are much too eclectic and evolving. But they do feel an affinity not just for the music, but also for the social struggle out of which hip-hop emerged. "We admire black culture a hell of a lot. And we identify with black nationalism." But, they go on to say in a 1993 interview, "we [also] like hardcore groups a lot. There's a spirit in common between what they do and what we do. . . . Anyway, we're closer to, say, Fugazi, than to any rap group" (Ross 1993).

Negu Gorriak is attracted to a bit of the musical style and some of the imagery of hip-hop. But not all forms of hip-hop, and not just its style, but the social struggle to which hip-hop gives voice. In his study of African American hip-hop, Jeffrey Decker (1994) has argued that we might look upon "nation-conscious rappers" such as Ice-T or Chuck D as something akin to what Gramsci would call an organic intellectual. Straddling the boundary between entertainers and community spokespersons, these rappers retain strong ties to their communities of origin and the struggles of the urban poor. They see their music as a form of political speech against the distorted representation the mainstream media regularly puts out about African Americans. This is something Negu Gorriak and its brigades can relate to. The group had its roots in and remained connected to the social institutions and concerns of radical Basque youth culture—gaztetxes (youth houses), free radio, the antimilitary movement—both by doing surprise concerts to promote these causes and by supporting smaller groups that continue to emerge out of this milieu. What makes the appropriation of rap—or of reggae and raï, for that matter—oppositional in the work of Negu Gorriak is precisely that this historical context of struggle is not erased. Rather, it is used to help illumine power relations in the Basque situation and recognize similarities across differences.

That militant rappers have appealed to the group should probably come as no surprise. One can easily understand why, after years of armed conflict with the state's repressive forces, young Basque radicals, especially males, would find the militaristic, antipolice imagery of Public Enemy appealing. One can see how they might find notions of black pride a particularly meaningful discourse exportable to their own cause, particularly at a time when the legitimacy of the radical Basque political position has come under such sustained attack in the press and by government institutions. The support the Basque nationalist Left once had from Spanish socialist and communist intellectuals and parties at the end of the Franco regime has steadily diminished, and government inquiries have revealed that under the Socialist government of Felipe Gonzalez, the Spanish Ministry of Interior was pursuing a dirty war of illegal assassinations of presumed ETA members throughout much of the eighties. *Egin*, the daily newspaper of the nationalist Left, created in 1978 during the optimism and liberalization of the immediate post-Franco years, suffered years of boycotts and police harassment in the 1990s in its efforts to keep the perspectives of the radical Left and youth movements in the public sphere. The newspaper has finally been closed. The turn to the right in Spanish politics does not promise to bring any improvement. Youth inclined to radical Left politics throughout the 1980s and 1990s frequently found themselves criminalized, censored, and harrassed by the police as breeding grounds for future "terrorists." In this immediate context and looking at the social problems of racism and inequality that loom large in the rest of Europe, radicalized Basque youth, like many other youth in Europe, find in the language and iconography of militant hip-hop a set of concerns with police violence, nationalistic aspirations, and the media that speaks to their frustrations. Rap, as Juan Flores writes, provides a mortar of remarkable potency. "Its unifying potential has certainly been one of its strongest legacies and source of appeal among youth in countless settings across the world" (Flores 1994: 93; see also Greenawalt 1996). Using a common set of codes allows youth to literally "pump up the volume" and feel as though they are part of a larger social struggle. Aside from its imagery and political messages, hip-hop artistry also offered a stance toward mass culture that is uncommon in the nationalist Left. Sampling and juxtaposing sounds and images from popular culture, television, and so on, hip-hop artists turn commodity culture into a resource to be exploited—to be used rather than refused.

The consequences of this are not without potentially paradoxical consequences. On the one hand, the recycling of signs and symbols might be seen as decontextualization, perhaps even flattening out differences in the struggles to which these hip-hop signs allude—certainly a recognized problem with commodity culture. It explains why, for example, in thinking about political dimensions of this music, we want to consider the broader set of practices and social relations generated by the group, not simply its tracks. But we also want to consider how elements of hip-hop incorporated into an eclectic musical mix have afforded this radical group a means of reconfiguring the Basque political imaginary. A fusionist strategy of musical expression does not, in the view of these *abertzales* (Basque patriots) undermine their self-understanding as patriotic or authentically Basque, but it does change what being patriotic or authentic might mean and what its cultural signifiers might look like. And this is of critical importance for the larger Basque social movement. Negu Gorriak expands the boundaries of membership in the radical Basque political community both by going beyond the borders of the Basque Country to name friends and allies in other social struggles, and by transgressing internal borders. Negu Gorriak's music invites nonethnic Basques, the children of Spanish immigrants who were born and live in the deindustrialized cities of the Basque north, into the Basque nation by affirming that membership is based not on ethnicity or blood, but on adherence to a cultural, linguistic, and working-class struggle. In their lyrics, in their performative style, in their practice, they demonstrate that being Basque does not mean closing oneself off to a larger world of cultural tastes and social concerns. It does not require renouncing bomber jackets for berets, or trading in Fishbone CDs for Benito Lertxundi. But it does mean speaking Basque, or at least learning Basque, and it means understanding the interconnections between economic, cultural, linguistic, racial, and sexual forms of domination. Ethnic and nonethnic Basques become part of the radical vision of the Basque nation not simply by sentiment, but by participating in these struggles and carrying them into daily life through practical commitments to language revival and social justice.

Domestication, rather than imitation, might be a useful way of describing how some musical transplantations do their semiotic work. As Marc Slobin writes, domestication "literally means bringing into the house" (1993: 90). The term could not be more appropriate for describing the semiotic work of Negu Gorriak. *House* is a term that has rich multivocal resonance in African American hip-hop culture and Basque nationalism, where it stands metaphorically for the nation (Aretxaga 1988). Through its music Negu Gorriak brings black activists, Zapatistas, Arab guest workers, and ethnic and nonethnic working-class youth into their house. The house of Negu is a different house from that of the Basque bourgeois nationalists who have held governmental power. Patriotism in most bourgeois nationalist imaginaries is about drawing and defending borders. In Negu's vision, the nation is imagined as a permeable sodality, built upon and strengthened by intercultural and working-class alliances with others.

These alliances are figured through performances and forged through touring. But, as George Lipsitz reminds us, popular music is a crossroads of collisions as well as connections. Negu Gorriak was to find this out in a dramatic way when Public Enemy, the group's heroes, came to give a concert in Bilbao and greeted the enthusiastic audience with a big "Hello, Spain!" Negu's disappointment with Public Enemy as a result of their Bilbao concert was clear in an interview the members gave to Paul Ross, from the San Francisco–based 'zine *Maximum Rock and Roll*. Having organized a bus to go see the group in Paris a few years back, Fermin angrily described to Ross Public Enemy's much-anticipated performance in the Basque Country as armed robbery: "They came to take the money and run. If they are really a group that is trying to put forward some ideas, they should find out about the place where they are playing, what kind of people go to see them beforehand. I think it's essential that there be some kind of communication" (quoted in Ross 1993). Negu was even more disappointed when Public Enemy expressed their dissatisfaction at playing to what they perceived to be a white audience and announced to the press that they preferred to play at the U.S. Army base outside Madrid, where they would have more of a black audience. The gulf between the two groups revealed by this incident seemed unbreachable. For Public Enemy, race solidarity proved to be the stronger of the bonds. For Negu Gorriak, it was hard to understand or sympathize with the race and class politics that drive many African Americans into the enlisted ranks of the army. It was even harder to accept that these militant rappers did not perceive a U.S. Army base in Spain to be a symbol of U.S. imperialism. And it was a disappointment that Public Enemy's black-nationalist politics did not lead the group to embrace white Basque nationalists as their allies. As Kaki Arkarazo explained it to me, "[W]hat I think happened with them is a problem you see in the U.S. as a whole. The people there see themselves as the center of the universe, and everyone else's struggle is insignificant. I don't know if it's misinformation, lack of information, or not wanting to be informed."

In closing, we might recall the warning that the cultural critics Greg Tate and Angela Davis have issued to the African American community against rushing to proclaim hip-hop as the political revolution or solution. The political role (if any) played by music and musicians in a social movement is both complex and sometimes contradictory. Musicians can be spokespersons for certain causes, singing about issues and "spreading the word."

They can do this through their lyrics and, as we have seen, through the creation of new networks of communication. But I suggest that the political agency of a group like Negu Gorriak lies also in the role they play in shaping the Basque political imaginary. The way in which the group musically and visually figures Basque nationality and alliances with other forms of social inequality and struggles shifts the terms in which activists understand themselves, their social reality, and their own political subjectivity. And shifting the terms under which social actors understand their reality and their own agency is a critical dimension of any struggle for social change (Aretxaga 1988: 8–9). Rather than dismiss popular music as remote from "real" politics, we might more fruitfully "explore the potential of popular culture as a mechanism of communication and education, a site for experimentation with cultural and social roles not yet possible in politics" (Lipsitz 1994: 17). Public Enemy's visit to the Basque Country made clear that the figured intercultural alliance between radical Basque youth and North American blacks has yet to become a political reality. Among other reasons, unequal relations between the United States record industry and Basque radical music mean that Public Enemy's message reaches the Muguruza brothers in Irun, and not vice versa. Nevertheless, in the connections these youth make with Spanish working-class youth in their own country and with other social movements through their tours, in the information they spread, and in the heteroglossic imagined community they call into being via their albums, performances, and videos, they are contributing to a reshaping of what it could mean to be Basque and speak Basque in the years to come.

NOTES

I would like to thank Negu Gorriak for their music and for the interviews the members have granted to writers like me interested in their work, thereby helping us to help them disseminate their message. In Usurbil, special thanks go out to Kaki Arkarazo for the initial interview and his patience, and to Jakoba Rekondo and Jokin Eizagirre for their invaluable assistance in this project. My analysis owes a debt to many audiences who have heard early versions of this paper. I am especially grateful to Sharryn Kasmir, Brenda Bright, Joan Gross, Brad Weiss, Val Carnegie, Susan DiGiacomo, and George Lipsitz for discussions and commentary that helped to sharpen my analysis, and to Tony Mitchell for editorial counsel. Fieldwork for this project was conducted in 1994. I am grateful to the School of American Research for funding during the writing of this work.

1. For a sense of some of the enormous variability in European adaptations of rap, see Gross and Mark 1994; Gross, McMurray, and Swedenburg 1996; Mitchell 1996.

2. For critiques of this view as it relates specifically to music, see Robinson et al. 1991; Slobin 1993; Lipsitz 1994.

3. As the ethnomusicologist Steven Feld (1994: 262) notes, "[E]xotic world musics will always be financially and aesthetically remote from the historical loci of international recording consolidation — control and ownership of approximately ninety-three percent of the world musical sales market is now concentrated among six European–North American–Japanese companies: Time-Warner, CBS-Sony, MCA, Thorn-EMI, BMG/RCA, and Philips-Polygram."

4. On this critical point, see Fusco 1995. In this essay, Fusco warns against purely formalist analyses of intercultural borrowing, which, in focusing on the operations of the sign, run the risk of forgetting the historical circumstances that make formally similar acts of recontextualization take on very different meanings for distinct audiences. Only by bringing into the framework of analysis the historical relationships between peoples can we begin to understand, for example, why it is that artists and activists of color often perceive Anglo-European "borrowing" as "ripping off." See also Kobena Mercer's influential essay "Black Hair/Style Politics" (1990).

5. On Laboa and the New Song movement in the Basque Country, see Aristi 1985; Urzelai et al. 1995.

6. In some respects, Negu Gorriak's clearest predecessor is Hertzainak, a group that sought to forge an alliance between the hardcore sounds of punk and radical Basque nationalism. Like Negu Gorriak, Hertzainak served to unsettle the provincialism associated with *abertzale* (radical nationalist culture), which was often mocked by punks as being musically conservative and tied to folklore (see Espinosa and López 1993). On the tension between punk rock and Basque nationalism in Basque radical rock, see also Lahusen 1993: 266–67. For a more general discussion of the radical rock movement, see the special issue of *Punto y Hora* (1986). The newspaper *Egin* is an important source on the music movement (see especially the insightful contributions of journalist Pablo Cabeza), as is *El Tubo: Euskal Herriko Musika Aldizkaria.*

7. The public outcry against this act of censorship was immediate and widespread. There was virtually unanimous support not only from the Basque music world (everyone from Mikel Laboa and Txomin Artola to La Polla Records), but also from well beyond it — Lluis Llach, Fugazi, Body Count, the various free radio stations of Euskadi, rising stars of the new Basque cinema (Juanma Ulloa, Julio Medem, Alex de la Iglesia), well-known *bertsolaris,* and the world of literature, including Bernardo Atxaga and Alfonso Sastre, both of whom wrote short statements for the CD *Ustelkeria.* The concert was ignored by the Spanish and international press but not by youth: it sold out two days before it began. Pablo Cabeza, a longtime observer of the Basque music scene, declared the concert of fifteen

groups with wide-ranging styles the "artistically most complete festival in the history of our rock . . . on Saturday evening and night something special took place underneath the tent. A mysterious spirit exacted the best of each group" (Cabeza 1995). Whether there was a "mysterious spirit" or not, the concert was yet another demonstration of the group's capacity for mass mobilization and strong support in the world of Basque culture, arts, and alternative politics and their ability to merge music with political protest.

8. Interview with Fermin Muguruza by Jakue Pascual for *El Tubo: Euskal Herriko Musika Aldizaria*. Reprinted in *Negu Gorriak* 10, the 'zine of the group produced in conjunction with their last CD, *Ideia Zabaldu*.

9. This title has no easy translation into English. The album gives "Por Cojones" as the Castilian translation, and "Damn Right!" for the English. Given that the track is said to be "inspired by those who have cocks for brains" (CD insert), we might want to translate it as "Cock Sure."

10. Negu Gorriak's vision is exemplified more broadly in radical Basque youth culture. For a very insightful discussion on the classed nature of the national imaginary in radical Basque youth culture, see the forthcoming work by Sharryn Kasmir, "Classing National Identity: Radical Nationalist Bars and the Basque Working Class in Mondragón," in *American Ethnologist*.

REFERENCES

Agirre, Lorea. 1995. "Erritmo Aldaketekin Gabe ez Genuke Negu Gorriak Ulertuko." *Egunkaria*, 31 March, 25.

———. 1995. "Ideia Zabaltzen Helburu." *Egunkaria*, 31 March, 24.

Aretxaga, Begoña. 1988. *Los funerales en el nacionalismo radical vasco*. San Sebastian (Spain): Primitiva Casa Baroja.

Aristi, Pako. 1985. *Euskal Kantagintza Berria, 1961–1985*. Donostia, Spain: Erein.

Bousfield, Jonathan. 1994. "Mixing with Glamorous Guerillas." *European*, 9–15 December, 12.

Cabeza, Pablo. 1995. "Inmensa Solidaridad." *Egin*, 30 October, 27.

Canclini, Néstor García. 1995. *Hybrid Cultures: Strategies for Entering and Leaving Modernity*. Translated by Christopher Chiappari and Silvia López. Minneapolis: University of Minnesota Press.

Decker, Jeffrey Louis. 1994. "The State of Rap: Time and Place in Hip Hop Nationalism." In *Microphone Fiends: Youth Music and Youth Culture*, edited by Andrew Ross and Tricia Rose. New York: Routledge.

Espinosa, Pedro, and Elena López. 1993. *Hertzainak: La confesión radical*. Vitoria, Spain: Ediciones Aianai.

Fanon, Frantz. 1967 [1952]. *Black Skin, White Masks*. Translated by Charles Lam Markmann. New York: Grove Press.

Feld, Steven. 1994. "From Schizophonia to Schismogenesis: On the Discourses and Commodification Practices of 'World Music' and 'World Beat.'" In *Music Grooves,* edited by Charles Keil and Steven Feld. Chicago: University of Chicago Press.

Flores, Juan. 1994. "Puerto Rican and Proud, Boyee! Rap Roots and Amnesia." In *Microphone Fiends: Youth Music and Youth Culture,* edited by Andrew Ross and Tricia Rose. New York: Routledge.

Flores, Juan, and George Yudice. 1990. "Living Borders/Buscando America: Languages of Latino Self-Formation." *Social Text* 24: 57–84.

Fusco, Coco. 1995. "Who's Doin' the Twist? Notes toward a Politics of Appropriation." In *English Is Broken Here: Notes on Cultural Fusion in the Americas.* New York: New Press.

Gilroy, Paul. 1987. *There Ain't No Black in the Union Jack: The Cultural Politics of Race and Nation.* Chicago: University of Chicago Press.

Greenawalt, Alexander. 1996. "RijeKKKa's Most Psycho: Ugly Rappers after the War." *Village Voice,* 3 September, 31–33.

Gross, Joan, David McMurray, and Ted Swedenburg. 1996. "Arab Noise and Ramadan Nights: Raï, Rap, and Franco-Maghrebi Identities." In *Displacement, Diaspora, and Geographies of Identity,* edited by Lavie Smadar and Ted Swedenburg. Durham, N.C.: Duke University Press.

Gross, Joan, and Vera Mark. 1994. "Language Use in Popular Music: The Occitan Rap of Les Fabulous Trobadors." Paper delivered at the American Anthropological Association Meeting, December, Atlanta, Ga.

Lahusen, Christian. 1993. "The Aesthetic of Radicalism: The Relationship between Punk and the Patriotic Nationalist Movement of the Basque Country." *Popular Music* 12, no. 3: 263–80.

Lipsitz, George. 1994. *Dangerous Crossroads: Popular Music, Postmodernism, and the Poetics of Place.* London and New York: Verso Press.

Mercer, Kobena. 1990. "Black Hair/Style Politics." In *Out There: Marginalization and Contemporary Cultures,* edited by Russel Ferguson, Martha Gever, Trinh T. Minh-ha, and Cornel West. New York: New Museum of Contemporary Art and MIT Press.

Mitchell, Tony. 1996. *Popular Music and Local Identity: Rock, Pop, and Rap in Europe and Oceania.* London and New York: Leicester University Press.

Punto y Hora de Euskal Herria. 1986. *Al trepidante ritmo de Euskadi* [special issue]. Cuadernos Monograficos 442 (August).

Robinson, Deanna Campbell, Elizabeth Buck, and Marlene Cuthbert, in association with the International Communication and Youth Consortium. 1991. *Music at the Margins: Popular Music and Global Cultural Diversity.* Newbury Park: Sage Publications.

Ross, Paul. 1993. Interview with Negu Gorriak. *Maximum Rock and Roll* 120, May.

Slobin, Marc. 1993. *Subcultural Sounds: Micromusics of the West.*
    Hanover, N.H.: Wesleyan University Press.

Urla, Jacqueline. 1997. "Outlaw Language: Creating Alternative Public Spheres
    in Basque Free Radio." In *The Politics of Culture in the Shadow of Capital,*
    edited by Lisa Lowe and David Lloyd. Durham, N.C.: Duke University Press.

Urzelai, Pello. 1995. *Mikel Laboa.* Donostia, Spain: Elkar.

Zulaika, Joseba. 1988. *Basque Violence: Metaphor and Sacrament.*
    Reno: University of Nevada Press.

DISCOGRAPHY

Negu Gorriak. 1989. *Negu Gorriak.* Elkar.

———. 1991. *Gure jarrera.* Esan Ozenki.

———. 1993. *Borreroak baditu milaka aurpegi.* Esan Ozenki.

———. 1995. *Ideia zabaldu.* Esan Ozenki.

———. 1995. *Ustelkeria.* Esan Ozenki.

Chapter 8

Fightin' da Faida

The Italian Posses and Hip-Hop in Italy

TONY MITCHELL

STYLE WARS, ITALIAN RAP, AND THE MAFIA

he Italian television miniseries *La piovra* (The Octopus),
broadcast on channel 1 of RAI, the Italian national state network, is the country's most widely watched and longest-
running television drama. A police thriller about the ongoing
battle between the *carabinieri* and the Mafia, it has been broadcast in more than fifty-five countries throughout the world to
an estimated global audience of four billion viewers (Oliver
1996). By 1998 it had reached its ninth installment, "The Pact,"
set in Sicily in the 1950s. *Octopus 7: The Cattani Murder Mys-
tery*, first screened in Italy in 1995, introduced a solo pirate
radio broadcaster, Radio Tam Tam, who set out to unmask and
expose corrupt practices and Mafia connections in Palermo
from a brightly painted and graffitied silver van converted
into a mobile broadcasting unit. The soundtrack to the political disclosures of Radio Tam Tam's DJ Rannisi, the stepson of a
countess with Mafia associations, consisted mainly of Italian
rap tracks by the Sicilian group Nuovi Briganti, the Neapolitan
ragga-dub posse Almamegretta, and the chart-topping pop-
rapper Jovanotti. But most notably, Frankie Hi-NRG's well-
known "dis" of the Mafia, "Fight da faida" (Fight the Blood
Feuds) is featured prominently during a climactic scene in
which the Barroti gang, a group of motorcycle punks involved
in a local extortion racket, blow up a series of commercial
properties after scrawling graffiti over them. They then splat-
ter the Radio Tam Tam van with paint and threaten Rannisi,
who has been offering poetic freestyle comments on the "cold
wind of fear sweeping through the city." This injection of Italian rap into a prime-time television crime drama series serves
to illustrate that it has become an important identity signifier

of oppositional Italian youth culture and of struggles against the Mafia, and has been acknowledged as such in Italian mainstream culture. It also further serves to illustrate the "glocalization" and "indigenization" of hip-hop culture.

In *La piovra,* Italian rap signifies in the crime-ridden, deprived, Mafia-dominated "peasant" contexts of Sicily and southern Italy, which provide something of an equivalent to the ghettos of U.S. cities. And it is worth recalling that the term "ghetto" is of Italian origin, having first been used in the sixteenth century to denote the Jewish quarter in Venice. The word derives from the Italian *gettare,* which means "to cast," referring to the traditional employment of Jews in metal foundries, but also taking on the meaning of "to cast aside." "Graffiti," one of the four principal elements of hip-hop culture, is of course also of Italian origin, coming from the Italian word *graffiare,* "to scratch." This suggests that Italian hip-hop was an historical inevitability.

"Fight da faida," the most well-known and often-compiled Italian rap track of the early 1990s, first appeared in 1990. As a single, it sold more than 15,000 copies for the small Bologna-based dance and acid jazz label Irma, and many Italian ten- and eleven-year-olds are said to have learned its lyrics by heart and understood them. It calls for a halt to the family blood feud practices of the Camorra and the Mafia, which it identifies as a fundamental cause of Italy's social and political evils. As Frankie Hi-NRG MC conceded, it offered a small but not insignificant protest: "when you speak about the Mafia, you have to make sure that you're small enough for them not to worry about you. From this point of view, I don't have any problems" (quoted in Harpin 1993: 60). Frankie, a transplanted southerner, had emerged from the northern Italian disco and dance-music scene, which meant his track was frowned upon by more underground, politically oriented "combat rappers," who found it too commercial, despite its political offensive.

But the main focus of "Fight da faida" is its text, as is emphasized in the video clip of the track: the lyrics run continuously across the images, in the style of Prince's typographic video for "Sign of the Times." The musical arrangement of Frankie's track employs only a Jew's-harp and a drum machine, along with samples from Sly and the Family Stone and the Jungle Brothers. There is also a saxophone break reminiscent of "La Raza" by the U.S. Latino rapper Kid Frost, with whom Frankie performed in Rome in 1992 in a freestyle session along with other Italian rappers. Built around the English refrain "You gotta fight," the track uses standard Italian to give maximum comprehensibility to its message, although it includes a segment in which a woman's voice raps in Sicilian dialect. The extended critique of the Mafia is expressed through a rapid-fire proliferation of internal rhymes that cannot be rendered adequately in English, but that contrast sharply with the tendency of U.S. gangsta rappers to embrace uncritically a Mafia imaginary. It begins:

> Father against father, brother against brother,
> born in a grave like butcher's meat;
> men with minds
> as sharp as blades,
> cutting like crime
> angry beyond any limits,
> heroes without land
> fighting a war
> between the Mafia and the Camorra, Sodom and Gomorrah
> Naples and Palermo
> Regions of hell
> devoured by hell flames for eternity,
> and by a tumor crime
> while the world watches
> dumbly, without intervening.
> Enough of this war between families
> fomented by desire
> for a wife with a dowry
> who gives life to sons today
> and takes it away tomorrow,
> branches stripped of their leaves
> cut down like straw
> and no one picks them up:
> on the verge of a revolution
> to the voice of the Godfather,
> but Don Corleone is much closer to home today:
> he sits in Parliament. It's time to unleash
> a terminal, decisive, radical, destructive offensive
> united we stand, all together, now more than ever before,
> against the clans, the smokescreens,
>   the shady practices maintained by taxes,
> lubricated by pockets:
> all it takes is a bribe in the right pocket
> in this obscene Italy . . .
> . . . you gotta FIGHT THE FEUD!!!
>   (In Branzaglia 1993: 109).[1]

Nuovi Briganti were among a number of militant rappers who accused Frankie Hi-NRG of betraying the independent, grassroots, oppositional principles of the Italian hip-hop movement in the early 1990s represented by the *centri sociali,* the computer-linked national network of "underground" occupied "social centers." These developed indirectly from the Italian Communist Party's *case di lavoro,* or community centers, and functioned as more than simply music venues, providing nurturing places for the development of indigenous Italian rap styles and "posses," as they became widely known, adopting the Jamaican sound-system expression. The centri sociali were indicators of authenticity, political militancy, and street credibility, as opposed to more opportunistic appropriations of hip-hop into pop contexts by rappers such as Frankie Hi-NRG MC, DJ Flash, Jovanotti, and Articolo 31. In the late 1990s these four exponents of a more party-oriented rap (albeit with political overtones in the case of Jovanotti and Frankie Hi-NRG) became extremely successful in the pop charts—Jovanotti's and Articolo 31's albums sold more than half a million copies—and were instrumental in developing a distinctively Italian strand of pop or party rap.

In a widely diffused cover story titled "Rissa nelle posse" (Riot in the Posses), a special summer 1992 issue of the Italian music monthly magazine *Fare musica* (Making Music) set Frankie Hi-NRG MC up in opposition to a centro sociale rapper, the Salento-born and Bologna-based Papa Ricky. The story, by Paolo Ferrari, contrasted Ricky's "street credibility," which came from the "collective and political hip-hop of the centri sociali," with Frankie's more individualistic "funky sensibility" (Ferrari 1992: 11). The centri sociali rappers' appropriation of claims to a monopoly on authentic hip-hop practices and their strategies for excluding those who had not "paid their dues" in the centri sociali could alternatively be regarded as the demagogic posturings of a self-defining, politically correct orthodoxy. Such ideological and territorial conflicts over claims of authenticity versus fashion, popularity, and opportunism are, of course, common in popular music scenes everywhere, particularly hip-hop scenes. What they illustrate most is the heterogeneity of most local music scenes, to which Italian rap is no exception. This is affirmed by Ferrari, who invokes Gramsci's concept of hegemony in distinguishing the diversity and multiplicity of the Italian rap scene from "homogenous nuclei who run the risk of becoming sectarian in their need to defend themselves against business and banality. Italian hip-hop follows a lot of different paths and has a lot of schools: it is important that each individual works within their own course, as hegemonic claims don't help anyone" (1992: 11). This chapter attempts to trace some of the different paths Italian hip-hop and rap have followed.

*Comitato. Photo by Stefano Giovannini. Courtesy of
Manuela Calomba/BMG Ariola S.p.a.*

RAP'S ITALIAN ROOTS AND THE CENTRI SOCIALI

The first Italian rap recordings and performances in English, as featured on Irma's 1990 compilation *Italian Rap Attack* (where "Fight da faida" is the only track in Italian), quickly gave way in the early 1990s to the use of standard Italian, and then regional dialects, by individual rappers and crews. These included Papa Ricky and his Isola Posse All Stars (Bologna) and other ragga-inflected regional posses such as Almamegretta (Naples), Possessione (Naples), Comitato (Milan), Lion Horse Posse (Milan; the group later became Piombo a Tempo), Mau Mau (Turin), 99 Posse (Naples), Sud Sound System (Salento), Nuovi Briganti (Messina), and Onda Rossa Posse (Rome), many of whom were associated both with what was referred to as "Mediterranean reggae" as well as the centri sociali.

Italian rap tends to combine the influences of Jamaican ragga and dance hall, traditional Mediterranean folk music (often featuring accordion and drums), "world music" elements and vocal styles, and samples, scratches, and breakbeats derived from both African American and Latino rappers such as Kid Frost. This distinctively syncretic combination of global and local musical forms led to the coinage of the term "rappamuffin" in a 1992 Flying Records compilation of Italian rap and ragga entitled *Italian Posse: Rappamuffin d'Azione*. A politically militant, more rock-inflected form of rap, best illustrated by the Rome-based Communist group Onda Rossa Posse (Red Wave Posse) and their offshoots AK 47, Assalti Frontali, and Lou X, developed alongside a resurgence in the Italian "Second Republic" of the early 1990s of 1970s-style mass oppositional political activity, which rap both reflected and provided a soundtrack for (Jee Militant 1998; Wright 2000).

Donadio and Giannotti (1996: 212) have located the social and political origins of Italian rap in the series of university and school occupations, protest demonstrations, and sit-ins that took place throughout Italy in January 1990 disputing the Ruberto law, which invited private sponsorship of universities. They focus in particular on the Pantera (Panther) Occupation in Rome, named after an escaped panther that was still at large in Rome at the time, having resisted all attempts to catch it. These protests, reminiscent of the 1968 student revolutions in France, Italy, and elsewhere in Europe, adopted graffiti writing and rap music to propagate their cause. Rome-based groups such as Onda Rossa Posse and Assalti Frontali performed their hardcore, politicized rap at the occupied Roman building known as La Pantera and the centro sociale at Forte Prenestino, and elsewhere in Italy rappers began performing in the various centri sociali (see Militant 1998).

The centri sociali had emerged all over Italy in the mid-1980s in the wake of the *riflusso* (recession and resignation) of 1970s left-wing militant students and disaffected young people, as semi-illegal, alternative, self-organized activity centers. Self-organized groups occupied and refurbished disused buildings, often in the outer suburbs of the large Italian cities. The centers were run along collective and cooperative lines, and developed into underground drop-in centers, youth clubs, and drug rehabilitation centers, as well as recording studios, cinemas, video and postindustrial art galleries, and even cyberpunk computer centers for *hackeraggio* (hacking) in some cases. They also provided rehearsal rooms and concert venues for punk rock groups, eventually transforming into centers for hip-hop music and graffiti art. In some cases there was a direct line of continuity between the politically committed wing of the Italian punk rock scenes of the 1980s and the hip-hop movement of the 1990s. The Florentine rapper Il Generale, for example, began as a punk rocker, as did Papa Ricky. As well as being influenced by the 1960s French situationists, the appropriation and transformation of disused urban spaces involved in the centri sociali also aligns them directly with Hakim Bey's philosophy of "temporary autonomous zones," which is often applied to 1990s rave culture and dance music. The appropriation of space by the centri sociali can also be directly linked to the appropriation of rap by the posses, who used the term "posse" in the sense of an open, fluid collective subject to rearrangement and change. The graffiti symbol for the centri sociali was a bolt of lightning inside a circle, symbolizing "breaking through the confines of the urban prison" but also "an autonomous microsociety, jealous of its own independence, bound to its own territory, but ready to forge links with the other islands in the archipelago" (Lipperini 1993).

A 1992 book about the Italian posses, *Posse italiane,* lists fifty-three centri sociali in thirty-three Italian cities from the 1980s to 1992. The list includes twenty-six in Rome, thirteen in Milan, five in Florence and Bologna, three in Naples, and two in Turin (Branzaglia et al. 1993: 141–42). Perhaps the most prominent were the Leoncavallo in Milan (which originated in 1975), the Isola nel Kantiere in Bologna, the Forte Prenestino in Rome, and the Officina 99 in Naples. It was here that the Italian posses, along with punk, ska, and reggae groups, cut their teeth and sometimes their first recordings, although the first two of these centri sociali were subsequently closed down and cleared out by local city councils. The Italian posses were part of a subcultural movement that discovered a new rhetoric of political militancy, using rap music to criticize a whole range of social and political ills they attributed to an increasingly visibly corrupt Christian Democrat government. Rap music could even be seen as one of the main cultural catalysts of a political renaissance of oppositional Italian youth movements, and it became the accompaniment of a new upsurge of political demonstrations against the Christian Democrat government in the early 1990s and then the Berlusconi government of 1994. Rappers like Frankie Hi-NRG, the 99 Posse, and Fratelli Soledad gave performances in support of the left-wing alliance of *progressisti* (progressives) in the 1994 elections.

Although some rappers, like Speaker Dee Mo' of the Isola Posse All Stars, publicly disassociated themselves from communism, Ferrari (1992) identifies a communist "radical wing" of Italian rappers. It includes Assalti Frontali and AK 47, who both emerged from the Rome-based Onda Rossa Posse, one of the earliest Italian rap groups to use Italian. The name of this group, "Red Wave Posse," emphasizes the connection between Italian rappers and 1970s left-wing political activity, deriving from an extreme-left-wing pirate radio station of the 1970s that also formed a centro sociale in Rome. Employing what Liperi (1993: 203) refers to as "combat rap"—a term also used to describe the Basque rock-rap group Negu Gorriak—Onda Rossa Posse combines hard-line political lyrics with dramatic orchestral samples, thumping bass lines, scratching, a mournful flute solo, and a saxophone break embroidering the saxophone refrain from Kid Frost's "La Raza." Their self-produced debut mini-album, *Batti il tuo tempo,* with its refrain, "Batti il tuo tempo per fottere il potere" (Beat your own time to fuck up the power), and a clenched fist, a red flag, and a black panther on its cover (reflecting both the Rome Pantera occupation and the U.S. Black Panthers), was an emotional but clearly telegraphed call to political action. It expressed rebellion against the "criminal bastards" who represented all forms of political, institutional, and Mafia-controlled power in Italy. Dropping expletives into their discourse and attacking drug dealers in the style of U.S. gangsta rappers such as N.W.A., sampling national television news reports and police sirens, celebrating the courage of political prisoners, and chronicling examples of police violence against civilians, Onda Rossa Posse presented an angry, emotive, highly rhetorical view of a "fucked-up country" riddled with violence, injustice, and greed.

Gramsci's notion of the "organic intellectual," referred to in the previous chapter, which is sometimes dubiously evoked by U.S. commentators in reference to African American rappers, (e.g., Decker 1994; Potter 1995), actually has some credibility and relevance when applied to these groups, who could reasonably be expected to have far more familiarity with Gramsci's ideas in their Italian political context than any U.S. rappers. As with MC Solaar and other rappers in France, whose sophisticated wordplay has caused them to be included in French language textbooks, some Italian rappers are college educated and engage with political, social, and philosophical ideas with some degree of intelligence, wit, and dexterity. Raiss of Almamegretta, for example, has invoked Walter Benjamin's essay about the spongelike "porousness" of Naples to describe the openness of his native city to African migrants and international influences, as well as its "Africanization" (in Pestalozza 1996: 56). He has also referred to the "reification" involved in selling hip-hop recordings (64).

The lyrics of Italian rap provide alternative modes of social and political discourse that have spoken out about local social problems such as homelessness, unemployment, and police repression, as well as attacking political corruption, the Mafia, and the Northern League and celebrating the pleasures of marijuana. It could be argued that some of the more "combat-oriented" Italian rappers such as AK 47 at times produce little more than a crude form of humorless political sloganeering. But the use of regional dialects and instrumentation by Almamegretta, Sud Sound System, Mau Mau, 99 Posse, and others often gives rap music the function of a cultural repository for local regional expressions and a folkloric dimension that distinguishes it from rap music in many other Western countries. Lorenzo Coveri has identified two functions in this incorporation of dialect in Italian rap: one is its scope "for providing a wider range of metric and rhythmic solutions than standard Italian" together with "new sonorities"; the other is "a strong ideological choice by groups who are more aware of their autonomy, including linguistic autonomy" (1996: 35). This has resulted in regional dialects' "reacquiring dignity and prestige at the very moment when they are disappearing from everyday use" (37).

ITALIAN INDIGENIZATION AND "CONTAMINATION" OF RAP

The Italian posses' appropriation of Jamaican and black American vocal styles saw words like *rappare, scratchare,* and *ragga* enter the Italian language, and *rispetto* (respect) and *nella casa* (in the house) take on new specific meanings. "Rap" also inevitably became a label for marketing Italian sports clothing, as well for a new model of Fiat car. Sud Sound System appropriated Jamaican English expressions like "Hear me nuh!" "Ah bwoy!" and "Come in!" into their southern Italian dialect equivalents, "Sienti moi!" "Ahi li guai!" and "Camina!" Italy is also one of the few countries to have appropriated rap into classical music, in the form of a surreal, dreamlike stream of free-associating, rhyming vocalizations titled *Rap,* written by the poet Eduardo Sanguineti, with music composed and performed by Andrea Liberovici with a chamber ensemble, an electronic sampler, and the singer Ottavia Fusco. This work combines breakbeats, visual spectacle, and classical instrumentation, with help from the "offstage voice" (via a television monitor) of the prominent alternative television personality Enrico Ghezzi, and was premiered at the Teatro Carlo Felice in Genova in 1996. Reviewing it in the Italian monthly theater magazine *Sipario,* Andrea Balzola commented: "Amongst all the phenomena which have innovated the recent musical panorama, rap has established itself transversally with a real sense of contagiousness which has spread from the music of mass consumption to the more cultured byways of contemporary poetry and musical composition. . . . Sanguineti has found in [rap's] formal characteristics of repetition, alliteration, rhyme and word play occasion for an oneiric, poetic journey which is entirely consistent with his own research" (1997: 73). Liberovici's *Rap* could perhaps be compared to the African American composer Gregory T. S. Walker's 1993 classical composition *Dream N. the Hood* for rapper and orchestra, which was dedicated to Frank Zappa and used texts by Martin Luther King and others, or the same composer's *Bad Rap* for violin and orchestra. A U.S. compilation released in 1997 titled *The Rapsody Overture* combined raps by LL Cool J, Run-DMC, Warren G, Mother Superia, Redman, Onyx, Nikki D., and others with operatic arias by Puccini, Delibes, Hoffman, and others, revealing in most cases a surprising degree of confluence between the vocal techniques of rap and opera that has sometimes been reflected in Italian rap. Papa Ricky is the son of an opera singer, and both Sud

Sound System and Bisca 99 Posse have sampled Figaro's aria from the first act of Gioacchino Rossini's *Barber of Seville* (Plastino 1996: 116).

There are a number of homegrown historical and traditional precedents to some of the styles and idioms of Italian rap. In a review of Vincenzo Perna's Italian translation of David Toop's study of the origins of U.S. rap, *The Rap Attack,* Loredana Lipperini argues that the ritual insults and verbal jousting endemic to the idiom can be traced to the calls of washerwomen portrayed in baroque madrigals as well as in the "dozens" (ritual insults) of U.S. black ghettos (1992: 25). Lipperini also argues that Italian rap music could be said to have dual origins in the oral traditions of the griots of Africa and in the *recitativo* used in early Italian operas in Florence in the 16th century, with their *imitar con canto chi parla* (imitating in song a person speaking). As a way of keeping the narrative in opera moving, early Italian opera developed *recitativo secco* (dry recitative), which required the words to be metrical, and one had to be able to beat time to the music, which meant that the speech patterns were both melodic and rhythmical. By the time of Gluck, audiences had grown weary of the single voice in operas, and the duet form was borrowed from comic opera, which enabled two characters to "quarrel and call each other names" (Dent 1949: 105).

Rap's use of ritual insults also finds equivalents in other Italian cultural traditions. Carla Locatelli has drawn affinites between rappers and traditional Sicilian *cantastorie* (singer-storytellers), who perform stories accompanied by a guitar and placards illustrating their main plot points (1996: 113). The popular Roman dialect tradition of exchanging sung ritualized insults is illustrated in the opening scene of Pier Paolo Pasolini's 1962 film *Mamma Roma,* in which Anna Magnani as the title character exchanges improvised abusive strophes with her former pimp (Franco Citti) and his new bride. Signifying, "sounding," or "flyting," as Joan Magretta and William Magretta have indicated, is a strong feature of many cultures throughout the world, and Italian popular culture's own particular carnivalesque variation of it goes back to medieval times. It is also powerfully reflected in the exchanges of abuse between Giancarlo Giannini and Mariangela Melato in the films of Lina Wertmuller, particularly the 1974 *Swept Away* (Magretta 1979: 33–34). Many of the ritual insults used in Italian hip-hop tend to be directed at right-wing political parties such as the right-wing separatist Lega del Nord (Northern League), which has been the subject of both "Legala" (Put the League in a Straitjacket) by La To.sse (whose name is a pun on "Turin posse" and the Italian word for "cough") and "Slega la lega" (Smash the League) by Fuckin' Camels 'n' Effect. Other rappers "dis" judges, industrialists, and Mafiosi, sometimes all together, as in the Venetian reggae group Pitura Freska's ragga-rap "Na bruta banda" (An Ugly Mob), which launches a generalized attack on all "those who command."

A number of the Italian posses incorporate elements of traditional regional Italian music, from the Apulian peasant shouts and chants used by Suoni Mudu and Sud Sound System to the Neapolitan shepherd's horn used by 99 Posse. The *fisarmonica* (piano accordion), violin, *djembe* (an African drum), *requinto* (Mexican guitar), tub bass, balalaika, and other arcane instruments used by Mau Mau represent a more syncretic and international combination of traditional instruments. Mau Mau, whose name means "tramp" or "vagabond" in Piedmont dialect, as well as referring to both the Kenyan revolutionary group and a deprecating Torinese term for southern Italian immigrant Fiat workers, call themselves an *acustica tribu* (acoustic tribe) because they play only acoustic instruments when they perform live. The group's ragga-inflected music, which sounds very much like an Italian version of the Algerian raï- and Celtic-influenced French groups Les Negresses Vertes and Mano Negra, is a syncretic mixture of Mediterranean, African, and Jamaican influences. The singer and main composer of Mau Mau, Luca Morino, has emphasized that the group does not play traditional music and is not part of the Italian posse movement (although they are continually identified with it by critics, commentators, and other musical groups), quoting the Senegalese musician Baaba Maal to indicate that they are more concerned with a "universal music." The fact that the group's first two albums were mixed at the Real World studios in Bath and that the second, *Bass paradis* (1994), was issued on EMI with English translations of the Piedmontese lyrics, indicates Mau Mau's connections with world music.

Mau Mau also mixed English lyrics with Piedmont dialect in their song about U.S. migrants, "Ellis Island," on their third album, *Viva Mamanera* (1996). Their world music orientations are shared by other Italian rap, ragga, and dub-oriented groups such as the Kunsertu and Sensaciou, both of which produce Middle Eastern musical inflections and record on the Anagrumba label. Sensaciou's "Ramadan Dub," on their 1995 CD *In scio bleu* (In Blue Mode), for example, which invokes Buddha, Shiva, Christ, Jah, Mohammed, and Allah, combines Jamaican toasting, Mediterranean melodies, dub rhythms, and Arab inflections, mixing raggamuffin with the ancient Genovese song form *trallallero* to create a new genre called "Trallamuffin." The group's proliferation of musical influences caused them to split up into two groups in 1996, with Senza Fiato (Breathless) devoting itself to trip-hop, with Italian rather than dialect vocals, and Sensaciou settling into a more roots-oriented sound, combing Arab elements with rap in dialect, dub, and trance (Pacoda 1996: 161).

Also on the Anagrumba label are Almamegretta, a highly distinctive Neapolitan group that combines traditional Neapolitan music with rap, rock, Algerian raï, and other Middle Eastern influences, along with ragga and dub, in what provides evidence of a distinctively original musical and ideological direction in Italian rap. "Almamegretta" is Neapolitan dialect for *anima migrante* (migrant soul), which is the title of the group's debut 1993 album, produced by Ben Young, an associate of the Bristol-based Massive Attack. It displays the range of the group's combination of "roots" music with migratory musical "routes." In their 1993 debut EP "Figli di Annibale" (Sons of Hannibal), Almamegretta explores rhetorical notions of African roots in Italy. Based on a speech by Malcolm X, the song claims that when Hannibal, the "great black general," brought 90,000 African men across the Alps along with his famous elephants, there was considerable cross-breeding during the fifteen to twenty years he remained in Italy after his defeat of the Romans. This explains "why so many Italians have dark skin . . . dark hair . . . dark eyes . . . a trace of Hannibal's blood has remained in all their veins." (It is also worth noting that southern Italians are referred to derogatively in Piedmont as *moru*—Moorish, African, or Saracen—and that Sicilians, as Akhenaton of the French rap group IAM has pointed out, are of Islamic origin.) The track also suggests that during World War II a large number of African Americans "filled Europe with black babies," both sources having a particularly strong impact in the south of Italy. "Figli di Annibale" was written as an ironic attack on racist notions of racial purity, and to avoid its being taken at face value the group released a remix that placed a question mark after the title. But it remains an anthem of Almamegretta's politics of support for the deprived people of southern Italy as well as Italy's African migrants, and a symbol of their musical and rhetorical adoption of Afro-Caribbean influences. It was also adopted as the title of a 1998 film by Davide Fennario about southern Italian criminals on the run, which also used music by Almamegretta.

Almamegretta's second album, *Sanacore 1.9.9.5.*, combined a traditional Neapolitan composition by Salvatore Palomba with vocals by Giulietta Sacco and a *tammurriata* by the folklore group E Zezi, and the influence of the Neapolitan blues rock of Pino Daniele and others. A strong, driving ragga and dub beat produced a surprisingly harmonious syncretic result that was mixed by Adrian Sherwood and Andy Montgomery of the London-based dub unit On U Sound System. According to *Billboard,* "the industry phrase 'musical contamination' fits this band's blend of electronic ambient music and traditional Neapolitan roots, spiced with flavors from the Casbah quarter of Naples" (Dezzani 1995: 74; the term *contaminazione* in Italian is equivalent to "syncretization" or "hybridization"). As the group's vocalist, Raiss, has explained, the syncretism of the group's sound is seamless and spontaneous:

> If we sketched out an experiment in associating Naples with reggae in *Anima migrante,* in *Sanacore* we took it much further, to the extent that you can no longer tell if our music is more reggae or more Neapolitan: the amalgamation of the two elements was created naturally, in a spontaneous way. It's almost as if we pretended that reggae was Neapolitan music. . . . Reggae is melancholy and languid music played in minor chords, like melodic Neapolitan music, which is why it is the closest of all other styles of music to our sensibility. This also explains why the Italian language is more adaptable to reggae than to rock, punk or other forms: reggae is music that allows one to communicate in a relaxed way. (In Campo 1995: 53)

After performing in the Neapolitan centro sociale Officina 99 and on tour with fellow Neapolitan rappers Bisca and 99 Posse in the mid-1990s, Almamegretta moved further away from rap into reggae and dub with their 1996 album *Indubb,* which consisted largely of dub-styled remixes from *Sanacore.* Their 1998 album *Lingo* took them further into dance, trip-hop, drum 'n' bass, and electronica territory, although they maintained their use of Neapolitan dialect and song, with Pino Daniele collaborating on one track. Influenced by the underground Asian dance scene in London, the group collaborated on the album with three former members of Transglobal Underground, Count Dubulah, Larry Whelan and Neil Sparkes, and Dave Watts from Fun-Da-Mental. The album's lineup also included the ubiquitous New York dub producer and bass player Bill Laswell, following Almamegretta's transnational, migratory impulses into more diverse forms of musical fusion (Moretti 1998: 41). But as Raiss has stated, the group's roots are paradoxically based more in reggae and "black music" than in Neapolitan music:

> Dub means access to us, a ticket which gets you on a ship that takes you around the world. The possibility of escaping from an ethnic and cultural cage, and an attempt to be free in every sense: to play Indian music without being Indian, black music without being black, Neapolitan music without being Neapolitan, because in the end we know more about black music than Neapolitan music. . . . In the beginning I took famous reggae pieces and when I translated them into Neapolitan they became Neapolitan songs, and if you take *Nun ti scurdà* [I Won't Forget You], which is undoubtedly a Neapolitan song, and translate it into English, it could easily be a reggae song. (In Pestalozza 1996: 61)

Almamegretta is the most distinctive Italian group to have emerged from the posse movement and have perhaps come closest, after Jovanotti, to receiving attention outside Italy. In 1995 they were invited to do a remix of the British trip-hop group Massive Attack's track "Karmacoma," and they have continued to have close connections with the English group, one of whose members, 3D (a.k.a. Robert Del Naja), is himself of Neapolitan origin. Del Naja has indicated that it is only language barriers that have prevented Almamegretta from being internationally recognized: "I like [Almamegretta's] album very much and I find it nonsensical that countries that are cut off from the major distribution circuits purely for language reasons, like Italy, are reduced to export only music for clubs sung in English" (in Pestalozza 1996: 76).

DIALECT RAP AND TRADITIONAL FOLK

The use of regional dialects by a large number of other Italian posses has contributed to building a distinctively local and historically based culture out of Italian hip-hop, drawing on rap and ragga in conjunction with local popular folkloric traditions, and frequently using peasant songs as a basis, along with dance forms like the tarantella. (According to a 1997 survey referred to by RAI International's program *Italia News*, only about 23 percent of Italians continue to speak regional dialects, which means these musicians represent something of a cultural vanguard.) In "In Sa La" (The Road), for example, Sa Razza uses Sardinian dialect as a matter of local pride in their Sardinian heritage to express the dilemma of being forced away from their roots onto the "road" of immigration to mainland Italy because of growing unemployment and economic hardship:

> We prefer Sardinian rap slang
> And to boast about being Sardinian, brother,
>   you've got to defend yourself,
> This is the cause we're rapping for
> This is the only hope for my people
> To survive—survive on the road.
>   (In Branzaglia et al. 1993: 105–6)

Papa Ricky's eponymously titled 1995 debut album begins with a similar invocation of the constraints on southern Italians to emigrate to the north of Italy:

> The south is an ancient, wise and generous land
> Where bread tastes like bread and oranges are abundant

But the people's smiles hide the bitter tears
Of those who are stuck in the shit and forced to emigrate.

The importance of this emergence of a distinctive southern Italian ragga-rap scene was acknowledged by the Academy Award–winning Italian film maker Gabriele Salvatores in his 1993 film *Sud* (South), about a group of Neapolitan left-wing militants who attempt to subvert a local election dominated by a northern candidate. Salvatores's soundtrack used Papa Ricky's ragga version of "O sole mio"—which he interprets as "not just a song for southern Italians, since the sun heats up all the land"—along with cuts by Nando Popu of Sud Sound System and the Neapolitan rappers Possessione, Bisca, and 99 Posse. Sud Sound System's "tarantamuffin," which uses ragga combined with samples of traditional southern Italian instruments, represents a particularly vital example of "Mediterranean reggae" in which the group has discovered a vehicle for exploring and preserving their own southern Italian dialect and musical traditions:

> Reggae, like jazz and blues, has value as a universal protest, because it has an immediate application to the listener's private, intimate spheres, rather than to external antagonistic attitudes. At first we were attracted by reggae's rhythmic hypnosis, which we found was able to express the musicality of our dialect. Then we noticed that in these Jamaican texts there was an infinite sense of southern [Italian] culture. There is the same attachment to roots, the desire to sing about love and sentimentality, and intolerance for the oppression of school and military service. But above all we liked reggae's desire to fight against human malaise. It's an interior music. (In Branzaglia et al. 1993: 97)

Such is the cultural importance of the use of traditional regional dialects and musical elements by Italian rap and ragga groups that in 1992 the Milan-based Istituto De Martino, which carries out research into traditional genres such as work songs and ritual chants, made contact with a number of rap groups, seeing Italian rap as a genre with analogies with traditional forms of musical improvisation. Italian rappers and the *centri sociali* have also received a considerable amount of academic attention (see Plastino 1996, which contains a six-page bibliography.) In the late 1980s the controversial French ethnomusicologist George Lapassade and his Italian associate Piero Fumarola began carrying out research on affinities between traditional folk music forms and the raggamuffin-rap of the Occitanian rap group Massilia Sound System in France and Sud Sound System and Salento Posse in Italy. Lapassade, who saw Italian rap as "a new form of social communication which threatens to change our lives" (in Pacoda 1996: 17), invited rappers and graffiti artists to Lecce University (earlier he had also invited performers to the University of Paris; see Cannon 1997). He also organized festivals and tours and encouraged Sud Sound System to collaborate with traditional Salento musicians. He was particularly interested in exploring the continuity of the ancient tradition of *tarantismo,* which involves going into a trance and dancing after being bitten by a tarantula spider; this is the supposed origin of the tarantella, a dance traditionally done to the frenzied music of a *tamburello* (drum), violin, guitar, and accordion. This involved notions of "raggafolk" and "ethnorap" and tracing a lineage of oral tradition that was somewhat forced; although the groups involved used some of the instrumentation of the tarantella, this tended to derive more from the Italian folk revival movement of the 1960s than from any continuity of musical tradition. Lapassade claimed there were affinities between the *pizzica-pizzica* ("bite"; the Salerno variant of the tarantella) and the reggae rhythms used by the Salento Posse and Sud Sound System, and he set about attempting to prove it. His research generated considerable debate among other academics and journalists in Italy and is discussed at great length by Plastino, who argues that there is little evidence of tarantismo in the music of either Sud Sound System or the Salento Posse, an argument backed up by members of the groups themselves (Plastino 1996). What does emerge, as Plastino claims, is that traditional forms of Italian music are used syncretically and virtually in the sonic mix of a number of rap groups as an indication of Italian roots.

GEOGRAPHIC SHIFTS, ANTAGONISM, AND COMBAT RAP

According to Paola Zukar, the first Italian vinyl rap release was the single "What's the Rhyme," released by the Turin-based Devastatin' Posse (a name perhaps influenced by the Hispanic New York rapper of the 1980s Devastating Tito) in 1989, which was strongly influenced by Public Enemy (1998: 120). Prior to that, breakdancing, graffiti writing, and hip-hop clothes had all been introduced to Italy, as elsewhere, through the films *Wild Style* and *Beat Street.* Rapping began at a series of monthly evenings titled "Ghetto Blaster" at the Isola nel Kantiere, a centro sociale in Bologna, where the public were invited to try their hand at rapping into an "open microphone." The Isola Posse All Stars' 1991 single "Stop al panico" (Stop the Panic), featuring Papa Ricky, was one of the first major Italian-language rap releases. This was a hardcore rap with ragga inflections about the Gulf War. The video of the song, which was featured regularly on the national music channel *Videomusic,* used newspaper headlines and newsreel footage about

Mafia and racket killings together with street scenes in which the group raps, U.S. gangsta-style, and crowd scenes that emphasize their community orientation.

Rather than reproducing the traditional rivalry between Rome and Milan as cultural capitals, the Italian posses tended to emerge around Turin and Naples, which represented focal points for hip-hop scenes in northern and southern Italy respectively, while Bologna became the most active hip-hop scene in central Italy. A number of Neapolitan and southern Italian groups mixed Neapolitan and southern dialects and musical influences with ragga and rap, and the Mediterranean migratory patterns from the south of Italy, Africa, and the Middle East that converged at the Fiat factory in Turin also produced a number of ethnic influences in that city's hip-hop scene. As Raiss has commented:

> Turin and Naples are the two poles of Italian music in the 1990s: the periphery of the world begins at Naples, which is the port that opens to the south and filters through all its problems. Turin, on the other hand, is the port that opens to the north, but it is also the most Italian city in Italy, the place where the ethnic mixture between races, and between north and south, is most pronounced: it's a kind of laboratory. The Turin groups are the result of those processes: Africa Unite mixes music of the south and cultures of the north, and Mau Mau does likewise, as well as having a Senegalese member, Nsongan. (In Campo 1995: 53)

The summer of 1992 in Italy saw the real emergence of the distinctively local, politicized, and decentralized Italian posses in the Italian mass media. They were arguably one of the most important phenomena in the ongoing history of the often vexed relationship between music, politics, and the appropriation of U.S. and other foreign influences in Italian popular music. The Italian posses signaled a renewal of oppositional political practices in Italian popular music and youth culture, and in its sincere and direct attention to local political and social problems, its creation of a distinctive youth subculture, and its recourse to dialect and Mediterranean folk music sources, Italian hip-hop echoed the attempts to create a "national popular culture" (to use Gramsci's often-quoted term) by some Italian rock groups like PFM and Area in the 1970s. If, as Zygmunt Baranski has suggested, Italian distinctions between popular and mass culture originated in "the need to differentiate between what was felt to be popular and 'genuinely' indigenous, and what was seen as popular but 'foreign,' or rather 'transatlantic'" (1990: 11), Italian hip-hop could be said to have originated in the latter but progressed toward the former.

A defining epithet of militant Italian rap is "antagonistic." The word indicates a culture of opposition that during the 1980s had lost the means of articulating itself. As Liperi explains,

> [I]f, on the one hand, antagonism in Italy has continued to accumulate not only political connotations but also social and territorial ones (such as the renaissance of the *centri sociali*) on the other, it has not succeeded in giving expression to any identifiable culture. The linguistic forms of hip-hop culture offered an immediate connection with the world of social opposition because it was the immediate, direct result of it. If rap in its crudest form can be considered as a means of making political speeches *[comiziare]* through music, this is one of the main reasons that it offered the most direct vehicle of expressing anger against corruption, organized crime, and social upheaval. (1993: 199)

One prominent example of this use of rap as a rhetoric of political opposition was the 1994 tour by the Neapolitan 99 Posse, in tandem with their fellow Neapolitan group Bisca. The often punning discourse of 99 Posse is aimed at representing a form of *rappresaglia* (reprisal) — the title of one of their tracks. After they had performed nearly sixty concerts over five months at a series of locations between Bergamo, Naples, and Sardinia, a selection from Bisca 99 Posse's "Incredible Opposition Tour" was subsequently released as a live double album. Rapping mostly in Neapolitan dialect over a ragga beat with saxophone and rock guitar embellishments, the group dealt with subjects ranging from Naples, "a city that has been forgotten, exploited, abandoned and despised by everyone except [Fiat boss] Agnelli" (a chant-like song performed with Arab music and a piano accordion), to the Gulf War. They also dealt with guaranteed salaries for the self-employed, "two thousand years of exploitation" of immigrants, illegal employment, unemployment, "a smart bomb" (a Bisca contribution), hatred, the "idiocy" of the mass media and politicians, and a revival of antifascism. Few of Bisca 99 Posse's songs deal with anything other than political subjects, and they run the risk of browbeating their audiences to the point of exhaustion, as do some of the other Italian "combat" rappers, many of whose political subject matter, critical targets, and musical frames of reference overlap. The group 99 Posse is one of the few posses to continue its strong associations with the centri sociali, touring twenty of them in December 1998, although the militant, agitational nature of the group's music had by then been modified toward a more ragga and traditional Mediterranean folk idiom.

The British cultural critic Iain Chambers, a professor at Naples University, commented in 1993 that the insistence of the Italian posses and centri

sociali on alternative circuits to the major recording labels and institutionalized concert venues, as well as their antagonism toward capitalist ideology,
linked them to the 1960s as well as making them distinctively Italian. This
contrasted, he claimed, with youth cultures in other countries such as the
United Kingdom and the USA, who in the 1990s were more disposed to negotiate with capitalist institutions. Chambers also noted that the posses and
centri sociali were particularly local, regional manifestations, but at the same
time represented global phenomena: "The centers are profoundly linked to
territories: they use dialect, and at the same time they use the language of
youth cultures. The posses, for example, have appropriated rap, which is an
American musical form, and by applying dialect to it have created a new language: a global language" (in Lipperini 1993). But by the end of the 1990s
the oppositional stances of many of the Italian posses were beginning to
soften, and the influence of the centri sociali was not so strong. The polarization between pop rap and centro sociale rap was also beginning to erode,
and the Italian rap–and hip-hop scene became more homogenized, while re-
taining its distinctive regional characteristics.

JOVANOTTI AND POP RAP:
POLITICIZING THE COMMERCIAL MAINSTREAM

The strong sense of militancy and antagonism in the Italian rap aligned
with the centri sociali had an impact on more mainstream and commercialized examples of Italian hip-hop. The most popular Italian rapper in terms of
record sales and chart hits is Jovanotti, whose real name is Lorenzo Cheru-
bini, and who titled three of his top-selling albums *Lorenzo 1992, Lorenzo
1994,* and *Lorenzo 1997.* (*Jovanotti* literally means "young man.") As a television and disco star in the late 1980s, he was a *paninaro,* a mid-1980s Italian
version of the English mods who hung out on Vespas and Lambrettas at fast-
food joints, wore Timberland shoes, and were celebrated in a song by the
British Hi-NRG group the Pet Shop Boys (See Donadio and Giannotti 1996:
187–93). Jovanotti became famous for a teenage pop hit titled "Sei come la
mia moto" (You're Like my Lambretta) and reached the top of the Italian
charts in 1988 with the pop rap song "Gimme Five" and his album *Jovanotti
for President.* The journalist Paolo Zanuttini described him as "straddling
the hedonistic idiocy of the late 1980s with commercial dexterity" (1992:
77). He subsequently became the target of satirical barbs and scorn on the
part of centri sociali rappers, who saw his form of pop rap as a gross commercial travesty of the politicized "combat rap" that they were having difficulty getting radio and television air play for. At the other extreme, the
young Calabrese disc jockey and fledgling pop star DJ Flash released a

disco-styled rap hit song in 1994 titled "Un Lorenzo c'è già" (There's Already a Lorenzo); he apparently intended to displace Jovanotti as a pop icon.

Jovanotti developed a public political conscience in 1992, when he voted for the Partito Democratico della Sinistra (the Left Wing Democratic Party, which had resulted from the split in the Italian Communist Party) in the national elections, after composing an election rap called "Ho perso la direzione" (I've Lost the Drift). He also composed an "instant song" called "Cuore" (Heart) about the assassination of the anti-Mafia magistrate Giovanni Falcone. Although he continued to represent the flippant, commercial pop face of Italian rap, which had begun to be incorporated into the most conventional of Italian *musica leggera* (literally, "light music"), Jovanotti showed that even this idiom could incorporate ideological gestures.

Jovanotti achieved a considerable degree of popularity outside Italy, selling several million albums and joining Eros Ramazzotti and Laura Pausini as one of the most internationally successful Italian pop stars of the mid-1990s. In 1993 his "Penso positivo" (I Think Positive), which invoked the world as "a great church that goes from Che Guevara to Mother Teresa, passing by way of Malcolm X and Gandhi and Saint Patrignano" (in Pacoda 1996: 185), became something of an anthem for some Italian youth. In 1994 he headlined a series of fifteen concerts in Germany, Switzerland, Slovenia, Holland, Belgium, Portugal, and France with Eros Ramazzotti and Pino Daniele, as well as playing a twenty-five-date European tour of his own. In 1995 he was the only Italian artist at the Montreux Jazz Festival, and was the first Western musician to break the U.S.-dominated economic and cultural embargo against Cuba, performing at his own expense to an audience of 20,000 people in Havana, many of whom were familiar enough with his music to sing along with him. His outstanding contribution to the 1998 George Gershwin tribute album *Red Hot and Rhapsody,* where he does an Italian rap version of "I've Got Rhythm," gave him his first exposure to Anglophone audiences.

Jovanotti attained a new credibility in Italy with the release of his 1997 album *Lorenzo 1997: L'albero* (The Tree), a seventy-minute, fifteen-track marathon recorded in Johannesburg after a trek through Africa. Combining funky brass, jazz, rock, disco, and world music influences (including a didjeridu and samples of African music), the album also displayed the imprint of the respected bass player Saturnino. It went straight to the top of the Italian charts ahead of Zucchero and the Spice Girls and sold over half a million copies. His 1999 album *Capo Horn* continued in a similar vein and went straight to the top of the Italian charts ahead of the Backstreet Boys' *Millennium*, in its first week in June 1999, with the single "Per te" (For You) going straight to number 2, behind the Backstreet Boys' "I Want It That Way." The former contempt of the centri sociali rappers appeared to have been forgotten when Jovanotti was invited to write the introduction to Pierfrancesco Pacoda's 1996 anthology of lyrics by sixteen Italian rap groups and individuals, *Potere alla parola* (Power to the Word), in which he stated a collective ideology: "In rap there are no long careers or individual musical evolution. The sound of rap evolves with the latest arrival, who is substituted for the old innovator, who progresses from selling a million copies to none in the course of an ellipsis or two. This means that rap is more important than its practitioners, and precedes those who interpret it as the pulse of the moment; the language has more weight than the means" (in Pacoda 1996: 3). Along with Jovanotti's success, *rap leggera* (light rap) became a commercially successful category in Italy, its main protagonists including Articolo 31, Alta Tensione, Ottiere, and Radiotitolati. Articolo 31 produced a successful chart-scoring album in 1994, *Messa di Vespiri* (Vespers Mass), selling more than 70,000 copies. The group's 1994 single "Ohi Maria" was a lightweight rap panegyric to marijuana that announces itself as a tongue-in-cheek, Latin-style love song in the style of the *cantautori* (singer-songwriters) and ends with a plea to "legalize it," quoting Peter Tosh's reggae anthem, and showing the influence of Cypress Hill. It received considerable radio airplay in 1995, despite complaints against the song by the "Mamme Contro Il Rock" (Mothers Against Rock), an Italian equivalent of the Parents Music Resource Center in the United States. Articolo 31, who, along with the Varese group Sottotono, have provided rap soundtracks for television commercials, are one of a number of rap groups on the Crime Squad label, an offshoot of the Naples-based Flying Records. Flying Records emerged as one of the main independent labels promulgating the more pop-oriented Italian posses and are included on a 1994 Crime Squad compilation, *Nati per rappare* (Born to Rap), named after Articolo 31's debut single. Articolo 31 (which takes its name from an Irish human-rights law) won two of the Italian Music Prizes established by the newspaper *La Repubblica* in April 1997, and based on its readers' votes, for best Italian band and best Italian rap group. (Jovanotti's album *L'albero* was duly nominated for Best Album of the Year in 1998.) Articolo 31's third album, *Cosi com'è* (The Way It Is) sold more than half a million copies in Italy and was the third highest-selling album in Italy in 1996, while in the autumn of 1996 they performed their "hit-hop" to more than 100,000 people in twenty-two concerts. The relatively smooth progress of Italian rap music from the centri sociali to the pop charts has resulted in an almost complete indigenization of rap in Italy, along with its appropriation as a subgenre of Italian *musica leggera*. With 53.3 percent of the Italian music market occupied by domestic music, as opposed to 40.3 percent by international music, according to a 1997 *Billboard* report (Dezzani 1997: 58), this is perhaps hardly surprising, even if Italy represents only 2 percent of the global popular music market.

DIVERSIFICATION AND COMMERCIALIZATION

The recorded output of Jovanotti and other Italian pop rappers displays unmistakable traces of self-parody and irony, but their more politically oriented rap recordings could be seen to operate as "edutainment," designed to educate young people about drugs, safe sex, violence, political corruption, and other social issues. Most Italian rap continues to be almost exclusively male dominated, as is illustrated by the range of groups covered in both the standard textbooks on the subject, *Posse italiane* and *Potere alla parola*. Similarly, the 1992 film *Suoni dalla città* (Sounds from the City), a survey of the rap and ragga scene made in Turin, apart from showing two brief glimpses of subsidiary women rappers performing with La To.sse and Assalti Frontali, has an entirely male focus. Two rare examples of female rappers, apart from those involved in Assalti Frontali, are Carrie D., who is from Turin and part of the Century Vox crew, and La Pina, a member of the group Ottiere (OTR). AK 47, the Salento Posse, Suoni Mudu, and the Bari-based Zona 45 have also included female rappers in their lineups. Despite this male domination, most of the posses tend to avoid misogyny, although the reggae group Pitura Freska angered Italian feminists with graphically lecherous songs like "Biennial," which uses the tune of Harry Belafonte's "Banana Boat Song" to celebrate the volume of female flesh at the Venice Biennale art exhibition.

After 1995, when the first left-wing Italian government came into power since World War II, the Italian rap scene began to mellow and diversify. The centri sociali still provided venues for rap and reggae concerts but no longer played the vital nurturing role they had performed for hip-hop culture a decade previously. Some, like the Isola nel Kantiere in Bologna and the Leoncavallo in Milan, had been closed down, and others were transformed into more generalized cultural centers. "Softer" and more commercial forms of rap, some celebrating marijuana, took artists such as Neffa e i Messaggeri della Dopa and Sottotono into the pop charts. More reggae- and dub-inflected groups such as Almamegretta, Africa Unite, and Mau Mau drifted further away from the hip-hop posse culture, illustrating the increased idiosyncrasy of Italian hip-hop-influenced music. Other more militant exponents of rap and hip-hop, such as 99 Posse, subdued their style into more of a reggae-folk hybrid, and the often strident ideological conflicts of the early 1990s between politically engaged rappers and more commercially inclined rappers

Africa Unite. Courtesy of Manuela Calomba/BMG Ariola S.p.a.

subsided. Some rappers gravitated into the burgeoning Italian dance-music, acid-jazz, techno, and drum 'n' bass scene that proliferated largely around Irma Records in Bologna. One such example was Papa Ricky's 1996 album, with his new group I Cauti, which showed a mixture of drum 'n' bass and dub influences, its rap aspects considerably subdued. And the mainstreaming of the militant "combat rappers" of the early 1990s was aptly demonstrated by the release in 1999 on BMG of *Banditi,* the new album by Assalti Frontali—a group that had previously refused to have any involvement in any aspect of the recording industry, releasing recordings on their own label and selling them at gigs and through other alternative outlets (Campo 1999).

Banditi was produced by Ice One, the DJ with Colle der Fomento. This freestyle group, which uses Roman slang and whose name is based on the idea that the stage they perform on is an eighth hill of Rome where the positive energy of hip-hop is fomented, plays what it calls "Roman funk." They were described by Pacoda as "perhaps the real revelation of the end of 1996" (1996: 24) in their revival of hardcore rap, which connected them to the Onda Rossa Posse. Pacoda also profiled Sangue Misto (Mixed Blood), which formed from the remains of the Isola Posse All Stars, a group he claimed represented "the evolution of rap no longer content with the slogans of sonic manifestos, which sought out wordplay and other concoctions to explain in the best of possible ways that the instinct for survival of the tribes will resist being superseded by any fashion" (Pacoda 1966: 27). Both groups indicated a new diversity and maturity in Italian hip-hop that went beyond the polarization of centri sociali militants and party pop–rap factions.

The continuing growth, indigenization, and mainstream acceptance of Italian rap as a musical genre was illustrated in June 1997, when Mentos Hip-Hop Village, the first of what has become an annual free rap festival, was held. This featured fifteen Italian rap posses, including Frankie Hi-NRG MC, Neffa, Colle der Fomento, 99 Posse, and Sottotono, playing to a capacity crowd of more than 12,000 people in Milan. The event was headlined by Kool Herc, indicating a general shift toward reggae sound systems as the acknowledged roots of Italian hip-hop. Reviewing the event in *La Repubblica*, Enrico Assante summed up almost a decade of the genre's growth: "Italian rap has grown and matured and become capable of being not just a manifestation of anger and anxiety, but a rich and complex musical proposition, at once totally modern and linked to the real roots of Italian popular music. It is music that is international by vocation but Italian in spirit, with lyrics that often succeed in describing reality in a creative way" (Assante 1997: n.p.).

Assante's comments bear witness that by 1997 rap and hip-hop had become absorbed into "the real roots of Italian popular music" through a process that began with often inept imitations of English-language rap in the late 1980s, proceeded through phases of adoption and adaptation, and gradually became indigenized and domesticated. In 1996 Marcella Filippa described the "imaginative repertoire" of the Italian posses as "a veritable battlefield where different and in some cases mutually contradictory traditions meet and clash. They represent . . . continuity with the political generations of the 1970s and the more recent experience of the student antiestablishment activity linked to the *Pantera* movement" (1996: 340). By 1999 Italian hip-hop's syncretic blending of African American models, Afro-Caribbean musical forms, and traditional Italian musical and linguistic idioms and political militancy had become a vitally distinctive and heterogenous example of what Gramsci called a "national popular" music culture.

NOTE

1. All quotations from Italian sources are in the author's translation.

REFERENCES

Assante, Ernesto. 1995. "La lingua della strada diventa rap" [The Language of the Street Becomes Rap]. *La Repubblica (supplemento musica)* 12, 7 June.
———. 1997. "Il potere alla parola" [Power to the Word].
    La Repubblica, 31 May.
Balzola, Andrea. 1993. Review of *Rap. Sipario,* January.

Baranski, Zygmunt. 1990. "Turbulent Transitions: An Introduction."
In *Culture and Conflict in Postwar Italy: Essays on Mass and Popular Culture,*
edited by Zygmunt Baranski and Robert Lumley. London: Macmillan.

Bey, Hakim. 1991. *Temporary Autonomous Zone, Ontological Anarchy,*
Poetic Terrorism. New York: Autonomedia.

Branzaglia, Carlo, Pacoda Pierfrancesco, and Solaro Alba. 1993. *Posse italiane:*
Centri sociali, underground musicale e cultura giovanile degli anni '90 in Italia
[The Italian Posses: Social Centres, the Musical Underground, and
Youth Culture in Italy in the 1990s]. Florence: Editoriale Tosca.

Cachin, Olivier. 1996. *Il rap: L'offensiva metropolitana.* Trieste: Electa/Gallimard.

Campo, Alberto. 1995. "Reggae Mediterraneo: Almamegretta." *Rumore,* June, 53.

———. 1996. *Nuovo? Rock?! Italiano!* Florence: Giunti.

———. 1999. 'Banditi e b-boys: Assalti Frontali." *Rumore,* June, 48–51.

Cannon, Steve. 1997. "Paname City Rapping: B-Boys in the Banlieues and
Beyond." In *Post-Colonial Cultures in France,* edited by Alec Hargreaves
and Mark McKinney. London and New York: Routledge.

Coveri, Lorenzo. 1996. "Lingua e dialetto nella canzone popolare italiana
recente." In *Analisi e canzone,* edited by Rossana Dalmonte.
Trento: Università degli Studi di Trento.

Decker, Jeffrey Louis. 1994. "The State of Rap: Time and Place in Hip Hop
Nationalism." In *Microphone Fiends: Youth Music, Youth Culture,*
edited by Andrew Ross and Tricia Rose. New York: Routledge.

De Luca, Fabio. 1992. "Italian Rap Attack" and "Singoli-Speciale Rap."
L'Urlo, March–April, 43.

Dent, Edward. 1949. *Opera.* London: Penguin.

Dezzani, Mark. 1995. "Italian Acts to Follow." *Billboard,* 1 July, 74.

———. 1997. "Italy: The Billboard Spotlight." *Billboard,* 14 June, 48–58.

Donadio, Francesco, and Marcello Giannotti. 1996. *Teddy-boys, rockettari e*
cyberpunk: Tipi mode e manie del teenager italiano dagli anni Cinquanta a oggi
[Teddy Boys, Rockers, and Cyberpunk: Fashion Types and Italian Teenage
Manias from the 1950s to the Present]. Rome: Riuniti.

Ferrari, Paolo. 1992. "Rissa nelle posse" [Riot in the Posses].
Fare musica 135 (summer supplement): 11–15.

Filippa, Marcella. 1996. "Popular Song and Musical Cultures." In *Italian*
Cultural Studies, edited by David Forgacs and Robert Lumley.
London: Oxford University Press.

Harpin, Lee. 1993. "One Continent under a Groove." *i-D,* 16 May, 60.

Liperi, Felice. 1993. "L'Italia s'è desta: Tecno-splatter e posse in rivolta" [Italy
Gets Smart: Techno-Splatter and the Posses in Revolt]. In *Ragazzi senza tempo:*
Immagini, musica, conflitti delle culture giovanili, edited by Massimo Canevacci,

Alessandra Castellani, Andrea Colombo, Marco Srispini, Massimo Ilardi, and Felice Liperi. Genoa: Costa and Nolan.

Lipperini, Loredana. 1992. "Se sei un ladro dillo col rap" [If You're a Thief, Say It with Rap]. *La Repubblica,* 22 August.

———. 1993. "I sogni della metropoli" [Metropolitan Dreams] and "Combattenti del rap." *La Repubblica,* 22 October.

Locatelli, Carla. 1996. "Musica e società nella storia del rap." In *Analisi e canzone,* edited by Rossana Dalmonte. Trento: Università degli Studi di Trento.

Magretta, William, and Joan Magretta. 1979. "Lina Wertmuller and the Tradition of Italian Carnivalesque Comedy." *Genre* 12 (spring): 33–34.

Militant, A. 1998. *Storia di Assalti Frontali: Conflitti che producono banditi* [The History of Assalti Frontali: Conflicts Generate Banditi]. Rome: Castelvecchio.

Mitchell, Tony. 1995. "Questions of Style: Notes on Italian Hip Hop." *Popular Music* 14, no. 3: 333–48.

Moretti, Carlo. 1998. "Almamegretta international: Da Bombay a Londra passando per Napoli." *La Repubblica,* 29 January.

Oliver, Robin. 1996. "Octopus 7." *Sydney Morning Herald TV Guide,* 12 December, 17.

Pacoda, Pierfrancesco, ed. 1996. *Potere alla parola: Antologia del rap italiano.* Milan: Feltrinelli.

Pestalozza, Alberto. 1996. *Almamegretta.* Padua: Arcana.

Plastino, Goffredo. 1996. *Mappa delle voci: Rap, raggamuffin e tradizione in Italia.* Rome: Meltemi.

Potter, Russell A. 1995. *Spectacular Vernaculars: Hip Hop and the Politics of Postmodernism.* New York: State University of New York Press.

Wright, Steve. 2000. " 'A Love Born of Hate': Autonomist Rap in Italy." *Theory, Culture and Society* 17, no. 3: 117–35.

Zanuttini, Paolo. 1992. "Non è qui la festa" [The Party Isn't Here]. *Il Venerdi,* 28 August.

Zukar, Paola. 1998. "Rappresento per l'hip-hop." *Source,* January, 120.

DISCOGRAPHY

Africa Unite. 1991. *People Pie.* Newtone Records.

———. 1993. *Babilonia e poesia.* Vox Pop/Flying Records.

———. 1995. *Un sole che brucia.* Vox Pop/Flying Records.

AK 47. 1992. *0516490572.* [Self-produced.]

———. 1996. *Fuori dal centro.* Il Manifesto.

Almamegretta. 1993. *Anima migrante.* Anagumbra/BMG.

———. 1993. *Figli di Annibale.* Anagumbra.

———. 1995. *Sanacore 1995.* Anagumbra.

———. 1996. *Indubb*. Anagumbra.

———. 1998. *Lingo*. Anagumbra.

———. 1999. *Quattro Quarti*. Anagumbra/BMG.

———. 2001. *Imaginaria*. BMG/Ricordi.

Articolo 31. 1994. *Messa di vespiri*. Flying Records.

———. 1996. *Cosi com'è*. Best Sound/BMG.

Assalti Frontali. 1991. *Terra di nessuno*. [Self-produced.]

———. 1996. *Conflitto*. Il Manifesto.

———. 1999. *Banditi*. BMG.

Bisca 99 Posse. 1994. *Incredibile Opposizione Tour*. Io/Flying records.

———. 1995. *Guai a chi ci tocca*. Io/Flying Records.

Casino Royale. 1993. *Dainamaita*. Blackout/Polygram.

Frankie Hi-NRG MC. 1993. *Faccio la mia cosa*. RCA/BMG.

———. 1993. *Libri di sangue*. RCA/BMG.

Fratelli di Soledad. 1992. *Barzelette e massacri*. X Records.

Jovanotti. 1994. *Lorenzo 1994*. Mercury.

———. 1994. *Penso Positivo*. Soleluna/Polygram Italia.

———. 1997. *Lorenzo 1997: L'albero*. Mercury.

———. 1999. *Capo Horn*. Mercury/Universal.

LHP (Lion Horse Posse). 1992. *Vivi e diretti*. [Self-produced.]

Liberovici, Andrea. 1996. *Rap*. Nuora. Fonit Cetra.

Lou X. 1995. *Dal basso*. Disastro.

Mau Mau. 1992. *Sauta Rabel*. Vox Pop/EMI Italiana.

———. 1994. *Bass Paradis*. Vox Pop/EMI Italiana.

———. 1996. *Viva Mamanera*. Vox Pop/EMI Italiana.

———. 1998. *Eldorado*. Vox Pop/EMI Italiana.

Neffa. 1996. *I messageri della dopa*. Blackout/Polygram.

99 Posse. 1993. *Curre curre guaglio*. Esodo/Flying Records.

———. 1996. *Cerco tiempo*. Esodo/Flying Records.

Nuovi Briganti. 1996. *Camico*. Cyclope Records/Polydor.

Onda Rossa Posse. 1990. *Batti il tuo tempo*. Assalti Frontali.

Otierre, Featuring La Pina. 1997. *Dalla sede*. Polydor.

Papa Ricky. 1995. *Lu Papa Ricky*. Virgin Records.

Papa Ricky e I Cauti. 1996. *16 semplici ricette*. Giungla Records.

Piombo a Tempo. 1995. *Cattivi maestri*. Crime Squad.

Pitura Freska. 1991. *'Na bruta banda*. Psycho.

Possessione. 1993. *Il posto dove vivo*. San Isidro.

Sangue Misto. 1994. *SXM*. Crime Squad/Flying Records.

Sensasciou/Senza Fiato. 1996. *In scia lûnn-a*. Anagrumba.

Sottotono. 1996. *Sotto effeto stono*. Blackout/Mercury.

Sud Sound System. 1995. *Comu na petra*. Il Manifesto.

———. 2001. *Musica Musica*. Royality/Edel Italia.

Various artists. 1990. *Italian Rap Attack*. Irma Records. .

———. 1992. *Fondamentale*. Century Vox/Sony. [Includes Isola Posse All Stars, Sud Sound System, Sa Razza, Speaker Dee Mo', Devastatin' Posse, OTR, Papa Ricky, Fuckin' Camels 'n' Effect.]

———. 1992. *Italian Posse: Rappamuffin d'azione*. Flying Records. [Includes Sud Sound System, Frankie Hi-NRG MC, Comitato, Possessione, La To.sse, 99 Posse, Il Generale.]

———. 1993. *Sud*. San Isidro.

———. 1994. *Nati per rappare*. Crime Squad/Flying Records.

———. 1994. *Salento Showcase 1994*. Ritmo Vitale.

———. 1995. *Nati per rappare 2*. Crime Squad/Flying Records.

———. 1997. *The Rapsody Overture*. Def Jam.

———. 1998. *Red Hot and Rhapsody*. Antilles.

VIDEOGRAPHY

Almamegretta. 1995. *Sanacore Tour 1995: Live in Napoli*. Polygram Video.

Suoni dalla città. 1992. Turin: Cooperativa Zenit–Arti Audiovisivi.

SUD: Suoni Uniti Differenti. 1995. Melendungno, Lecce, Ritmi Vitali.

Chapter 9

A History of Japanese Hip-Hop
Street Dance, Club Scene, Pop Market

IAN CONDRY

yth making is often a part of music marketing, and Japanese hip-hop is no exception. On the introductory track of his 1997 album, the rapper ECD evokes "the beginning of the legend" by reciting the names of the seminal New York City DJs Kool Herc and Grandmaster Flash as well as the rappers KRS-1 and Rakim. It was, he intones, "a revolution, scratching two records and making one music" *(hitotsu no ongaku)*. He then describes the arrival of hip-hop in Japan as a flying spark *(tobihi)* that traveled from the Bronx across the ocean to light a fire.[1] This image of a flying spark is important, for it reminds us that although popular music styles travel on the winds of global capitalism, they ultimately burn or die out on local fuel. One of the challenges in understanding the shape of cultural forms in the contemporary world is to analyze the influence of enormous media conglomerates. To what extent do they guide the uses and meanings of popular culture in everyday life? What other actors and social spaces are key to grasping local appropriations of global styles? The story of hip-hop in Japan—how it was introduced, how it evolved—offers clues as to the dynamic interaction between culture and economics in the twenty-first century.

Japanese hip-hop and other versions around the world are interesting in part because they help us understand the significance of what seems to be an emerging global popular culture. The idea that the boundaries of nation, culture, and language are becoming more permeable and that "flows" need to be given more analytical attention has surfaced in a number of important ways (Appadurai 1996; During 1997; Featherstone and Lash 1995; Gupta and Ferguson 1992). Television shows such as *Who Wants to Be a Millionaire?* and *Big Brother* spawn copycat versions in different national settings. Hollywood films are reaching broader, more international audiences, MTV is beaming its images around the world, and geographically diverse urban youth are adopting the clothing and stance of foreign stars thanks to such new modes of communication. But at the same time, Japanese hip-hop has some intriguing local features. In its lyrics there are no guns, no misogyny, and little violence. Beer is the most common drug mentioned, and when other drugs are present the sentiment tends to be "marijuana good, amphetamines bad." Not a single Japanese rap lyric mentions crack cocaine. Japanese MCs engage in much of the same kind of boasting one might find elsewhere—"I'm the number one rapper"—but the language is Japanese, as are the images of schools, television, and daily life that pepper the songs. Moreover, hip-hop appears in its various aspects, from extensive graffiti walls in Yokohoma, to breakdancers in Tokyo public parks, to DJ shows on television. The focus of this essay is on the Japanese rap music scene, but it is important to recognize that there is a range of local takes on what hip-hop is and should be.

At the same time, it would be a mistake to ignore the interactions between foreign centers of production and the local forms. Japanese hip-hop artists and club DJs follow the trends in the United States very closely, adopting the music that they like the best, playing it in the clubs, and producing their own work in that context. One of the interesting aspects of the Tokyo hip-hop club scene is that East Coast styles—with their faster tempos, sharper rhythms and textures, and often more lyrically dense songs—tend to be more popular than the West Coast, often more mellow, G-funk style, with its slower tempos, more minimal bass lines, and sampled textures in an R&B vein. Some Japanese DJs suggest that this is because Tokyo is more like New York (subways, high population density, no beach) than Los Angeles. Some also point out that Japanese pop music, at least in the 1990s, tended to have a fairly quick tempo, and thus an East Coast style was more amenable to the clubbers' ears. It is also significant that New York is regarded as hip-hop's historical place of origin, so Tokyo fans and artists tend to view that area as producing the more authentic style. The prominence of New York artists in Japan, as compared to the United States where West Coast artists tend to sell more albums, points to one of the local aspects of the market and the fans. This also shows how foreign styles are used by Japanese listeners to define what Japan (or Tokyo) means to them. In this sense, hip-hop in Japan is part of a "global culture" because it cannot be understood solely in local terms.

There is, however, a wide-ranging debate about how one should interpret the significance of such forms. Connections arising from technologies of communication are what some analysts highlight. Scott Lash and John Urry, for example, argue that the structural basis of society must be reconceived because social structures that are national in scope are being displaced by global information and communication structures (Lash and Urry 1994: 6). Distinctiveness of new forms in local areas is emphasized by others. Daniel Miller (1995: 2) notes that although mass-consumption goods are commonly viewed as subsuming and suppressing cultural difference, in fact the opposite might be true. He argues that an "unprecedented diversity created by differential consumption" creates new forms of difference, which should be treated "not as continuity, or even syncretism with prior traditions, but as quite novel forms, which arise through the contemporary exploration of new possibilities" (Miller 1995: 3). This contrast between the standardizing or linking-up aspect of globalization and its diversifying or hybridization aspect is a key theoretical dilemma examined in more detail below.

In this chapter, I explore the history and current scene of Japanese rap music, from its origins in the early 1980s via seminal films to today's expression in all-night hip-hop clubs in Tokyo and its gradual appearance in mainstream pop. My aim is to show what an ethnographic perspective on Japanese hip-hop can tell us about the interaction between a global cultural form and local appropriations. I argue that Japanese hip-hop needs to be understood not as some disembodied flow of culture from one locale to another, but rather in terms of cultural production that is animated through the local scene and the national market. Local musicians and record companies are both involved in the production of music, but their orientations are somewhat different. The role of record companies is largely one of choosing among the musicians already out there and selecting from songs they have already produced. As I will discuss later, record companies' interest or neglect depends heavily on the appearance of crossover hits, especially those songs that sell over a million singles. In this case, the crossover is from a small core of committed fans to a larger, more mainstream mass of consumers. The primary orientation of Japanese DJs and rappers, however, is toward all-night hip-hop clubs, which they call the "actual site" (genba) of the scene. As discussed later, it is in the clubs that musicians hone their musical styles and lyrics in front of discriminating live audiences. Both the commercial pop market and the sweaty nightclubs are central to understanding the production of Japanese hip-hop. My emphasis is on cultural production, because in some ways the idea of "flows" gives the wrong impression. One could consider hip-hop as being like water, flowing underground before emerging into more visible mainstreams on the surface. But in other ways hip-hop does not flow unchanged from one locale to the next, as the variety of examples in this volume make clear. Instead, I would emphasize the flame metaphor, because it is the spark and the local fuel together that make the fire burn with its own particular range of colors.

JAPAN, GLOBALIZATION, AND MUSIC

The significance of Japanese hip-hop relies in part on how we analyze the link between cultural forms and economic power in an age of globalization. Fredric Jameson (1998) notes that evaluations of globalization tend to differ dramatically depending on whether one begins with a cultural or an economic frame of reference. If you focus on the cultural contents of global communication, he argues, "you will slowly emerge into a postmodern celebration of difference and differentiation: suddenly all the cultures around the world are placed in tolerant contact with each other in a kind of immense cultural pluralism which it would be very difficult not to welcome" (Jameson 1998: 56–57). If, on the other hand, you emphasize an economic perspective, "what comes to the fore is increasing identity (rather than difference): the rapid assimilation of hitherto autonomous national markets and productive zones into a single sphere . . . a picture of standardization on an unparalleled new scale" (1998: 57). The distinction could not be more stark, and it highlights both the excitement and the anxieties associated with globalization.

Is hip-hop *in Japan* merely "global noise" drowning out local song? Or is *Japanese* hip-hop an example of a vibrant hybridity of contemporary culture — global noise from the periphery shouting back? Jameson argues that the importance of any given region hinges on the vitality of its cultural products: "fresh cultural production and innovation—and this means in the area of mass consumed culture—are the crucial index of the centrality of a given area and not its wealth or productive power" (1999: 67). Although this formulation raises some thorny questions (for example, what is "fresh"?), it does focus our attention on the key issue of how we should relate local cultural production to the economic setting.[2]

The Japanese market is instructive for a number of reasons. Japan is the second-largest recorded-music market in the world, and sales are dominated by Japanese artists. With a population of 126 million people and per capita spending slightly higher than in the United States, 1997 sales of recorded music in Japan totaled ¥588 billion (U.S. $6.8 billion) (RIAJ 1999: 23). This is a little over half the size of the U.S. market.[3] Although Western artists are quite popular, Japanese artists dominate the market in a ratio of three to one. It was not always this way. From the end of World War II until 1967, Western records outsold Japanese albums (Kawabata 1991). But from 1968 on, Japanese artists have outsold their Western counterparts. Year by year, Japanese musicians have steadily increased their market share such that in 1998, Japanese artists accounted for 77.5 percent of sales (RIAJ 1999: 7). Japan's vibrant and at least semiautonomous national market supports a wide range of local artists.

Japan is also instructive because of its frequently cited proclivity to adopt and adapt foreign cultural forms. Certainly the Japanese have a long history of appropriating foreign ideas, objects, and systems to suit their needs. The writing system, for example, was imported from China in the eighth century. Roland Robertson (1992: 177–78) argues that the syncretism of Japanese religion, namely the importation of Buddhism and its linkage with indigenous Shinto forms, has given Japan a privileged role in the current round of globalization. Arjun Appadurai (1996: 37) notes that "the Japanese are notoriously hospitable to ideas and are stereotyped as inclined to export (all) and import (some) goods, but they are also notoriously closed to immigration." One could point to other historical examples of Japanese adaptation to ideas from the outside. In the late nineteenth century, after two hundred years of isolation imposed by the military government, Japan entered a rapid phase of appropriating Western traits from clothing styles to educational institutions to military tactics. After World War II, the Allied occupation forces also introduced a variety of Western ideas and institutions to Japan, not to mention a wide range of music and dance styles.

Despite these examples, it is dangerous to assert a propensity to appropriate foreign things as inherent in Japan's national character, as if Japanese of all times and circumstances have essentially the same openness to borrowing and syncretism. During the Meiji Restoration of the late nineteenth century, Japanese borrowed from the West to catch up to European colonial powers. After the devastation of World War II, the introduction of Western ideas offered a contrast to the wartime, militarist, and nativist ideology of the nation-state. In postwar Japan, the central dynamic is one of a highly advanced consumer society within the world's second-largest economy. Too often Japan is characterized by broad generalizations — for instance, that it is a nation of imitators, not innovators. We need a clearer sense of the specific dynamics of cultural imports; music offers a useful case study.

Western music styles have been incorporated locally at least since the beginning of the twentieth century, when marching bands and French chansons could be heard in Japan. In the postwar period, various styles have served as a backdrop for youth culture, including jazz in the 1950s, folk in the 1960s, rock in the 1970s, and teen idols in the 1980s (Hosokawa et al. 1991). A clear trend is that foreign styles are initially consumed as foreign, but gradually the local appropriations come to dominate the market. Japan's folk music scene of the 1960s, for example, began with Japanese groups singing Peter, Paul, and Mary songs in English. Over time Japanese artists began using the music of the West, but writing Japanese lyrics with pointed social critiques. Nakagawa Gorō's 1961 "Jukensei Burūsu" (Exam-Student Blues), for example, is a lament about the exam-oriented educational system, set to the tune of a Bob Dylan song. Today, some hip-hop artists liken their music to Japanese folk of the 1960s in that they are the voice of youth disenchanted by the dominant ideologies of what came to be known as "new middle-class" Japan.

Yet for the most part, the political pointedness of Japan's folk music of the 1960s is absent from today's hip-hop. When folk music was on the rise, Japan was subject to political unrest related to students' mistrust of the U.S.-Japan security arrangements.[4] The country was also in the midst of spectacular economic growth, increasing urbanization, declining birthrate, and a growing number of households of nuclear, not extended, families. In the mid-1970s the oil crisis and a sharp fluctuation in exchange rates led to a more uncertain period of adjustment. In the 1980s Japan emerged even stronger as an economic superpower, and today's young rappers spent their early years in this time of the bubble economy. From the early 1990s to the beginning of 2000, Japan's economy has been caught in a recession, and so the current generation of high school and college graduates is facing relatively bleak employment prospects as unemployment, especially among the young, continues to rise. This uncertain economic environment is part of the context of contemporary Japanese hip-hop. Songs by K Dub Shine, for example, consistently criticize the "heartless commercialism" of wealthy Japan. While these broader political economic trends are important to keep in mind, in many ways more personal social dynamics were more important for understanding the first imports of hip-hop.

The First Spark: A Breakdance Boom

One of the interesting features of hip-hop in Japan is that it came via breakdance. A common characterization of hip-hop in both U.S. and Japanese music magazines is to describe hip-hop culture as composed of four main elements: rap, DJing, breakdancing, and graffiti. Since rap albums have become more commercially successful, relatively speaking, than DJing, breakdancing, or graffiti, one might assume that flows along channels of global capitalism would be guided by record companies. Not so in Japan, at least not at first. There breakdancing was the first aspect of hip-hop to experience a "boom" (buumu), as fads are called in Japan. Over time DJing, rap, and graffiti appeared, in roughly that order. This is a reminder that transnational flows of popular culture are not driven solely by media companies' profit margins, but rather by a more complex interaction between foreign and local scenes.

The seminal moment for breakdancing in Japan was 1983, when *Wild Style,* a low-budget film featuring the first generation of U.S. rappers, DJs, and breakdancers, was shown in Tokyo theaters.[5] Performers who appeared in the movie, such as the breakdance team Rock Steady Crew, came to Japan at the same time and performed in Tokyo discos and department stores. ECD, now a key figure as rapper and producer, recalls one of these shows: "Actually, when I saw those guys, I didn't really understand what the rappers and DJs were doing. In terms of what left a lasting impact, I can't remember a thing except the breakdancing" (Fujita 1996: 9). Films conveyed the exuberant athleticism of breakdancing that mesmerized a range of Japanese youth, mostly boys. Another hip-hopper, Crazy-A, relates being reluctantly dragged by his girlfriend to see the movie *Flashdance* but then spellbound by the breakdance scene. Now the leader of the hip-hop outfit Rock Steady Crew Japan, Crazy-A believes that the appeal of breakdancing is its combination of aggressive showmanship without the violence of fighting. It is a dance form where one competes in a very masculine way.

These aspects of breakdance as competition and performance point to the need to develop teams in a place where people will watch. Tokyo in the 1980s had just the spot. Yoyogi Park, between the youth shopping districts of Shibuya and Harajuku in Tokyo, is a gathering point for all manner of youthful fans and performers, and it provided a central meeting point for Japanese breakdancers as well. Crazy-A had heard that breakers were gathering on Sundays on a street called Hokoten, an abbreviation of a word meaning "pedestrian paradise." There, every Sunday, traffic was stopped while diverse bands and dancers gathered to perform outdoors.[6] When Crazy-A went to see, however, "there was only this older guy who had a big Disco Robo [boom box] playing rap music." He continues: "But as time went on, people like me gradually gathered there to listen to the music. Once there were about three or four of us, we gradually started to adopt the posture *(soburi),* and move to the rhythm. More people would come by, and I'd ask if anyone knew where there was dancing going on, but no one was doing it. Then I suggested that maybe we should start, the four of us, and from the next week on, every week, we danced. At first we did it with a radio cassette and cardboard laid out on the ground. Sometimes there was a turntable and PA [public address] system. It was like a block party, a natural phenomenon *[shizen genshō].* And then people like B-Fresh started up too" (interview by the author 1997). That began in the winter of 1984. By the next year, Crazy-A was dancing on television on a weekly music show and also as a back-up dancer for a teen idol. This exposure, along with another movie, called *Break-dance,* released in 1985, is credited with initiating the first of several break-dancing booms. DJ Krush, something of a cult figure in Japan and abroad, also started out playing on Hokoten backing up B-Fresh, the first Japanese rap group to record with a major label.[7]

These early breakers learned primarily from movies and videos and then practiced outdoors with friends. I would stress that the effect of the films must be understood in the context of the weekly practices in the park. In other words, the breakdancing boom did not emerge simply because of the films, but because people who had seen the films also found places to meet and perform together. Interestingly, it seems that breakdancing in New York City owes a debt to movies from East Asia. According to Crazy Legs, a leader of RSC, "The only place I'd say we learned moves from, which was universal for a lot of dancers, was karate flicks on Forty-second Street, 'cause those movies are filmed the best, you could see the movement of the whole body" (Fernando 1994). A striking feature of global flows of popular culture, then, is that dance — movement of the body — moves easily across linguistic and cultural boundaries, and that movies and videos are a primary channel for this exchange. Nevertheless, breakdance also illustrates how media may convey images, practices, and ideas, but the social value of these imports depends on having a group of people get together and work on them. Hokoten, the pedestrian paradise, attracted both interested participants and curious onlookers in a way that generates the feedback between performer and audience critical to developing a new style. Another important space for the development of Japanese hip-hop were all-night dance clubs.

CLUBS: DISCO INFERNO

During the 1980s and the early days of hip-hop in Japan, discos were the trendiest spots for the in crowd. The first rap hit, "Rappers Delight," by the Sugar Hill Gang, is usually cited as the start of hip-hop history, and the song traveled even to Tokyo discos that year (Egaitsu 1997). As the 1980s progressed, rappers and DJs became more active in the club scene. As MC Bell of B-Fresh puts it:

When you talk about Japanese hip hop, you definitely have to recognize that there are two streams. One is that of Itō Seiko and Tiny Punx, what might be called the classy *[oshare]* style that started with the people who frequented clubs. The other stream started with Hokoten ("pedestrian paradise") in Harajuku. At Harajuku's Hokoten, it started with break dancing. If you consider that hip-hop culture developed in stages, the first way we [B-Fresh] took up hip hop was breakdance. (Bell and Cake-K 1998)

Clubs were the primary focus for musicians, and a variety of groups crossed over from other genres. Takagi Kan came over from punk, Chikada Haruo had already released several rock albums before he adopted the moniker President BPM and formed the band Vibrastone, and so on. The idea of clubs as "classy" locales is a reference to the new breed of conspicuous consumers known as the *shinjinrui,* who were twentysomething urbanites enamored of foreign brand-name items. They were symbolic of the wealth and ephemeral consumption of the 1980s bubble economy.

Two trends in the Tokyo club scene in the mid- to late 1980s are worth highlighting. As the decade progressed, people could get more timely access to U.S. music, and this contributed to an increasing compartmentalization of separate scenes. New songs and new artists were becoming known more quickly as Japanese fans, at least in Tokyo, were able to learn of the latest trends more or less immediately. In other words, mass culture was becoming more widely diffused, more quickly, another example of what David Harvey (1990) calls time-space compression. On the other hand, a growing depth of media exchange was occurring as well, gradually changing the equation for those wishing to be up to date. More specialized forums for hip-hop gradually appeared. In 1986 a club called Hip Hop opened in Shibuya and was the first space devoted solely to the genre. DJ Yutaka, who splits his time between Tokyo and Los Angeles and who works with Ice-T, was a regular there. That same year a Yokohama radio station began airing the "scratch mix" of the hip-hop DJ collective MID (Egaitsu 1997). In 1987 a television comedy show featured rappers giving the weather report. Specialty magazines began covering hip-hop in greater detail as well, which meant that there was also a deepening compartmentalization of the hip-hop scene as more and more media options became available. From 1988 to 1992 the scene picked up energy in part from a growing number of club events that featured contests for rappers, DJs, and breakdancers. Some were sponsored by companies selling DJ equipment (e.g., Vestax). The DJ Underground Contest, first held in 1988, featured many of the prominent artists of today. Major Force, a hip-hop and dance-music label founded by Takagi Kan and others, began producing albums in 1988. In 1989 ECD started the Check Your Mic contest, which continued off and on for five years; a live album was even produced. That same year a flood of U.S. artists traveled to Japan to perform, including the Jungle Brothers, 45 King, and De La Soul. After

Public Enemy's show, which featured armed security guards pretending to spray the audience with machine-gun fire, Japanese rap groups began to include motionless, silent, brooding "security" to their onstage shows, a practice laughed about today. The Little Bird Nation, led by the wordplay rappers Scha Dara Parr, coalesced in 1990, as did Zingi (DJ Bass, Dohzi-T, Zingi, etc.), a brash and noisy group of hip-hop artists whose name refers to a gang's moral code. The year 1990 also saw a second breakdancing boom when Bobby Brown visited Japan. A year later the television show *Dance yochien* (Dance Tournament) spread the excitement of breakdancing further.

This dual process, whereby big clubs became more specialized and television broadcast aspects of hip-hop music and dance, points to some underlying mechanisms in the spread of a new style. In his study of the growth of sugar consumption in Britain, Sidney Mintz (1985) traced the complex linkages between slavery, trade, and household habits. Two important concepts he used for analyzing changes in consumption habits are extensification and intensification. Extensification refers to the process whereby a broader range of people gain access to a given commodity. Sugar gradually changed from a luxury for the elite to a staple for the masses. With popular music, extensification comes through expanded media coverage in television and through the appearance of hit songs. Intensification is the process by which a taste becomes more important—for example, through a ritual such as taking one's daily tea with sugar. In the case of Japanese rap, movies, videos, and live performances were key means by which hip-hop was experienced with sufficient extensiveness to encourage emulation. But above all, for the style to develop locally, years of intensive back-and-forth circulation between would-be rappers and their audiences led to the emergence of diverse families of rap groups within the club scene.

Although the club scene was developing during the 1980s, record companies gave only a lukewarm reception to up-and-coming Japanese rappers, in part because of a deep-seated skepticism about whether the Japanese language could be used for rap music. It is this issue I turn to next.

Language: The Impossible Wall

Language is a key variable for understanding Japanese hip-hop and for transnational exchanges more generally. When we consider cultural globalization, we need to examine what actually moves across the cultural divide, because that is how to get a sense of what kind of divide it is. In Japan the lyrical content of U.S. rap songs is to a large degree unappreciated, though the flow of the rapper's voice is dissected and analyzed in quite fine detail.

The attraction is more the "grain of the voice," as Barthes says (1990: 293), than the meaning of the words. The puns, the slang, the sly references and often even the main ideas are lost on most Japanese listeners. A DJ friend, wondering about the lyrics of one of his favorite songs, was shocked to learn that "We love smokin' that chronic" refers to marijuana. Although Japanese releases of U.S. hip-hop albums often include translations of the lyrics, my experience interviewing clubbers and Japanese rappers indicates that not a lot of attention is paid to the subtleties of U.S. rappers' words. In contrast, there is intense discussion and analysis of the samples that make up the music track. There is even a book that describes the source of the original samples used in a variety of so-called Shibuya-style musicians' albums, such as those of Scha Dara Parr (Murata 1997). Thus, one of the effects of language differences is to make the importance of U.S. hip-hop albums depend largely on the music rather than the lyrics.

Language differences were also viewed as a major hurdle for Japanese rappers to overcome. The period between 1992 and 1994 is regarded as an ice age *(hyōgaki)* for Japanese rap, and few albums were released. For one thing, record companies were fairly unenthusiastic about the genre, which had failed to produce any big hits. But they were also skeptical because they viewed the Japanese language as inherently deficient for producing the rhythm and rhyme that characterizes rap vocals. Japanese, in contrast to English, is an unaccented language; that is, each syllable in a word receives the same amount of stress.[8] Rappers must artificially add stress to certain syllables to give the rap lyrics the necessary rhythmic punctuation. This makes it "sound" like English. Rhyming is difficult because of the grammatical structure, which places the verb at the end of the sentence: the limited number of verb endings makes it difficult to create striking rhymes. This was the story I heard from Japanese rappers and from record-company people during preliminary fieldwork in the summer of 1994. Microphone Pager, a group whose members include the rappers Muro and Twigy, even referred to this language difference as "the impossible wall" and, rhyming with the English phrase "got it goin' on," exhorted Japanese to cross over it *(fukanō na kabe nori koerō)*.[9] By the summer of 1996, when I began a year and a half of extended fieldwork in Tokyo, this deficiency of the language was seldom talked about, and the relationship between the recording industry and Japanese rappers had changed markedly. Why? One reason was that a range of new releases showed that it was possible to use the Japanese language to produce a rap rhythm. What convinced record companies to take another look at the genre, however, was the appearance of several million-selling Japanese rap hits.

Crossover Hits 1: The East End X Yuri Phenomenon

In 1994, the rap trio Scha Dara Parr teamed up with the guitarist-song-writer Ozawa Kenji to produce the first million-selling rap hit, a mellow funk song called "Kon'ya wa būgi bakku" (Boogie Back Tonight) that was an anthem to hanging out with friends and flirting with women in clubs.[10] Music magazines heralded this as evidence of the establishment of a bona-fide rap scene because it was now capable of producing hits. Then in the summer of 1995, East End X Yuri (the "X" is read "plus") produced a couple of million-selling hit songs ("Da Yo Ne!" and "Maicca"), both of which capitalized on using teenage slang combined with a carefree attitude toward everything from school to love affairs.[11] These commercial successes prompted a wave of publicity in music magazines, and the term "J-rap" was coined to represent the up-and-coming new genre. Major record companies began to show interest in a variety of hip-hop groups that had been languishing on independent labels. It is important to note that most of these groups had been performing for years when the major labels finally decided to record and promote their new work. Record companies did not create new acts; rather, they showed new interest in the hopes of cashing in on a new wave of interest. Groups that emphasized a more playful approach — "party rap" — were signed to several major companies. EDU was one of these groups, and they benefited from a vastly increased budget for promoting their work and for a weekly live event in a Harajuku club.

Not all rappers were enthusiastic about the J-rap boom. For some hip-hop groups, East End X Yuri's success meant that the sickening commercialism of Japanese pop culture had invaded even hip-hop. They viewed people like Yuri as posers who forsook the oppositional stance at the root of hip-hop culture in favor of a superficial pop song with a distinctive rap style. Party-rap groups countered that lighthearted rap was much more appropriate to Japanese teens than the preachy, self-important boasting of underground groups. The two perspectives built on each other as the fan base for party rap as opposed to underground hip-hop diverged. On television, East End X Yuri performed on the Japanese national network NHK's year-end musical extravaganza in 1995. Meanwhile, the underground hip-hop collective Kami-nari held to a tougher, more abrasive ethic, performing to packed clubs and eventually moving to Club Citta in Kawasaki, a venue holding over a thousand b-boys and b-girls for their semiregular event, called Onidamari (literally, "devils' gathering").

The composition of the fans for the two styles was almost completely different as well. The split in the scene is portrayed most starkly by a pair of outdoor concerts held only a week apart in July 1996. The first, Thumpin'

Camp, was organized by ECD and featured over thirty artists from the underground scene. The sellout crowd of 4,000 was roughly 80 percent male. The fashion, gestures, and atmosphere emphasized building an authentic hip-hop culture in Japan, which was defined largely by an oppositional stance to mainstream culture. K Dub Shine, for example, called on the audience to yell loudly enough to disturb the then scandal-ridden Ministry of Health. The next week, Scha Dara Parr and friends held the Dai LB Matsuri (Big Little Bird Festival) in the same outdoor amphitheater in a downtown Tokyo park. They too had a sellout crowd, but here the audience was 80 percent female, and the atmosphere was one of a playful romp with rap lyrics and style. Spoofs of popular Japanese television programs as part of the show exemplified a more sympathetic attitude toward mainstream popular culture. There seemed to be little overlap between the audiences of the two events.

Although the distinction between party rap and underground hip-hop is a recurring theme in the Japanese scene, the energy of the debate waned in the latter half of the 1990s. The J-rap boom had subsided significantly by mid-1997, when subsequent releases by East End X Yuri failed to live up to the high expectations held by their record company. Shortly thereafter Yuri and East End went their separate ways. Meanwhile, many of the groups signed to major labels were also let go, including EDU and Cake-K, who were also more closely aligned with the party rap style. On the other hand, so-called underground groups gradually became more established, if not in mainstream pop, at least in terms of building up a core of fans. Hip-hop music continued to be produced, but the main venues returned to being all-night dance clubs. In many ways, it is this setting that most helps us understand the particulars of Japanese hip-hop production.

The Clubs as "Actual Site": A Visit to Harlem (the One in Tokyo)

Doko ga riaru?	Where is the "real"?
Sore wa genba	In the clubs
Tsumari koko ni aru	In other words, right here
	—Rhymester[12]

In the spring of 1999, when I returned for a brief research trip, the flagship for the Japanese hip-hop scene was a club called Harlem. Nestled in the love-hotel area of Shibuya, a shopping district of Tokyo targeted at youth, Harlem was the largest hip-hop club in Tokyo, attracting upward of 1,000 people on a busy Friday or Saturday night. Incidentally, if you want to find the happening hip-hop shows, a good method is to check the flyers posted at

Manhattan Records, not far from Shibuya's main thoroughfare, and look for shows featuring popular club acts such as Rhymester, Zeebra, DJ Kensei, and DJ Krush. The flyers also have maps to the clubs, which is useful because there is no sign out in front of Harlem; a well-dressed bouncer with long hair is the only indication that a club is inside. It seems there are always a couple of clubbers out front talking on their tiny cell phones (it is too loud inside to use them). If we were going to a club, we would probably meet at around midnight, since the main action seldom gets started before 1:00 A.M., just after the trains stop running for the night. At the door, we head up the stairs, past a table filled with flyers advertising upcoming hip-hop events at Harlem and elsewhere. We pay our ¥3,000 each (around $30, which may seem expensive, but it is only about half again as much as a movie ticket), and move into the circulating and sweaty mass inside.

The first thing you notice is the booming bass coming from the enormous speakers. It literally thuds through your body, massaging your bones. The records are mostly U.S. hip-hop tunes, both classics and more recent releases, mixed in with an array of Japanese rap songs as well. On the wall behind the DJ stage, Bruce Lee videos and Japanese *anime* provide a background of violence and mayhem, but on the dance floor a detached coolness pervades the space. The clubbers dancing are split between couples and same-sex groups, with quite a bit of circulating and flirting going on. A Japanese MC occasionally shouts out encouragement to the audience to get riled up. DJ Master Key may be showing off his scratch technique, and a group of breakdancers may be holding an impromptu battle on the dance floor. There are an additional bar and dance area upstairs, as well as a VIP lounge where rappers and DJs of diverse groups will meet, gossip, and network. The live show will begin around 1:30 A.M., but in the meantime, people are circulating, flirting, and exchanging news and views in an environment of play heightened by loud music, alcohol, and cigarettes. There are usually more women than men, about a sixty-forty split. A few *gaijin* (foreigners) linger about, but for the most part the place is by Japanese for Japanese, a space where they can be b-boys and b-girls to their hearts' content, until they go back to school or their mindless service jobs the next day.

Clubs are regarded by musicians, promoters, and fans alike as the actual site *(genba)* of the Japanese rap music scene, where one finds the most devoted and most critical fans, where professionalism in performance is gauged most heavily, and where the health of the scene is on display. They all agree that you cannot understand Japanese hip-hop unless you spend time in the clubs. Thanks to the huge sound *(dekai oto)*, the physical intimacy of performers and audience, and the loosening effect of alcohol, clubs are a space where an ideal hip-hop world can be given free play, precisely because it is such a circumscribed location. The word *genba* is made up of the kanji characters "to appear" and "place," thus meaning "the place where something happens"—a crime, an accident, a job site, or, in this case, hip-hop itself. Clubs represent a kind of crossroads, where foreign and local music mix and are remixed and where fans, musicians, and media and industry people keep in touch with each other.

Clubs are central sites in part because they tell us about the pleasures of rap music in Japan, a pleasure that arises even when the lyrics of U.S. rappers (and often those of Japanese rappers too) cannot be understood. Because club kids play while almost everyone else sleeps, the clubber's experience is defined by the sense of moving against the stream in time and space, yet residing within the confines of a larger mainstream. It is analogous, perhaps, to the way a personal CD player eliminates the sound of the endless "be careful" announcements at Japanese train stations, though the train doors open and close at the same time for everyone. Moreover, club events encourage a heightened emotional intensity that becomes associated with the music. Ideally, one gets caught up in the drama of the show, and the excitement of the audience compounds the energy in the space. A key word is *moriagaru*, which means "to get thrilled" and has the connotation of emotion piling up on emotion. Emile Durkheim speaks of the effect of religious thought bringing about heightened mental activity, which he calls "effervescence," in terms that could easily apply to a hip-hop club: "Vital energies are overexcited, passions more active, sensations stronger; there are even some that are produced only at this moment. A man does not recognize himself; he feels himself transformed and consequently he transforms the environment which surrounds him" (Durkheim 1993: 99). It is analogous to Durkheim's notion of the sacred in being "something added to and above the real" (99). Clubs, by analogy, are b-boy heaven. At home, his parents ridicule his hair and his clothes. His sister hates his music. His teachers tell him to study more. But in the club, the time spent reading music magazines, listening to music, and scouring record store bins pays off as a form of cultural capital, a way of communicating among friends and acquaintances who may not live in the same area or work the same kinds of jobs.

How do the rappers speak to their fans? There is a wide range of hip-hop styles for almost every taste. Zeebra, arguably the most gifted stage presence on the Japanese hip-hop scene, offers an energetic hardcore style filled with references to sex and marijuana and lyrics with intriguing bilingual rhymes. The group Rhymester, which formed when the members were students at prestigious Waseda University, are notable for a wry sense of humor, jabbing fun at Japanese society and even their own fans. Buddha Brand presents a mellow funk mix of Japanese sprinkled with English slang, an outgrowth of their early years of performing in New York City. Some groups, such as You the Rock and Shakkazombie, have exciting stage shows, while others, such as Rino and K-Dub Shine, put forth a cooler, more restrained style. EDU offers an upbeat show focusing on relationships and emotions, while TAK the Rhymehead gives cerebral rhymes in a lilting delivery on subjects like the homeless and teens' amphetamine abuse. Dassen 3, one of the few groups from Osaka, combine their regional slang with humorous stories. Scha Dara Parr is recognized for its clever wordplay and smooth tracks. DJ Krush is arguably the most innovative instrumentalist of the Tokyo scene, his spacey compositions often featuring a distinctive brassy snare drum. This range of artists is a reminder that clubs are not only important for making listeners feel a close connection to the music, but are also sites for learning and experimentation.

Since the late 1980s there have been numerous contests for DJs, break-dancers, and rappers where the unsigned can hype their stuff. Clubs offer more informal means of education and testing as well. At most hip-hop club events, you will find DJ acolytes huddled around the booth, trying to read the names of groups on spinning albums, studying scratch tricks, and learning new transition techniques. On the dance floor at some point in the evening, three or four breakdancers are likely to begin an impromptu battle while a circle of onlookers judges with enthusiastic "oohs" or pained silence. After rap shows, there are usually freestyle sessions where a microphone or two is passed around the stage and newcomer rappers can step up and try out some new lines or, better yet, improvise. Indeed, there was something of an improvisation *(sokkyō)* boom in 1995, as rappers competed to perform the best "top of the head" rhymes.

Clubs also help us understand the way different styles within Japanese rap music emerged. The social organization of the Japanese hip-hop scene is best characterized as loose groups of "families" *(famirii)* who come together regularly at different club events. A family is a collection of rap groups, usually headed by one of the more famous Tokyo acts, with a number of protégés. These families arise primarily from the club scene and are the key to understanding stylistic differences between groups. In 1988 the DJ Underground contest featured in one show many of the groups (or earlier incarnations thereof) that are popular today: DJ Krush, Scha Dara Parr, Rhymester, Cake-K (of B-Fresh), and Gaku (of East End) (Egaitsu 1997). By the late 1990s each of these groups had built up a following of its own, organized separate club events, and amassed a group of like-minded performers, so that distinctive styles have gradually coalesced around the central artists. There are strong affinities among groups that perform regularly together and marked differences between the different collectives. The Little Bird Nation (with Scha Dara Parr), Kaminari (with You the Rock and Rino), the Funky Grammar Unit (with Rhymester and East End), and Kitchens (with EDU and NowNow) are all good examples of this, and they have each developed fairly separate groups of fans as well. Groups that perform together often have met at live shows, and it is common for younger artists to credit certain freestyle sessions as opening the door to later collaborations with more established groups.

This brings us back to Daniel Miller's insight that consumption be viewed not merely as a kind of syncretism with prior traditions, but rather as new forms. The variety of Japanese rap styles militates against an interpretation that the domestication of rap has involved a melding of "Japanese culture" with "hip-hop culture." Instead, we need to understand how specific social spaces, first Yoyogi Park and later the clubs, helped create networks of people. Thus, the kinds of communication these spaces have facilitated and the trajectories of different rap groups give us the key to understanding the kind of mixing involved. Some of the social interaction in clubs does arise out of very Japanese styles of behavior, such as respect for seniors, attitudes toward drinking, and ritual greetings. Age-graded hierarchies can often be read off from the order of microphone passing during freestyle battles. I know of at least one group that disbanded because one member demanded more respectful treatment since he was older. Getting drunk is in general positively evaluated, and acting cool (i.e., being drunk though seeming not drunk) is generally frowned on as acting cold. Hip-hop practices — rap music at high volume, the clothes, the music videos showing, and the performances themselves — are not regarded as excluding Japanese rituals. At an event I attended in January 1997, rappers and DJs in their Nike sneakers, baggy jeans, and oversized hockey shirts were going around the club giving the traditional New Year's greeting — "Congratulations on the new year; I humbly request your benevolence this year too" — without even a hint of irony. Japanese hip-hop is a collage of appropriations, experimentations, and refusals. Clubs are the settings that provide the critical link between the current array of styles and the history of media exchange.

One of the main points about clubs is that they help us understand the setting in which the production and consumption of hip-hop in Japan reach their most intense expressions. By identifying sites like these, where people build relationships and loose communities of friends, we can situate mass commodities in the situations and social relationships that make them meaningful. Taken out of this context, Japanese rap music often strikes listeners both in Japan and in the United States, as merely imitative. Indeed, this discourse of imitation and authenticity is an interesting topic, one that I explore elsewhere (Condry 2000). Significantly, the pleasures of clubbing make questions of authenticity meaningless. As Rock-Tee, a DJ and music producer, puts it, "We don't care that people say we're just imitators. Our fans understand, and that's all that matters" (interview by author 1999). Given the loud sound and enclosed spaces of clubbing, I would argue that this understanding is less intellectual than visceral. Not surprisingly, record companies and music magazines also pay closer attention to those artists that can move the crowd.

Crossover Hits 2: The Japanese R&B Boom

In the late 1990s, local hip-hop found another path into more mainstream pop music thanks to a Japanese R&B boom. Sparked by female artists such as Misia and Utada Hikaru and groups such as Double and Sugar Soul, this "new R&B" is characterized by melodic music and attractive young women singers. The music tends to be bass heavy with an emphasis on the rhythms, and always with a token DJ scratch solo. As these singers and groups produced hit songs, they often recorded remix versions with Japanese rappers accompanying them. Zeebra appeared with Misia and Sugar Soul, Rhymester with Double, Muro with Misia, and so on. One of the intriguing contrasts with the earlier J-rap boom that began with East End X Yuri and Scha Dara Parr is that the more recent artists hail from the underground scene as opposed to the party-rap world.

Even so, music magazines that focus on the club scene emphasize a sharp boundary between the dubious pop *market* and the authenticity that characterizes the club *scene*. In an article describing a then-forthcoming release by the rapper Zeebra, a writer for *Remix* magazine contrasts the flighty fad of Japanese R&B with what he calls the "mature foundation" of hip-hop. "Now that it seems the so-called Japanese R & B/melody-oriented songs are starting to fade, we've reached the stage where there will be some natural weeding out. . . . But there's no worry about that for Japanese hip-hop, because the scene itself is supported by people choosing the authentic over the fake. Now more than ever, true ability and originality will distinguish those artists who preserve 'realness'" (*riarusa*) (Kinoshita 2000: 14–15). This distinction between mere fads and "true ability" is just one of the many ways that musicians and music writers keep some distance between the fast-changing market and the more enduring club scene.

One of the interesting features of the new R&B boom is that it has brought a variety of the underground hip-hop artists into the national market spot-light. In the mid-1990s it was the lighthearted, feel-good party rap of Scha Dara Parr and East End X Yuri that created the first big break for Japanese hip-hop. In the late 1990s and the beginning of the new millennium, it is the resolutely masculine, outsider, tough-guy stance of Zeebra, Muro, and Rhymester that has provided a striking contrast to the melodic and feminine world of Japanese R&B. As the writer above points out, the R&B boom, like all fads, will lose energy, but it has provided a way for Japanese hip-hop to gain exposure to a much wider audience than it has seen since the mid-1990s.

In the end, it is a range of mechanisms at work that produces the expansion of foreign-based styles in Japan. Hit songs may extend the popularity of Japanese rap music, but the evolution of different styles is better understood in terms of the clubs where, out of the interactions between performers and fans, various styles emerge. Paul Gilroy points to the importance of rethinking our mapping of cultures. The notion of diaspora is in many ways more flexible and revealing than the metaphor of cultural flows. The idea of diaspora reminds us that it is the artists, writers, and consumers together who produce a new cultural phenomenon, and that no solid (or fluid) object itself actually flows. As Gilroy puts it, "Critical space/time cartography of the diaspora needs therefore to be readjusted so that the dynamics of dispersal and local autonomy can be shown alongside the unforeseen detours and circuits which mark the new journeys and new arrivals that, in turn, release new political and cultural possibilities" (1993: 86). Japan's hip-hoppers are part of this dispersal and local autonomy. They redefine and reshape hip-hop. For now, it is primarily for Japanese consumption, though it seems likely that transnational crossovers will also become more frequent in the future, as the Ricky Martin phenomenon suggests. Such crossovers may even, like hits in Japan, spark record companies' interest in experimenting with foreign artists.

Part of this cartography involves understanding the place of Shibuya in Tokyo in the world of Japanese youth culture. Japanese hip-hop is best characterized as youth music that focuses on the importance of young people's "speaking out," in a society that stresses seniority, and of questioning, in various ways, the hyperconsumerism of Japanese culture. In other foreign locales, rap music is also associated with the places of youth, but, more often, youth marginalized by class and ethnicity. In France it is the public housing projects for immigrants from the colonial empire that provides the home base for many rappers (Prévos 1997). In Italy, community centers originally set up by the Communist Party nurtured early Italian rap and encouraged political tendencies in the music (Mitchell 1997). In Australia, the western suburbs of Sydney, with its migrant communities, are analogous to U.S. ghettos and are seen as the historic center of local hip-hop culture (Mitchell 1997). Urla, in this volume, shows how Basque separatists turned the oppositional stance of a group like Public Enemy to their own ends.

The contrast is stark. In Japan, too, hip-hop is associated with place, but not any kind of marginalized residential neighborhood or region. On the contrary, Japanese hip-hop is generally associated with Shibuya, a trendy shopping district in Tokyo where many of the key nightspots and record stores are located. Shibuya is the epicenter for youth culture in Japan in many ways. Japan, like France but unlike the United States, is a nation with a single metropole. Partly this is a matter of density: the metropolitan region of Tokyo is home to roughly 40 percent of the nation's 126 million people. This concentration of people provides a critical mass for all kinds of extremely specialized youth movements such that people commute to play. The park with the "pedestrian paradise" where the first breakdancers congregated is typical of the kind of gathering place that brings enough people together so that something can happen. Above all, however, probably the main reason youth go to Shibuya is to shop. From enormous department stores to tiny boutiques, the range of choices is stunning. For music, the area is probably one of the best places in the world to find both new and rare items. Record stores such as Manhattan, Cisco, and DMR (Dance Music Records) that specialize in hip-hop LPs stock the latest U.S. releases as well as those of the few Japanese artists that make it to vinyl. It is not just the availability of goods that makes the area the epicenter of the latest fads. Print and television aimed at teens use the area to identify new trends in fashion, language, and music by interviewing and photographing youth on the street. Again we see the different levels between mass markets and more focused scenes that are both part of the mechanism explaining the spread and significance of popular culture.

CONCLUSION

My hero is Stevie Wonder. He is a god. But when I watch
kabuki, *I feel like I'm in a foreign country.*
—Como-Lee, a Japanese hip-hop producer

Many in the first generation of Japanese hip-hoppers were first exposed to the style in 1983 by watching the movie *Wild Style,* a homage to graffiti artists, rappers, and breakdancers in the Bronx. Over time a growing number of U.S. rap artists toured Japan, and record stores expanded their stock of the genre. By the mid-1990s a vibrant local scene was characterized by a diverse range of styles from unabashedly commercial to resolutely hardcore. One of the intriguing features of Japanese hip-hop is the way that crossover hits have influenced the relationship between the Japanese market and the underground scene. In 1994–95 there were three million-selling singles in the J-rap mode, sparking a fierce debate about the meaning of hip-hop in Japan. In the late 1990s the rise of Japanese R&B led to a very different kind of tension between the underground artists and the pop-music world. For many urban youth, hip-hop is the defining style of the era. In the 1970s the paradigm of high-school cool was long hair and a blistering solo on lead guitar. Today trendsetters are more likely to sport "dread" hair and show off their scratch techniques with two turntables and a mixer.

There is no reason to think that the transmission of cultural forms across national boundaries is likely to slow down. The capitalist logic of entertainment industries is to seek larger and larger markets. The general rule of information-based industries is that it is expensive to produce the original (e.g., a master tape for a CD) but inexpensive to reproduce subsequent copies. Hence, the larger the market, the greater the return, with increasing (not diminishing) returns as the scale grows. Japanese hip-hop musicians, however, are adamant about distinguishing between the market and the scene, not because they are completely separate worlds, but because they represent different orientations in defining the meaning of music. Record companies naturally focus on the market and respond to crossover hits with increased signings and production. But the musicians themselves produce the music with a focus on the clubs and a desire to get attention among a more focused group of fans and fellow musicians. For Japanese hip-hop at least, the local production of styles continues as a kind of craft industry focused in the all-night clubs. Only a few of the artists are making a living by music alone, but they continue working as best they can. The anxieties expressed by Jameson that from an economic perspective media conglomerates have monopoly control, thus creating extensive standardization, are accurate in the sense that record company monopolies do very much determine the kinds of music we can get access to on CD. On the other hand, there is a rich variety of cultural production that never sees the light of day. For these artists, the key factor is the crossover hit that brings a style and group of artists out of obscurity into the buzz of the style of the day. This happened in 1994–95 with three million-selling singles. It has also been happening to some extent at the turn of the new century thanks to the current Japanese R&B boom, though with a more underground style.

One goal of this chapter is to show how we must relate the economic to the cultural in order to understand the expansion of cultural forms across national boundaries. Music is an example of commodified culture where the style is related to specific social spaces and to a larger economic market. As we have seen, Japanese hip-hop is not driven solely by media companies, but neither is it immune to their influence. Similarly, despite declarations in music magazines of "keeping it real," Japanese rappers are not simply artists working out their rhymes alone in their apartment buildings, but also entrepreneurs trying to expand their network of fans. Thus, the example of hip-hop is intriguing for the insight it offers into changes in cultural forms. Clearly there is some currency in the idea that cultural forms are becoming increasingly deterritorialized, while people's connection to place is in ways growing more tenuous (Appadurai 1996). Japanese hip-hop fans are plugged into a wide-ranging scene that includes Tokyo club events and the latest album releases and interviews from New York City, while they also use streams of cultural capital in their everyday lives that are more geographically constrained, usually limited to travel by car or train or to telephone communication.

Although the Japanese are stereotyped as imitators, not innovators, the distinction is difficult to define in any rigorous way. To read into all uses of rap and hip-hop in Japan a traditional mode of borrowing is to blur the specificity of what is going on. Japanese hip-hop is both derivative *and* innovative; trying to define it as one or the other misses the point. Both the history of Japanese rap music and the location of the clubs as the "actual site" give us some clues to the pressures on artists to create certain styles of music. In addition, changes in media technology are creating a situation in which popular culture spreads more widely than ever before. Pop musicians, whether Western stars such as Celine Dion or Japanese pop groups such as Mister Children, are selling unprecedented numbers of albums. One scholar explains the rapid increase in the number of million-selling albums in 1990s Japan as resulting from new CD technology that makes it more accessible to a broader segment of the population (Asō 1997). This extensification is accompanied by a kind of intensification as well. As a Sony Records representative put it, "In the 1980s, we had reggae, punk, rap—really all kinds of underground things in the clubs . . . but with kids nowadays, they choose one thing—computers, *anime*, reggae, hip-hop—and go deeply into that" (interview by the author 1997). Understanding the social role of popular culture means moving back and forth between the style's constellation of meanings, understood in the practitioners' own terms, and the larger social economic context. For hip-hop in Japan, the movement between street dance, club scene, and pop market provides touchstones for understanding the globalization of popular culture more generally.

Finally, the path hip-hop has taken in Japan points to the distinctive role anthropology can play in understanding global media. Films were important initially for bringing the style to Japan, but so was Yoyogi Park, where spatially dispersed people with similar interests could come together to build a scene. Similarly, the tension between the music market and the club scene plays out in different ways depending on the presence or absence of hit songs. The point is that anthropology draws us to the social spaces, local meanings, and interpersonal relations that animate popular culture. The interaction between global flows and local settings is somewhat complex, but by unraveling the mechanisms we can get a clearer picture of the potential effects of global media products. Most important, we need to move beyond an overly simplistic dichotomy between the cultural and the economic aspects of globalization to explore instead how each affects the other.

NOTES

I would like to thank Tony Mitchell, Bill Kelly, members of the anthropology dissertation writing group at Yale, and Tim Soehl for their helpful comments and criticisms. The usual disclaimers apply. Funding for fieldwork on this project from September 1995 to February 1997 was generously provided by the Japan-U.S. Educational Commission (Fulbright). Thanks go to the Yale Council on East Asian Studies for generous support during the writing of my dissertation and for brief trips to Japan in 1998 and 1999.

1. ECD, "Intro," *Big Youth* (1997, Cutting Edge, CTCR-14075).

2. Obviously, Jameson is aware of the pitfalls in trying to define what would be "authentic" local production (authentic for whom? according to whom? etc.). Even so, the notion of "fresh" in many ways merely reproduces the problem of how to distinguish real versus imitation, or, in another, related dimension, local versus foreign, by transposing it into an opposition between fresh versus derivative. His formulation is useful, however, because it so accurately captures an ongoing concern in evaluating the power of media giants: do they, the artists, or the consumers control? I would argue that it is not only the features of the cultural product (e.g., a song) that need to be understood, but also the broader circumstances of production as well.

3. According to the Recording Industry Association in Japan, in 1997 per capita spending on music was $53.84 in Japan (pop. 126 million) and in the United States, $44.67 (pop. 267 million). U.S. recorded-music sales in 1997 totaled $11.9 billion (RIAJ 1999: 23).

4. For an excellent and concise overview of postwar Japan's history, see Allinson 1997.

5. *Wild Style,* originally released in 1982, was written, directed, and produced by Charlie Ahearn. A video of *Wild Style* with Japanese subtitles was rereleased in September 1996 through the record company Vortex (MLK-001). It also had a brief run as a midnight show at Parco Department store in Shibuya around the same time.

6. In the winter of 1997 live bands were banned from playing at Hokoten, but the area continues to provide a gathering place for such groups as the so-called rock 'n' rollers, who come every Sunday, wearing jeans and leather jackets and boots and sporting greased-back Elvis hairdos, and do a kind of twist to U.S. rock of the 1950s and 1960s. Female fans of the band X-Japan also gather nearby and engage in "costume play" *(kosu pure),* wearing lacy wedding-style gowns (white, black, or red), black lipstick and eye make-up, and colored, tormented hair.

7. The album is B-Fresh, *Brown-Eyed Soul* (1991, King Records, K-CP-110). This B-Fresh did not include DJ Krush but consisted of the two rappers Cake-K and MC Bell, as well as DJ Beat.

8. In particular, the Japanese language lacks stress accents. This means that each syllable in a word receives the same amount of stress. Japanese does, however, have tonal accents. A rising tone, for example, can indicate a question, as in the difference between "yes?" and "yes." Accent in this sense should not be confused with dialect. The Japanese language has a wide range of regional variations (dialects), which might also be called accents.

9. Microphone Pager, "Rapperz Are Danger," *Don't Turn Off Your Light* (1995, File Records, FR027D).

10. Ozawa Kenji, *Life* (1994, Toshiba-EMI, TOCT-8495).

11. Both songs appear on the album East End X Yuri, *Denim-ed Soul II* (1995, Epic-Sony, ESCB-1590).

12. Rhymester, "Kuchi kara demakase" (Speaking Nonsense), *Egotopia* (1995, File Records, 26FRO32D).

REFERENCES

Allinson, Gary D. 1997. *Japan's Postwar History*. Ithaca: Cornell University Press.

Appadurai, Arjun. 1996. *Modernity at Large: Cultural Dimensions of Globalization*. Minneapolis: University of Minnesota Press.

Asō, Kootarō. 1997. *Breeku shinkaron* [Theory of Increasing Music Hits]. Tokyo: Joohoo Sentaa Shuppankyoku.

Bell, MC, and Cake-K. 1998. Interview of B-Fresh, *Woofin'*. 9, 112.

Barthes, Roland. 1990. "The Grain of the Voice." In *On Record: Rock, Pop and the Written Word,* edited by Simon Frith and Andrew Goodwin. London: Routledge.

Condry, Ian. 2000. "The Social Production of Difference: Imitation and Authenticity in Japanese Rap Music." In *Transactions, Transgressions, Transformations: American Culture in Western Europe and Japan,* edited by Uta G. Poiger and Heide Fehrenbach. New York: Berghan Books.

During, Simon. 1997. "Popular Culture on a Global Scale: A Challenge for Cultural Studies?" *Critical Inquiry* 23, no. 4: 808–33.

Durkheim, Emile. 1993. "The Cultural Logic of Collective Representations." In *Social Theory: The Multicultural and Classic Readings,* edited by Charles Lemert. Boulder, Colo.: Westview Press.

Egaitsu, Hiroshi. 1997. "Japanese Hip Hop Scene Chronology." *Groove* 1, 34–35.

Featherstone, Mike, and Scott Lash. 1995. "Globalization, Modernity, and the Spatialization of Social Theory." In *Global Modernities,* edited by Mike Featherstone, Scott Lash, and Roland Robertson. London: Sage.

Fernando, S. H. 1994. *The New Beats: Exploring the Music, Culture, and Attitudes of Hip Hop.* New York: Anchor Books.

Fujita, Tadashi. 1996. *Tokyo Hip Hop Guide.* Tokyo: Ohta.

Gilroy, Paul. 1993. *The Black Atlantic: Modernity and Double Consciousness.* Cambridge: Harvard University Press.

Gupta, Akhil, and James Ferguson. 1992. "Beyond 'Culture': Space, Identity, and the Politics of Difference." *Cultural Anthropology* 7, no. 1: 6–23.

Harvey, David. 1990. *The Condition of Postmodernity: An Enquiry into the Origins of Cultural Change.* Cambridge, Mass.: Blackwell.

Hosokawa, Shuhei, Hiroshi Matsumura, and Shun'ichi Shiba. 1991. *A Guide to Popular Music in Japan.* Kanazawa, Japan: IASPM-Japan.

Jameson, Fredric. 1998. "Notes on Globalization as a Philosophical Issue." In *The Cultures of Globalization,* edited by Fredric Jameson and Mason Miyoshi. Durham, N.C.: Duke University Press.

Kawabata, Shigeru. 1991. "The Japanese Record Industry." *Popular Music* 10, no. 3: 327–45.

Kinosita, Mitsuru. 2000. "Zebra Recording Report." *Remix* [Tokyo], June, 14–15.

Lash, Scott, and John Urry. 1994. *Economies of Signs and Space.* London: Sage.

Miller, Daniel. 1995. "Introduction: Anthropology, Modernity and Consumption." In *Worlds Apart: Modernity through the Prism of the Local,* edited by Daniel Miller. London: Routledge.

Mintz, Sidney. 1985. *Sweetness and Power: The Place of Sugar in Modern History.* London: Penguin.

Mitchell, Tony. 1997. "Another Root: Hip Hop outside the U.S." Unpublished paper delivered at the annual meeting of the American Anthropological Association, Washington, D.C., November.

Murata, Tomoki. 1997. *Shibuya-kei Moto Neta Disc Guide* [A Record Guide to the Original Samples of Shibuya-kei Music]. Tokyo: Ohta Shuppan.

Prévos, André J. M. 1997. "Hip Hop, Rap, and Repression in France and the U.S." Unpublished paper delivered at the annual meeting of the American Anthropological Association, Washington, D.C., November.

RIAJ. 1995. *RIAJ Yearbook*. Recording Industry Association of Japan.

Robertson, Roland. 1992. *Globalization: Social Theory and Global Culture*. London: Sage.

DISCOGRAPHY

Best of Japanese Hip Hop, vol. 7. 1996. Nippon Crown.

B-Fresh. 1991. *Brown-Eyed Soul*. King Records.

East End X Yuri. 1995. *Denim-ed Soul II*. Epic-Sony.

ECD. 1997. *Big Youth*. Cutting Edge.

Kitchens [EDU, Cake-K, Now]. 1997. *Kitchens*. Kitchen Records.

Ozawa, Kenji. 1994. *Life*. Toshiba-EMI.

Rhymester. 1995. *Egotopia*. File Records.

Takagi, Kan. 1991. *Fruit of the Rhythm*. Epic/Sony.

Wild Style 1996 [1982] [video with Japanese subtitles]. Vortex.

Chapter 10

"Who Is a Dancing Hero?"

Rap, Hip-Hop, and Dance in Korean Popular Culture

SARAH MORELLI

atching a television camera descend into a basement practice space located in one of the poor sections of Pusan, South Korea, I was struck by the loud hip-hop music, Korean style.[1] Youthful voices, high-pitched synthesizers, and a strong, pulsing bass filled the air as teenage boys practiced their dance moves in front of a wall of mirrors. Other walls were covered with graffiti, including one slogan that translates as "If it is impossible, make it possible." This Korean saying, traditionally invoked by students preparing for exams, here inspires young people who see music as their means to success. The young men who come to this practice space devote hours after school honing what they believe to be their most marketable skill, dance.

For teens in Korea today, such hopes of stardom are not entirely misplaced. In a country where approximately half the population is under age thirty, rap, hip-hop, and other types of dance music are the best-selling styles.[2] Current pop music is said to receive 70 to 75 percent of available air time on Korean radio stations ("Inroads" 1998).

In the fifty years since South Korea's independence, it has grown into a modernized, industrial country where the sounds and styles of rap and hip-hop (as well as other Western musics) are now commonplace. In the shopping districts of Seoul or Pusan, roadside marketeers pass the time by watching the latest rap videos on portable televisions. Consumers are often greeted by rap music blasting from record shops or fast-food restaurants, or played at background levels at grocery stores and gas stations. Rap thrives in the newly flourishing coffee shops that cater to younger crowds dressed in the latest urban fashions. Music is an integral part of this rapidly urbanizing world.

To a newly arrived Westerner, these scenes may seem to exemplify the growing homogenization, the "cultural gray-out" cautioned against by the likes of Alan Lomax (1977) in the late 1970s. As a reading lesson from Korea's national high school English textbook states: "The world seems to be getting smaller" (Lee et al. 1995). However, as scholars have recently observed, seemingly unchallenged appropriations by those on the periphery of a globalized cultural network are often embedded with new and unique meanings. Arjun Appadurai writes, "If 'a' global cultural system is emerging, it is filled with ironies and resistances sometimes camouflaged as passivity and a bottomless appetite in the Asian world for things Western" (1990: 3). The seeming homogenization of music in the case of Korea, in other words, is replete with new innovations, both musical and societal.

Strictly speaking, rap does not exist as a category of popular music in Korea.[3] The untranslated English term "rap" is used to indicate a style of vocalization, but until recently no music groups performed exclusively what could be called rap music. In the late 1990s a few groups such as Uptown were marketed and recognized as rap groups, but more frequently rap has been used as just one of many styles that go into the production of a dance-music album.

A mix of Western genres is common in *gayo*, or Korean popular music.[4] Genres are both juxtaposed within an album and overlaid within one song. Album jackets at times explicitly label the genres represented in each song. In one rather extreme example, the group Solid designated a genre for every song on their album. The broad range of genres and creative descriptions included a cappella, Latin house, R&B ballad, hip-hop, techno, 1970s ballad, funky, house, and P-funk (Solid 1995).

Though this patchwork of styles and representations might be problematic for American listeners, who, as Mark Slobin (1993: 86) claims, are often "highly sensitive to finely tuned distinctions in style," they do not hold the same symbolic meaning for Korean musical consumers. In the words of one Korean student, this simply "keeps the album from becoming boring" (H. J. Lee, interview by author 1996). In this case, the genres have been lifted from their historical and cultural contexts, resituated and "indigenized" (to use Appadurai's term) into Korean culture. In the process, these Western popular genres have been emptied of some of the extramusical associations that would disrupt a listener's expectations of stylistic coherence. Instead, this music has been transformed and new musical associations created.

This amalgamated style of popular-music is an important marker of identity for Korea's *shinsaedae,* or "New Generation": "[Korean] newspapers are filled with stories about the New Generation—those born after 1970—whose values and customs seem alien and irresponsible to their elders. These are youth who cut holes in new jeans, prefer pizza to rice, and don't believe that the old are necessarily wise (Kim 1993). Kim Byong-suk, a professor of sociology at Seoul's Ewha Women's University, further described this group: "The New Generation is loosely identified as those in their twenties, with rap music and Seo Taiji at the center" (Kim 1993).

Seo Taiji, the most successful popular-music performer of the 1990s, provides a useful starting point for an introduction to the musical culture of the *shinsaedae.* His group, Seo Taiji and the Boys, burst onto the Korean pop music scene in 1992 with "Nan arayo" (I Know), one of the first rap tracks to use the Korean language. This extremely popular single—described in *Billboard* (Suh 1992: 6) as "the fastest-selling record since 1982"—paved the way for a proliferation of dance-music groups that utilize rap as well as other sounds and techniques of contemporary Western pop music. Like many to follow, in "Nan Arayo" Seo Taiji employs rap only during the verses, singing choruses in a pop style.

Formerly a bass guitarist for the underground heavy metal group the Sinawe, Seo Taiji greeted the popular media in the early 1990s with his long hair cut short and a new, youthful image. True to this image, the lyrics of Seo Taiji and the Boys' first rap song are rather innocuous:

> I really only loved you—you, who left me with so much sorrow.
> Please don't tell me that you are leaving.
> You are everything to me.
> Oh, please don't go. Are you really leaving me?
> Oh, please don't go. I'm crying now.[5]

As his career progressed, Seo Taiji's lyrics became more critical of society, and his music gained a new edge, employing more elements of his harder musical past. On the group's third album (1993), he critiques the educational system in "Kyo-shil idaeyo" (Classroom Ideology):

> Enough . . . Enough of that kind of learning. . . .
> Every morning at 7:30 we are forced into a little classroom.
> All nine million children are forced to learn the same things.
> In classrooms closed off by four walls,
> In the dark that eats away at us,
> I am wasting my youth. . . .
> Enough. Enough already. We don't need that kind of learning any more.[6]

Live concert footage of this song begins with the soothing strains of a Western classical string quartet. Its sound then becomes disquieting as silent images loom large on three multiscreens in the darkened stadium. These pictures include textbooks filled with Hangul (the Korean written language), desks, lockers, and the silhouette of a teacher shaking a student's shoulders. The child folds his hands in appeal, tests are passed out, and an iron lock fastens the school gates. Suddenly the music in the stadium changes. A pipe organ replaces the string quartet, and a spotlight fixes on Seo Taiji. Dressed in a quasi-military school uniform, he addresses the cheering audience from behind a podium: "All students have to think of only one thing—getting into a good university. All this studying is like slavery: why should we memorize so much? We have the right to learn what we want. Why do the schools force us to all have the same goals, though we all have differing abilities?"(Seo Taiji and the Boys 1996).[7] Seo Taiji is then joined by "the Boys," Yang Hyun Suk and Lee Juno, a troupe of dancers, and a speed metal band that launches into the song.

As can be seen from this description, Seo Taiji masterfully utilizes diverse sonic styles and images as well as lyrics to convey his meaning. A number of Korean students I interviewed cite this song as being particularly meaningful to them. As one of them stated, "The song was about the fact that all Korean youngsters are under tremendous pressure to study to get into colleges and they don't have any other options."[8] The pressure for a place in a university often leads parents to enroll their children for extra training at a *hogwan,* or institute. From an early age, many children in the middle class not only attend a full day of school, but also go to their hogwan between roughly 4:00 and 10:00 P.M. It is a common sight in Seoul to see girls slumped over each other, napping on the subway ride home before they eat dinner and study late into the night. Such children are given little or no free time, and activities such as sports and the arts go virtually unexplored—with the exception of an enthusiastic interest in popular music and musicians.

In the 1980s, when most popular groups were made up of either college students or working musicians, Seo Taiji was one of the few musicians who quit high school before graduating. Though such an act is traditionally a source of shame for parents, Taiji's success and the message of songs like "Classroom Ideology" has opened up discussion in Korean society about such nontraditional paths.

With their fourth album (1995), Seo Taiji and the Boys' music became even more socially and politically charged, targeting problems such as teen runaways and political corruption. The song "Sidaeyugam" includes lyrics that have been interpreted as being critical of the Korean government:

The era of the honest is gone.
Today you can hear screams and cries in all the pretense.
How much do you think you can fly with your broken wings
I hope we can uproot everything for the new world.
You burnt your conscience and hid your sharp claws.[9]

The Korean censorship board banned portions of the song, so instead of changing the lyrics, the group released the song as an instrumental. The second issue of the album included the remaining lyrics that were permitted, and to make their audience aware that the song was being censored, the group replaced the outlawed lyrics with bleeps. Finally, the third issue of the album included the song in its entirety. The following story explaining the release of the banned lyrics has been told to me many times in slightly varying forms, though I have never seen it in print. It is said that in reaction to the second version of the album, the group's audience, mainly high school girls, began a letter-writing campaign to the government. These letters demanded that the lyrics be allowed in their entirety. Their writers threatened not to take the national college-placement exams at the end of the year, and some even threatened suicide if this demand was not met. Finally, only days before the college-placement exams, as the story goes, the government repealed its censorship laws. The Korean government did, in fact, repeal its censorship laws at approximately this time. However, I have no evidence to establish causality.

This account illustrates a few significant aspects of Korean youth culture. First, it emphasizes the deep reverence that many young people in the 1990s had for Seo Taiji (and the extent to which Korean youth idolize many pop groups). In one Web site dedicated to Seo Taiji and the Boys, titled "To the greatest korean musicians ever *[sic]*," the author announces, "Seo Taiji . . . has become the best there was and the best there is, and the best there will ever be."[10] Another claims him as "the god of korean music *[sic]*."[11] Second, the story reveals gender patterns common to contemporary popular-music culture in Korea. Few women perform as musicians in this music scene, yet they play strong roles behind the scenes as fans. Those who do perform are often ballad singers or are in the minority within larger pop groups. In music videos as well, females are, to use Walser's term (1993), "excripted"— conspicuously absent from situations that articulate ideals of masculinity and exhibit male bonding.

The video for one of Taiji's songs, "Hayeoga" (Anyway), illustrates different levels of endogamous and exogamous male bonding. The video begins with a crowd of men gathered at the bar of a nightclub. Korean and

African American men dressed in trendy clothing, some with dreadlocked hair, sway back and forth to hip-hop music. When they begin to dance, the three African American males jeer (in English with Korean subtitles) at their Korean counterparts: "Man, these guys can't dance!" The Korean men do their best to impress their critics, without success. At this point, one anxious Korean makes a phone call to Taiji, whom he asks to come and help them out. Predictably, Taiji and the Boys step in and save the day. We then cut to a studio location, where standard backdrops provide the setting for the music video, in which the unnamed black men continue to play cameo roles (Seo Taiji and the Boys 1996).

This video clip is not only a celebration of Afrodiasporic cultural aesthetics, but a competition as well. Through this contest of masculinity as well as dance, we see the reification and expansion of a racialized hierarchy of hipness, in which, globally, the African American man now defines the standard. This scenario compares remarkably with a long-standing social dynamic in the USA in which, as Tricia Rose states, "young white listeners [are] trying to perfect a model of correct white hipness, coolness, and style by adopting the latest black style and image" (1994: 5). By gaining the respect of these black men and saving face for his fellow Koreans, Taiji establishes both alliances. He not only proves his own capability to compete in this now international music space, but also suggests that his superior capabilities are something for other Korean men to aspire to.

Other groups in Korea also try to demonstrate their authenticity through the use of English words and Western cultural markers. Adopting specifically African American phrases to give authenticity to nonblack versions of rap music is prevalent, though certainly not unique to Korea. Many current groups employ one member who specializes in rapping.

Though black cultural aesthetics are highly valued by urban Korean youth, it is important to note that locally produced popular music, including rap, is much more popular than its U.S. counterpart.[12] This indicates that Korean youth are not so much uncritically mimicking black culture as they are (with the help of the record industry) appropriating it and using it as a guide to fashion similar musical products for their own use.

As the highly respected music critic, composer, and writer Moon Pyong Hwang observed of the trends of the 1990s in Korea, the focus of popular-music "is moving from aural to visual" (interview by author 1997). Seo Taiji and the Boys, like other groups, have often been featured in the media because of their appearance as well as their music. Taiji and his two singers were banned from television after they showed up to promote their second album in dreadlocks, ripped jeans, and earrings. They were told that in order to appear on television, they had to cut their hair and alter their appearance. They replied that they would not make such compromises again: "'I'm not cutting off my hair again, and if the stations have a problem with that, then we won't perform,' says Lee Juno, 24, twirling his braids. . . . 'Television stations have no right to tell people what to wear. Who do they think they are?' said Seo [Taiji]" (Kim 1993).

As with most youth-oriented popular-music trends, the music makes up only part of a group's overall style, which includes dance movements, clothing, and hairstyles. Much of it has been adopted from U.S. hip-hop culture. Music groups such as Solid, H.O.T. (High-Five of Teenagers), Uptown, Jinusean, and D.J. Doc not only use rap, R&B and other "black" musical styles, but also model their visual images after the b-boy styles of the USA. These extramusical elements of dance music are just as important as the dance music itself in fostering image and creating meaning within this social context.

The importance of the visual and somatic elements of this music has been recognized from the beginning. Taiji, whose music was instrumental in establishing rap's popularity in Korea, chose the other two members of the group—"the Boys"—based not on their musical but their dancing abilities. According to fans, their role within the group continued to be primarily dance and image oriented throughout the group's career. Likewise, the most important criterion for record-company scouts is the ability to dance well, and they often find new talent at dance competitions for high school–aged people.

At one such dance competition, held outside the Lotte department store in Pusan, signs flanking the stage asked, "Who is a dancing hero?" Though the question seems trite, to be discovered is indeed a heroic act for the very poor of Pusan. Two young men from the neighborhood described at the outset of this essay were discovered at such an event and now perform in the popular dance group Sechs Kies. Stardom has enabled them to move out of their neighborhood—something that would otherwise hardly have been possible. Their success has created a stir within that impoverished community; families have constructed dance practice spaces, like the one described at the outset of this chapter, at tremendous expense, in the hope that their sons too will be able to lift them out of their economic conditions. The support of these working-class parents suggests how thoroughly Korean values are shifting. Popular music not only is a vehicle of escapism for middle-class kids, but often provides an alternative both for high school dropouts like Seo Taiji and for the underprivileged. Where the "impossible" once referred to success in exams, it now often refers to making it in the music business. In the case of the very poor in Korea, the "dancing hero" could be the teenager who finds success not through studying, but through pop stardom.

APPENDIX: SONG LYRICS

"I Know" (Nan arayo) by Seo Taiji; translated by Eundeog Hwang, and Hee Kyong Lee (University of Pennsylvania, May 1997).

I know. Someone will leave me if the night passes by.
Now, I know the reason.
I didn't tell that person "I love you."
It's too late now.
What was I doing then?
That beautiful smile,
I really only loved you—you, who left me with so much sorrow.
Please don't tell me that you are leaving.
You are everything to me.
Oh, please don't go. Are you really leaving me?
Oh, please don't go. I'm crying now.
I know. If the night passes, I will try to forget the memory of you leaving.
My heart will ache with thoughts of our last kiss.
Are you really leaving me?
I want to love you, everything about you.
Your breath still runs through my body.
That smile, those tears, your secretive heart
You don't have to write me a letter. Our hearts are one.
I can see your true self.
Do I still have a place in your heart?
I am forever yours.
I really only loved you—you, who left me with so much sorrow.
Oh, please don't go.
Are you really leaving me?
Oh, please don't go. I'm crying now.

"Classroom Ideology" (Kyo-shil Idaeyo), by Seo Taiji; translated by Eundeog Hwang, and Hee Kyong Lee (University of Pennsylvania, May 1997).

Enough. Enough already. (Enough)
Enough of that kind of learning. (Enough)
I'm satisfied. I'm now satisfied. (Satisfied)
Every morning at 7:30 we are forced into a little classroom.
All nine million children are forced to learn the same things.

In classrooms closed off by four walls,
In the dark that eats away at us,
I am wasting my youth.
I will make you into a better you.
You will step on the child sitting next to you to get what you want.
You can be a better you.
Why don't you change?
Why do you wander in your youth?
Why don't you change?
Why do you want others to change instead?
From elementary school to middle school, then to high school,
    they are trying to present us in nice wrapping paper
    like what they do in a gift wrapping store.
They are wrapping us in a wrapping paper called "college."
Think now.
Hiding behind a college degree, trying to act cool
These times have passed.
Try to be more honest.
You will come to know.
I can make you better than the child sitting next to you.
Step on others to get what you want.
You can be a better you.
Why aren't you changing?
Why do you wander with an anxious heart?
Why don't you change?
Why do you want others to change instead?
Why do you want . . . Oh . . .
Enough. Enough already. We don't need that kind of learning any more.

NOTES

The question in the title is taken from a sign that flanked either side of the stage at a teen dance competition held outside the Lotte department store in downtown Pusan, South Korea, 17 July 1997.

1. This was for a documentary aired at 9 P.M. on PBS (Pusan Broadcasting Corp.), Korea, 5 August 1997.

2. Figures as of 1996, Asian Demographics Ltd.
<*http://www.asiandemographics.com*>.

3. I presented an earlier version of this discussion of genre at the IASPM (International Association for the Study of Popular Music) conference in Kanazawa, Japan, August 1997.

4. The term *gayo* can refer to contemporary popular-music or to older popular song styles of this century, including *shin-min-yo* and *man-yo*.

5. Translation by Eundeog Hwang and Hee Kyong Lee of the University of Pennsylvania, Philadelphia, June 1997. A complete version of this song's lyrics appears in the appendix.

6. Ibid.

7. Translation by Jin Hee Mun, Pusan, August 1997.

8. Chul Y. Chung, <*http://www-scf.usc.edu/~chulyc/seotaiji.html*>.

9. Translation as in note 7.

10. This and other Web sites on Korean popular music are listed in the bibliography.

11. <*http://www.geocities.com/SunsetStrip/Mezzanine/6026/Taiji.html*>.

12. Korean music has outsold foreign music by an average of 23 percent every year from 1990–97. (Figures provided by KOMCA [Korea Music Copyright Association], Seoul Korea. Personal communication, February 1998.)

REFERENCES

Appadurai, Arjun. 1990. "Disjuncture and Difference in the Global Economy." *Public Culture* 2, no. 2:1–22.

Kim, Ju-Yeon. 1993. "Rap Setting New Beat in S. Korea." *Chicago Sun-Times,* 29 November.

Koo, Hagen. 1994. "Middle-Class Politics in the New East Asian Capitalism: The Korean Middle Classes." In *Culture, Politics, and Economic Growth: Experiences in East Asia,* edited by Richard Harvey Brown. Williamsburg, Va.: College of William and Mary.

"Inroads of Pop Music" [editorial]. 1998. *Korea Herald,* 18 January.

Lee, Kee-Dong, Kurt Weigett, and Kim Jong-Seng, eds. 1995. *English for Everyone.* Seoul: Jihangsa.

Lomax, Alan. 1980. "Appeal for Cultural Equity." *African Music* [South Africa] 6, no. 1: 22–31.

Rose, Tricia. 1994. *Black Noise: Rap Music and Black Culture in Contemporary America.* Hanover, N.H.: Wesleyan University Press.

Sinclair, David. 1992. "Rapping the World." *Billboard* 28 November, R16.

Slobin, Mark. 1993. *Subcultural Sounds: Micromusics of the West.* Hanover, N.H.: Wesleyan University Press.

Suh, Byung Hoo. 1992. "An Unexpected Rap Eruption Rocks a Traditional Music Market." *Billboard* 22, August, 6.

Walser, Robert. 1993. *Running with the Devil: Power, Gender, and Madness in Heavy Metal Music.* Hanover, N.H.: Wesleyan University Press.

DISCOGRAPHY

D. J. Doc. [N.d.] *Fourth Album*. King Record Co.

———. 1995. *DJ. Doc*. Sinchon Music.

H.O.T. [N.d.] *Volume 2, Wolf and Sheep*. S.M. Entertainment.

Jinusean. 1997. *Jinusean*. Samsung Music.

Sechs Kies. 1997. *First*. Samsung Music.

Seo Taiji and the Boys. 1992. *Seo Taiji and the Boys*. Bando Records.

———. 1993. *Seo Taiji and the Boys* [2d release]. Bando Records.

———. 1994. *Seo Taiji and the Boys* [3d release]. Bando Records.

———. 1995. *Seo Taiji and the Boys* [4th release]. Bando Records.

Solid. [N.d.] *Volume 1*. King Record Co.

———. 1995. *Solid*. Daehong.

———. [N.d.] *Solidate*. World Music.

Uptown. [N.d] *Volume 1*. World Music/Samsung Music.

VIDEOGRAPHY

Seo Taiji and the Boys. 1996. *Goodbye Music Video*. Seoul: Moonhwa Chíeyook bu.

WEB SITES

"Dennis' Music Page." <*http://www.geocities.com/SunsetStrip/Mezzanine/
     6026/music.html*>.

"GS Korean Music Page: Seo Taiji and Boys." <*http://www.imsa.edu/~hoonie/*>.

"Hong's Gayo Server." <*http://www.sori.org/gayo/*>.

"Kconcept–Korea Town." <*http://www.kconcept.net/ktown.htm*>.

"Seo Taiji." <*http://www.geocities.com/SoHo/Studios/3507/seotaiji.html*>.

"Seo Taiji and Boys." <*http://www.geocities.com/Tokyo/5327/*>.

"Seo Taiji and Boys' Band: SeoTaiji and Boys Homepage for Japanese."
     <*http://www2h.biglobe.ne.jp/~taiji/main.htm*>.

"To the Greatest Korean Musicians Ever." <*http://www.geocities.com/
     SouthBeach/6217/taiji.html*>.

"Welcome to Taijiboys." <*http://www.geocities.com/Hollywood/Hills/
     6749/taiji.html*>.

Chapter 11

Sydney Stylee

Hip-Hop Down Under Comin' Up

IAN MAXWELL

"They'll tell you it's a black thing, man"—fixing me with his gaze, index finger jabbing once, emphatically, Ser Reck speaks as if for the record, making sure that I understand exactly where he is coming from: ". . . but it isn't . . . it's *our* thing."

Ser Reck is not black. He has not been to America; his ancestors were never slaves, although they may well have been convict stock (in Australia, perversely, that is actually something to boast about); he is not identifiably anything other than "Anglo": a white man, a father, by now in his mid-twenties, with a long ponytail and a goatee.

It is 1995. Ser Reck (he is also known by his tag, "Unique") lives in the far western suburbs of Sydney, Australia. The constituency for whom he claims to be speaking, whom he *represents* — the "us" whose *thing* this is — is the social imaginary that sometimes refers to itself as "the Sydney hip-hop community": a geographically, ethnically, and socioeconomically heterogeneous collection of (predominantly) young men who share this sense of belonging, who (the referent is now revealed in all its tautologicality) share this *thing:* "I speak for all those who are like me; they are like me because I speak for them." It does not matter whether you are black, white, yellow, red, brown, pink. And though, admittedly, it does help if you live in the far west — if you are, in the vulgar class demographics of Sydney (west = poor; east = privileged), part of the "westie" (a pejorative epithet) underclass — even that is negotiable. What matters is that hip-hop is your *thing*.

But above all, remember this: all other things being equal, here, in the far western suburbs of Sydney, Australia (but anywhere really), hip-hop is not a *black* thing.

What might justify and sustain such a claim? Or the claim that an authentic hip-hop culture exists (or existed, for things change) in Sydney, Australia? How does *that* thing become *our* thing? Note that what is at issue is not an ontological question: whether or not hip-hop in Australia is authentic in any kind of objective sense, or in terms of a "real" hip-hop that might be found somewhere else. Rather, my questions take as their epistemological horizon Ser Reck's simple statement of belief: "it's *our* thing." What then needs to be understood is how it is that the individuals claiming this belonging to this thing, this hip-hop, understand this belonging not in terms of any necessary continuity with the putative, celebrated origins of hip-hop (everyone knows that story), but through a kind of elective affinity: a process of identification revealing of the intensely mediated labor of making a culture of one's own. This chapter, then, mounts an argument about the affective grounds of hip-hop: what it is that is felt, that allows someone (anyone, regardless of race, color, history) to claim belongingness to something called hip-hop now here, in Sydney, Australia?

That there is a radical experiential and contextual disjuncture between the "originary" African American[1] hip-hop culture of urban North America and hip-hop culture as it developed in Australia, is, of course, self-evident. The development and maintenance of a hip-hop community down under relied (and, to an extent, continues to rely) upon the efforts of various social agents to reinscribe their own social world with logics, truths, actions, and interpretations that arrived in Australia nor through a physical diaspora, not through the embodied importation of cultural form or memory, but predominantly through (mass-)mediated channels: television, radio, and imported fanzines and recordings.

A Sydney writer tells me of his desire to see the graff work on the New York subways. He has read—no, he has assiduously studied—Cooper and Chalfant's *Subway Art*. ("You won't find it [this book] in any library, man," I was told; "they all get racked by writers.") He knows about the buff, that the lush photographs of full-train pieces ripping through the anonymous grey emptiness of the Bronx are things of the past. "But it's like the *home* of hip-hop, man," he explains; "you've just gotta go [there]." Cultural material accessed at a distance like this carries with it both the distorting effects of the mediation itself and the tendency of the relatively isolated interpreters of that material toward reification: to perhaps overinvest in their interpretation, immobilizing that material as a cultural essence rather than as a snapshot of cultural process, a synchronic sliver of illusory coherence plucked out of the less stable diachronic flow of history. Such reifications are a commonplace of the experience of repatriated migrants, who upon returning to their homeland find that, simply put, life goes on; that the cultural purity they remember and live with in their (remote) present no longer exists "at home" where it should; that things change.

The making of (a) hip-hop culture, community, or nation in Australia, if not a utopian project, is at least what Foucault called a heterotopia: the inscription upon this place, the sunburnt expanses of Australian suburbia, of an idealized cultural form drawn from the mediated imaginary of the inner-urban 'hoods of New York and Los Angeles. For hip-hop is not an historical continuity, or a formal substratum or "universal," self-similar throughout the world, manifesting homologically in specific geographical contexts as a variation on an internally coherent structure (the "essence of hip-hop"). The story I can tell is about imagination, about the attempt to make culture and traditions in the absence of traditions or cultural continuity. It is a story that privileges the experiences, investments, interpretations, and practices of the social, in the context of radical discontinuities. In other words, it is a phenomenology, in particular, a phenomenology that engages with the performative, embodied encounter between a "hereness" and a "thereness"—an encounter that is always a series of interpretations, carrying with them the potential for the institution of new habits, new performances, new embodiments. And in this process of interpretation and embodiment, perceived analogies between the "here" and the "there" become understood as homologies: the labor of remaking the here in the image of the there is masked, or at least forgotten, through the formation of a habit of logic: the hip-hop here is not just *like* the hip-hop there; it becomes understood as *the same thing*.

In the absence of historical, cultural, racial, socioeconomic, and other continuities between the "original" context of hip-hop and its local (Australian) manifestation, the locus of identification with an abstracted idea about "hip-hop" is necessarily placed, and, therefore, to be found, within the realm of affective, embodied experience. Hip-hop is something that is felt in particular bodies, almost (and certainly in the accounts of those who have experienced this connection) as an irreducibly primary experience: either you get it, in which case you're one of us, or you do not, in which case you are not, an assertion supported by the irreducibility of the embodied experience of hip-hop. In the words of a contributor to a Sydney hip-hop fanzine: "So how do you get there [to the hip-hop nation]? Put the needle on the record and 'It'll take you there.' And if you still can't find it, chances are you never will" ("Fibular," in *Vapors* 8 [1992]).

"Mass mediation." "Disjunction." "Making culture." "Global cultural flows." All the catchwords of postmodernism. But this is not pastiche. For although the world certainly may be characterizable as postmodern (or "postindustrial," as Rose [1994] would have it) and is increasingly determined by increasingly complex cultural flows (Appadurai 1993), it is not simply the case that, in the borrowed and often repeated words of one Australian cultural commentator, "we no longer have roots, we have aerials" (Wark 1994: xiv). McKenzie Wark's aphorism (appropriated from Brazilian singer Gilberto Gil) rings true to the extent that it registers the increasing mass mediation of cultural material in the late twentieth century; less ethnographically sustainable, in the context of which I am writing, is Wark's extrapolation to a world inhabited by Net-surfing *bricoleurs,* cutting and pasting at will cultural material from the vast expanse of the transnational, transhistorical mediascape in the spirit of a postmodern playfulness. It was absolutely not the case that those who professed to belong to the hip-hop community in Sydney understood their practices, their commitment to hip-hop, in such a light. The seriousness with which Ser Reck and many like him went about their cultural project suggests anything but a bricoleur's sensibility. Rather, the decidedly premodern preoccupations with ideas of (pure) "community," "nation," and "culture" evidenced throughout the Sydney hip-hop scene might more profitably be seen as a reaction against, and not a celebration of, a postmodern — and, perhaps more tellingly in this Australian context, a postcolonial — absence, or at least an instability, of sustaining cultural, national, and communitarian narratives.

Indeed, in that Australia might be seen as an archetypal postcolonial society, the negotiations of cultural and community identity that Ser Reck and his colleagues are engaged in must be understood within the context of a broader set of identical negotiations contemporaneously unfolding in Australia.[2] The effort of cultural transcription (of hip-hop from idealized "there" to quotidian "here") involves an almost oxymoronic doubling of the discourse of nationalism, in order to accommodate the apparently centrifugal incitement to, on the one hand, hip-hop transnationalism with, on the other, a more general, contextual incitement to a specifically Australian nationalism.

Homi Bhabha recognizes the experiential dimension of such negotiations of social identity in his description of "the nation as narration." All cultural agents, he writes, are engaged in processes of signification, locating themselves — their subjective experiences and their performances ("terms of cultural engagement," Bhabha writes, "are produced performatively" [1994: 2]) — within an objective narrative, or to use Bhabha's term, a *pedagogy.* In order to sustain a social imaginary, this pedagogic narrative must constantly be articulated to unfolding (and, I would add, embodied and affectively experienced) performance: the potential disjunction between one's own experience and the narrative to which one wants to belong, within which one desires to be placed, must be papered over, the performative lined up with and integrated with the pedagogy.

Slightly recasting Bhabha's argument, the process of the narration of nation involves a moment in which the phenomenological subject of a living, embodied human life identifies itself as the object of a nationalist pedagogy. Practice, or "performance," is not simply generated by "tradition" (pedagogy), but, in all its difference, all its potential inequality and specificity, is articulated to a body of discourse. "Tradition" becomes an explanation for practice: what one does in synchronic time is accounted for in terms of the body of discourse that precedes, diachronically, that embodied performance.

Ser Reck can legitimately claim to be hip-hop, as it were, because he recognizes the same truth that Bhabha recognizes: belonging is a function of work, not a simple birthright. And Ser Reck's cultural work—specifically, his performative credentialing, as we will see—is unimpeachable. He has knowledge. He commands respect. Through the careful management of what becomes, within his world, what Sarah Thornton, after Bourdieu, refers to as "subcultural capital" (1996), Ser Reck was able to align his own narrative with a master narrative of hip-hop and to position himself within the field of Sydney hip-hop as a tastemaker, as an arbiter of authenticity: to determine the boundaries of hip-hop propriety, and in so doing, mark out his difference from the apathy, the emptiness that he saw in mainstream Australian culture.

The claim to a down-under hip-hop authenticity, as I have already hinted, is specifically grounded in the meaningfulness attributed to particular relationships of bodies to place—in Sydney, that place has been the city's far western suburbs—and the remaking, or at least, the semiotic recasting of that place in the light of these attributed meanings: processes that, as I have already suggested, we can understand through Michel Foucault's notion of the heterotopia. "There are," Foucault wrote, "probably in every culture, in every civilization, real places—. . . which are something like counter-sites, a kind of effectively enacted utopia in which the real sites, all the other real sites that can be found within a culture, are simultaneously represented, contested, and inverted" (1986: 24). Hip-hop in Sydney (at least, in the slice of time—the heterochronie that Foucault sees any heterotopian project as being linked to—during which I watched that scene) is precisely such a utopian project, as I have been arguing, *affectively* enacted. "Utopian" in that the discourses of hip-hop in the raps, autobiographical accounts, broadcasts, and conversations that I encountered in Sydney, in the mid-1990s, not only positioned hip-hop as an epistemology (that is, as a way of knowing the world), but offered it as a teleology: hip-hop as a world to come. "Enacted" in that the evidence of the consistent performance of key practices (rapping, breaking, piecing) over a sustained period of time enabled those claiming hip-hop authenticity to argue their case. And "affective" in that in the absence of a cultural, ethnic, geographical, or historical continuity with the origins of hip-hop (or, at least, with what I have elsewhere called the "standard narrative" of the origins of hip-hop), the identification of one's own experience with an essentialized "hip-hopness" is a matter of affect: it is something to do with feeling, a sense of bodily knowing experienced as irreducible and therefore as unimpeachably authentic. In such moments it does not matter if you are not black, if you are middle class, if you live in the eastern beach suburb of Bondi or the far west of Mt. Druitt. If you feel it—this hip-hopness—then it is true. *Put the needle on the record . . .*

Interestingly, each of the three modalities of social semiotic practice referred to by Foucault at the end of the passage quoted above—representation, contestation, and inversion—has a special resonance in the world of hip-hop. In that world, the execution of core practices, even the wearing of appropriate clothes, using appropriate speech, and playing appropriate music, is representing. As I will show below, inversion operates as a key trope in the construction not only of hip-hop in general as an underground counter-culture, but in the Australian context, this trope is redoubled as a series of authenticating self-otherings: Australian hip-hop is not only underground, but "down under" as well; in Sydney, hip-hop's heartland is not the cosmopolitan center of the inner city, but the peripheral outer suburbs. Finally, in this environment, far removed culturally, historically, ethnically, and geographically from the putative site of authentic hip-hop (the [imaginary] Bronx or South Central Los Angeles), the question of what hip-hop is, is itself always up for debate: the right to claim one's own practice (as a Sydney breaker, writer, rapper, and DJ) as being "true to hip-hop" is always a move in a micropolitical struggle, predicated upon one's access to authenticating cultural capital—the latest album, the latest issue of *The Source*, contact with writers in New York, Copenhagen, and London, the latest news, or having been to Compton, or being up, and, perhaps most significantly, the ability to demonstrate one's long-term commitment to representing. Here is Ser Reck, stopping his rap in mid-flow, leaping to the floor in front of the low stage and executing a series of ground moves, burning his back in the circle cleared amongst the pogoing bodies; sweat slicking his brow, he leaps back to his spot—and affirms his commitment to hip-hop, countering the idea that hip-hop is just a style, a passing thing: "Ten years," he punches out, "is not a fad."

More recently, Hakim Bey (1991) has used the term "temporary autonomous zone" (TAZ) to designate what de Certeau would call "strategic" re-appropriations of space. There is a burgeoning body of scholarship (much of it unpublished, but thriving in the TAZian expanses of cyberspace[3]) using the TAZ to theorize various dance communities' uses of industrial, sporting, and recreational facilities for raves (and the various permutations of the rave macrogenre), often in a modality of playfulness itself informed by scholarship in the area. The hip-hop heterotopia of western Sydney—the "Westside"—however, falls short of the theoretically informed strategic ideal of the TAZ. For those engaged in the making of the Westside, it was not so much a question of temporarily inverting or subverting extant geographies as of investing feeling in a making of a "real" to redress a (felt) absence. The Westside, as heterotopia, is then, an affectively enacted utopia (as well as, as I have suggested, a dystopia): its being is grounded not only in strategy and playfulness, but also in an earnestness that was anything but playful.

Further, notwithstanding the imaginary dimensions of such a project as the predication of a hip-hop culture or community down under, this project is one taken on "for real"; the hip-hop imaginary exists in a real place, in real bodies, across a real geography that is itself reinvented as heterotopia. Hip-hop is a map preceding, and making, a new place, in which it is possible for the agents to think and experience their own being in a manner or modality that previously had left them feeling denied. "While U2 were talking about 'The Streets with No Name,'" writes Brian Cross, "Eazy and Cube were talking about Crenshaw, Slauson, Gauge and Figeroa. U2 may have meant well with their liberal rhetoric, but they missed the kind of naming that occurs from below, even when there are no street signs. How else do you find your way home? Hip-hop in many ways is a map for precisely this purpose" (1993: 3).

Hip-hop generically demands geographical specificity, and just as North American rap has mapped Compton, South Central, Los Angeles, and the Bronx into the global hip-hop collective consciousness, so it has been the desire of local Australian rappers to name their place. As a corollary, too, my writing must map this reality; my account names Bondi (a name that will resonate, perhaps, for some readers: sun, surf, an arc of golden sand), and also Mt. Druitt, St. Marys (names evocative of no such imagery), Oxford Street, Villawood, and Kings Cross, for the practices I am describing not only take place in place, but are practices in and of place.

Now, as I have already noted, Foucault uses the word "heterochronie" to describe the temporally specific slice of time to which any heterotopian project is linked (Foucault 1986: 26). Indeed, this present writing is about a slice of hip-hop in Sydney, Australia, in the early to mid-1990s: it cannot be a history of hip-hop in Australia. It is not particularly up to date. It is to no small extent an outsider's account: my account of an encounter with a world of which I was not a member, in which I was a guest, and, therefore, a critical account.

Foregrounding this criticality positions this account away from two pitfalls of much writing about youth culture: on the one hand, the historico-documentary approach, subsuming specific cultural experiences to totalizing narratives (for example, the kind of writing that takes as its theme an unproblematized transcontextual continuity—say, "hip-hop"—and views any local narrative engaging this theme as an effect of that continuity); on the other, the (to my mind more pressing) problem of the "curse of fandom": the tendency of insider accounts to take up positions of advocacy for their chosen cultural project. The result in the latter camp often tends to be work that over-emphasizes a purported "political" dimension to cultural practices, overreading them perhaps, from the position of a nonreflexive organic intellectualism. This lack of reflexivity leads to a failure to acknowledge methodological biases.

For myself, during my own fieldwork, these questions were thrown into high relief: my status as a researcher frequently elicited highbrow explanations for a given person's involvement or engagement with hip-hop. Virtually everyone I met could, to one extent or another, talk the talk: hip-hop was "the voice of the streets"; it was "giving a voice to people who don't have one"; it was, simply, "political." I am not denying that this is, to an extent, the case. It is not, however, the whole story, and it is the other side of the story that does not get written about enough: "young people don't really get into the politics of hip-hop," Blaze, the publisher, editor, chief journalist, reviewer, and layout artist of *Vapors,* told me one day ("what Blaze doesn't know about hip-hop," I was assured, "isn't worth knowing"); "they're more into, like, the groove of it." And although this statement cannot be taken at face value—for some "young people" do get into it precisely because of the politics—it is worth looking (critically) at the, like, groove of it. So here is where I first encountered the groove of it.

Sydney, Australia, early 1980s. I am at a club, up on Oxford Street in the heart of the city's night-life district. The club's name is, I kid you not, even at this early, early point in time, The Hip-Hop Club. I was young, an undergraduate in the process of dropping out of a psychology major, looking toward a more exciting, visceral life. I did not go to clubs terribly often—I actually remember very little about them, or the music that was played, although I do remember the burgeoning Sydney gay scene of the time (Oxford Street then as now being the city's gay quarter) having a particular fascination with Culture Club and Boy George's (even stranger) fellow-traveler, Marilyn. (After all, this is the country that pioneered kitsch gay chic: think Kylie Minogue, the Lesbian and Gay Mardi Gras, and *Priscilla, Queen of the Desert.*) I do not think that the Hip-Hop Club was a "gay" venue, nor, despite its name, a place where black music was played in particular. It was simply another link in the Oxford Street–East Sydney–Darlinghurst–Paddington club daisy chain, the name simply taken, I suppose, from the latest wash of pop culture to sweep across the Pacific.

And here is the Sydney hip-hop creation myth, the standard narrative of the local scene: Back in 1981, the video clip for Malcolm McLaren's novelty single "Buffalo Gals" was screened on *Sound Unlimited*, a weekly music show broadcast each Saturday morning. Staged in a Manhattan basketball court against a sprawling graff piece by Bil Blast ("Sky's the Limit," in Chalfant and Prigoff 1987: 20), the clip featured breakers (and rope jumpers). The following Monday morning (the creation myth goes), dozens of school playgrounds were full of kids trying their first break moves. Graffiti appeared, and after a specialist youth radio station started broadcasting hip-hop (usually late at night, on new release–type programs), boys would congregate at the handful of import record stores happy to ship in the new sounds from New York, Miami, and Los Angeles. Crews were generated through this kind of encounter, rather than geographical propinquity. And why were these kids drawn to hip-hop? Some apprehended in the world elicited by McLaren's clip a density and excitement they did not feel in the suburbs of Sydney: here was a deep, multifaceted culture replete (apparently) with traditions, with histories, with meaning, while here in the antipodes, there was only sport (cricket in summer, one of the rugby codes in winter), empty suburban landscapes, and heat. And of course, the USA was (and still is, and always has been), the future: hip-hop as a kind of folkavant garde.

Australia, on this account, got a complete hip-hop package deal: just as emigré populations tend to preserve the moment of the culture that they left behind and are shocked to discover on returning to their homeland that history has moved along, in Australia hip-hop, even in the mid-1990s, referred to these old-school days as a kind of prelapsarian golden age. Breaking, writing, and rapping: the three pillars upon which hip-hop is built, freeze-dried as markers of authenticity, as indices of culture.

A decade later, in their late twenties and early thirties, these original b-boys spoke of their sense of not belonging to the "Aussie" world of rugby and pub rock, of surfies and beer: in hip-hop they found something of more substance. And of course, ten years on, you have an interest in this thing, this hip-hop being real; if you've given your life to it, man, it has to be more than just a fashion, a fad, a style. Others recall the breadth of appeal of hip-hop, its catholic vocational openness: if you were not athletic, you can still write graffiti; if you were a show-off, you could grab a mic; if you were more reserved, technically minded, perhaps, or enjoyed collecting, DJing was the thing. And if you felt like rebelling, if you felt angry, if you felt somehow marginal or even oppressed, well, here, too, were anger, passion, and ideas. And it was sexy. Writers tell me of strutting into clubs: "you'd always pick up . . . girls like the outlaws." The networks of shared interest skeined across the huge suburban sprawl of Sydney created a sense of community, of mutual recognition and respect.

And of course, as Blaze pointed out, there are the sounds themselves.

I remember one night, perhaps in 1984, being on the dance floor at the Hip-Hop Club and hearing (feeling) for the first time the music that only later I would later come to know as hip-hop. It was Grandmaster Flash and Melle Mel's "White Lines," pumped through the room: a driving and some-how, simultaneously, a mellifluous bass riff; the even smoother harmonies of the crew, melodiously singing the chorus ("White lines . . . going through my mind . . .") counterpointing Mel's sassy rap delivery chronicling (always somewhat unconvincingly to my ears) the dangers of cocaine use. Wow. This was some music. The room really *grooved:* a deep, affective, embodied groove, all hips and stomach. A beat you sat back into and flowed with, the subterranean riff pulling all us white, middle-class kids—refugees from Aussie pub rock—along, the samples, electronic scratching ("D-d-d-don't do it-t-t-t") and horn breaks snapping us up and out of the all-consuming funk.

It is 1992. Public Enemy are touring Australia, playing the Hordern Pavilion in the Showground precinct just south of Sydney's Central Business District (the precinct now subsumed, thanks to a massively overgenerous series of state government tax incentives and subsidies by Rupert Murdoch's "Hollywood down under" Fox Studios—a detail not out of place in a piece of writing concerned with the transnational flow of cultural material). The performances themselves that night were, on reflection, fairly unremark-able. It was the first time I had encountered Australian rap: the opening band was Sound Unlimited, a local crew who were, under the auspices of Pub-lic Enemy, negotiating a breakthrough recording deal with Sony-Columbia. In all honesty, though, that night I was completely underwhelmed. The male vocalists sounded, to my ears at that time, as though they were affecting a drawling, American style of delivery over unremarkable, repetitive beats.

Between raps, the boys would stalk the stage, spending what seemed to be an inordinate amount of time with their backs to the audience, in apparent obeisance to the DJ at the upstage console. There was little or no communication with the audience, the performance failing to establish any great momentum or energy. The lone female vocalist sang, rather than rapped, and although later I would be able to locate T-Na's singing in the R&B genre, at the time, and, I suppose, my expectations buoyed by the vigor and attack of *Fear of a Black Planet,* I was more or less completely unaffected.

The same goes, really, for Ice-T, the main support that night. Ice-T's performance was my first experience of braggadocio, and although I was not quite as amused as the reviewer from the *Sydney Morning Herald* (see Maxwell and Bambrick 1994: 2), his strut and swagger certainly bemused. Public Enemy, obviously having saved the best of the public address system for themselves, were a much slicker proposition: the carefully choreographed SIWs ("Security of the First World"), Chuck D's down-the-barrel-of-the-microphone intensity, and Flavor Flav's horseplay, notwithstanding the "stadium rock" ambience of the venue, created a more engaging performance.

But I did learn some very important things that night. I learned that we were, collectively, as an audience, in a place called "the House." In fact, more than that, the whole of Sydney was, apparently, in the motherfucking House. And even better than that, Sydney was "the capital of the hip-hop world." This (to my ears at least) extraordinary claim, repeated dozens of times, elicited a kind of lethargic antiphonics, which reached their zenith for me as Ice-T managed to get what seemed to be the entire audience chanting back to him that they were "original gangstas."

The rules of this performative genre, however, demand even more hyperbole: Sydney was, in fact, the *motherfucking* capital of the hip-hop world. The Hordern Pavilion, was, Ice-T assured us, "surrounded by the *po*-lice," who had been persecuting Ice and his entourage (there had been a problem with visas and criminal records, apparently). The *po*-lice did not want him here, in Australia, and nor, Ice told us, did our parents. Later, as we left the show (and, of course, to be fair, it was a show; the whole thing was, quite self-consciously, [don't believe the] hype), I looked around but could see only barrel-chested private security guards (largely of Polynesian extraction, upping the evening's ethnic ante) ringing the building, and, beyond them, a wagon train of anxious-looking parents in family sedans waiting curbside, to pick up their kids.

Now, it is pretty easy to poke a bit of fun at the theatrics of that evening. It was, after all, show biz, and apart from Public Enemy's recognition of Aboriginal land-rights issues and Sound Unlimited's multiethnic appearance, there was little about the performance that was anything other than, as I have suggested, generically "by the numbers." We might have been anywhere, but for Public Enemy's parading of an Aboriginal flag on stage and Chuck's speaking of his "Aboriginal brothers" and their "struggle."

A few days after the concert, Public Enemy traveled to inner-city Redfern, which contains one of the densest indigenous populations in Australia and is consistently demonized as a "no-go zone," as Sydney's one true, authentic ghetto. Two Aboriginal women (themselves rappers) later told me that when Public Enemy arrived at the Block, a particularly notorious strip of dilapidated terrace houses, Chuck D spent ninety minutes talking and signing autographs, while Flavor Flav "spent the whole time sitting in his limo talking on his mobile phone." Another (white) informant was less than impressed with Public Enemy's identification of the Australian Aboriginal struggle with that of African Americans, arguing that African American rappers seemed to have little if anything to say about Native American land rights, a situation far more closely analogous to local Australian issues of indigeneity. Instead, my informant argued, the African American rappers invoked an identification with Australian Aboriginals solely on the grounds of skin color, grounds apparently capable of transcending all cultural context and difference. This informant wanted to argue for another grounds for his own engagement with hip-hop, something other than blackness.

Another white middle-class informant, a prominent figure in the local hip-hop scene, extended this argument even further: the two Aboriginal girls mentioned above wrote and performed raps as Blackjustis, appearing at local festivals (including the Invasion Day concerts, an annual event marking the arrival of the first fleet of British settlers and convicts in 1788 and celebrated by mainstream Australia as Australia Day). Blackjustis rapped about their Aboriginality:

Taking our land our souls our beliefs
Rape, murder and all the white lies
Resulting in black genocide
Clear the land with whiteman tools
With the land the stars the moon and the sun
They should have left us alone

40,000 years living in peace
And now 200 years the peace has ceased
Motherland no longer smiles
Vanished bushland around for miles

But Blackjustis were not, my informant explained, "really *hip-hop.*" Sure, they rapped, they were black and marginalized, and their raps conformed to the message rap genre. But just because you rap does not mean that you are part of hip-hop.

This, then, is hip-hop as a cultural phenomenon, as opposed to rap, the performative genre. Hip-hop as *culture,* as *community,* and, most intriguingly of all, as *nation:* the hip-hop nation, a transnational entity manifested, in this antipodean context, in the absence of an existential shared grounding of participants in race, class, or physical proximity (either to each other, in terms of a 'hood, or to their brothers over the oceans), means a commitment in the first instance to the three key hip-hop practices — rapping, writing, and breaking — and to something variously referred to as the "essence," the "ideology," the "hard core," or the truth of hip-hop, a truth that, in the circular logic of the far western Sydney crew Def Wish Cast's rap, could be found in the affective thrall of the music itself. Arguing for his hip-hop credentials, the eponymous Def Wish raps that he is "always hardcore / 'cos hardcore means true to the music." This a formula is expanded upon by DJ Vame: "true to the music," he tells me, means being "faithful" to the "original instruments" of hip-hop: two turntables and a microphone.

And here is the other appeal of the tautological ascription of authenticity to a sensation, or of coming up with something as circular as "hardcore" meaning "true to the music" (which is, of course, "hardcore"). "Hip-hopness," in such formulations, operates as a purely transcendental signifier. It has no simple referent; just this: it *feels* a certain way ... *that's it,* there, in that beat! Can't you feel it? Yes, that attitude, that's it! How do you know? Because I do, because I feel it. The "truth" of hip-hop is a slippery thing, it would seem. It is open to dispute, arbitrated by key figures who are able to name, to discern, to include and exclude, and to police the boundaries of authenticity.

Two rappers battle with each other, the first a self-styled "hard rhymer," the other a freestyler, an improviser, less concerned with being "hard" than with his flow and with the responsibilities he feels toward his community. The battle revolves around a simple problematic: my hip-hop is more authentic than your hip-hop. The freestyler wins the battle: he is, after all, in his element, exchanging off-the-cuff rhymes, thinking on his feet. His flow cuts the other to pieces, and the vanquished rhymer steps down. The winner is able to announce to his audience that that was an authentic hip-hop tradition, and that his rap was *real* rapping: the other guy (younger, an upstart, unable to *flow*) was out of line, claiming an authenticity he had not earned.

Afterward, the young men shake hands, promise each other "peace";

later another informant, incensed by the upstart, tells me that had he been there, he would not have been so restrained: "I'd have bashed him," he says.

Hardcore means true to the music. The track that this grab comes from is Def Wish Cast's anthemic "A.U.S. Down Under Comin' Upper," on their 1993 independent CD release *Knights of the Underground Table* (subtitle: *Twelve Moons of Finely Mastered Hip-Hop Ritual*). "A.U.S." was Def Wish Cast's finest moment: in fact, each and every time I saw and felt it performed was astonishing. Four T-shirted boys from the outer suburbs: Def Wish himself, the slight, crop-haired exponent of ragga-rap syllable ballistics; Ser Reck, sharp of face and glaring of gaze; and Die C, shaven headed, olive complexioned, swapping verses as they prowled the stage. And on the upstage turntables, DJ Vame, an island of calm in the shrieking maelstrom. Three of the four young men, Simon, Shane, and Paul, were decidedly Anglo-Saxon; the fourth, Pablo, of Latin blood. Their audience pogos in front of the stage (a dance that started, Def Wish told me, at a gig in Melbourne), punching fists in the air as the rappers name-check Sydney's far-western suburbs, antiphonically responded to with a distorted sample on the DAT:

St. Clair's	*in the house*
St. Mary's	*in the house*
Mt. Druitt's	*in the house*

culminating in the climactic

Aaaah . . . Penrith's   *in the house!*

and Ser Reck rips into his rhyme, his voice ragged, guttural, barking: the signifiers of Aussie hip-hop authenticity (there is none of the smooth, mellifluous flow of a NAS or Dr. Dre here); broad, bent, nasal *Aussie* syllables, as his cartography of hip-hop Down Under spreads outward from its western-Sydney epicenter: "Pieced with Brisbane, drank with Adelaide boys / Perth kicks, Melbourne society makin' the noise."

Here is a motor-atlas index of Australia's major cities. Ser Reck has been there, done that all over the country. He has witnessed and participated in hip-hop the length and breadth of the land. This is the argument for Australian hip-hop authenticity that I was presented with time and time again, grounded in an unimpeachable performativity: hip-hop in Australia is real, tangible. All over the country, b-boyz (even some b-girls) are piecing, breaking, DJing, rapping. Australia is, Ser Reck continues,

An island with more than just a dream
With a stand in hip-hop, a definite mark

... a journey to embark
All bands on an outbreak, not a remake
A.U.S.T. on a path to overtake ya!
And back into the chorus:
A.U.S. down under comin' upper.

In this construction of place, the familiar spatial metaphors of hip-hop (and indeed of the popular discourses of subcultures as subversive undergrounds), in which a street-level wisdom is seen as rising up against the oppressive powers that be, are redoubled: Australia is down under, comin' up. Sound Unlimited, also from Sydney's western suburbs and including members of Russian and mixed Chilean and Filippino origin, spelled out this doubling in the title of their 1993 album *Postcards from the Edge of the Underside*.

This spatial othering morphs easily into a chrono-narrative (Appadurai 1993: 273), with quite specific resonances in the context of a local Australian ideo- and mediascape preoccupied with notions of cultural and national maturation, in which Australia figures predominantly as being temporally anterior to the United States, and to a lesser extent, to Europe.[4] In publicity material circulated to accompany the release of their album in 1993, for example, Sound Unlimited presented a narrative of origin in comic-book form in which the members of the crew appear as already constituted, identifiably hip-hop personae who have come from "the future" to "save" a moribund local music scene from "an onslaught of mediocrity" (see Maxwell and Bambrick 1994: 11–12). Of course, the future (as well as the past) of hip-hop is figured as the USA, and this is the source of yet another ambivalence in the Australian hip-hop milieu: the USA is where "it all began" and "where everything happens first," and yet, in order to assert the authenticity and "reality" of the local scene, it was important to deny that what was happening locally was in any way imitative or derivative of an "original" American hip-hop. Hip-hop needed to very carefully, then, negotiate its fidelity to what I have called "the standard hip-hop narrative" (gleaned from the hip-hop mediascape: album covers, fanzines, Web sites, folklore, and even quasi-academic sources such as Toop, Jones, and Nelson), a narrative of *that* place, the USA, while simultaneously perpetrating a parallel narrative of belongingness to *this* place, Australia. In the absence (with very few exceptions) of a diasporic African American community through which the cultural substrate of hip-hop might be embodied, the "arrival" of hip-hop in Australia was, as I have noted, completely media-ted. The American past and future constituting the narrative grounds of hip-hop was, of necessity, an imaginary America, an America delivered to the lives of proto-rappers, breakers, and writers down under by way of Hollywood (Dennis Hopper's *Colors* or John Singleton's *Boyz n the Hood)* and the hyperbole of gangsta rap.

For the press and electronic media, this imaginary America tended to figure as a radical dystopia. At the bottom of the media food chain (the tabloids, both print and electronic), the Los Angeles of color gangs, drive-bys, fear, and no-go areas was invoked as Sydney's future as part of the journalistic tradition of moral outrage (see Maxwell 1994b), accompanied by absurd maps purporting to show "color gang" territories. Such journalism made no distinction between organized criminal activity and loose confederations of youth; a report commissioned by the New South Wales Police in 1994 concluded that, in fact, there was no reason to believe that the American experience of gangs was being reproduced in the suburbs of Sydney (Godbee 1994). At the same time, the state Labor government was legislating increased powers for the police to break up gatherings of three or more youths — the state premier making electoral capital out of the media-hyped climate of fear, indexed by the apparently pandemic outbreaks of baseball caps and baggy clothes across the suburbs.

At the top end of the market, serious broadsheets fretted about American cultural imperialism, but the message was the same: an "authentic" Australian culture (a snark if ever there was one) under threat from without. Rap offered an easy target for such analysis, with the baseball cap the ultimate icon of cultural infection. And, back on the streets (or more precisely, in middle-class bedrooms), the crews were rapping about the same questions. Here is Illegal Substance, a crew from Bondi, in Sydney's eastern (i.e., beach-side) suburbs, rhyming about a celebrated incident "out west":

What the fuck is happening?
Is Sydney turning into the home of Rodney King?
Los Angeles is the city we're becoming
In the west of Sydney we saw people running
From a gang involved in a drive-by
The first one for S-Y-D-N-E-Y
Why on earth does it happen here?
A gang involved in a drive-by
He was only eighteen — why did he die?

DJ E.S.P. explained to me the story behind the rap: "Friends of ours were performing in Villawood and we went to see them and after the show, after everything was finished late at night . . . inside there was a fight, between the Lebs and the Blacks, and the Lebs got kicked out, and they came back and did a drive-by." His MC, Mick E, elaborated: "I mean that's American . . .

but then it happened in Australia, therefore I wrote about it as an Australian issue," thereby taking on the role of rapper-as-street-journalist, telling it like it is. For E.S.P., this gets to the heart of the question of authenticity: "'Cos to start with, things do happen in Australia that do happen in America, like the drive-by and all that, like people say, mate, they'd call Australian rappers fake, but.". . . Mick E leaps in: "Nah, they're not, because we're talking about things that happen in Australia, even though they may be American things happening. . ." And E.S.P. clears up this potential confusion by asserting a *necessary* chrono-logic in which Australia is figured as developmentally anterior to the dystopian devolution of urban America: "They did happen in America [then], but they're happening here [now]."

Here is an imaginary landscape, rapped into being: a landscape of "Lebs" (Lebanese) and "blacks" (in this instance, neither the African American nor the Australian Aboriginal blacks, but Polynesians), each staged as discrete ethnic identities, designated by the definite article, apparently waging identity wars in the mean streets of the far western suburbs (see Maxwell 1994a, 1994b). And here, of course, the specific, contextual valencies of place must be weighed up: there are few better archetypes of "westie" Sydney than Villawood, site of one of the notorious migrant hostels that sprang up around Sydney in the years following World War II. Diane Powell takes the title of her 1993 ethnography of Sydney's western suburbs from this quote from Robin Boyd's 1968 *The Australian Ugliness*:

> Out west, the wooden villa, or Villawood zone . . . is a fairly typical Australian working class development, repeating the dreary, ill-considered housing growth on the outskirts of every Australian town. . . . [T]he Housing Commission of NSW, speculative builders and private owners compete with one another to reduce the bush to a desert of terra-cotta roofs relieved only by electrical wires and wooden poles. (Powell 1993: 24–25)

For E.S.P. and Mick E., two middle-class boys from the eastern suburbs, Villawood could represent more or less pure otherness. In their rap we can read the ambivalence of what Powell refers to as the "slummer journalist" (1993: 20ff.): the prurient fascination with the underworld that marks the other as simultaneously desirable and undesirable. (Indeed, Mick E. uses the by now standardized hip-hop trope of rapper-as-reporter, telling it like it is, as another index of his own hip-hop authenticity: "we're talking about things that happen.") The young men, notwithstanding their affected outrage ("what the fuck?"), seem to relish the prospect of Los Angeles down under.

Hip-hop's eschatological promise ("we [hip-hop] are the future," Ser Reck would tell me) is bound to the jingoistic nationalism of proto-republican Australia. Die C raps:

A.U.S.T. defender Die C delivering strong and aggressive
Lyrics heard clearly in every barricade across the world
On an island that many never look twice at as being associated
    with rap—
On hip-hop charts they come across a new discovery:
US, U.K., U.S.—what A.U.S.T.?
Where's the pride? Many'd rather just step aside
See what the rest of the world's doing and live their lives
Lounging. Followers stand up and make the time
No longer behind, step to the front of the line
Representing leaders, hold up a new flag
Our own turn for the better
The letters that stand alone, not in the shadow of any other country
Def Wish Cast from the A.U.S.T.

Even better, Def Wish Cast invert the center-periphery model of North American urban hip-hop, in which hip-hop speaks from and represents the demographic hole in the urban doughnut: the inner city 'hood. St. Marys, Mt. Druitt, St. Clair, Penrith: these are on the *outside,* the sprawling, sunburnt expanses of Sydney's suburbia, thirty miles from the picture-postcard, Olympic-touted cityscape of Harbour Bridge, Opera House, and sapphire-blue surf. A single railway line transects mile after mile of quarter-acre blocks set amidst the gum-tree haze of the Cumberland Plain. These are the western suburbs, or, even better, the *far* western suburbs, demonized dystopia of media (Powell) and a popular mythology that styles "westies" as the monstrous other antithetically opposed to the vigor and health of the cosmopolitan center —a local with no locality, a space without a sense of place, as Def Wish explained to me one baking summer day, sitting at St. Marys station. I had asked him what he would show someone who wanted to see "the Westside," the heterotopic hip-hop imaginary from which he and his crew claim to speak—which they claim to *represent.* "That's it, man," he told me, echoing Gertrude Stein's apocryphal assessment of Oakland, California; "there's nothing here" (Maxwell 1994a).

Things, of course, change. The ethnographic present rapidly becomes historical past. By the late 1990s, new generations of rappers were appearing in Sydney, many of whom made none of the claims to cultural belongingness that characterized the old school. Genres proliferated as freestylee rappers forged partnerships with jazz and funk musicians, moving away from a claim to hip-hop authenticity grounded in particular signifiers ("no live instruments" or "two turntables and a microphone") to one based even more overtly upon intangible felt qualities, governed by increasingly fragile logics of cultural capital. Cultural capital, of course, shifts: what was unthinkable in 1992 (I remember one informant snorting at the very idea of *Doo-Bop*, the 1992 Miles Davis collaboration with Easy Mo Be) becomes orthodoxy in 1995 (another informant, fingering Guru's *Jazzmatazz* album, told me, "Hip-hop and jazz . . . they're the same thing"; but then again, Guru had the subcultural clout to authorize such a pronouncement). Even "Westside" is a floating signifier: the mid-1990s Westside of Def Wish Cast is located a good twenty or thirty kilometers farther west than the late-1980s Westside of Sound Unlimited's earlier incarnation, the Westside Posse.

By the end of 1997, Miguel d'Souza, writing for the entertainment section of the city's leading broadsheet, the *Sydney Morning Herald,* was able to nominate his "top 10" local hip-hop releases for the year. While this represents an extraordinary multiplication of product, given that the combined local hip-hop releases of the previous five years would barely have reached that number in total, a nagging sense is also in there of hip-hop as genre, rather than as culture: another product offered up in the "supermarket of style" (Polhemus 1994), hip-hop not as a way of life ("I eat, breathe, and sleep hip-hop," said one old-school writer), but as a Grammy Award category, or section in your local record store. D'Souza told me in early 1998 that those who were into rap—the new crews—did not seem to be so concerned about hip-hop culture any more. "I think you'd find," he told me, "that people who are into rap now don't use terms like 'community,' 'culture,' or 'nation' so readily." All sorts of clubs and club nights now market themselves as "hip-hop," d'Souza laments, and we together recognize the collapse into that most familiar of youth-culture analytical refrains: the fall into the commercial, the commodification of youthful rebellion, the selling out of the authentic.

But even in that moment, I find myself thinking, instead, of Ser Reck's eyes fixing me, shaking me, challenging anyone to prove otherwise: "It's *our thing.*"

NOTES

1. *Pace* Juan Flores (1987, 1994), and Regan Kelly (1993), both of whom offer useful correctives to the hegemonic New York–African American–centered narratives of the origins of hip-hop.

2. The 1998 Constitutional Convention resolved in favor of putting to the Australian people a referendum seeking approval for reforms that would, potentially,

have seen the present constitutional monarchy, under which the queen of the United Kingdom is the Australian head of state, replaced by a republican model. But the referendum was defeated, due to a rallying of conservative promonarchy elements and confusing semantics in its presentation. Much of the republican movement's momentum was derived from the success of Sydney in bidding for the 2000 Olympic Games and the wish that those games had been opened by an Australian head of state.

3. See, for example, the Youth-Sound-Space site at <*http://www.cia.com.au/ peril/youth/*>.

4. The corollary is, of course, a national preoccupation with "world first" and "world class"-ness, a syndrome recognized way back in the 1950s by the literary critic A. A. Phillips as Australia's "cultural cringe": a sense of dependence upon (at that time, anyway) English cultural forms and institutions, by the 1980s manifesting as overstated attempts to assert Australia's "global" status. A 1998 furor in the Australian arts scene involved the Victorian state premier crowing about his state's "world-class culture." A prominent theater director, Barrie Kosky, responded by quoting John Ralston Saul's *The Doubter's Companion:* "[W]orld class is a phrase used by provincial cities and second-rate entertainment events, as well as a wide variety of insecure individuals to assert that they are not provincial or second-rate, thereby confirming that they are."

REFERENCES

Appadurai, Arjun. 1993. "Disjuncture and Difference in the Global Cultural Economy." In *The Phantom Public Sphere,* edited by Bruce Robbins. Minneapolis: University of Minnesota Press. Originally published in *Public Culture* 2, no. 2: 1–24.

Bey, Hakim. 1991. *Temporary Autonomous Zone, Ontological Anarchy, Poetic Terrorism.* New York: Autonomedia.

Bhabha, Homi K. 1994. *The Location of Culture.* London and New York: Routledge.

Chalfant, Henry and James Prigoff. 1987. *Spraycan Art.* London: Thames and Hudson.

Cross, Brian, ed. 1993. *It's Not about a Salary: Rap, Race, and Resistance in Los Angeles.* London and New York: Verso.

Flores, Juan. 1987. "Rappin' Writin', and Breakin'." *Dissent* 34, no. 4: 580–84.

———. 1994 "Puerto Rican and Proud, Boyee! Rap Roots and Amnesia." In *Microphone Fiends: Youth Music and Youth Culture,* edited by Andrew Ross and Tricia Rose. New York: Routledge.

Foucault, Michel. 1986. "Of Other Places." *Diacritics* 16, no. 1: 24–27.

Godbee, Graham. 1994. *Street Gangs: Study for the NSW Police Service.* Beecroft, N.S.W.: Pulse Consultants.

Kelly, Raegan. 1993. "Hip Hop Chicano: A Separate but Parallel Story."
In *It's Not about a Salary: Rap, Race, and Resistance in Los Angeles,*
edited by Brian Cross. London and New York: Verso.

Maxwell, Ian. 1994a. "Busting Rhymes." *RealTime* 3, October–November: 4–5.

———. 1994b. "True to the Music: Authenticity, Articulation, and Authorship
in Sydney Hip Hop Culture." *Social Semiotics* 4, no. 1–2: 117–37.

———. 1997a. "Hip Hop Aesthetics and the Will to Culture."
Australian Journal of Anthropology 8, no. 1: 50-70.

———. 1997b. "How to Make a Rap Recording."
Sounds Australian 15, no. 50: 22–23.

———. 1997c. "On the Flow: Dancefloor Grooves, Rapping, 'Freestylee,'
and the Real Thing." *Perfect Beat* 3, no. 3: 15–27.

Maxwell, Ian, and Nikki Bambrick. 1994. "Discourses of Culture and
Nationalism in Sydney Hip Hop." *Perfect Beat* 2, no. 1: 1–19. ;

Phillips, A. A. 1958. "The Cultural Cringe." In *The Australian Tradition*.
Melbourne: F. W. Chesire.

Polhemus, Ted. 1994. *Street Style*. London: Thames and Hudson.

Powell, Diane. 1993. *Out West*. Sydney: Allen and Unwin.

Robbins, Bruce, ed. 1993. *The Phantom Public Sphere*.
Minneapolis: University of Minnesota Press.

Rose, Tricia. 1994. "A Style Nobody Can Deal With: Politics, Style, and the
Postindustrial City in Hip Hop." In *Microphone Fiends: Youth Music and Youth
Culture,* edited by Andrew Ross and Tricia Rose. New York: Routledge.

Ross, Andrew, and Tricia Rose. 1994. *Microphone Fiends: Youth Music
and Youth Culture*. New York: Routledge.

Thornton, Sarah. 1996. *Club Cultures: Music, Media, and Subcultural Capital*.
Hanover, N.H.: Wesleyan University Press.

Wark, McKenzie. 1994. *Virtual Geography: Living with Global Media Events*.
Bloomington: Indiana University Press.

DISCOGRAPHY

Def Wish Cast. 1993. *Knights of the Underground Table*. Random Records.

Illegal Substance. 1994. *Off da Back of a Truck*. Illegal Records.

Sound Unlimited. 1992. *A Postcard from the Edge of the Under-Side*. Columbia.

Chapter 12

Kia Kaha! (Be Strong!)

Maori and Pacific Islander Hip-Hop in Aotearoa–New Zealand

TONY MITCHELL

AKONA TE REO: NATIVE LANGUAGE RAP

In 1992 the Maori group Moana and the Moa Hunters, who combine rap, soul, and reggae with traditional Maori chants and musical instruments, won a New Zealand Music Industry award for Best Maori Recording with their rap-inflected song "AEIOU (Akona Te Reo)." The song, whose title translates as "Learn the Language," was addressed primarily to Maori *rangatahi* (young people), many of whom do not speak Maori, which could be regarded as a dialect of the language spoken throughout Polynesia. (Only 3 percent of the population of Aotearoa–New Zealand speaks Maori fluently. This population of 3.8 million is made up of 81.2 percent Europeans, 9 percent Maori, and 3 percent Pacific Islanders, mostly Polynesian migrants from Tonga, Samoa, Fiji, Niue, and the Cook and Tokelau Islands.) "AEIOU" is also a plea, mostly in English, to the Maori people of Aotearoa to preserve their native culture (Maoritanga), study their history, and take part in the global movement of indigenous peoples for self-preservation. Its use of rap inflections combined with traditional Maori *waiata* (song) was an apt illustration of the indigenization of rap and hip-hop in Aotearoa–New Zealand as well as its strategic use as a vehicle of expression to address Maori youth. Receiving the award, Moana Maniapoto-Jackson accused New Zealand radio of racism in continuing to ignore Maori music, commenting that fewer than twenty people present at the awards ceremony would have heard all three finalists in the Best Maori Recording category. Airplay on national radio remains a rarity for Maori popular-music groups, especially those who sing in Maori (Reid 1992a: 36). Four years later, in 1996, a remixed version of "AEIOU, Akona Te Reo '95" was again nominated for (but did not win) a New Zealand Music Industry Award. This time it was included in a new separate category called Mana Reo (Maori Language and Culture), which indicated that little had changed as far as mainstream acceptance of Maori music in New Zealand was concerned. And in 1998, Maniapoto-Jackson again summed up the continuing marginal position of Maori-language rap and popular-music in the local media and industry on the release of Moana and the Moa Hunters' second album *Rua* (Two):

> Basically, if you use Maori language you've blacklisted yourself off the radio anyway, anything that has a discernible Maori style to it is out. I didn't realize until I looked at the track listing [of *Rua*] the other day, every song has got Maori language in it. I have no expectations whatsoever that we're going to get mainstream radio play. . . . It's almost like Maori music —and I'm not just talking about us—it's underground here. Everyone talks about "alternative" music, Flying Nun or whatever, but anything that's got Maori language in it is just so alternatively alternative it doesn't rate. (Russell 1998a: 22)

But despite the difficulties of radio and mass-media access, the adaptation of rap and hip-hop by Maori musicians in Aotearoa–New Zealand has brought some degree of local commercial success. This began in 1984, when the Patea Maori Club reached number 1 in the New Zealand charts with "Poi E," a remarkable blend of Maori chanting, *poi* dancing (the poi is a small ball made of flax, which is swung around on a string in traditional Maori dance), rap, and breakdancing. (As with "Akona te reo," a video release of the song was vital in reinforcing traditional Maori musical elements.) "Poi E" combined traditional Maori vocals and show-band and concert-party idioms with gospel and funk, and was even named "Single of the Week" in Britain's *New Musical Express,* eventually winning a New Zealand Recording Industry Best Polynesian Record award on its rerelease in 1988 (Dix 1988: 331, 344). The Patea Maori Club, which Geoff Lealand has described as "the group that comes closest to capturing some of the unique nuances of life here . . . due to its unique coupling of two unmatched musical traditions" (76) also won Best Polynesian Record in 1984 for its second single, "Aku Raukura (My Feather)," and were the original performers of "Kua Makona (Satisfied)," which Moana and the Moa Hunters also recorded in 1993. This absorption of elements of rap and hip-hop culture into a tradition of Maori popular-music provides an example of both the syncretism of indigenous musical cultures and the indigenization of rap in seemingly remote ethnic contexts. Produced and led by Dalvanius, a flamboyant singer-composer who provided a link between the traditional Maori show bands of the 1950s and earlier and Maori hip-hop, "Poi E" was produced as a Maori musical with fifteen additional songs in 1995, and an album version was released in 1996. Dalvanius and a traditional Maori cultural group subsequently performed selections from the musical in Sydney in 2000 at the Waitangi Day Concert, an annual event celebrating the signing of the treaty between Maori chiefs and the British colonial government on 5 February 1840.

MULTICULTURAL NOISE: U.S. APPROPRIATIONS
AND THE AUCKLAND HIP-HOP SCENE

And what about Mangere? the "lazy"

volcano, quarried for its scoria,

renowned for significant suburban wildlife: punks, streetkids, rastas, heavy metal,

    Ronald McDonald is headmaster of the local primary

(it's true!)

. . . In Mangere

the PMs's the MP:

everyone and everything's in an inverse universe: you get karanga'd on the shopping malls,

    the tangata phenua live in genuine chipboard

whares

overlooking the beautiful hei-tiki-shaped sewerage system,

the streetkids pop smack, listen to Grandmaster Flash, rap Michael

Jackson's BAD LP:

I'm Bad, shimon you know it, and of course they sleep in the public dunnies

    with the hole in the cubicle to prick your dick through.

Yeah Columbus

discovered Mangere, but meaty chicken breasts in sesame seed burger buns

    are really insensitive: it's just the way, aha aha, you like it?

No wonder

they spraybombed KILL A WHITE on the local Kentucky Fried.

—Robert Sullivan, "Message from Mangere," *Jazz Waiata,* 1990

The young Maori poet Robert Sullivan shows the direct impact of black American hip-hop culture, along with other less welcome forms of U.S. im-port culture, on the predominantly Maori, Polynesian, and poor-white popu-lation of the sprawling, topsy-turvy South Auckland suburb of Mangere, the constituency of the former New Zealand Labour Party prime minister David Lange. Situated near the airport, Mangere is largely made up of what David Eggleton has described, quoting another Sullivan poem invoking Public Enemy and the Polynesian gang the Mongrel Mob, as "state houses for the urban dispossessed where 'the Mongrel mob fights the power' of the dominant culture. . . . In a way the deracinated centerless sprawl of Mangere is repeated all over Auckland, as if the whole city is merely some Los Angeles spillover" (1991: 380, 381). The affinities with Los Angeles extended to Auckland street gangs, named Crips and Bloods after their Los Angeles prototypes, who were featured in February 1995 in *Families at War,* a two-part exposé on New Zealand TV2's local version of *Sixty Minutes.* This offered, in the words of the U.S.-accented narrator, "a rare and disturbing glimpse into the mind of an active gang member." Although the teenaged gang member in question was white, the musical accompaniment to the story was performed by unidentified Polynesian rappers. Mangere, Otara, and a number of other South Auckland suburbs are appropriate centers of origin for the New Zealand hip-hop scene, which also has crews in Wellington and Christchurch, and which involves a significant number of Maori, Samoan, Niuean, European, and even Malaysian Chinese performers. As with a cappella, the essentially oral and vocal dynamics of rap have been adopted with ease by both Maori and Pacific Islander musicians and performers.

Breakdancing was a prominent and prototypical example of a black American import culture that was adopted widely by Maori youth in the early 1980s, as a study of breakdance as an identity marker in the North Island city of Palmerston North by Tania Kopytko indicates. According to Kopytko, breakdance first arrived in New Zealand in 1983 via Western Samoa, and by 1984 local breakdance teams, consisting mostly of young Maori and Pacific Islanders, were appearing on local television programs, and Television New Zealand even sponsored a national breakdance competition. Kopytko argues that for Maori and Pacific Islander young people with little chance of achieving recognition through conventional channels such as school, sport, and social position, "breakdance provided a very strong and positive identity that did much to raise their self esteem and realize their capabilities" (1986: 21–22). She also claims that, despite the local mass media's association of breakdancing with street gangs, glue sniffing, and petty crime, which gave it pejorative connotations and contributed to its decline by 1985, it provided Maori youth in particular with a viable substitute for their own culture (Maoritanga): "Amongst Maori youth the association with an international Black identity compensates in part for the lack of a thorough knowledge of Maori culture. Also, popular culture movements are more readily accessible without the commitment and effort necessary for a knowledge of Maoritanga" (1986: 26).

Following the adoption of breakdancing by Maori and Pacific Islander youth, rap music and the other elements of hip-hop culture inevitably became a vehicle for vernacular expressions of Maori militancy. (One prominent example of Maori graffiti in Auckland in the mid-1980s read, "Aotearoa: the land of the wrong white crowd"; Aotearoa means literally "the land of the long white cloud.") In an examination by the Maori cultural magazine *Mana* in 1993 of the adoption by Maori youth of African American music, films, television programs, and clothes such as baseball caps, baggies, T-shirts, and jackets, Maniapoto-Jackson suggests that this acculturation of the artifacts of another black minority by Maori young people was mainly due to the absence of Maori culture from the mass media: "It comes down to what you see on television and what you hear on the radio. We don't hear enough of our own culture, so we co-opt the next closest thing. . . . Maori kids identify with the stereotypical Afro-American they see on television, who's funny, sassy, streetwise, who's funky, who plays sports, who's into music, who's got all the quick one-liners and who's got all the gear on" (Ihaka 1993: 12). In the same article, the Maori filmmaker Merata Mita blamed the absence of strong Maori leadership and the enforcement of *tapu* (taboos) and preservation restrictions on elements of Maori culture by Maori elders for alienating Maori youth and forcing them to seek black American role models and cultural icons: "If you put a Maori pattern on your shirt, people accuse you of prostituting the culture or selling out or it's too tapu. We've created such a mystique and negative enforcement that it's much easier for young Maori to take Afro-American symbols and wear them. Nobody's going to attack them for it" (13).

As Kerry Buchanan has argued, hip-hop's associations with African American culture became an important reference point and example for musical expressions of a local Maori and Pacific Islander vernacular culture, with which it shared strong roots in church and gospel singing:

> With our links to the land broken, our alienation from the mode of production complete, our culture objectified, we have become marginalised and lost. . . . This is not to say beaten. And this is what we have in common with black America. When Maori hip-hop activists Upper Hutt Posse visited America recently, these political, social and racial links were brought into perspective. Upper Hutt Posse were welcomed as people involved in a common struggle, linked symbolically through hip-hop culture. (1993: 27)

Comparing the imagery and ideals of the Maori Ratana Church with the Nation of Islam, Buchanan argues that there is a "homology, a symbolic connection" between Maori and African Americans expressed through hip-hop and rap in terms of a culture of resistance to dominant white culture:

Like black Americans, Maori have witnessed the total failure of the assimilationist ethic, with biculturalism meaning an exclusion of Maoritanga
from the dominant culture. There will be no biculturalism until there is
Maori sovereignty. The only bicultural impulse of any strength is to link
with black America, to be involved in the international struggle to form
new hegemonic ties. This is what Maori and Polynesians are doing through
hip hop. (1993: 27)

While developments in U.S. rap and hip-hop since 1993 have made this homology with Maori struggles more fractured and problematic, it is important to note this Maori espousal of hip-hop as what Buchanan calls "a symbolic war of resistance" against assimilation.

A 1994 survey of the local New Zealand rap scene by Otis Frizzell (a.k.a.
Rhythm Slave), of the Pakeha (European) group M.C.O.J. and Rhythm Slave,
featured a dozen groups and individuals and mentioned five more,[1] many
of whom had released recordings. Frizzel emphasizes the multicultural heterogeneity of the scene but cites the Wellington-based Maori group Upper
Hutt Posse as an important influence on the development of a distinctively
local style. Frizzel concluded: "I believe Hip-Hop in Aotearoa is still growing and improving, and has an authentic and original style. We have a lot
to thank Maori and Pacific Islanders for, in as much as a South Pacific feel
goes, but us honkies have definitely also helped to form the New Zealand
rap culture we have today. New Zealand is a multi-cultural society, and this
is reflected in most music, but none more so than hip hop" (1994: 45). Frizzell released *One Inch Punch* in 1995 together with the Maori rapper DLT and
OJ under the moniker Joint Force, with mixed results, as an attempt to forge
what they described as an "A.K. [Auckland] 95" hip-hop moment. The predominantly drum-heavy, scratch-drenched sound was perhaps summed up
by the track "Too Much Static," two versions of which were included, and attempts at ragga and dub styles on "Homie Phobic" and "Burntime" were not
entirely convincing. Snatches of uncharacteristic rock guitar and American
accents also did not help, and the end result was rather patchy. But in 1998
Frizzel compiled an important eighteen-track compilation album, *Aotearoa
Hip Hop, Vol. 1*, which documented ten years of largely Maori and Pacific
Islander rap music in Aotearoa–New Zealand, from Upper Hutt Posse's first
single, "E Tu" (Stand Proud), originally released in 1988, to DLT and Che Fu's
1996 number 1 hit "Chains" and the young Samoan rappers Losttribe's 1997
track "Summer in the Winter." This album, which included tracks in both
Maori and Samoan, was released on the major label BMG, and provided evi-

dence of the significant role rap and hip-hop had taken on in multicultural Aotearoa–New Zealand.

The first New Zealand hip-hop group to achieve any commercial success were the West Auckland Maori rappers 3 the Hard Way. Their pop-rap single "Hip-Hop Holiday," a hip-hop transposition of 10CC's 1970s hit "Dreadlock Holiday," topped the charts for several weeks and went gold in New Zealand in 1994, reaching number 12 on the Australian top 20. Describing themselves as "old school prankstas" (the title of their debut album), 3 the Hard Way maintained a commercial, ragga-based, accessible, party-rap sound which helped to smooth their way to the top of the charts.

Few other local hip-hop groups had any chart success until 1996, with the exception of 3 the Hard Way's Auckland Deepgrooves label-mates Urban Disturbance, who were voted Most Promising Group at the 1994 New Zealand Music Awards. Urban Disturbance's 1994 album *37° A-ttitude*, which paid homage to the Wu-Tang Clan's 1993 debut album *Enter the Wu-Tang (36 Chambers)*, was a sophisticated, witty, swing beat–influenced collection of distinctively local tracks. An overlooked milestone in New Zealand rap music, it included the single "Impressions," which describes the frustrations and ambitions of the group's hip-hop lifestyle in Auckland. Sampling debates from New Zealand Parliament and other sources and including some impressive saxophone solos by the Pakeha jazz musician Nathan Haines as well as creative input from the prominent Polynesian DJ Manuel Bundy, the album deserved to be noticed more widely than it was, and the group was impressive in live performance. The album was produced by the Niuean group member Zane Lowe and featured the Maori rapper Danny Haimona (of the Dam Native crew) and the Pakeha rapper Hame (Hamish Clarke) on the track "Relay." Lowe and Clarke later formed Breaks Co-Op, whose 1998 album *Roofers,* released just before the duo translocated to London, represents another landmark, this time in "abstract" hip-hop in New Zealand, with its predominantly sonic textures and only one track featuring Clarke's vocals. But it also represents the end of an era, for the album was conceived of as a farewell to the frustrations of producing hip-hop in isolation in New Zealand. As Clarke explained: "The first part is saying goodbye to hip-hop and the second part is saying goodbye to our ability to do hip-hop/electronic music and achieve the level that we want in New Zealand. Hip-hop is always New Zealand to me. I listen to it in other places but I always did it in New Zealand. And Zane did as well. We just grew more despondent with the state of what hip-hop meant to us as we grew older" (in Jewell 1998a: 63).

Another musician who made a similar transfer from hip-hop to trip-hop was Jody Lloyd of the Christchurch-based Dark Tower, one of the few rap groups in the predominantly Anglocentric South Island of New Zealand. Incorporating Pacific and Polynesian elements into their music, Dark Tower were featured on a 1996 compilation of Christchurch dub, hip-hop, and dance-music artists titled *On the Beat 'n' Track*. Their track "Too Much" showcased a distinctive, if self-consciously nationalistic, use of New Zealand idioms, accents, and cultural references, also emphasized by the title of their debut album, *Zealmen*, with Lloyd comparing himself to the Auckland vernacular poet Sam Hunt. The compilation also included rap tracks by Beats and Pieces, who in "Worldwide" celebrated rap as a global phenomenon, and Nil State, who in "Most Importantly the Pacific" located hip-hop in a diaspora in Oceania. The three groups also collaborated as Aposse Cut on the compilation's title track, which expressed their joint struggles to overcome criticism and mockery and create a Pakeha mode of New Zealand hip-hop:

> In the beginning Kiwiana was never meant to be
> Now the only way to have an identity
> Is by gripping and sifting through icons from the past
> Doesn't suit you because the future is moving so fast
> Folks being choked by the American yoke
> So now anything New Zealandy looks like a joke
> Kiwi music, now that's a Kiwiana laugh
> (A strange mind frame — you gotta be half cut mate)
> I took stories from my childhood and put them to verse
> And then got bombed, a Kiwiana curse
> I can think of worse, but still it's a taint
> It isn't nice being labelled as a joke when you ain't.

Lloyd was inspired to start rapping after watching Upper Hutt Posse on television — an interesting example of local influence rather than the usual U.S. sources — and in 1998 released a largely instrumental trip-hop album titled *Shadows on a Flat Land,* featuring members of Dark Tower. Attempting to forge a consciously local southern New Zealand sound — Christchurch is frequently alluded to as "flat city" — Lloyd is suspicious of what he regards as the "Americanisms of Auckland" (Jewell 1998c: 52; see Mitchell 1997 on the "Christchurch sound"). This transference from hip-hop influences to the more abstract, electronic beats represented by British drum 'n' bass and trip-hop, itself influenced by hip-hop, was echoed in Australia, with an almost simultaneous release of an instrumental hip-hop album by Moonrock, formerly a rap group called Easybass. It is also found in Italy, where there has been a noticeable shift by groups such as Almamegretta, who worked with the British group Massive Attack, toward a more dub–inflected, drum 'n' bass–oriented sound where rapping is less predominant.

Dam Native's debut album, *Kaupapa Driven Rhymes Uplifted (KDRU)*, which was released in 1997, was another important milestone in Maori hip-hop. Described by group leader Danny Haimona in the container insert as "an accumulation of 10 years hard work in Music and learning Tikanga Maori (Maori customs)," the album seamlessly combines rapping, scratching, and sampling with Maori cultural forms of expression. It includes the single "Behold My Cool Style," which features the Maori woman rap artist Teremoana Rapley, and contains a reference to the phenomenal Tongan All Black rugby player Jonah Lomu. The album's aim is to encourage positive associations for Maori cultural themes *(kaupapa)*. Another single, "Horrified One," in the manner of Niggaz with Attitude, attempts to reverse the derogatory connotations of the colloquial word "Hori," referring to Maori. "The Son," featuring Che Fu, promotes Maori unity and cultural tradition, and "Extremities" describes the "trials and tribulations" of a "nocturnal wanderer" and alludes to the group's name in the lines "America doesn't give a damn about me / I've got the influence and I'm sure to keep it Maori." The song "4 Realms of Existence" celebrates both New Zealand and global breakdancers, graffiti artists, DJs, and MCs. On "Revolution," Haimona explains that "being pro-Polynesian doesn't mean being anti-white," and "Battle Styles" expresses his commitment to producing kaupapa (theme-driven) rhymes and lyrical poetry.

In the video for "Behold My Kool Style," Haimona and the rest of the group dress in nineteenth-century European style, in the manner of Mario Van Peebles's black western *Posse* (1993), but also in the style of Maori "Puha Westerns" (see Parekowhai 1993) such as Geoff Murphy's *Utu* (1983). Haimona holds a hand-carved Maori public speaking staff, in the manner of the Canadian-Jamaican rappers the Dream Warriors, but also suggesting Maori traditions of oratory. Reviewing *KDRU* in the long-standing New Zealand monthly music magazine *Rip It Up*, Troy Ferguson (1997: 31) praised its "flax roots credibility" (flax is a local native plant traditionally employed by Maori for basketweaving, among other uses). Ferguson also praised Haimona and the group's often low-key delivery and its incorporation of hip-hop into a Maori context, describing it as "an album with both indigenous relevance and an international flavour — and maybe one of the finest local releases this year." Dam Native was duly nominated for Top Group and their album for a Mana Maori (Maori Culture) award at the 1998 New Zealand Music Awards. In 1997 the group won Most Promising Group and Haimona won Most Promising Male Vocalist, but like the Raskals in Canada, he saw these awards as token gestures, and they were not backed up by any local music-industry support.

Danny Thompson, a former member of Dam Native who left because he found the group too hardcore, had chart success in 1997 as DLT with his single "Chains" and made some further commercial inroads into the mainstream for local Pacific hip-hop. But there is still considerable pressure on New Zealand recording artists to produce radio-friendly, pop-oriented singles, even to get airplay on the predominantly Polynesian Auckland station Mai FM, which plays mainly U.S. R&B. This was illustrated by Losttribe, whose ragga- and "Samoan soul"–inflected "Summer in the Winter" appeared in five different versions, leading off with what John Russell described as "designed for radio mix . . . as it has that slick, laidback, easily digestible (ie. bland) swingbeat groove that so many Top 40 USA R&B groups are fond of. That said, Mai FM could be 'scared off' by the words 'Samoa' and 'Aotearoa' — 'too hardcore and offensive, bro'" (1997a: 33).

PROUD AND THE OTARA SOUND

Another important manifestation of rap music in Aotearoa–New Zealand occurred in 1994 with *Proud,* an "Urban Pacific Streetsoul Compilation" of South Auckland Polynesian rap, reggae, soul, a cappella, swing-beat, and traditional musicians that topped the New Zealand compilation charts for three weeks that year. The project, which involved Samoan, Tongan, Niuean, Fijian, and Cook Islander as well as Maori musicians, also included a twenty-five-date nationwide tour by most of the artists featured on the album. Produced by Alan Jannsson for Second Nature, the New Zealand branch of Sydney-based Volition records, the album included Sisters Underground, a Samoan and African American a cappella duo whose feisty, street-smart rap "In the Neighbourhood" set the tone for the compilation. This song later received a nomination for Best Single at the 1995 New Zealand Music Awards (and Sisters Underground was nominated for Most Promising Group) and even found its way into *Heartbreak High,* Australia's multicultural high school television drama series. With the exception of the Semi MCs, a mixed Maori and Samoan swing-beat group whose "lovers' rap" single "Trust Me" had been released on Volition in 1993, and DJ Payback, who had been involved in one of New Zealand's first rap groups, Double J and Twice the T, the groups featured on the *Proud* album had not previously recorded, and many had been involved in the local community Otara Music and Arts Centre. The ironically named Otara Millionaires Club (a.k.a. OMC, whose sole remaining member, Pauly Fuemana, later almost became a millionaire due to the worldwide success of his single "How Bizarre") had done a number of live performances as a hardcore rap group playing underground clubs to audiences that included members of Auckland's branches of the Crips and Bloods gangs. The Pacifican Descendants were regarded as one of New Zealand's leading live rap performers, along with Radio Backstab and DJ Playback. The Samoan a cappella group Di-Na-Ve, the gospel-based Rhythm Harmony, and the seven-man team of log drummers Puka Puka completed the lineup. Perhaps the most distinctively local, community-oriented track on the album is MC Slam's rap about street violence in Auckland, "Prove Me Wrong," which was adopted as a theme song by the South Auckland Manukau borough "Safer Communities" Council:

> our city streets are tainted with thugs
> cruising around selling off their drugs
> this wonderful city used to be safe
> you could walk around from dawn til late
> but these days nobody's caring
> you want to crack me for something that I'm
> wearing?

Proud was lauded by music reviewers as a new landmark in New Zealand popular-music, despite its release on an Australian label and "cringe" reactions to the final track, an a cappella version of the national anthem "God Defend New Zealand." Colin Hogg of the *Sunday Star Times* described *Proud* as "the best compilation of new Kiwi music in a decade" (1994) an evaluation affirmed by its rerelease in 2000. Hogg also suggested that the album's "Otara sound" may have ushered in a "new era" of Kiwi music, displacing and supplanting "the challenging new sounds of New Zealand contemporary music . . . from the bedsits of Dunedin, the garretts of Grey Lynn [an Auckland inner-city suburb] and the garages of Christchurch." Russell Baillie in the *New Zealand Herald* found it "a truly ground-breaking and purposeful local compilation . . . that captures a time and an attitude, and one to point to as a starting point in years to come" (1994). But the fact that by 1995 only one of the groups involved in the *Proud* project, the Otara Millionaires Club (shortened to OMC, and by then consisting only of Pauly Fuemana), was still in existence indicates that the album was an expression of potential rather than actuality and had little or no local music-industry support (Vui-Talitu 1996: 5). Jeremy To'omata, formerly DJ Playback, resurfaced in a hardcore underground rap group called Overdose who released an obscure cassette album, *The First Chapter,* in 1996, described by Grant Smithies as "pulling no punches in their portrayal of the violence, poverty, racial tension and urban desolation that is the flipside to south Auckland's cultural pride and creativity" (1996: 18).

Nonetheless, Hogg's comments suggest that the extent of young Polynesian musical talent displayed in the *Proud* project indicated that the syncretic hip-hop, swing-beat, soul, and funk music of the loosely defined "South Auckland sound" of the 1990s may have replaced the jangling indie guitars of "the Dunedin sound" that dominated New Zealand popular-music in the mid-1980s. The U.S. influences in the *Proud* compilation (Arrested Development, Cypress Hill, A Tribe Called Quest, Sly Stone, KRS1, Teddy Riley, etc.) are unmistakable, but the distinctively Polynesian rhythms and harmonies in the singing are just as discernible. A desirable solution to some of the anxieties of influence expressed about the *Proud* project was a balance between the indigenous and the imported, as the project coordinator Phil Fuemana stated in an interview in the *New Zealand Herald* in March 1994, after the *Proud* tour:

> The performers were all dressed like Americans when we first went out and I don't dis that because we're all affected by American music and culture . . . but the trick is to get something of ourselves into the music. It might take a couple of *Proud* albums to do it, but it'll happen. We are aware that at the moment we are Polynesians using Polynesian culture and it's just a token right now. We can sometimes be accused of using our culture as a fashion and we make no apology for how we sound now because that's where we're at. (In Reid 1994)

Take away the log drums and ukuleles from *Proud* and what is left is a group of English-language songs and raps that reflect the Pacific Island migrant status of most the performers. It expresses a strong "urban Polynesian" perspective but lacks any equivalent to the use of *te reo Maori* (Maori language) by artists such as Moana, Upper Hutt Posse, Survival, or the te reo rappers Ruaumoko. These groups struggled to make an impact in 1995, designated Te Tau o te Reo Maori (year of the Maori Language). The Maori-language content of New Zealand television also remained at less than 0.1 percent (Muru 1994: 28).

UPPER HUTT POSSE: A BRIEF HISTORY

The most prominent Maori rap group in the late 1980s and early 1990s was Upper Hutt Posse, whose Public Enemy–influenced hardcore rap, often featuring Teremoana Rapley, had some impact in both New Zealand and Australia. In 1990 the group toured *maraes* (Maori community centers) to "show them there's more to Maori music than just guitars" (Gee 1990: 16), supported Public Enemy on their New Zealand tour, and performed with the ragga artist Macca B. and the Zimbabwean group the Bhundu Boys in Australia. Upper Hutt Posse released the first 12-inch hip-hop record in New Zealand, "E Tu," in 1988, combining African American revolutionary rhetoric with an explicitly Maori frame of reference. "E Tu" pays homage to the rebel Maori warrior chiefs of Aotearoa's colonial history, Hone Heke, Te Kooti, and Te Rauparaha. It also praises the 28th Maori Battalion, a celebrated volunteer force in World War II whose high casualty rates resulted in the loss of almost an entire generation of Maori men: "Yes yes the Maori was a strong warrior / Strike fear in the heart of a Babylon soldier." The record also included the track "Intervention," which targets British colonialism and the French government–sanctioned bombing of the Greenpeace ship *Rainbow Warrior* in Auckland harbor, and "Hardcore," which celebrates Malcolm X. In a 1988 survey of the group, Buchanan commented on Upper Hutt Posse's U.S.-N.Z, syncretism: "Upper Hutt Posse is modern Maori music with links to the spirit of hardcore black American hip hop, as in the reference in the rap 'Hardcore' — 'Like Malcolm X him preach the hard truth / And we'll remember him and what he did contribute.' In the Posse's rap Hone Heke and Malcolm X can exist side by side, because they represent the spirit of resistance against the dominant power structure" (1989: 35).

But the group's 1989 album *Against the Flow,* delivered in a mixture of Kiwi and American accents, and including a paean to U.S. basketball, combined some rather inchoate political rhetoric with an overriding ambition to emulate U.S. hip-hop styles. The singles taken from the album, "Do It Like This" and "Stormy Weather," achieved some degree of popularity in New Zealand and Australia, but there was a notable absence of any of the specific Maori references or use of the Maori language that distinguished the group's earlier recordings. It was as if they had decided to delocalize their songs in the interests of a broader international appeal while maintaining a nominal militant rhetorical pose. Of the eleven tracks on the album, only the title track, which begins with a reference to New Zealand's sesquicentenary in 1990, has any local frame of reference, but is otherwise a vague and nonspecific tirade against generalized oppression. "Against the Flow" and "Stormy Weather," which contains references to Jews and Nazis and Central America, but does not mention New Zealand, are the only two tracks that have any specifically political frame of reference at all. The video clip of "Stormy Weather" used footage of 1977 Maori land rights demonstrations at Bastion Point in Auckland, protests against the 1981 South African rugby tour of New Zealand, and opposition to French nuclear tests in the Pacific, together with scenes of a Kanaka laborers' strike in Queensland and demonstrations in South African townships. This attempt to contextualize the song's claim that "People's culture's not respected . . . madness rules the world" remains a rather unconvincing domination of hardcore rap styles and rhetoric over content, as does the fist-pumping but context-free dance track "Do It Like This." While leader Dean Hapeta continued to speak out on racism and local political issues in the local mass media, Upper Hutt Posse's music and lyrics seemed to have become more homogenized into a mode of "black" music that was losing its local features, reflecting the group's ambition to move into the overseas market. Hapeta's visits to the USA, initially at the invitation of the Nation of Islam, were also a strong influence on the group's music.

But subsequent releases by the Upper Hutt Posse were much more powerful expressions of what is referred to as the "staunch" attitudes of Maori militancy. Hapeta's "Whakakotahi" (To Make One) was first released as a single in 1993 by E Tu, an offshoot of Upper Hutt Posse, to mark the United Nations' International Year for Indigenous People. Like Jane Campion's film *The Piano*, the video for it was filmed on a West Coast Auckland beach (Zepke 1993: 41), but by Hapeta himself at a cost of $1,200. While it includes some snatches of rugged bush and coastline, its uncompromisingly rough, in-your-face indictment of colonialist violence against Maori, presented in the style of traditional Maori challenges, meant that both the song and the video got little airplay. Incorporating quotations from speeches by Louis Farrakhan and Khallid Mohammed of the Nation of Islam along with a *haka* (war dance) and the sound of the *purerehua* (bull roarer) and *ngutu* (nose flute), its message of unity "to the indigenous people of the world" was also barely noticed in the local music press. The lines "Fuck New Zealand, ya call me a Kiwi / Aotearoa's the name of this country" necessitated a specially edited version with expletives deleted for radio play.

A definitively syncretic version of "Whakakotahi" opens the Upper Hutt Posse's powerful 1995 album *Movement in Demand* (a title derived from Louis Farrakhan), welding together Maori traditional instruments and militant *patere* and *karanga* (raps and shouts) and invocations of the spirits of the forest (Tane Mohuta) and the guardian of the sea (Tangaroa) with Nation of Islam rhetoric. This version also draws on the group's reggae and ragga inclinations, funk bass rhythms, blues guitar riffs, and hardcore gangsta-style rapping, which switches from English to te reo Maori. It ends with a patere (abusive chant or rap) — for which, as for all the other te reo Maori lyrics on the album, no English translation is provided — exhorting the Pakeha to leave the land, the sea, the indigenous people, and the world, and to get away from Maori space and children at once for ever. One of the album's tracks, "Tangata Whenua" (People of the Land), is entirely in te reo Maori and was rere-leased as a single in 1998 acompanied by a powerful video about the pollution of waterways and the disruption of Maori fishing rights.

The cover of *Movement in Demand* assembles fourteen Maori chiefs, warriors, prophets, and leaders, from Hone Heke in the early nineteenth century to Princess Te Puea Herangi in the twentieth century. The sleeve notes include historical notes on all of them, under the banner of a slogan attributed to the Maori activist Rewi Maniapoto and used in Maori demonstrations: *"Ka whawhai tonu matou, ake, ake, ake"* (We will continue to fight forever more). Knowledge of past Maori battles, struggles, and victories over the Pakeha informs the whole album. Reference is made in a new version of "Hardcore" to Bob Marley, Marcus Garvey, and the English dub poet Linton Kwesi Johnson, along with Malcolm X, Steve Biko, Crazy Horse, and a number of Maori militants past and present, whom D Word (Hapeta) claims and appropriates as part of his *whakapapa* (lineage). The album's musical heterogeneity of influences mirrors its political array of black militant role models, and the track "Gun in My Hand" disturbingly adapts the violent rhetoric of African American gangsta rap and ragga boasting into a biblical-style diatribe against the evils of Babylon: "The way you go on and on /Murdering mis-education fornicating and creating / Pain and strife for the people of the land / I'm lettin' ya know there's a gun in my hand." The track expresses a rhetorical confluence between ritualized Maori challenges and U.S. gangsta rap threats.

Due to their uncompromising political stance of total support by whatever means necessary for *mana* (integrity) and *tino rangatiratanga* (absolute Maori sovereignty), and their musical and political strategy of "push(ing) it furterer," the Upper Hutt Posse have never been far from controversy. Hapeta sued the evening newspaper the *Auckland Star* (and won) over claims that they had barred two Pakeha youths from one of their shows, and the scandal tabloid *The Truth* claimed controversially in 1990 that the group had behaved in a racist fashion in telling Samoans at a concert to "go home" (Gracewood 1995: 11). Hapeta's comments about the local hip-hop scene emphasize its smallness, fragility, and deracination, but also rap's compatibility with Maori formations of oral discourse, illustrated by the way concepts such as patere (rap), *whakarongo mai* (listen up), and *wainua* (attitude) are easily assimilated into hip-hop discourse:

> NZ Hip-Hop is a fallacy! Hip-Hop is a culture—rap music, breakdancing, graffiti, clothes, language. This country lacks a connection between, and a socialisation of, these components of Hip-Hop. True Hip-Hop will only

exist, for the moment at least, in the inner city suburbs of Black America where it was created as an everyday "living" thing. . . . We can emulate certain areas of Hip Hop, as we do with rap music, and did with break-dancing back in the early 80s, and still do with other components of Hip-Hop today, but, just as experiencing Maori culture today is done best on the Marae, Hip-Hop can only truly be experienced fully at its home. . . . Although I love and respect Hip-Hop, being Maori I only take from it what doesn't compromise my own culture. But in spite of this I have found them both very compatible. (Frizzell 1994: 48, 50)

Hapeta denies that hip-hop is merely a "music style," emphasizing that the music is an expression of a culture and way of life that originated in inner-city black ghettos in the USA. This makes it difficult, if not impossible, to transpose to an isolated country at the bottom of the world like Aotearoa–New Zealand. But Hapeta and other Maori and Pacific Islander rappers and musicians have attempted in convincing fashion to substitute Maori and Polynesian cultural expressions for the black American context of hip-hop, while borrowing freely from the U.S. musical styles of the genre. (And it is an indication of the strong position traditionally held by women in Maori and Pacific Islander societies that the misogynist aspects of much U.S. hard-core rap are totally absent from its Maori and Pacific Islander appropria-tions.) The result is a further syncretization of an already syncretic form, but one capable of having strong musical, political, and cultural resonances in Aotearoa. As Danny Haimona has stated, 'We don't own [hip-hop]. All we can do is inject our own culture into it. *Kia kaha*'" (in Frizzell 1994: 50). But Haimoana also sees the popularity of U.S. gangsta rap and R&B amongst young Maori and Pacific Islanders in New Zealand as the biggest threat to the rise of local indigenous hip-hop:

There's such an influx of American stuff, and we need to quell it, and we need to give these kids some knowledge on what's really up. . . . Kids don't want to be preached to, so what I'm trying to do is put it on their level, and take all the good influences from hip hop, and bring it close to home. There is a good vibe out there for New Zealand hip hop, but it's being poisoned by the Americanisms—the Tupacs and the Snoop Doggy Doggs. You have to have a balance, and Dam Native are trying to help kids work out that they have their own culture, they don't have to adopt Americanisms. (Russell 1997b: 18)

The importance with which rap music and reggae are regarded by Maori as legitimate forms of expressing "official" Maori oral kaupapa are illustrated by the inclusion of lyrics by Hapeta and others in *Te Ao Marama* (The Dawning of the Light), a five-volume anthology of Maori literature edited by the novelist and former New Zealand consul Witi Ihimaera (1993).

In December 1998 a Maori rap-R&B group, Iwi (Tribe), consisting of five vocalists and twelve musicians, released the first hip-hop album in Aotearoa–New Zealand to be almost entirely in te reo Maori. Apart from a few passages in English, the Maori lyrics to the album are printed on the CD container insert without any translation into English. Formed in 1995 at a *hui* (meeting) in a *marae* (community center), Iwi was founded to express the predominant concerns of Maori people in the twenty-first century, based on four key principles: the Maori language, the Maori people, the marae, and self-government. The group's kaupapa (theme or strategy) includes health issues, political issues, and Maori cultural beliefs and customs, and the various tracks express acknowledgment of Maori ancestral guardians, a karanga (call) for Maori to return to their roots and their marae, a caution against government policies which are detrimental to Maori, a tribute to Maori land occupations, advice to Maori youth to be guided by their ancestors, support for Maori language and customs, references to characters in Maori mythology, and a reiteration of Maori proverbs. Musically, the album combines traditional Maori waiata chants and harmonies, haka vocal styles, rapping, scratching, ragga, soul-oriented vocals, and funky bass lines. It represents an important example of the indigenization of rap and hip-hop in Aotearoa–New Zealand and its incorporation into traditional forms of Maori cultural expression. This example of indigenized Maori hip-hop was eclipsed on 1 January 2000 by *Ko Te Matakahi Kupu* (The Word that Penetrates), a solo Maori hip-hop album by Dean Hapeta of Upper Hutt Posse under his Maori MC title Te Kupu (the Word), which was released in two different versions: one entirely in Maori, the other in both Maori and English. This highly politicized Maori "concept album" included a summary of Te Kupu's hip-hop career in "Autahi" (The Emanation) and a video version of "Te Kairaupatu" (Vision) featuring a Maori land occupation at Paraparaumu airport. In November 2000 the Upper Hutt Posse released an album entirely in te reo Maori, returning to their reggae roots with *Mā Te Wā*, which was produced in Te Kupu's computerized home recording studio.

ONCE WERE WARRIORS AND NEW URBAN POLYNESIANS

In 1992 Upper Hutt Posse had also returned to its reggae origins, releasing four different mixes of "Ragga Girl," a ragga-dancehall single that rose in the local charts and was subsequently included on the soundtrack to the Maori director Lee Tamahori's highly successful film *Once Were Warriors*.

Based on the prominent and controversial Maori writer Alan Duff's novel about a dysfunctional urban Maori family, this film achieved an unprecedented success in its country of origin. It was the first film to gross more than $6 million in cinemas in Aotearoa–New Zealand (more than *Jurassic Park*), going straight to the top of the national ratings in its first week of release on video, and being seen by more than a third of the population, as well as winning nine of the fifteen national film and television awards. (It also won an Australian Film Institute award in 1995 for Best Foreign Film.) It also had some success abroad, winning prizes at the Montreal, Durban, and Rotterdam film festivals. Having been sold to more than twenty countries and running for more than six months in Sydney, it provided a focal point for current conflicts in New Zealand over issues of Maori land and cultural rights and social deprivation. In the largely Polynesian Otara market in South Auckland, T-shirts went on sale featuring the film's protagonist, "Jake the Muss," and one of his most notorious sayings, "Make the man some eggs!" along with the wife he batters, Beth, and her riposte, "Make your own damn eggs!"

Tamahori, who translocated to Hollywood after the success of *Once Were Warriors,* has indicated that the film's title had entered the national vocabulary in a particular way: "people are using the title to express an entire range of feelings, whether it's in anger management or rape crisis, they say 'I've got this problem and it's a *Warriors* kind of thing.' It unlocks something they weren't able to articulate before"(1994: 17). One illustration of this pentration of the film into New Zealand culture occurs in the Upper Hutt Posse's 1995 remix of their track "Hardcore," which extends the film's warrior rhetoric in "Harder than Jake da Muss I kicked his sorry ass / I'm a warrior with knowledge of the past."

Tangata Records, which was established in 1991 by Neil Cruikshank in Wellington and George Hubbard in Auckland to record and promote music by Maori musicians, acted as musical advisers for the soundtrack of *Once Were Warriors.* The label was given a much-needed boost by the platinum-selling (i.e., more than 15,000 units) soundtrack album, which stayed at number 2 in the New Zealand album charts for two months and was the second-highest selling album in the country in 1994. It was released in forty-two countries, sold more than 22,000 units in Australia, and was particularly popular in Italy, with "Ragga Girl" striking resonances with the widespread ragga–rap music movement there.

The Maori musician Hirini Melbourne, who specializes in reconstructing and playing traditional Maori musical instruments from bone, wood, stone, shells, and even flax snails, was the film's Maori music consultant. Melbourne's musical presence in *Once Were Warriors* is evident from the opening credits, which introduce the whirring sound of the *purerehua*. This is an oval or diamond-shaped blade of wood, bone, stone, or greenstone attached to a two-meter rope and swung around the body. It is used by different Maori tribes to attract rain, accompany funerals, or lure lizards. The purerehua recurs throughout the film at moments of anger and violent confrontation, particularly in the scene where Jake beats Beth up, and serves as a subliminal, elemental commentary on both Jake's aggressive state of mind and the frequent eruptions of violence in the film. Also used in the main theme and other atmospheric contexts in the film are *koauau*, bone or wooden flutes whose vibrato sound is described by their generic name, and which join with the purerehua and Tama Renata's distorted Hendrix-style electric guitar in the main theme to combine the sounds of the earth with an urban rock lament. Melbourne also performs a patere, a rhythmic vocal chant, on the soundtrack, while other traditional Maori chants such as the karanga that opens the soundtrack album and the haka performed at the funeral at the end of the film, are also included. Melbourne's work has since been influential in the work of a number of Maori popular-musicians, including Moana and the Moa Hunters and the Upper Hutt Posse.

The *Once Were Warriors* soundtrack's inclusion of a number of important popular Maori recording artists is also a significant indication of the paradigm shift the film achieves, away from the predominantly negative, "victim" perspective of Duff's novel toward a much more positive portrayal of Maori cultural and social potential. Using a wide range of recent (and some not-so-recent) Maori rap, soul, reggae, and rock music, the soundtrack demonstrates the syncretic, African American–influenced music of Maori youth in the 1990s as an expression of a vitality in urban Maori culture that has combined with some of the traditional aspects of Maoritanga into a vibrant mix of old and new.

This kind of energy is maintained by the inclusion of Che Fu and DLT's "Chains," Che Fu's "Waka," DLT's "Black Panther," and Dam Native's "Horified One" along with traditional Maori waiata on the soundtrack of the 1999 generic Maori gang warfare sequel to *Once Were Warriors, What Becomes of the Broken Hearted?* These tracks contrast with the music that is heard predominantly throughout the bikie gang scenes in the film, which are mostly imported rap and reggae tracks such as the American Samoan crew the Boo Ya Tribe's "R.A.I.D." and Desmond Dekker's "Shanty Town," and they have interesting syncretic indigenous implications. Scripted by Duff from his own novel and directed by Pakeha Ian Mune, *What Becomes of the Broken Hearted?* takes the form of a populist revenge story in which Beth and Jake's estranged son Sonny tries to avenge the death of his brother Nig in a gang fight and is assisted by Jake. The Maori rap tracks are sonically aligned with the fight for justice and Maori dignity represented by Sonny and by Nig's girl-friend Tania, brutally murdered by gang members whose decadent and violent lifestyle is presented as a modern urban aberration of traditional Maori warrior values. The associations with Che Fu, DLT, Dam Native, and traditional Maori waiata that the film makes also contrasts with Jake and his drinking buddies singing "Slippin' Away," a 1960s hit for the Pakeha group Max Merritt and the Meteors that implicitly comments on Jake and Beth's estrangement. And as in its predecessor, *What Becomes of the Broken Hearted?* embodies Duff's view of music as having redemptive and self-fulfilling capacities for displaced urban Maori: here Tania's self-doubt is overcome by her singing a song to an appreciative audience in a record shop. Although not as incisive in its impact on the national psyche as *Once Were Warriors*, *What Becomes of the Broken Hearted?* continues its predecessor's assertion of Maori cultural pride and dignity, indexed musically through rap and hip-hop.

POLYNESIAN FUSIONS

By 1995 the term "urban Polynesian" had become a buzzword in the New Zealand mass media and music industry, and it was not always to the liking of the musicians it was used to refer to. One example was the Wellington-based Samoan recording artist Igelese, who explores "Polynesian fusion" on his 1995 debut single "Groovalation." This incorporates a native-language dialogue between Maori and Samoan rappers with U.S. soul, funk, dance, and rhythm and blues influences, as well as including Polynesian log drumming and Maori chants. A church choirmaster, pianist, and university music graduate, Igelese claimed he had some fresh ideas that nobody else had done and was getting sick of watching Polynesians imitating African Americans. "Groovalation" advocates racial unity, reworking the slogan "One nation under a groove," and its (albeit self-consciously national) syncretism indicates a possible future musical direction, combining different elements of the multicultural diversity of Polynesian Aotearoa. It provides a musical illustration of a historical process in which a complex but distinctively Pacific and indigenous local identity has emerged in formations of popular music in Aotearoa–New Zealand.

In July 1996 news of the first major mainstream crossover of what the prominent New Zealand music journalist Graham Reid described as "the cross-cultural sound of urban Polynesia" reached the front page of *Billboard* in an article recounting the success of Pauly Fuemana's OMC's record-breaking dance–rap single "How Bizarre." This catchy, upbeat pop-dance song, influenced by Mink DeVille's "Spanish Street Stroll" and cowritten and produced by the producer of *Proud,* Alan Jansson, won several New Zealand music industry awards, sold 142,000 units in Australia and New Zealand, and stayed at number 1 in the Australian charts for five weeks in April and May 1996. It was reportedly the first New Zealand–produced single to go top 10 in Australia since Ray Columbus's "She's a Mod" in the mid-1960s (Reid 1996: 1, 16). It also reached number 1 in Sweden and Canada. By August 1996, "How Bizarre" had also sold 65,000 copies in the United Kingdom, risen to number 11 on the United Kingdom singles charts, and been released in twenty-one countries. Fuemana became an overnight celebrity, with local media coverage emphasizing his past involvement in gangs, drugs, and petty crime, and he was flown to London for two appearances on the BBC TV program *Top of the Pops*. "How Bizarre" subsequently gained "Heatseeker Impact" status on the *Billboard* top 200 in July 1997, reaching number 79 and remaining there for six months. By July 1997 it had sold an estimated 83,000 units in the USA (Reece 1997: 1), and in August 1997 OMC gave a sold-out concert at the Whiskey Au GoGo in Los Angeles, supported by a live band that included the DJ Manuel Bundy and the saxophonist Nathan Haines. Fuemana's commercial success in the United States seemed complete when his version of Randy Newman's "I Love L.A." was included in the soundtrack of the British comedian Rowan Atkinson's film *Bean: The Ultimate Disaster Movie*.

But OMC's follow-up singles to "How Bizarre"—"Right On,"which debuted on the national charts at number 11, but then fell, "On the Run," and "Land of Plenty" (a moving eulogy of the New Zealand countryside from the perspective of a Pacific Islander immigrant), failed to repeat its success. This suggested "How Bizarre" had been something of a novelty hit with its low-riding, Latino-styled beats and lyrics, but after its success other hip-hop-style releases by Polynesian artists began getting more media and chart attention. In August 1996 "Chains," by DLT, with vocals by the Maori singer and rapper Che Fu, who had fronted the former chart-topping group Supergroove, went to number 1 in the local charts, after debuting at number 2. Described by Andy Pickering in *Rip It Up* as "possibly the strongest hip-hop single ever released in New Zealand" (1996: 20), "Chains" featured soul and gospel-style vocals augmented by ragga and rap segments by the reggae artists the Mighty Asterix and Ras Daan and combined a tuneful melody with slow, loping beats and lyrics about the hardships of life in the city. Thompson was a prominent member of the Trueschool Posse, presenters of a hip-hop program on the Auckland music video channel Max TV and student radio station bFM, and a producer for other hip-hop groups such as Joint Force (featuring M.C.O.J. and Rhythm Slave) and Native Bass. "Chains" is the most commercially oriented track on Thompson's top 20 album *The True-school,* which incorporates a wide range of styles, from the blues-funk of the Maori guitarist Billy TK through old-school hip-hop to jungle. The album illustrates Thompson's perception that successful charting songs in New Zealand require U.S.-style rhythm and blues elements rather than Polynesian rhythms to be prominent (Pickering 1996: 20). Che Fu subsequently emerged as a solo artist in his own right with a successful single, "Scene III," and an album, *2B Spacific,* which set something of a benchmark in New Zealand hip-hop, being described by John Taite in *Rip It Up* as "without a doubt one of New Zealand's classic must-own recordings" (Taite 1998: 22). Unlike the more hardcore beats of Upper Hutt Posse and Dam Native, with their prominent use of Maori-language raps, instrumentation, and striking political video imagery, DLT and Che Fu's less threatening and less noticeably Maori hip-hop was more inclined to gain acceptance in the mainstream, combining soul, reggae, and Pacific musical influences with scratches and breakbeats (provided by the highly developed skills of the DJ Manuel Bundy). As a result, in 1998 the style magazine *Pavement* announced a "renaissance" in New Zealand hip-hop, profiling the *Aotearoa Hip Hop, Vol. 1* compilation and new releases by the Polynesian rappers and DJs Che Fu, Manuel Bundy, King Kapisi, Losttribe, Mu and Dallas, and Ermehn (Jewell 1998c). King Kapisi's album *Savage Thoughts,* described as "Samoan hip-hop to the world!" was a particularly important release in 2000, and Kapisi gained popularity in Australia. DLT's release of *Altruism,* consisting of collaborations with a number of rappers around the world, also in 2000, indicated another facet of the globalization of Polynesian hip-hop. But as Reid pointed out in his *Billboard* profile of Pauly Fuemana, this apparent revival of Polynesian hip-hop was still not reflected adequately in music industry and media outlets: "While the sound of urban Polynesia has long been part of the substructure of New Zealand's music . . . there have been only fleeting glimpses of Polynesian artists cracking the charts. . . . Maori and Polynesian music is a constant in the cultural landscape, if not on the country's radio stations" (1996: 16).

These "fleeting glimpses" of urban Polynesian hip-hop artists illustrate that despite its health and variety, it remains a marginal, fragile phenomenon in commercial and industrial terms due to its limited accessibility within Aotearoa–New Zealand and almost total inaccessibility outside the country. Aotearoa is a country still marked by its geographical isolation as a peripheral "other" in the global economy of popular music, where it represents less than 1 percent of the international market, and its hip-hop scene is a marginal factor even within this tiny economy.

Writing in the Auckland newspaper the *New Zealand Herald* in 1996, Zane Lowe, a founding member of Urban Disturbance and the producer of Dam Native's debut album, expressed this sense of fragility and marginality along with a strong sense of independence and dedication to hip-hop culture. He summed up ten years of hip-hop in Aotearoa–New Zealand in terms of "what was a child looking towards its American forefathers for inspiration (who) has developed into a teenager keen to break free and make its own mark on the world of hip hop." Citing Che Fu's calls for a nuclear-free Pacific rather than the U.S. gangsta rap of Ice Cube and Dr. Dre as a more important influence on the local hip-hop scene, he noted increased audiences for local hip-hop gigs but also a dearth of live performing experience and "a continuing lack of support from mainstream radio." He warned against exaggerated expressions of nationalism, which risked "alienating the rest of the world," and merely trying to be different within "an already overprotected American market." Cautioning local rappers against infighting, he concluded, "It's what you can do with a mike and a pair of turntables that counts" (Lowe 1996). As Che Fu indicated in 1998, "Aotearoa hip hop, MCs, DJs, rhymers. breakers, they're discovering an identity and it is something that should be pushed forward . . . they're coming up with something fresh, that's totally distinctive, but it can still stand up on an international level" (Russell 1998b: 23). This is something he proved in Sydney in July 1999 with three live performers attended by a significant proportion of Sydney's Maori community, and when he was featured in a 1999 television program about New Zealand as a significant part of the cultural landscape of Aotearoa on the U.K. "alternative" tourist series *The Rough Guide to the World*. But what is still lacking, as with other emergent indigenous hip-hop scenes, is an adequate industrial infrastructure of recording, distribution, and radio airplay to provide that essential push forward.

NOTES

The lyrics reproduced as the epigraph to the section "Multicultural Noise" are reprinted courtesy of Robert Sullivan and Auckland University Press.

1. The rappers featured in the *Pavement* article were Urban Disturbance (European and Niuean), 3 the Hard Way (Maori and Samoan), Upper Hutt Posse (Maori), Dam Native (Maori and Samoan-Maori), Otara Millionaires Club (Niuean-Maori), Ermehn (Samoan), Field Style Orator (Samoan), Rhythm Slave (European), Teremoana Rapley (Maori), Man Chu (Chinese Malaysian), DLT (European-Maori), and Justice (European). Also mentioned were (all since defunct) Sisters Underground (Samoan and African American), Gifted and Brown (Maori and Samoan), Pacifican Descendants (Samoan), Rough Opinion (Maori), and the Semi MCs (Maori and

Samoan). Of these, all were from or based in Auckland, with the exception of Upper Hutt Posse, Gifted and Brown, and Rough Opinion, who were from Wellington.

REFERENCES

Baillie, Russell. 1994. "Our Streets Are Grooving." *New Zealand Herald,* 25 March.
———. 1996. "Getting DeaLT To [sic]. . . . ". *Real Groove,* September, 6–7.
Buchanan, Kerry. 1989. "The Upper Hutt Posse: Music with a Message."
    Music in New Zealand (summer):
———. 1993. "Ain't Nothing but a G Thing." *Midwest,* 3: 25–27.
Dinnen, Naomi. 1994. "Hip-Hop Hooray." *Drum Media,* 19 July, 52.
Dix, John. 1988. *Stranded in Paradise: New Zealand Rock and Roll, 1955–1988.*
    Paradise Publications.
Duff, Alan. 1990. *Once Were Warriors.* Auckland: Tandem Press.
Eggleton, David. 1991. Review of *Jazz Waiata. Landfall* 45, no. 3 (September).
Ferguson, Troy. 1997. Review of Dam Native, *Kaupapa Driven Rhymes Uplifted.*
    Rip it Up, October, 31.
Frizzell, Otis. 1994. "Hip Hop Hype." *Pavement,* December, 44–50.
Gee, Kirk. 1990. "DAT's the Way I Like It: Upper Hutt Posse." *Rip It Up,* January.
Gifford, Alan. 1994. "Warriors Once Again." *Planet,* spring, 41–43.
Gracewood, G. 1995."What's New Posse Cat?" *Real Groove,* August, 11.
Hogg, Colin. 1994. "'Otara Sound' Creates Proud New Kiwi Era."
    Sunday Star Times, 17 April.
Ihaka, Jodi. 1993. "Why the Kids Wanna Be Black." *Mana,* August–September.
Ihimaera, Witi, ed. 1993. *Te Ao Marama: Contemporary Maori Writing,* vol. 3,
    Te Puawaitanga o Te Korero, The Flowering. Auckland: Reed Books.
Jewell, Stephen. 1998a. "Leaving Home: Breaks Co-Op."
    Pavement, February–March, 63.
———. 1998b. "NZ Hip Hop." *Pavement,* August–September, 78–83.
———. 1998c. "Southern Exposure." *Pavement,* April–May, 52.
Kopytko, Tania. 1986. "Breakdance as an Identity Marker in New Zealand."
    Yearbook for Traditional Music 28: 21–22.
Lealand, Geoff. 1988. *A Foreign Egg in Our Nest? American Popular Culture
    in New Zealand.* Wellington: Victoria University Press.
Lowe, Zane. 1996. "State of the Nation." *New Zealand Herald,* 28 November.
Mitchell, Tony. 1994. "He Waiata Na Aotearoa: Maori and Polynesian Music in
    New Zealand." In *North Meets South: Popular Music in Aotearoa/New Zealand,*
    edited by Philip Hayward,Tony Mitchell, and Roy Shuker.
    Sydney: Perfect Beat Publications.
———. 1997. "Flat City Sounds: The Christchurch Music Scene."
    Popular Music and Society 21, no. 3 (fall): 83–106.

Muru, Selwyn. 1994. "Maori and the Media." *Planet* (summer): 28–29.

Parekowhai, Cushla. 1993. "What Do You Mean We, Whiteman? The Lone Ranger and Tonto in a Puha Picture Show." *Midwest* 3: 27–29.

Pickering, Andrew. 1996. "Walking the Razor Blade." *Rip It Up,* August, 20.

Reece, Doug. 1997. "Huh!/Mercury's OMC Finding Fans at Top 40."
    Billboard, 3 July, 1, 36.

Reid, Graham. 1992a. "New Zealand Awards Display Diversity."
    Billboard, 25 April.

———. 1992b. "New Zealand's Maori Music a Genre Melange." *Billboard,* 30 May.

———. 1993. "Kiwi Scene Makes Strong '93 Showing." *Billboard,* 24 July.

———. 1994. "Tour Teaches Pride." *New Zealand Herald,* 25 March.

———. 1996. "Polygram's OMC Unearths Polynesia." *Billboard,* 6 July, 1, 16.

Russell, John. 1997a. Review of Losttribe, "Summer in the Winter."
    Rip It Up, September, 33.

———. 1997b."Rhymes and Real Grooves: Dam Native." *Rip It Up,* August, 18.

———. 1998a. "As Easy as 1, 2 . . . Moana and the Moahunters." *Rip It Up,* March, 22.

———. 1998b. "Hoodies Up! Che Fu." *Real Groove,* October, 22–23.

Smithies, Grant. 1996. Review of Overdose, *The First Chapter.*
    Real Grove, October, 18.

Sullivan, Robert. 1990. *Jazz Waiata.* Auckland: Auckland University Press.

Taite, John. 1998. Review of Che Fu, *2B Spacific. Rip It Up,* December, 22.

Tamahori, Lee. 1994. "Directing Warriors." *Midwest,* 6.

"Urban Disturbance and 3 the Hard Way." 1994. *NZ Musician,* April,

Vui-Talitu, Sara. 1996. "AEIOU: Music Video and Polynesian Communication."
    Perfect Beat, January, 78–88.

Walker, Clinton. 1995. "Pacific Pride." *Rolling Stone* [Australian ed.], June, 28.

Zepke, S. 1993. "Dean Hapeta: The Medium Is the Message."
    Music in New Zealand 23 (summer): 2

Zemke-White, Kirsten. 1999. "'I Greet the Funk with My *Mauri*': Indigenous Elements in New Zealand Rap Music." Paper presented at the Tenth International Conference of IASPM (International Association for the study of Popular Mustic), University of Technology. Sydney, July.

DISCOGRAPHY

Breaks Co-Op. 1998. *Roofers.* Deepgrooves/Festival.

Dam Native. 1997. *Kaupapa Driven Rhymes Uplifted.* Tangata Records.

Dark Tower. 1996. *Zealmen.* Curious Records.

———. 2001. *Canterbury Drafts.* Universal.

DLT featuring Che Fu. 1996. *The True School.* BMG.

DLT. 2001. *Altruism.* BMG.

Double J and Twice the T. 1989. "All Wrapped Up." Definitive Records.

———. 1990. "Def to Be Green." EMI.

Ermehn. 1998. *Samoans: Part 2*. Deepgrooves/Festival.

E Tu. 1993. *"Whakakotahi."* Tangata Records.

Che Fu. 1998. *2b Spacific*. BMG.

———. 2001. *The Navigator*. Sony Music.

Gifted and Brown. 1993. "So Much Soul." Tangata Records.

Igelese. 1995. "Groovalation." Papa Pacific Records.

Iwi. 1998. *Iwi*. Tangata Records/BMG.

Joint Force. 1995. *One Inch Punch*. BMG.

Lloyd, Jody. 1998. *Shadows on a Flat Land*. Universal.

Losttribe. 1997. "Summer in the Winter." Urban Pacifika Records/BMG.

Melbourne, Hirini, and Richard Nunns. 1994. *Te Ku Te Whe*. Rattle Records.

Moana and the Moa Hunters. 1992. *AEIOU (Akona Te reo)*. Southside Records.

———. 1993. *Tahi*. Southside Records.

———. 1998. *Rua*. Tangata Records.

Moonrock. 1998. *Moonrock*. Creative Vibes.

OMC (Otara Millionaires Club). 1996. *How Bizarre*. Huh!

Overdose. 1996. *The First Chapter*. A & Entertainment Cassette.

Patea Maori. 1996. *Poi E*. Maui Records/WEA.

Semi MCs. 1993. "Trust Me." Volition.

Sisters Underground. 1994. "In the Neighbourhood." Second Nature.

Supergroove. 1994. *Traction*. BMG.

Te Kupu. 2000. *Ko Te Matakahi Kupu*. Kia Kaha/Universal.

3 the Hard Way. 1994. *Old Skool Prankstas*. Deepgrooves.

Urban Disturbance. 1993. *No Flint, No Flame*. Deepgrooves.

———. 1994. *37° A-ttitude*. Deepgrooves.

Upper Hutt Posse. 1987. *"E Tu. "* Jayrem.

———. 1989. *Against the Flow*. Southside.

———. 1992. "Ragga Girl." Tangata Records.

———. 1995. *Movement in Demand*. Tangata Records.

———. 2000. *Mā Te Wā*. Kia Kaha/Universal.

Various artists. 1989. *AK 89: In Love with These Rhymz: BFM Rap Trax*. BFM Music.

———. 1994. *Once Were Warriors* [soundtrack album]. Tangata Records.

———. 1994 (and 2000). *Proud: An Urban-Pacific Streetsoul Compilation*. Second Nature/Volition.

———. 1996. *On the Beat 'n' Track*. Curious Records.

———. 1998. *Aotearoa Hip Hop,* vol. 1. BMG.

———. 1999. *What Becomes of the Broken Hearted?* [original soundtrack recording]. BMG.

Chapter 13

Rap in Canada

Bilingual and Multicultural

ROGER CHAMBERLAND

t has taken a long time for rap to be recognized as a musical genre in Canada. Of course, the proximity of the United States has made material circulating on the other side of the border more accessible and facilitated the broadcasting of rap music on television and as well as radio. But proximity is not everything; big Canadian urban centers also have their immigrants and disenfranchised people who rapidly adopted rap as a mode of expression. In addition, hip-hop culture exercises a power of fascination over a new generation of youth in search of new heroes. In order to understand properly the dynamics of hip-hop culture in Canada, one must know how popular music is produced and distributed, as well as how culture is transferred from one country to another.

First, I will focus on the marketing of popular music in Canada. Then I will look at the development of rap music from its "natural" points of emergence in Canada (Toronto, Vancouver, and Halifax) to its spread across the country, where it eventually developed strong foundations in the urban centers of each of the ten provinces. Quebec will be dealt with independently from the rest of the country, as more than 85 percent of the province is French speaking and benefits from both American and French influences. Rap has been welcomed in France, and "passeurs" have adapted rap to pop music, at least that which is exported directly to Canada, and made it more acceptable to radio broadcasters.

Having defined the social, political, economic, and cultural structures of rap, I will examine a few pioneering groups and several Canadian productions in the hope of defining the characteristics of an indigenous form of rap. By studying texts and music, fields of influence as well as fundamental differences can be identified and observed. Finally, I will analyze the network of hip-hop culture that, while formerly considered as a subculture, appears to have become a part of official culture in Canada as we find it filling music time slots on television and radio, and even on the Internet, where a group from Ottawa is broadcasting rap music nonstop.

THE POPULAR MUSIC MARKET IN CANADA

Listening to music is one of the most important cultural practices in Canada; even without studies on a national basis, the conclusions of one survey undertaken in Quebec from 1992 to 1994 may be extrapolated for the whole country. According to these data, more than 84 percent of the population say they listen to music very often, and most of them via radio. Radio is a not a free enterprise; it is bound by a series of rules managed by the CRTC (Canadian Radio and television Broadcast Commission), which imposes quotas to protect the market. On top of that, a radio broadcaster in Canada is obliged to broadcast at least 35 percent Canadian content; in Quebec these restrictions touch on language as well as broadcasting, and broadcasters are obliged to broadcast 65 percent French content. Television is also regulated, and channels specializing in video clips (Much Music in Toronto and Musique Plus in Montreal, the equivalents of MTV) are obliged to present at least 10 percent Canadian content. Adding to this issue is the fact that a radio broadcast permit is always associated with specific commitments related to music time slots. There are different networks for soft rock, country and western, retro, classical, jazz, blues, and so on. Adherence to the mandate by each radio broadcaster is guaranteed by the CRTC, which exerts constant and steady surveillance. In other words radio, and to a lesser degree television, are held captive by an indigenous production code that valorizes its music through accessibility and profitability.

In this context, it is difficult to promote alternative music, except perhaps for those who present themselves as its representatives or as being marginal, such as advocates of punk, heavy metal, and of course rap. In other words, these genres are confined to negligible listening periods in the broadcasting time schedules in order not to upset the popular tastes of listeners and DJs. Alternative or avant-garde music is more the domain of community and university radio stations, which have mandates giving priority to music that commercial stations would never risk playing or very seldom play. The three types of radio stations in Canada—the large national and regional CBC/Radio Canada networks, private commercial stations, and community and student radio — are all bound by particular, regulated time slots within which it is difficult to be innovative, except for the first, which tends to capitalize on the different musical genres.

If radio is the most widespread medium supplying musical tastes, listening to cassettes and CDs runs a close second. The cassette is primarily the domain of youth from ages fifteen to twenty-four years because of its low cost and its versatility (including recording from the radio and solitary listening thanks to the personal cassette player, and use on cheap sound systems). The compact disc, which is more expensive and less versatile, tends to be preferred by adults. These factors are essential to understanding the dynamics of the popular music market, since they highlight the fact that all musical innovations are always undertaken outside the margins of mass circulation and later developed into subcultures until they reach a level of popularity that facilitates the production of commercially produced CD albums. In other words, the commercialization of a new musical style correlates to its short-term saleability. Thus the recording companies are seldom disposed to promote new artists unless their musical style corresponds to the dominant radio listening culture. Radio shapes musical taste and is still the main source of novelty and discovery motivating the purchase of cassettes and CDs. But the causal nature of this system is not as watertight as it seems at first sight. Listeners must still rely on networks of friendship at school, for example, where cassettes and CDs are actively circulated, as is revealed in the study mentioned earlier. The development and refinement of musical tastes are exerted in cultural subcategories. For instance, in high schools we see groups developing around punk, heavy metal, rap, indie rock, pop, and so on, each adopting the vocabulary, clothing, body language, and other codes of its music subculture.

Cable and satellite television is to a certain extent subject to the regulations of the CRTC but takes advantage of a greater flexibility in its range of programming. MTV (USA) is accessible by cable all across Canada except in Quebec, while the U.S. network entirely devoted to broadcasting rap clips can be picked up via satellite. It goes without saying that U.S. video clips circulate freely from one end of the country to the other and offer a wide spectrum of the various aesthetic tendencies of the genre, including East Coast and West Coast styles.

This portrait of the Canadian music market would not be complete without the recording companies (which are, of course, one of the first links in the consumption chain) and their natural interface, the music stores. Both have simply "gone with the flow," as we will see.

Rap music was slow to develop in Canada, owing partly to the fact that ghettos are rare even in the largest Canadian cities, where Canadian rap was born. Unlike in the USA, rap soon moved away from Canadian black communities and had a reverse "integration" effect, its fashions, slang, and behavior adopted by predominantly white, middle-class youth.

From the very beginning, word of mouth and live concerts were the best way to spread this black urban art form, or "black noise," to quote Tricia Rose's idiomatic expression (Rose 1994). Despite its growing popularity in the United States, rap was introduced only gradually in Canada, gaining new listeners thanks to the initiative of a few people living within black communities, mostly from Caribbean backgrounds, in Toronto, Halifax, and Montreal, where the first rappers emerged. These initiators—the MCs Supreme, Brother A., Sunshine, and Ebony Crew—performed successfully on the local scene but never recorded. In the mid-1980s the major Canadian record labels showed no interest in black music in general, according to Ron Nelson, a former rap DJ in a student radio station who later became the director of Advance Productions, a recording house that produced album tracks for the Dream Warriors' *And Now the Legacy Begins:* "What is keeping rap from taking off is a general misunderstanding and rejection of this type of music and its audience, not to mention media and public prejudice against the power of black urban music."

But new management and production enterprises devoted to promoting rap music were eventually created. For example, Beat Factory Productions and Management in Toronto, founded by Ivan Berry, enabled Michee Mee (Michelle McCulloch) and L A LUV (Phillip Gayle) to record a number of singles, "On This Mike," "Elements of Style," and "Victory Is Calling," on the British label Justice Records. Michee Mee, who is a native of Jamaica, was considered for a while to be the major hope of Canadian rap. Her perform-ances as the opening act for LL Cool J, Salt 'n' Pepa, and Sinead O'Connor in Toronto and Montreal brought her recognition and enabled her to sign recording contracts in New York and London. For Berry, it was Mee's ragga-muffin style that made her typically Canadian, given the importance of the Jamaican population in the Toronto region at the time, and Canadian rap at the end of the 1980s was a harmonious mix of rap and reggae. Despite the advantages Michee Mee enjoyed in the production and distribution of her albums, her career was limited to Canada, and she did not succeed in the U.S. market.

In 1990 the first Canadian rapper to achieve any degree of international success was Maestro Fresh Wes (real name Wesley Williams, born in Toronto of Guyanese parents). He was backed by a large Canadian recording company, Attic, which had decided to test the rap market. Wes's album *Symphony in Effect* sold more than 150,000 copies, and his singles "Let Your Backbone Slide" and "Drop the Needle" were given extensive airplay on alternative radio. They were even heard on a few commercial stations, owing to their similarity to dance rap à la MC Hammer and Vanilla Ice, who were having their period of glory in the same year. Soon other rappers, such as MCJ, Cool G, HDV, and the better-known Dream Warriors, began to break onto the scene and succeed beyond the Canadian borders. MCJ and Cool G were a duo from Montreal consisting of James McQuaid and Richard Gray, both natives of Halifax, whose R&B–influenced style ensured that two of their singles, "So Listen" and "Smooth as Silk," enjoyed reasonably wide distribution. In contrast, the provocative, pornographic rapper HDV (Sean Merrick, from Toronto), in tracks such as "Pimp and the Microphone," rapped about the harsh conditions in which black people were living in Canadian cities. But the Dream Warriors were most successful on the international scene, thanks to Ivan Berry from Beat Factory Productions, who signed them to Island Records' London-based label. Even when they were little known in Canada, the Dream Warriors (Louis Robinson and Frank Albert, alias King Lou and Capital Q, both from Toronto) had three high-rating singles released from *And Now the Legacy Begins,* "Wash Your Face in My Sink," "My Definition of a Boombastic Jazz Style," and "Ludi," which assured them of exposure first in England, then in the rest of Europe and the USA.

The Dream Warriors' music and lyrics were highly eclectic and seductive, owing partly to the presence of a constant melodic line. A number of other groups, including Simply Majestic, Krush and Skad, Main Source, Razor-Blayd, Top Secret, Slinky Dee, Self-Defence, and K4ce (K-Force), all of which consisted of black musicians, soon evolved, attempting to follow in the footsteps of the Dream Warriors' success. But white rap crews were also quick to respond to the spread of hip-hop in the mid-1980s. The Shuffle Demons from Toronto released the rap-inflected singles "Spadina Bus" and "Get Outta My House" in 1986 and 1987; they were among the first Canadian recordings on which scratching and recitative were used. The video clips of these tracks were given high rotation on Much Music, partly because of their spectacular elements. The Shuffle Demons' music was primarily jazz fusion, though it overlapped into other musical territories to obtain previously unheard sonorities and surprise the listener. Right from their beginnings in 1984 they sampled television theme tunes, movie soundtracks, recent pop hits, rap tracks, and jazz classics within the textures of their own original compositions. Laymen Twaist, a bilingual and multiracial trio from Montreal, made a brief foray into rap's sphere of influence with their rap version of Lou Reed's "Walk on the Wild Side," even if their album tended to privilege pop rock. Kish (Andrew Kishino), from Toronto but of Japanese origin, also made his mark on the Canadian rap scene with his first recording, released in 1991, "I Rhyme the World in Eighty Days." Produced by First Offence, a new production house created in Toronto, it bore witness to the growth of a Canadian rap repertoire that involved a growing awareness of ethnic communities struggling against problems of oppression and racial tensions in the big Canadian cities.

If Toronto rapidly became the capital of Canadian Anglophone rap, Montreal is a hub of both U.S.-influenced Anglophone rap and Francophone rap of French origins. But it would be misleading to say that the synthesis of these two styles, U.S. and French rap, which contain notable differences, took place through a simple transference of music and texts. The acclimatization of rap was strongly affected by the social, political, and cultural context of Quebec. In this province, more than 85 percent of the population speak French, and political campaigns and acts of protest are carried out in ways similar to those seen in oppressed communities in the U.S. ghettos. The group French B from Montreal (Jean-Robert Bisaillon and Richard Gauthier) initiated the rap genre in Quebec with their hit single "Je m'en souviens" (I Remember; 1987) which addressed the issue of Law 101, on bilingualism. A few years later the Francophone rap movement formed by Kool Rock, alias Ghislain Proulx, and Jay Tree, alias Jean Tsarzi, released "M.R.F. est arrivé" (The French Rap Movement Has Arrived; 1990), in an attempt to initiate hip-hop culture in Quebec. Le Boyfriend (Stephan Chetrit) and his "Rapper Chic" (1991) did not contribute a great deal to the evolution of this culture by proposing a watered-down version of rap similar to that of Vanilla Ice and M. C. Hammer. It was left to Maleek Shahid (John Morrow), a white Muslim based in Montreal, to reposition rap in its rebellious protest vein by writing politically committed tracks delivered in Spanish, French, and English. But lack of any commercial success stymied these rappers' careers, and they were largely consigned to anonymity.

On the whole, neither Quebecois recording companies nor the major labels, with their relatively discreet presence in Quebec, have been prepared to risk producing rap albums. Commercial prospects are hazardous given that many people judge rap only in the light of the scandals, murders, and arrests reported in the mass media. In Quebec as well as in the rest of Canada, the production, distribution, and broadcasting of rap remains confined to the margins. Its evolution has been very slow, and the major recording companies have yet to be convinced of its viability.

THE CURRENT RAP SCENE

The Canadian hip-hop Web site features more than 200 rap groups scattered throughout Canada. It is not surprising to learn that nearly half of them are located in Ontario, the majority in Toronto. Vancouver and Montreal are the other important foci; hip-hop activity there is most perceptible in terms of live performances. Within these cities, to which we must add Quebec City and Halifax, where there is a vigorous network of clubs and a not inconsiderable hip-hop circuit, supported by fans from various ethnic origins. But despite their fans, rap groups rarely achieve record contracts or hits. In this respect the USA has a very clear domination. As Ken Lewis, the director of Criminal Law Records, emphasizes: "The big labels ignore rap. No wonder: they have always ignored black Canadian music. In order to survive we have always had to look to the USA. All the time I receive cassettes from young kids who want to rap, but I can't help at all here. We can sell up to a certain point only. I want to distribute my music in the USA, specially in Miami, where the bass-boom type of reggae and rap is massively popular. From there we'll pass to Jamaica" (Caudeiron 1989: 35).

Another problem rap has to face is the rivalry between the Canadian regions, with each one making claims for its own territory without ever attempting to build a common front. On this point Lewis is eloquent: "The producers, the DJs, the MCs, the promoters are chasing each other, but nobody helps each other and consequently nobody wins. Everybody wants to be number one. It's a vicious circle: the major labels and the big distributors don't want to know about people who are fighting each other" (Caudeiron 1989: 35).

After ten years or so of relatively unsuccessful self-produced singles, cassettes, or CDs, the recording industry is content to stay in tune with mainstream Canadian musical tendencies and radio listening patterns, which condition the purchase of albums. Those few artists, like Michee Mee or the Rascalz, who have had the advantage of the support of a major label are still virtually unknown and have barely managed to break into either the U.S. or the Canadian markets. This was emphasized by the Rascalz' refusal to accept their Juno Award (the equivalent of the American Grammy and the French Victory Awards) for best rap recording at the 1998 Canadian Academy of Recording Arts and Sciences Awards. The group saw the award as a token gesture that merely exposed its lack of music-industry support, as well as a general lack of acknowledgment of black urban music. The Urban Music

Awards (for rap, reggae, soul, and R&B) were all presented prior to the televised portion of the Juno Awards ceremony.

But a number of radio stations throughout Canada have assigned a time slot to rap, and on television the situation has improved since Much Music introduced its show *Rap City* and Musique Plus scheduled *Hip Hop,* which allow for a certain opening in "the televisual universe." But in many respects rap is still confined to a parallel and marginal scene, even if rap and hip-hop shows are multiplying in the large cities as well as the smaller ones. In a center like Quebec City, with 450,000 inhabitants, rap events are programmed on a regular basis at small and mid-sized venues such as bars and community spaces. All-ages shows indicate that rap is appealing not only to young adults, but also to teenagers. Another ray of hope is the considerable popularity of the Montreal Francophone group Dubmatique, which since the release of its album *La force de comprendre* (The Power to Understand) in the spring of 1997 and the bilingual, R&B inflected single "Soul pleureur" (Weeping Soul) has succeeded in selling more than 100,000 units and performing to full houses throughout most of the country.

TENDENCIES IN CONTEMPORARY CANADIAN RAP

Canadian rap has great difficulty creating its own market owing to the music industry's lack of confidence in it. Consequently, many groups have created their own labels, which are nevertheless backed by big distribution companies, a hint that maybe attitudes are changing (or simply that profit is the primary law of the music market). Even the relatively ephemeral success of the Dream Warriors and Maestro Fresh Wes in the early 1990s has taken a considerable amount of time to repeat. Vancouver has taken over from Toronto as the emerging center of Canadian rap. It is now possible to speak of a West Coast style and a North Coast style to indicate Canadian hip-hop coming from British Columbia. This category appeared with the group the Rascalz, whose album *Cash Crop* (1997) was soon noticed in both Canadian and U.S. rap milieus. Their single "Dreaded First" was played by more than forty radio stations in the USA. According to one of the group's press releases, "The lyrical flow is the fluid Rascalz style layered over smoothed out rhythms in a mixture of what may have once been called abstract and what is known as hardcore" (Desmond 1997). For the members of Rascalz, Red 1, Misfit, Kemo, Dedos, and Zebroc, images of rap such as those on both the East and the West Coasts of the USA, marked with violence, sexism, racism, and homophobia, have to be reexamined. Their work in the studio requires the participation of every member of the group. In every piece the whole group sings the lyrics of Red 1 and Misfit, as well as organizing the samples.

The Rascalz are aware that their music is not suitable for radio, and it is not created for the purpose of airplay. They regard the rapper behind the microphone as needing to develop a social consciousness that goes far beyond denunciation or declamation. As one member of the group has stated:

> Misfit reasons that part of the problem is a lot of rappers simply don't realize they have a social responsibility when they're behind the microphone, and that they should be aware that a rapper's lifestyle isn't as glamorous as has been depicted, particularly in music videos. "There aren't three girls in the bed, there aren't people drinking champagne and there aren't fifty people in the pool. That's not a rapper's lifestyle. I don't think there's any rapper that has that [way of life], with the super mansion and the whole nine, and who got that money strictly from rapping." (Desmond 1997)

Cash Crop was released barely two weeks after the death of Notorious BIG, which followed the murder of Tupac Shakur in 1996. For the Rascalz, this battle between the East Coast and the West Coast in the USA has fueled the idea that rap sounds like an ongoing open war between two gangs. Their texts try to initiate a softer approach to rap, more anchored in the reality of their daily lives: "An experienced angle in that we only talk about things we know and experience and things that go through our heads that we want to put across to every one else. We grew up in Canada and all our experiences are here, so the things we're gonna rap about are different from every one else. We don't talk about guns and all that, we deal with topics like temptation. We got tracks like 'Solitaire' and 'The Dreaded First,' nothing hardcore though" ("The Rascalz" 1997: 8). For the moment, the Rascalz are assured a certain degree of leadership in the hip-hop community of Vancouver, where more than twenty groups are active. Among these, Social Deviantz are worth noting. Their album *Essential Mental Nutrients,* released in 1997 on the independent label Sugarshack, subscribes to Rascalz's line of thought and defines what has become the North Coast style: samples borrowed from many musical genres, television series, radio, and ambient and homemade sounds sustained by a melodic line of drum 'n' bass with breaks to allow for rhythm changes, coupled with a soundtrack of everyday events resulting in more or less developed stories. Like the Rascalz, Social Devianz's social and political commitment is evident: A-Train, Fatbone, and Junya, the three members of the group, attack the media, the alienating structures of social life, and abuses of drugs, sex, and alcohol. Like a number of other rappers, they also defend themselves against the vices of a music industry subordinate to the laws of capital.

Another important group from Vancouver is the Swollen Members, who record their brand of underground rap on the Battle Axe label. One of their strengths is a theatrical delivery that can barely contain the explosive force of their lyrics. For the Swollen Members, it seems that the time for compromises is over, and they speak aloud what others only timidly acknowledge, even if it means the doors of widespread distribution will be closed to them. The compilation *Chocolate Park Soundtrack* contains tracks by a dozen active groups from Vancouver, including the Swollen Members, as well as other less well known groups such as the Incredible Ease, Factor F, Mike D'Zire, All about Us, DJ Maximum Possible, J Ras, Kwan Solar, Mad Child (who also works with Swollen Members), Sol T, and Mysta Puka.

Between Vancouver and Toronto are the prairie provinces, where a small number of rap groups are very active. The black and West Indian populations are much less evident here than elsewhere, and rappers are mostly white. On the other hand, unlike in Vancouver, hip-hop communities are well defined by leading groups: in Alberta by the group Black Rose from Calgary; in Saskatchewan, the Beat Comber Family rallies the groups of Saskatoon; in Manitoba, Peanuts and Corn Records is a dominant presence in Winnipeg. Curiously, they manage to produce CDs, but without any significant distribution, and their circulation is restricted to live shows and events.

Ontario, the most highly populated province, is with Toronto the "fortified castle" of Canadian rap, in that most of the groups and major production industries are located in these two places. The Beat Factory serves the interests of a number of groups and distributes their music beyond the limits of Ontario's territory. In 1996 and 1997 Beat Factory released *Rappessentials,* volumes 1 and 2, in order to present an overview of the work of emerging groups. These included the Rascalz, Concrete Mob, Down to Erf, Kardinal Offishall, Black-I, Wio-K, Redlife, Dan-E-O, Scales Empire, Choclair, and Citizen Kane on volume 1, and Infinite, Grimmy Grimmy, Tara Chase, Madlocks, Asia, Michee Mee, Arsenal, Marvel, Sic Sense, ST8 of Mind, Furee, M.A.D, Motion, Illegal Justice, and Crooks of da Round Table on volume 2. Except for the Rascalz, all the other groups come from Toronto and surrounding areas and display remarkably diverse styles and lyrics. Apart from the diminished presence of West Indian rap since Canadian rap's first wave, all forms of rap seem to be present on *Rappessentials,* including both East and West Coast styles. Most of these rappers have had a single or two produced by Beat Factory Production and Management, whose philosophy allows its artists to create their own CD cover designs. Beat Factory places at its artists' disposal a high-tech studio installed in the Caribbean where they can record their master "in a relaxing climate" — as the company states — offering them artistic direction and the best technicians around.

Among the groups on these compilations, two stand out: Concrete Mob and Choclair. Concrete Mob released their first album at the end of 1996 and place themselves within the purest tradition of hip-hop. As Deuce Deuce, a member of the group, acknowledges: "We rap about real life, family issues, and politics. We're about concrete rap, concrete rhymes." Listening to "Boiling Point," the single that first brought them to public attention, one hears how close they stay to their sources: a bottom line of drum 'n' bass, some repetitive piano notes, and lyrics about the frustrations of daily life. Choclair's approach is quite different. His album *What It Takes* was reviewed in June 1997 by *Hip Hop Connection* in Europe and the U.S. magazine *The Source*, which described him as follows:

> He's a talented MC from up there with a knack for flippin' styles. Diverse in his own right, he sounds like a student fresh out of the Flow University —a school which boasts alumni like Ras Kass and Common Sense. His material seems tight enough to press. Specially "Twenty-One Years" and "Just a Second," two tight cuts that made their way into the underground circuit for a hot second, thus bringing himself to the attention of today's picky audience. In closing, props to Choclair and people of his kind— those who prove that the basic flavors of hip-hop can rub off on anyone anywhere, in any country, if you can find 'em sign 'em. (Morales 1997)

Choclair's style is direct and sincere, and he is conscious of the power of words and language:

> My style will lock you down and get your brain stimulated
> decapitating people while my pen orchestrated
> mad flavor on the paper
> and I'll Behavior be favoring some sky scrapers
> I be looking over sides like snipers
> watch the crossfire
> when my shots ring to bust up a cipher
> and lighters by flicking
> so fluids on empty, indeed
> my style rolls like a stampede
> causing mad casualties
> mics smoked like (inhaling)
> so the second hand from the M.I. got you high
> and made your doves cry
> so people check my slang
> the Borough Side Representative's who I be
> styles be nice-ly spreading rhymes like jam

people, I'll strand y'all
for all your propaganda
talking trash about this flow-er
without knowing the ramifications

This single, "What It Takes," from the album of the same name, won him a Juno Award for best rap recording in 1997. In the track "Twenty-One Years," Choclair reviews the course of his life and defends traditional values like family and religion:

Understand I
never seen my dad since grade 9
maybe years before or after, I don't know
but I know that time flies
so I just rely on my family
my mother and brothers and my boys is first before these others
and try to stay strong through the hard times and tough times
my heart dies every time my mom cries
twenty-one years of my lifetime

We are a long way from the drugs, prostitution, gang wars, and police oppression of gangsta rap. Choclair, Rascalz, and many others display an understanding of hip-hop culture and, rather than trying to copy what is being made in the USA, have developed a musical style and discourse more appropriate to who they are and where they live. The work of Thrust, Dr. Frankenstein, and Kardinal Offishall has developed in a similar way.

Frankenstein appears to be the best-known Canadian rap artist outside Canada. Up to now, "the mad scientist who's on everyone's mix," as he describes himself, has appeared on three international compilations, one in Japan, one in England, and another in the USA, on which he featured alongside, among others, Method Man and Guru. Since 1995 he has sold 20,000 vinyl releases, and his records have been played on radio stations in New York and Los Angeles. A "general practitioner," Dr. Frankenstein independently produces, composes, performs, and mixes all his creations himself in his own studio, known as "the ill laboratory where it all begins." *Uv,* his recently launched EP, provides substantial proof of his professionalism.

Thrust is one of the pioneers of Canadian hip-hop. He has been in the music industry for fifteen years, formerly as a b-boy, now as an MC, and has performed in the company of the Pharcyde, Blackmoon, and KRS-One, to name just a few. He has earned a solid reputation from a number of singles ("Lights, Camera, Action," "Rage," etc.), but his first album has yet to be released.

The cover of the September 1997 issue of the Canadian rap 'zine *Mic Check* features Kardinal Offishall, a member of the Figurez of Speech and the rap movement known as the Circle. Kardinal was first noticed when he released his first single, "Naughty Dread," after which he appeared regularly on radio and television and in the music press. His main drawcard remains, however, his live performances, where he plays with the crowd, who let themselves go under the MC's command. "My speciality is the scene, I am a performer naturally because I can vibrate with the audience," he declares in the *Mic Check* interview.

Another center of Anglophone rap is located in Halifax, Nova Scotia, where more than twenty groups animate the hip-hop scene. More than anywhere else in Canada, these groups have to survive and stay visible by their own means and self-produce their own recordings. A number of Halifax rappers have produced cassettes and CDs without the aid of any major producers. Classified, Quency, the Goods, Kaspa, Renegade Synapsis, Chaos Theory, Buck 65, and Witchdoc Jo-Run all have one or more recordings to their credit. The rap made in Halifax is very different from rap anywhere else: the lyrics lean on a musical basis that is closer to rock, with punk accents, creating music similar to that of groups such as Rage against the Machine.

Classified, a rapper from Halifax, finds himself following storytelling tendencies. His song "Hold Your Own" describes an attitude he shares with Kaspa and Witchdoc Jo-Run:

> What would rappers try to do if they ain't ever had a rhyme,
> trying to be a story teller having no say like Helen Keller,
> but I'm a dweller, so I'm a speak what's going in my mind
> taking days, months, years, that don't matter it's just time
> I'm a climb, the ladder of life for real,
> so what's the deal how ya trying to make me out to be a killer,
> the check 1, 2 mic thriller, that's how I feel ya,
> so don't be pushy or I'll be the one to up and spill ya,
> Yeah, that's how I prove to be committed with my very own words
> five years paying dues, never thought I would lose,
> but yo, I never won a thing so I lost,
> and if I'm going down then I guess I paid the cost,
> only time will tell if I made it back,
> but four tapes later kid I'm still making raps,
> guess I'm just an addict, gotta get some more
> but all you other rappers what the fuck you go commercial for.

Jo-Run is a pioneer of the hip-hop scene in Nova Scotia. As early as 1984 he began performing shows—along with, among others, Run-DMC, Public Enemy, and Michee Mee—and he created his own CD and cassette label (Jo-Run Records), which endorses the projects of a number of artists as well as producing their live shows. In 1994 he founded the Haltown Projex with Badi of Plain of Fascination in order to promote the development of hip-hop in Halifax. On the other hand, groups like Renegade Synapsis, Keltic Rebels, and others have been influenced by Celtic traditional music, which they sample as a framework for their compositions.

RAP IN QUEBEC

Situated at the crossroads of U.S. and French music, Quebec rap had a recent boost with the release of Dubmatique's *La force de comprendre,* which combines soul music with a French hip-hop approach. French rappers such as IAM, MC Solaar, Ménélik, 2Bal2Nèg (with whom Dubmatique recorded a song), and NTM are well known in Quebec and frequently broadcast on radio and television, demonstrating the viability of French rap in this Francophone city. Nonetheless certain Montreal rap groups such as Shades of Culture, Obscure Disorder, and Eye Spy Crew continue to perform in English, although their influence is restricted to the Montreal region. In contrast, Dubmatique's debut album sold 100,000 copies and succeeded in capturing the media's interest, with two of their songs reaching the airwaves: "Soul pleureur" (Weeping Soul) and "La force de comprendre" (The Power to Understand). The reasons for their seemingly spontaneous success are many: the group's stage performances reveal a sense of spectacle that excites their audiences; they express an optimistic and humanist, even pro-religious view of life in their lyrics; and their music incorporates the sounds of soul and gospel. In "Soul pleureur" the loss of a loved one becomes the occasion for a reflection on the injustices of life and a sense of culpability:

> I confess it's hard for me to keep my calm
> And come to terms with the idea that jealousy can cause drama
> Blame the one who takes a weapon against his brother
> Evil brings pain and sorrow to others
> The reality is that the best come first

Using both English and French, Dubmatique appropriates the rhythms of French rap texts (such as IAM's and MC Solaar's styles), where the refrains are often entrusted to soul voices, giving an emotional depth to the songs. Dubmatique is also a group that succeeds in synergizing their audiences—not in any aggressive way, but in a direct relationship, tinted with a certain seductive naiveté. The group won a Félix trophy for best alternative band at the 1997 ADISQ (Association québécoise de l'industrie du disque, du spectacle et de la vidéo) Gala Awards—Montreal's Francophone music awards and followed this with 1998 group of the year and album of the year, as well as 1999 hip-hop album of the year for the eponymous *Dubmatique*. They draw on the Senegalese and Parisian origins of two members of the group, O.TMC and Disoul (the third member is DJ Choice, formerly of Zero Tolerance and Shades of Culture), in addition to the influence of both U.S. and French rappers, to produce a distinctively local, but also hybrid and international form of rap, summed up in the title of one of their singles, "Montreal/Paris/Dakar." They also celebrate Montreal as a welcoming, multicultural city, open to all, and the focal point of a musical hybridization they wish to participate in, thanks to hip-hop, in "Un été à Montréal" (A Summer in Montreal) and "Jamais cesser d'y croire" (Never Cease to Believe). With their ragga- and soul-inflected rap and their politically and morally conscious lyrics, they are the first rap group in Quebec to succeeded in breaking into both the Francophone and Anglophone national broadcast and recording markets, as well as getting radio and video airplay in France and the rest of Europe. They even performed as a backup for the teen-pop group the Backstreet Boys, reaching 180, 000 people all over Canada, and their album was described in the Montreal French-language weekly newspaper *Ici* (Review of Dubmatique 1997: 13) as "making Montreal less of a small town and more of a city on the musical planet." Their second CD, titled simply *Dubmatique,* released at the end of 1998, consolidated the success of their first one. But for this CD, the French rappers Akhenaton and Shurik'n, from the group IAM, remixed the song "La force de comprendre."

Two members of the Montreal Francophone rap group La Gamic are also members of the Tox label, producers of Dubmatique. DJ Choice and Barney Valsaint are in charge of sampling and backup vocals in the studio. La Gamic owes its originality to two women, Pittsbury So and Natty Soyha (backed by Rakoon), who write and perform the group's lyrics. Each tells stories of her own life, fears, and anxieties and defines rap and hip-hop culture as the new voice of a youth in search of itself, as in the track "Mine de rien" (Nonchalant):

> I come from afar with lots of hate
> In my veins, my oriental look is pale
> I hide my critical side, when they want to structure my thoughts
> I panic. There are certain points that you haven't understood
> You cause me problems, see if I care

The female causes envy, jealousy but not taboos
Women of quality we can but count on our fingers
You don't have to look, they're right in front of you

Unlike Dubmatique and their soul music, La Gamic prefers scratching atmospheres sustained by a discreet melodic line following a drum beat. But like Dubmatique, La Gamic gives all they have onstage in their highly energetic performances. Natty Soyha has also begun performing with popular Québécois artists Jean Leloup and Bran Van 3000, both of whom borrow elements of rap in much of their work. Of all the Quebec rock groups, Bran Van 3000 borrows from hip-hop the most; their music is hard to define, as their eclecticism covers a broad spectrum from trip-hop to funk, rock, and punk, but in the background we hear clearly the work of a DJ playing turntables, which often serve as a spring board for the rhythm.

Another group attempting to follow in the footsteps of Dubmatique is Les Messagers du Son (LMDS; the Messengers of Sound). Their influences are far more French than American. What all these groups have in common is that they emerged from the suburbs rather than the city centers, and above all from the surroundings of the island of Montreal where neo-Quebecois install themselves, creating ethnic ghettos that are characterized not necessarily by poverty, but by racial conflict.

The situation in Quebec City is very different. The relative homogeneity of the population (more than 95 percent are white and/or French) shifts the focus of rap to the demands and protests of youth. The group Eleventh Reflektah capitalizes on a complex and very refined recording process, all computer generated, of samples ranging from well-known film themes (such as Ennio Morricone's "Once Upon a Time in the West") to tiny fragments, not more than one or two bars, of classical and contemporary music, to snatches of traditional Quebecois songs. Unlike many other groups, Eleventh Reflektah does not employ scratching, except sometimes in live shows, when DJ Nerve, one of the best DJs in Canada, performs on the turntables. The group's first EP was successful in Vancouver and Seattle and gained them recognition by Beat Factory in Toronto, who will include an Eleventh Reflekta track on their next compilation. The group have opened for Rascalz, Thrust, and Dr. Frankenstein in Quebec City, and they have been praised for their elaborate compositions.

By the spring of 1998 Eleventh Reflektah had decided to call itself La Constellation and to sing in French rather than to mix English and French, as they had done previously. Their choice was motivated by the facts that Deux Faces (Two Faces), Onze (Eleven), and their listening public were

Francophones. Recruited by the record label Tacca Musik, a major Quebec recording company, their first album, *Dualité,* appeared in the fall 1998, promoted by a provocative video clip that made them popular. The musical style of the group came into its own by virtue of its originality, in particular through the participation of Kassis and also Frankenstein and Danny-O, two Toronto rappers. The originality of their lyrics distinguished them from other groups owing to their poetic range, well adapted to their thematics. In contrast to other French Quebecois groups, which developed their texts from a certain *doxa* (common sense), La Constellation avoided moral preaching and sang about the facts of life and its minor anxieties without extolling the use of drugs and alcohol to evade reality.

> Turn around, come back, too late already too far
> To forget tomorrow, come, it's for your own good
> To make a point to all these problems, a single road
> Jump, swallow or lean, no you can't do anything
> Our perspective is negative, anything but not that
> Abandon not, hang on, time will fix it all
> For certain, not all men will live as a hero
> But nobody should put an end to such a beautiful thing
> Hey, yo, Two Faces, try at least to leave some traces
> Before you give up and the wind erases all
> Know that you hold the key in your hands
> So think about it well, yo, you know tomorrow can be yours
>   ("Duality")

The title of the album at this point reveals the two faces that all humans possess; positive and negative. The poetic style of the group is better defined by its presence of mind, because they changed the stakes of traditional rap music to express their own way of life.

A number of other rap groups are intensely active in the principal cities of Quebec, each adding its own contribution to a growing hip-hop culture. There are regular live performances, which often mobilize audiences as large as 200 to 300 people, even in the smaller cities where one would expect a certain resistance.

HIP-HOP CULTURE IN CANADA

Hip-hop has become widespread in Canada and developed into a strong subculture, despite being overlooked by the major record labels. This has its share of disadvantages, such as restricted distribution, but also its advantages, such as a certain freedom of expression and the establishment of a cultural network with its own radio time slots and its own 'zines (at least three important ones) and magazines (about ten). Shops specialize in rap clothing and equipment. Rap has its own record stores, bars, clubs, and Web sites, one of them the radio station in Ottawa mentioned earlier that broadcasts rap music nonstop, twenty-four hours a day, seven days a week.

The days when Canadian rappers sought to capture the attention of producers in a suicidal rivalry are long gone. Up to now there has been an underground solidarity among different groups from both Vancouver and Halifax, at either extremity of Canada, separated by at least 6,000 kilometers. Even if Vancouver seems to have become the main focus of Canadian rap, Toronto, because of its strong concentration of recording-industry apparatus, remains the center of hip-hop music distribution.

On the other hand, although Quebec City offers more shows and a livelier hip-hop community, Montreal remains the focal point of Francophone rap, thanks to the presence of record companies who are prepared to risk recording hip-hop groups. Despite the proximity of the USA, very few U.S. rappers perform in Montreal because street fights between ethnic groups are feared. A performance by the Wu-Tang Clan scheduled for October 1995 was postponed because of pamphlets circulating that stated, "Rap is Black, White Forbidden." Eventually the group performed in an amphitheater located in a no-man's-land outside the city. Most black people and members of other ethnic communities in Montreal who are drawn to rap (West Indian, Caribbean, African, etc.) speak English, but they recognize that the rap that reaches out for popularity is often produced by French speaking people, white or mixed race, who have appropriated a musical genre that bears many distinctive aspects of their own culture. In contrast, the black Anglophones who rap in Montreal hold little or no appeal for record companies in Quebec, and even less so in Toronto. The major labels can, of course, already count on an abundance of African American rap recordings. Nonetheless, there is a certain conviviality that is particularly noticeable at rap contest evenings that take place in Montreal every fall.

It is reasonable to expect, given the recent success of the Rascalz and Dubmatique, that within a few years rap music will be better distributed in Canada and will get a friendlier reception from recording companies, as it has with radio and television, thus helping to develop this musical genre, albeit in a minimal way. From east to west, Canada can boast at least 200 rap groups (despite limited means of distribution), their messages echoing from province to province.

Translated from the French by Denis Belley and Madonna Hamel.

REFERENCES

Adams, John. 1991. "La musique rap." *Compositeur Canadien/Canadian Composer* (summer): 18–19.

Billy, Hélène de. 1990. "Rap around-the-clock." *L'actualité*I, 1 June.

Caudeiron, Daniel. 1989. "Le hip hop d'ici." *Compositeur Canadien/ Canadian Composer* (November): 30–35.

———. 1990. "Le maître du hip hop." *Compositeur Canadien/Canadian Composer* (spring): n.p.

———. 1993. "L'échantillonage." *Compositeur Canadien/Canadian Composer* (fall): 12–13.

Caudeiron, Daniel, and Mark Miller. 1993. "Rap." *Encyclopédie de la musique au Canada*. Montreal: Éditions Fides.

Culture en pantoufles et souliers vernis [report of an inquiry on cultural practices in Quebec Montreal]. 1997. Les Publications du Québec.

Desmond. 1997. "Rascalz." *Peace Magazine,* April–May, 12.

Doole, Kerry. 1990. "The Maple Leaf Rap." *Music Express,* August, 150.

Galloway, Matt. 1997. "Toronto Rhymer Choclair Sweeter than All the Rest." *Now,* December–January, n.p.

Gudino, Rod. 1997. "Rascalz Reap a Cash Crop." *RPM,* 31 March, 8.

Jennings, Nicholas. 1990. "The Big Rap Attack." *Maclean's,* 12 November, n.p.

Kelly, Brendan. 1997. "Hip hop de chez nous." *Montreal Gazette,* 25 November.

Litorco, Frank. 1997. "Second Coming, West Coast Style." *FFWD,* 7 May, 3.

Morales, Rigo. 1997. "Behold the Second Coming: Choclair." *Source,* June, n.p.

Nazareth, Errol. 1988. "La musique rap." *La scène musicale/Musical Scene,* July–August, 362.

———. 1997. "Dragon Rap's Magic for Rascalz' Red 1." *Toronto Sun,*16 May, 5.

Quinlan, Thomas. 1997a. "Rascalz, *Cash Crop*." *Watch,* March, 10.

———. 1997b. "Rascalz, Elemental Journey." *Watch,* April, 11.

Philips, Colin. 1995. "World Play." *Word,* April, 5.

"Rascalz, The." 1997. *HHP (Hip Hop Connection),* June, 8.

Review of Dubmatique. 1997. *La force de comprendre.* *Ici,* 27 November–4 December, 13.

Rose, Tricia. 1994. *Black Noise: Rap Music and Black Culture in Contemporary America*. Hanover, N.H.: Wesleyan University Press.

Wallace, Jay. "Vancouver, B.C.: Introducing . . . the North Coast." *Source,* January, 114.

DISCOGRAPHY

Bran Van 3000. 1997. *Glee*. Audiogram.

Choclair. 1997. *What It Takes*. Kneedeep Records.

Different Shades of Black. 1994. *Crazy Fiction*. Peanuts and Corn Records.

Dream Warriors. 1991. *And Now the Legacy Begins*. Island.

Dubmatique. 1997. *La force de comprendre*. Disques Tox.

———. 1998. *Dubmatique*. Disques Tox.

Frek Sho. 1997. *Mocean*. Vagrant Hobby Records.

Haltown Projex. 1991. *Haltown Projex*. Jo-Runs Records.

———. 1994. *Haltown 2*. Jo-Runs Records.

———. 1996. *Haltown Junior*. Jo-Runs Records.

Kish. 1990. *Order from Chaos*. A & M.

K-OS (Kardinal Offishall). 1997. *Eye and I*. Capitol Hill, Entertainment.

La Gamic. 1998. *La Gamic*. Disques Tox.

La Constellation. 1998. *Dualité*. Tacca Musik.

Laymen Twaist. 1990. *Walk on the Wild Side*. Isba.

MCJ and Cool G. 1990. *So Listen*. Cap.

Maestro Fresh-Wes. 1989. *Symphony in Effet*. Attic.

Michie Mee and LA Luv. 1991. *Jamaican Funk-Canadian Style*. First Priority/Atlantic.

Mood Ruff. 1996. *Fluid*. Peanuts and Corn Records.

Rascalz. 1993. *Really Livin*. Figure IV/BMG.

———. 1997. *Cash Crop*. Figure IV/BMG.

———. 1999. *Global Warning*. BMG/U.K.

Shades of Culture. 1997. *Payin' Rent*. 2112 Records.

———. 1998. *Mindstate*. 2112 Records.

Social Deviantz. 1997. *Essential Mental Nutrients*. Sugarshack Records.

Swollen Members. 1997. *Swollen Members*. Battle Axe Records.

Various artists. 1996. *Bassments of Bad Men* [compilation]. Halifax Artists.

———. 1996. *Beatfactory Rapessentials,* vol. 1. Beatfactory/EMI.

———. 1997. *Beatfactory Rapessentials,* vol. 2. Beatfactory/EMI.

———. 1997. *Chocolate Park Soundtrack* [compilation]. Chocolate Park Entertainment.

———. 1991. *Cold Front* [compilation]. Attic.

———. 1991. *Je rappe en français* [compilation]. Station 12.

WEB SITES

http://www.wRAPradio.com/ [Canadian rap radio site].

http://griffin.multimedia.edu/~kkraft/chho/index.html [Canadian hip-hop site].

http://www.hiphopca.cihost.com/ [Canada hip-hop site].

Notes on Contributors

Roger Chamberland has a Ph.D. in literature from Laval University, Quebec, where he has taught as an associate professor since 1990. The author and editor of *Anthologie de la musique québecoise* and codirector of an education manual on the literature of Quebec, he has also taught in Germany, France, and Belgium and published a number of articles. His research includes Quebec literature and the aesthetics of the videoclip. He is a member of the International Association for the Study of Popular Music (IASPM).

Ian Condry is an assistant professor in the Department of Anthropology, Union College, N.Y. His Ph.D. thesis is titled "Japanese Rap Music: An Ethnography of Globalization in Popular Culture" (Yale University, 1999). He is currently writing a book on Japanese hip-hop.

David Hesmondhalgh works in the Faculty of Social Sciences at the Open University in Milton Keynes in the United Kingdom. He is the author of *The Cultural Industries* (Sage, 2002) and coeditor (with Georgina Born) of *Western Music and Its Others: Difference, Appropriation, and Representation in Music* (University of California Press, 2000) and (with Keith Negus) of *Popular Music Studies* (Arnold, 2002).

Claire Levy is a musicologist and member of IASPM. She is an associate professor and research fellow at the Institute of Art Studies at the Bulgarian Academy of Sciences in Sofia, researching different aspects of popular music. Her Ph.D. dissertation is on contemporary message song in Bulgaria. She has taken part in several collaborative projects and in 1994–95 visited Indiana University in Bloomington on a Fulbright to research African American music and modern pop styles. She has presented numerous papers at IASPM conferences around the world and published extensively (in Bulgarian and English) on a variety of issues in pop, rock, jazz, and world music in the journals *Bulgarsko Musikoznanie, Bulgarska Musica,* and *Popular Music.* She is general secretary of the IASPM.

Ian Maxwell is a lecturer at the Department of Performance Studies at the University of Sydney. He has written about a range of performance practices, from Australia rules football to courtroom practice, actor training, theater and performance forms, and youth culture. He is currently researching contemporary performance practice in Sydney's western suburbs.

Caspar Melville is researching a Ph.D. on black dance music in London in the Department of Media and Communications at Goldsmiths College, University of London. He has worked as a music journalist for many publications in the United Kingdom and United States, and writes regularly for the London-based street-culture monthly *Touch*.

Tony Mitchell is a senior lecturer in writing and cultural studies at the University of Technology, Sydney. He was secretary-treasurer of the Australia–New Zealand branch of IASPM from 1993 to 1995, secretary treasurer of the international executive of IASPM from 1995 to 1997, and chairperson of IASPM from 1997 to

1999. He is the author of *Popular Music and Local Identity: Rock, Pop, and Rap in Europe and Oceania* (University of Leicester Press, 1996) and (with Philip Hayward and Roy Shuker) *North Meets South: Popular Music in Aotearoa/New Zealand* (Perfect Beat Publications, 1994), as well as numerous articles on popular music in *Popular Music, Ethnomusicology, Media, Culture and Society, Popular Music and Society,* and *Perfect Beat.* His book *Dario Fo: People's Court Jester* was published by Methuen in 1984.

Sarah Morelli is completing a Ph.D. in ethnomusicology at Harvard University. In addition to her work on popular music in Korea, she has studied in Russia and India and is currently engaged in doctoral fieldwork in the San Francisco Bay area, where she studies the sarod with Ustad Akbar Khan and kathak dance with Pardit Chitresh Das.

Mark Pennay is editor for the Research Institute for the German language (DSA) at the University of Marburg, Germany. An independent researcher and language professional based in Germany since 1992, he has an honors degree in social anthropology from the University of Sydney and has published a number of papers on ethnicity, disability, and popular music. His most recent work is a translation of *The Shadow of the Dalai Lama,* a critical analysis of Tibetan Buddhism.

André J. M. Prévos received his Ph.D. from the University of Iowa and is an associate professor of French at Penn State University. He has published numerous book chapters, essays, and articles on blues, jazz, French popular music in the USA, and French rap, and translated Robert Springer's book *Authentic Blues* into English.

Ted Swedenburg is associate professor of anthropology at the University of Arkansas, the author of *Memories of Revolt* (University of Minnesota Press, 1995), and coeditor of *Displacement, Diaspora, and Geographies of Identity* (Duke University Press, 1996). He is currently working on a book, provisionally titled *Sounds from the Interzone,* that deals with border musics from or connected to the Middle East.

Jacqueline Urla is associate professor of cultural anthropology at the University of Massachusetts, Amherst. She is the coeditor of *Deviant Bodies: Critical Perspectives on Difference in Science and Popular Culture* (Indiana University Press, 1995). She is currently completing a book on cultural politics and language revival in the Basque Country.

Mir Wermuth was born in Holland of Indonesian parents. She was associate researcher at the Department of Communication Studies at the University of Amsterdam from 1991 to 1996 and now works at OMD Netherlands as media director and part of the management team. She is completing a Ph.D. dissertation on the way rap music and hip-hop in the United Kingdom and Holland developed from subculture to mainstream pop culture. Her prize-winning M.A. thesis is on the emergence of rap in Holland. She is a member of the boards of the Dutch Rock Foundation and the Dutch Rock Academy and president of the Dutch Pop Journalism Award and has published articles (mainly in Dutch) on black dance music, migrant cultural participation, the socialization of youth through music, the representation of migrants on television, and education via new media.

Index

Library of Congress Cataloging-in-Publication Data

Global noise : rap and hip-hop outside the USA /
edited by Tony Mitchell.

p. cm. — (Music/culture)

Includes bibliographical references and index.

ISBN 0-8195-6501-6 (cloth : alk. paper) —

ISBN 0-8195-6502-4 (pbk. : alk. paper)

1. Rap (Music) — History and criticism.

2. Hip-hop. I. Mitchell, Tony, 1949– II. Series.

ML3531.G56 2001

782.421649'09 — dc21   2001046705